RESEARCH MIDDLE EAST INSTITUTE

University of Pennsylvania

M.E.R.I. Special Studies

New Zionism and the Foreign Policy System of Israel

Ofira Seliktar

SOUTHERN ILLINOIS UNIVERSITY PRESS
Carbondale and Edwardsville

Copyright © 1986 by Ofira Seliktar
All rights reserved
Printed in Great Britain
Published in Great Britain by Croom Helm Ltd.,
   Beckenham, Kent

First published in the United States of America by
Southern Illinois University Press, P.O. Box 3697,
Carbondale, Illinois 62901

Seliktar, Ofira.
   New Zionism and the foreign policy system of Israel.

   (M.E.R.I. special studies)
   Includes index.
   1. Israel—foreign relations.   2. Zionism—Israel.
I. Title.   II. Series.
DS119.6.S45   1986   327.5694   85-26103
ISBN 0-8093-1287-5

This book is Number 4 of MERI
Special Studies series. Other books
in this series may be obtained from:

   Middle East Research Institute
   University of Pennsylvania
   3808 Walnut Street
   Philadelphia, Pennsylvania 19104
   USA

To my family which perished in the Holocaust and to my sons, Yaron and Dror, who provide the continuity.

CONTENTS

TABLES

PREFACE

Traditional studies of foreign policy, which was often equated with foreign relations and diplomatic history, have long outlived the 'classical' international system. The more rigorous methodology of the late 1960s generated the systems approach to international behaviour. A great deal of this endeavour concentrated on the macro-analysis of the global system which emphasised the political, social and economic factors of the international environment.

The psychological properties of foreign policy were a minor offshoot in this development. Psychology was most frequently applied to the study of leadership, producing some notable contributions such as the research on the operational code of elites. However, foreign policy issues have increasingly become a part of the domestic system in many countries. Massive popular participation has been dramatised by the rise of revolutionary groups, fundamentalist religious movements and new forms of international guerrilla warfare and terrorism.

To understand the psychology behind these new forms of international behaviour, we have to go beyond the study of the 'psychological prism' of the elite. Some current developments demonstrate that studying the attitudes of the ruling elites can sometimes limit our understanding of the changes in the popular belief system and their effect on foreign policy. The fundamentalist revolution in Iran is a good case in point. Excessive emphasis on the 'psychological prism' of the Westernised elite of the Shah has obscured our vision of the extent and depth of the change in popular beliefs. The psychological dynamics of this change which, once set in motion, produced an extremely rapid transition from a semi-westernised monarchy into an authentic fundamentalist republic, have left many academic and political analysts overtaken by events.

This book is the outcome of my intellectual quest for a research framework which could explain and predict such events. The choice of the concept of a belief system is based on the assumption that it can integrate individual and elite attitudes into a useful analysis of the psychology of a foreign policy system. This concept is discussed in the introductory chapter, which is methodological: however, the lay reader can understand the book without dwelling on the research design.

Israel is ideally suited for an analysis of a changing belief system and its impact on foreign policy. After some thirty years of dominance by the Socialist Zionist movement, Jewish society evolved a new belief system, New Zionism, which brought Likud into power in 1977. In line with its belief system, the Likud leadership proceeded to restructure the *modus operandi* of Israel's foreign policy system which subsequently resulted in the 1982 war in Lebanon.

The major task of this book is to recreate the long and extremely complex process of change in the belief system. To this end, I have reviewed and analysed most of the empirical studies which are relevant to the subject. My detailed scrutiny of the empirical data is especially important in understanding how the Socialist Zionist system was delegitimised and transvalued into New Zionism. I also hope that this large compilation of empirical evidence will contribute to a better understanding of the psychology of the Arab-Israeli conflict. While the Middle East struggle has attracted enormous attention, there is a relative paucity of empirical work as opposed to the preponderance of traditional foreign relations studies and polemical accounts.

In this book I use the term New Zionism to define the belief system which replaced Socialist Zionism. The term does not imply that New Zionism is a new ideology. The name was first used in the early decades of this century by the Revisionists, whose ideology forms the core of the new belief system. I have decided to employ the original term without apologetic quotation marks, which may imply that the belief system is somehow not authentic.

The term 'Greater Land of Israel' used in the book is an inaccurate translation of the Hebrew term *Eretz Israel Hashlemah* which means 'the Whole of the Land of Israel'. I decided to use the former term because of its widespread currency in English language publications.

Throughout the book I use the term 'Israelis' as synonymous with 'Jews'. This form is a literary convenience rather than a political statement. The book makes it clear that 15 per cent of Israel's population, or one in six Israelis, is an Arab and a citizen of the State of Israel.

In the two years it took me to research and write the book I received help, encouragement and ideas which contributed to the intellectual contours of my work. I am especially grateful to Merle Thorpe, the President of the Foundation for Middle East Peace, who invited me to lecture at the Metropolitan Club to a group of Washington policy makers and media representatives. I first conceptualised the phenomenon of New Zionism while preparing the lecture. Joseph Montville from the US State Department was a particular source of personal and intellectual inspiration. Shlomo Avineri from the Hebrew University in Jerusalem has commented on the methodological chapter. Our personal discussions and his many writings on Zionism and contemporary Israeli politics were invaluable for my understanding of Zionist ideology and practice.

I would like to take this opportunity to thank William Maynes, the editor of *Foreign Policy*, for publishing my article on New Zionism. The large response to the article, both positive and critical, encouraged me to turn it into a book.

Above all, I am deeply indebted to my colleagues and staff of the Middle East Research Institute at the University of Pennsylvania. Thomas Naff, the Director of MERI, provided the necessary help and moral support, without which this project would have been impossible. Ruth Matson, James Whitaker, Robyn James, Claire Gilmore and Mary Arnett diligently edited various parts of the book. Marsha Pripstein and Arieh Grumet assisted me in data collection. Catherine Mulhern co-ordinated the data entry and retrieval. Hilda Pring, Faculty Liaison, Van Pelt Library, University of Pennsylvania, was enormously helpful in tracking down missing information. Magida Abboud, Patricia Falciani, Nona Sachdeva and Keith Yoder patiently typed the manuscript. On this, as on previous occasions, they all went beyond the call of duty to meet my various deadlines. In a sense this book is a collective effort of the Institute.

Ofira Seliktar
Philadelphia

1 FRAMEWORK OF ANALYSIS: IDENTIFYING A SOCIETY'S CHANGING BELIEF SYSTEM

Research in foreign policy has historically evolved from single- or multi-country studies to those of general system theory. One product of this conceptual development is an integrated systemic analysis of the foreign policy of single countries. These studies view the foreign policy of a country as a system which comprises the operational environment of the country, the psychological environment of the decision makers and the process through which decisions are formulated and implemented.[1]

Whereas the operational environment and the structure of the decision-making process of a foreign policy system are relatively easy to analyse, the psychological environment of the decision makers is conceptually more challenging. Following the pioneering work of Boulding and his colleagues, it became almost commonplace to assume that decision makers act upon their perception of reality rather than 'objective' reality. 'Cognitive behaviouralism', as the principle is sometimes called, means that elites (as well as followers) have 'cognitive maps' or sets of images which condition their foreign policy behaviour.[2] These cognitive maps and their related images are used to order and make inferences about complex realities which are contained in the operational environment of the decision makers.

Yet the terms 'cognitive maps' and 'images' share the problem of other theoretical constructs, namely that their links with observed reality do not lend themselves easily to empirical analysis. Boulding himself admitted to the difficulty when he stated that, in reality, the image cannot be represented as a 'set of quantities or variables' and is the product of a weighted interaction between the images of a large number of people.[3]

Perhaps the most difficult part of the construct pertains to Boulding's notion that individual images grow out of *a complex process of interaction with the national images disseminated through the value system of a society*.[4] In other words, in order to understand the psychological environment of the foreign policy system, the analyst must account for the idiosyncracies of decision makers, the national and sub-national belief systems, and the patterned interactions between them.

1

Conceptual and Methodological Problems

The term 'belief system' is one of the most popular concepts in political psychology but two problems obscure its clarity. One is that of diverse meanings which include, among others, ideology, political culture and even culture. It is impossible to discuss the enormous literature on the subject, but it can safely be assumed that, while these terms are not identical, there is a fair degree of implied overlap among them. In a sense, they all refer to sets of ideas which men use to arrange and explain physical and social realities and to justify social actions aimed at ordering these realities.[5] The second and more difficult problem stems from the need to reconcile what may be broadly termed the macro-sociological or 'holistic' perspective with the microsociological orientation which focuses on the individual psychological processes.

The 'holistic' position that emergent group properties are not reducible to the sum of the individuals is an intellectual outgrowth of the sociology of knowledge perspective. This view is most clearly associated with Mannheim, but it is also influenced by Marx, Durkheim and Althusser. In their respective approaches, they all share the view that belief systems are formed through a complex interaction between intellectual standpoints and a sequence of human experience.[6]

The microsociological perspective derives from a number of disciplines which deal with individual psychological states. Cognitive psychology postulates that, in order to survive, human beings have developed an ability to extract essential clues out of the extensive flow of information to which they are constantly exposed. This selective perception is called a 'perceptual representation', 'cognitive representation', 'cognitive map', or 'perceptual-representational system'.[7] At the most fundamental level, such a private belief system informs the individual about the nature of reality by providing him with a series of explicit and implicit assumptions about causality, time and space orientation, and ethical codes of social morality and justice.

Motivational psychology, known also as the functional school, assumes that 'manifest' attitudes and beliefs are instrumental in expressing and imposing order upon the repressed conflicts and drives of an individual. Perhaps the best-known work of the functional school is Adorno's study of the authoritarian per-

sonality which found that anti-Semitism and strong ethnic prejudice correlate with repressed aggression and hostility.[8] Seen this
way, beliefs are used by an individual to resolve the problems
arising out of an interaction between self and society.

The respective analysis of the collective and the individual belief
system can be conceptually reconciled by adopting the interactionist view. Because societal beliefs constitute complex
symbolic sets, they are seen as both a product and a determinant of
individual beliefs generated through continuous social interaction.
This perspective was articulated in the phenomenological analysis
of Berger and Luckman which postulates a cyclical phenomenon.[9]

> The subjective mind creates a subjective reality (ex-
> ternalization) which, as time goes by, turns into institutions,
> tradition and culture (objectification), and then finally acts
> back on the subjective mind and shapes it (internalization).

This perspective, though conceptually elegant, cannot solve the
question of what unit of analysis should be used in an empirical
investigation of a societal belief system. The macro-sociological
approach is most rigid in its insistence that the 'collective consciousness' should not be constructed as the sum total of the
various types of 'individual consciousness'.[10] Although this view
implies that the belief system is a property of a certain collectivity
— nation, class, ethnic group, religious community — it is not
clear who are the ideational bearers of the system. Ashcroft
argued that much of contemporary political theory is still influenced by the notion that the 'collective consciousness is
embodied in the great philosophers'.[11] Sociology, anthropology
and, increasingly, political science have looked at group interaction in both institutional and informal settings in order to decode
the belief system of the different collectivities. Work as varied as
Lowi's discussion of the 'public philosophy', Crozier's bureau-
cratic phenomenon, and 'operational code' research are representative of this approach.[12]

The individual psychological approach is uncompromisingly
clear in its choice of the single individual as the basic unit for the
empirical analysis of collective belief systems. Almond and Verba,
who define political culture as an internalisation of the political
system through the cognition and feelings of the population, are
representative of this approach.[13] The conceptual premise under-

lying this perspective is that a belief system can be described in terms of statistically derived modal characteristics and modal personalities in a given population. It should be emphasised that it is empirically impossible to determine to what extent a societal belief system is equivalent to the collective attitudes of its constituent individuals.

In the absence of conceptual clarity, research on group belief systems has used a bewildering number of approaches. Billig, who reviewed some of them, found that one of the common analytical devices is reductionism, that is conceptualising a social phenomenon in terms of individual psychological processes. Another common device is to treat the group and the individual as isomorphic constructs. Such an approach, often used in foreign-policy studies, is likely to produce the 'group mind fallacy', that is, the 'attribution of mental predicates to social collectivities'.[14]

A more systematic way to discern a societal value system is to study the beliefs of elites. The notion that elites represent the collective belief system more faithfully than ordinary citizens has a long intellectual tradition dating back to Plato's philosopher-kings. These groups are variously known as 'power elites', 'castes', 'networks of meaning', 'strategic social groups'[15] or 'communication communities' (*Kommunikationsgemeinschaften*)[16]. None the less, the study of collective belief systems through the attitudes of the elites is vulnerable to 'a circulatory effect'. Elites define the parameters of the belief system and invest psychologically in established patterns of thought. Measuring the beliefs of elites may not take into account what Elliot and Schlesinger call the 'disjunction between administrative and electoral politics'.[17]

One way to solve the dilemma of the unit of analysis would be to condition the choice on the specific aim of a given piece of research. In studies which focus on the role of belief systems as mediators of individual decisions and behaviour, the only logical unit of analysis is the individual. On the other hand, research which deals with decisionally-oriented complex organisations — most notably the foreign policy system — should at least touch upon the macrosociological definition of the belief system. Used in this way, a belief system may be seen as a set or range of discrete rather than deterministic alternatives upon which decision makers can act. Given the constraints imposed by the external and internal environment of the foreign policy system, one cannot infer directly from a collective belief system to a particular decision.

Nevertheless, the belief system can serve as a collective 'cognitive map' of the foreign policy environment.

General Belief System and Political Beliefs: The Problem of Autonomy

Another major difficulty is that of relating a political belief system to the general belief system. It stems from what Goffman defined as 'boundary collusion', that is, the problem of constructing or interpreting a social occasion within the boundaries of a larger unknown social paradigm.[18] The problem of 'boundary collusion' is especially pertinent to foreign policy studies which tend to take a rather narrow autonomous view of the political belief system. Yet the basis of political beliefs, embedded as they are in the broader cognitive and affective organisation of general beliefs, raises the perplexing question of how autonomous the political belief system is.

A perusal of the literature reveals that the question of autonomy has not been systematically discussed. Rather, the boundaries of the political belief system have been defined *ad hoc*, to a large extent implicitly, by the methodological thrust of the various studies. Traditional historical and political science studies imply the existence of a fairly autonomous realm of the 'political'. These studies are permeated by what Frank described as the 'humanistic-scientific belief system which dominates the American scientific community'.[19] They assume a single reality existing independently of the actors and a relatively simple cause and effect structure. Moreover, the scholars impute rationality as they define it to the actors.

The work on social conflict provides a less autonomous vision of the political realm. These studies rest on the theoretical assumption that changes in a collective belief system, which are seen as a necessary prerequisite for social action ranging from civil unrest to revolution, are based on psychological states such as perceptions of relative deprivation and the 'demonstration effect'.[20] Other studies point to displacement mechanisms which lead to ethnic strife, 'scapegoating' and the emergence of anti-outgroup beliefs which have become firmly embedded in the collective belief system. Anti-Semitism, which at least partially derives from ego need-oriented displacement, and the role it plays in many belief systems, is perhaps the best researched case, but other examples abound in the literature.[21] Studies in political mobilisation often reveal the use of potent affective symbols as a means of manipulating the emotional responses of individuals. Occasionally, this leads to mass outbursts of the difficult-to-research 'mercurial variables' such as collective aggression, murderous frenzy and vindictive warfare.[22]

The porous nature of the collective political system is undoubtedly most emphasised in the psychoanalytical tradition. Even before Freudian psychoanalysis took intellectual roots, philosophers such as Nietzsche, Bergson, Kierkegaard, Pareto, and Sorel dwelt extensively on the undercurrents in man's 'stream of consciousness'. Jung systematised this theme by introducing the notion of 'archetype images', i.e. archaic types of mental imagery embedded in man's collective unconscious. They originated in a specific historical milieu, but later became intrapsychic constructs which surfaced subsequently as national and social myths.[23] As a special form of shared fantasy, the myth serves to bring the individual into a relationship with other group members and through this interaction becomes fused in complex belief systems.[24]

Even without accepting the psychoanalytical perspective, a wide variety of studies seems to imply an almost intuitive agreement that collective political belief systems reflect both the rational cognitive and the conscious and subconscious inner needs of the individuals and the collective. The ideology of the utopian and millenarian movements is a particularly good case in point. Research which links individual psychological responses to ideational consolidation at the collective level is another case in point. For instance, Socialist Zionism is said to have included elements derived from a personal rebellion against the father.[25] Tucker gives an impressive account of how Stalin's neurotic childhood caused him to strive for omnipotence which was subsequently institutionalised in the personality cult of the official Soviet ideology.[26]

Political Belief Systems and the Level of Analysis: The Problem of Cognitive Style

One of the most difficult problems in analysing political beliefs is the question of the level of analysis. The potential implication of this problem was not fully realised in the past, because historically the empirical study of ideology grew out of the analysis of the conservative-liberal continuum in Western democracies. For reasons which are too complex to elaborate here, few studies followed Converse's dictum to employ 'over-arching dimensions on which large arrays of events' may be understood.[27] Of course, these higher abstractions refer to the influence of cognitive styles on political belief systems.

Rokeach's study on dogmatism popularised the notion that beliefs at the individual level are linked to cognitive styles.[28] In collective belief systems this assumption has surfaced under a bewildering array of terms such as 'superordinate values', 'core beliefs', 'cultural referents', 'latent attitudes' or 'rockbed sedimentation', to mention just a few. The vision of the less-than-universal process of thought that the concept of cognitive style invokes was explored by comparative cognitive psychology but has not been systematically incorporated in the study of collective belief systems.

One rather paradoxical reason for this neglect pertains to the fact that these higher abstract constructs are so integrated in the belief system that they are taken for granted. In Lane's term, 'these most fundamental beliefs, embedded in the cultural matrix of behaviour and expectation are so pervasive and dense that one mistakes it for the natural environment'.[29] The second reason stems from a measure of ethnocentrism in the methodology of political science. It involves what Booth calls the 'privileging' of the researcher's own cultural conceptual system, and the tendency to use it in analysing aspects of other cultures.[30] Whether such bias is caused by beliefs in the superiority of one's own culture, by a lack of cross-cultural sophistication, or by a scientific socialisation which results in equating one's cultural 'givens' with universal laws of human behaviour, it inevitably distorts the theoretical perspective and hampers empirical research.

Even when the investigator is aware of the pitfalls of ethnocentric methodology, finding cross-cultural conceptual equivalents is not easy. Wilson dwells on the problem of translating the meaning of one culture into the language of another and the use of scientific terms to explain super-empirically oriented beliefs.[31] Przeworsky and Teune note the non-equivalence in the meaning of reality and time across cultural boundaries.[32]

Nowhere is the problem more acute than in determining what

constitutes a 'rational' belief system at either the collective or the individual level. Lukes's remark that the 'use of the word "rational" and its cognates has caused untold confusion and obscurity' is probably an accurate comment on the state of the art.[33] Yet assumptions about rationality are the backbone of research in foreign policy and strategic studies.

A major source of confusion in discussing the construct of rationality pertains to the fact that there are three different ways of defining it. One definition derives from *formal logic*. The requirements of formal logic define the parameters of a rational decision. Such a decision must satisfy three criteria: consistency, instrumentality, and transitivity. Consistency is defined in terms of preferences about outcomes. If one prefers outcome O1 to outcome O2, one cannot prefer at the same time O2 to O1. Instrumentality is defined in terms of the relation between action and outcome. If one prefers outcome O1 to outcome O2, one should also prefer action A1 to A2 assuming that A1 leads to O1 and A2 leads to O2. Transitivity is a preference in a polyadic pattern of options. For instance, in a triad, if one prefers O1 to O2 and O2 to O3, then one should prefer O1 to O3.

Because of the restrictive nature of these parameters, violation of logical rationality is extremely pervasive in human action. Some types of violations are related to cross-cultural differences. Rapoport points out that consistency can be undermined 'when a decision maker changes his mind for no apparent reason'. Such a change can be whimsical or patterned, as in the example of the man who prefers meat to fish, but chooses fish on Friday. Such behaviour can be labelled 'irrational' only at the peril of ignoring cultural factors. If the man is a Catholic, the pattern may be consistent in religious terms.[34]

Moreover, the use of formal logic in evaluating individual or collective belief systems is of little help in discerning 'empirical rationality'. This seems paradoxical in face of the popular belief that logic somehow equates with 'empirical truth'. Unfortunately the deductive system of formal logic deals with logical certainty or *validity*, not with 'factual certainty'. In her classic study on formal logic, Langer pointed out that 'we can start with premises that have no foundation in fact at all and elaborate a perfectly . . . consistent deductive system'.[35] Only if the society is committed to the scientific paradigm as well, is there some guarantee that its belief system will be empirically rational.[36] Traditional or religious belief systems can often be logically constrained, but are never structured in a way which renders their theorems liable to empirical verification.

A second definition of rationality derives from the *Theory of Games* by Von Neumann and Morgenstern.[37] The paradigm of the rational behaviour of an individual is based on the *minimax principle*. This principle postulates that a rational decision maker will use a techinque for maximising his utilities at a minimum cost. The major pitfall of this formulation is that the rationality of a decision can only be evaluated if the individual's subjective scale of utility can be converted to some objective and comparable scale. Because of individual and cross-cultural differences in utilities, the assumption of rationality had to be relaxed to the point where it was simply defined as social choice. Laboratory tests of gaming theories, such as Prisoner's Dilemma or the Trucking Game, reveal that subjects deviate from the rational behaviour prescribed by such games.[38]

The third and by far the most popular notion of rationality is defined in terms of the process through which individuals select means in order to achieve their ends. The *means-ends rationality* is subjective; it is based on the phenomenological assumption that individual perceptions define the context of the decision. An objective evaluation of the quality of the means-ends rationality involves an analysis of the process through which individuals or groups reach a decision.

Scholars offer three models for evaluating this process: the analytical, the cybernetic and the cognitive. The analytical model assumes that decision makers go through the following steps: comprehensive search for options, optimal revision, complete evaluation, and value maximisation. The cybernetic model assumes that decision makers use a programmed operation to select appropriate means for the given ends. The core of the cybernetic procedure is known as 'satisficing', i.e. the reduction of uncertainty and complexity by small and marginal changes. The cognitive model assumes that decision makers act somewhat like 'intuitive scientists'; they can construct causal explanations and show some capacity for formal logical rigour.[39]

Extensive psychological research devoted to evaluating these processes is quite unanimous in documenting that the quality of means-ends rationality is rather low regardless of which of the models is adopted. Some deviations stem from cognitive errors of the individual, such as flows in logical reasoning, low tolerance of cognitive dissonance, commitment to a central concept, or cognitive simplicity. Other factors pertain to the affective states of the decision makers, such as emotional involvement and stress. Still others are related to group biases, such as 'group think' or 'risky shifts'.[40]

While these deviations can occur within one culture, means-ends rationality becomes even more complicated when analysed across cultures. This difficulty is epitomised by the classic anthropological query as to whether praying for rain is a rational act, given the fact that, objectively, prayer is less likely to produce rain than cloud seeding.[41] The means-ends rationality of an act can be evaluated only within the context of a particular societal belief system and depends on the extent of the knowledge of means within the society, i.e. options and their legitimacy. In pre-scientific societies, extraordinary events which seemed opposed to the order of nature, such as drought or flood, were regarded as signs of heaven's wrath. Prayer was used to mollify God or the heavens, and therefore can be seen as a rational act. In addition, not all known means are accepted by a society as legitimate means for problem solving. For instance, birth control techniques, though objectively effective in controlling population growth, are not perceived as legitimate by a number of contemporary belief systems.

The use of cognitive style has an immense but largely unrealised potential for explaining belief systems as they relate to foreign policy matters. Elkins and Simeon advocate the use of super-ordinate values, such as assumptions about the order of the universe, the nature of causality, or perceptions of competitiveness.[42] Lane asserts that perceptions of resources, dichotomised into scarcity and abundance, may become embedded in a society's belief system.[43] If the former predominates it can create a zero-sum game perception, i.e. a competitive international outlook; if the latter prevails, it will lead to a variable-sum game perception, i.e. a co-operative outlook.

Another concept of considerable relevance for the study of collective belief systems is the perception of time. One instance of cross-cultural variability in perceptions of time is the religiously-inspired cyclical notion of time, as opposed to Western secular concepts of time which postulate a linear progression from one event to another. Cyclical notions of time imply a fusion of past, present and future. One such cycle is the Chinese concept of time as world age; time was assumed to start all over again every twenty-three million years. Cyclicality is also implied in the Talmudic concept of Redemption which, though consigned to the remote future, would restore the glory of the past.

The perception of time can influence the political belief system of a society in many ways. Sivin argues that the cyclical notion of time created an ambivalence in the way the Chinese perceived progress and modernisation. On the one hand, there was an awareness of progress and change, but on the other hand, the recurrence of situational contexts made the past relevant to the present.[44] The notion of fused time can hold a major moral significance because it organises events in a moral sequence leading to a transcendental goal such as Redemption.[45] The normative purposiveness implied in such a time concept has quite different implications for a society from the value-neutral notion of linear progression.

Another instance where time can be differentially perceived is in what Lane calls utopian as opposed to incremental thinking. The utopian mode has a certain 'timeless' quality in experiencing time which influences profoundly the perception of political possibilities in the belief system.[46] The utopian sense of time, with its perceptual corollary of unlimited possibility, can produce a more initiating posture in national or group policies than the more cautious incremental appreciation of time.

Cross-cultural analysis provides some additional insights into the understanding of foreign policy and especially conflict and co-operation. The first is the cultural variability in perceptions of the moral order. Each group moralises its code of behaviour in order to enhance group cohesion and collective commitment to law and order. But societies differ greatly in the degree to which they perceive their code as the ultimate form of universal morality. In the extreme case of the absolutist perception of morality, or what Mannheim calls 'total conception of ideology', the group questions the opponent's *Weltanschauung*, including his conceptual apparatus. When the moral perception is more relative, that is, Mannheim's 'particularist ideology', the group will try to 'refute lies and eradicate sources of error [in the adversary's belief system] by referring to accepted criteria of objective validity common to both parties'.[47] Needless to say, the absolutist morality involves a much sharper zero-sum game perception of inter-group relations than the alternative outlook.

The second insight derives from attribution theory, which comprises the set of theoretical principles proposed to explain how people draw causal inferences about each other's behaviour. Based on Heider's work on phenomenal causality, attribution theory assumes that the linking of events to causal sources is crucial in the way an individual or group perceives its environment.[48] Perception of causality depends on perception of intention, and it is here that large cultural differences exist. For example, in the Jewish Talmudic culture, an action is scrupulously evaluated according to the intention of the actor; in some cases, the intention is judged to be more important than the action. Anthropological research has documented the elaborate procedures for ascertaining intention in tribal cultures.

That different perceptions of intentionality may affect causality is of great importance for theories of international relations and even for some applied fields such as intelligence. When acts are ambiguous and difficult to interpret, as most acts in international relations are, the reaction, including the 'benefit of the doubt' calculus, will depend on variable national perceptions of intentionality.

Domestic Belief Systems and Foreign Policy Beliefs: The Problem of Correlation

The correlation between domestic belief systems and foreign policy beliefs is difficult to ascertain, as the literature on linkage in international relations demonstrates. For instance, Rosenau's representative volume on the subject reveals that national foreign policy may be either interactionist or isolationist because of a variety of reasons, ranging from the structure of domestic advocacy groups to geographical insularity.[49]

The collective domestic belief system is a poor predictor of a country's foreign policy for several reasons. First, countries are universally committed to preserving basic values such as physical survival of the population, territorial integrity and political sovereignty. More national variation can be expected in what Brecher called 'context specific' beliefs, that is, foreign policy issues which are defined by the countries as 'high priority'.[50] However, unlike the internal sovereignty of the domestic environment, rules of international interaction allow less leverage in pursuing such subjectively defined beliefs. As a result, foreign policy beliefs exhibit less national variation than domestic beliefs.

Second, domestic belief systems may affect the international outlook of a country indirectly and in ways which are empirically difficult to investigate. Jervis raised the intriguing possibility that some societies tend to develop a more Hobbesian foreign policy culture than others. A Hobbesian outlook tends to create a zero-sum game perception of the external environment and can prompt a country to choose the spiral, i.e. highly competitive, model of international interaction.[51] Other countries have a more co-operative foreign policy cognition and abide by the rules of the deterrence model.

Third, there is the theoretical and methodological difficulty in delineating foreign issues and beliefs. Rosenau and others have dealt with the formidable problems which have to be overcome in order to isolate foreign policy issues from domestic attitudes. Yet Rosenau's conclusion that foreign policy issues may or may not constitute an area with clear-cut boundaries and distinguishable characteristics bears testimony to the confusion surrounding this problem.[52]

This confusion arises from two interrelated questions which can be separated only in analytical terms. One is the degree of correlation between domestic and foreign policy beliefs and the second is their respective degrees of autonomy within the framework of the total societal belief system. These questions can best be answered by looking at the structure of individual beliefs.

At the most general level of discourse we accept McClosky's opinion that foreign policy attitudes do not differ from other political and social attitudes; they spring together with other attitude phenotypes from common personality genotypes.[53] Nevertheless, a perusal of the empirical literature raises doubts that domestic and foreign policy beliefs correlate. This is especially noticeable in research aimed at identifying clusters of domestic and foreign policy opinions which can be scaled along the traditional left-right or liberal-conservative continuum. In fact, evidence points out that such a cluster is at best not universal and at worst non-existent.[54]

The explanations which are normally offered for these findings range from the methodological shortcomings of undimensional and multidimensional scaling to the impact of privatism. The theme of privatism is derived from the sociologically-oriented perspective which argues that mass beliefs in post-industrial society are based on a non-ideological interest in those features of political life which are instrumental to the private life of an individual.[55] Privatism tends to produce issue-specific responses towards domestic and foreign policies. Such responses may 'swing' in all directions, reminscent of the 'issue voting' which was identified in recent literature on elections in Western democracies.

Perhaps the most important explanation is based on the functional rationale behind belief formation. Individual belief systems are functional in relating the self to society. Societal beliefs are functional in solving group conflict arising out of problems concerning the authoritative allocation of values. The domestic context provides the individual with what Abelson calls 'episodic concrete information' with which he can formulate and shape his beliefs. Such nationally focused beliefs are difficult to apply to an international context which may be equivalent to Abelson's 'abstract information environment'.[56] Rosenau and Holsti provide an especially perceptive illustration of this difficulty when describing the foreign policy thinking of the American elite. 'In thinking about domestic affairs, one is inclined to develop integrated beliefs about justice, equality, representation . . . values that have little applicability to the conditions to which foreign policy is addressed.'[57]

The second analytical problem relates to the question of whether foreign policy opinion enjoys a greater autonomy in the total belief system of the individual than do domestic beliefs. The limited number of studies which address themselves to this issue are quite uniform in concluding that the former are even less autonomous than the latter. Given the normally remote and abstract nature of foreign policy, these findings are a non-obvious result, which can be explained in terms of motivational and cognitive psychology.

First, people have generally only a limited knowledge of a foreign environment. Under conditions of information scarcity, individuals tend to rely more on stereotyped thinking. Research on perceptions of outgroups and foreign nationals has documented that only a small proportion of ethnic and national stereotypes is positive. Negative stereotyping and prejudice are often used by members of a national group to channel aggression and build up internal cohesion.[58]

Second, an unfamiliar environment over which the individual and his country have no control appears to be potentially threatening, regardless of the intrinsic character of the issue involved. Moreover, the content of foreign policy debates is often ambiguous, the messages confused, contradictory and unfamiliar to a person. Such a confusing set of stimuli can generate cognitive dissonance, anxiety, fear and other deep emotions. Third, foreign policy issues are often invested with symbolic meaning, that is, they are ideal 'sources of arousal' which can trigger highly emotive responses. Attacks on officially designated national symbols abroad such as diplomatic posts and personnel are especially arousing, but more pedestrian issues such as international water rights can provoke highly emotive responses. Decolonisation, even in the case of marginal possessions, can create a massive psychological trauma, as Lijphert's study on Dutch divestiture of its West New Guinea colony showed.[59]

Indeed, highly emotive responses to foreign policy issues have been occasionally manipulated for mobilisation purposes, especially in non-democratic regimes. Some political leaders use highly symbolic foreign policy issues in order to overcome domestic difficulties and promote national cohesion. In some cases, domestic failures are redefined in such a way as to be perceived as an outcome of the hostile international environment.

Of course, the least autonomous response is elicited in international conflicts which threaten the physical survival of a group, or struggles which are couched in terms of a clash between total belief systems. Religious wars, the struggle between the big 'isms' such as Nazism, Fascism, Communism and Capitalism, and the emergent fissures between the North and the South pose an immense threat to the very identity of an individual. This type of conflict, which mobilises the entire psychological defence system of a person, generates the most profound emotive responses.[60]

The conclusion that foreign policy beliefs are not structurally aligned with domestic beliefs, and that their boundaries are virtually undeterminable, is echoed in McClosky's seminal study on the psychological origins of isolationism in America. 'It may spring from psychological needs and impulses as well as from social, intellectual or political elements and it need not serve the same function or possess the same meaning to all persons who embrace it.'[61] For obvious reasons, most foreign policy research which has to account for numerous structural and objective factors in both the domestic and the international environment cannot delve into the psychology of the individual or collective belief system of a society. But the complex psychological grounding of any foreign policy system should be recognised as an important parameter of any discussion in international relations.

Identifying the Political Belief System of a Society: The Process of Legitimisation

The porous nature of the political domain creates a number of problems in defining the contours of a political belief system. The most difficult problem stems from the fact that the process of forming a collective belief system has to be analysed through a duality of focus between the psychological states of the individual, on the one hand, and the macrosociological realities, on the other hand, which is filtered through the psychological state of the researcher. This process is circular — individual psychological states in constant interaction with the sociopolitical environment consolidate beliefs into ideology which generates, sustains, and changes social order.

The sheer complexity of such a conversion process requires a conceptual framework which can interrelate in a systematic way personal beliefs and the macrosociological level of the social order. This framework must also possess a methodology which can equate the language of empirical research in individual psychology with the conceptual constructs developed by political science and sociology which treat individuals as high-level abstracts or molar groups. The conceptual framework proposed here is based on a number of assumptions.

According to cognitive psychology, humans have developed an elaborate system for selecting information which is essential for survival. The relatively limited amount of information which humans can process constitutes the basis of perceptions. These selective perceptions are variously known as 'cognitive maps', 'cognitive representation', or 'perceptual-representation systems'.[62]

Collective belief systems are created by individuals whose survival has always depended upon group existence. To facilitate social interaction and cope with the environment, individuals must reach a certain consensus on the definition of the situation. Tajfel described this process as the cultural 'interpretation of the information provided by our senses into coherent patterns'.[63] Mannheim suggested that such a process leads to a 'collective definition of the situation' — 'a situation is constituted as such when it is defined in the same way for the members of the group'.[64]

Such a collective belief system constitutes the parameters of the social order of a given society in a given period of time. The selection of elements which make up the belief system is not arbitrary or random. Known as the *imperative of selection*, these elements represent a limited matrix of beliefs which are perceived by the group to be most instrumental for its survival and cohesion. This matrix includes basic postulates about the nature of the world and of men. Such *existential postulates* provide the framework for generating additional beliefs and values.

In addition to its meaning-giving function, a collective belief system is also normative. Reflecting the normative-evaluative needs of individuals, each dominant belief system includes a set of implicit or explicit assumptions about what constitutes 'good' or 'bad'. These assumptions are called *normative postulates*.[65] Together with the existential postulates, they provide the *Weltanschauung* of a society, or the frame of reference for the group and the individual.

Another property which is co-jointly generated by the individual and the collective belief system pertains to the affective dimension of human existence. Known also as 'affective loading', it colours the perceptual-representational system of an individual. Affect is partially idiosyncratic and partially social in origin. It is formed by the individual in the process of developing a social identity. Social identity is composed of congeries of subidentities, such as national, ethnic, religious, social, and gender roles.[66] Affect is thus shaped by the extremely complex interaction of these subidentities which differ in multiplexity, hierarchical arrangement, centrality, salience and valence. For instance, subidentities which have high valence, i.e. attractiveness, for the individual would generate positive affective loading for the range of attitude objects subsumed under the particular subidentity.

The concept of identity-mediated affect emphasises the importance of the *symbolic* meaning of a collective belief system. Anthropologists who specialise in the study of persistent collective identity systems have always maintained that such systems are sustained by the preponderance of symbols which affectively bind the individual to his community. The selection of symbols — a form of linguistic manipulation — is not based on any logical relationship between them, and has only limited universal meaning. Symbols can be best understood in terms of a given culture. Neither are the symbols immutable. Symbolic referents are selected, altered and dropped as part of the ongoing adaptation of a group to a changing environment.[67]

Treating the collective belief system as a range of beliefs which define the social order of a group can help us to delineate its political dimension. In the most general Weberian sense, we can define the political system as the subset of beliefs *which conceptualise the authority system of a group*. The probability of any particular belief being included in such a subset depends upon its being *legitimised* by the individuals and the collective. A dominant political belief system contains the set of such normatively binding prescriptions.

Legitimisation, like any other hypothetical construct, is not easy to define. Apter's comment that 'legitimacy is too complex, related as it is to personal identity, and ultimately, to the individual's need for immortality, meaning and purpose . . .' is probably a painful reflection on the state of the art.[68] A perusal of the literature reveals that definitions of legitimisation and its cognate concepts, *legitimacy* and *legality*, differ immensely. At the risk of simplifying the various treatments of the concept, two major approaches can be identified. The first approach perceives legitimacy in terms of legality. An authority-system is considered to be legitimate if it operates according to a certain set of rules. Lawful descent in monarchies or adherence to rules stipulated by the social contract of a given society, such as its constitution, were assumed to satisfy the conditions for legitimacy.[69]

The second approach is analytically more diffuse. Its lowest common denominator is based on a phenomenological view of legitimacy, i.e. legitimacy as an outcome of individual psychological states. Fraser, who reviewed this approach, summed up its essence as follows:[70]

legitimacy does not refer to whether authorities or structures follow some concrete set of objective rules, but to the extent to which members of a political system believe that the authorities and structures are adequate to meet the members' own expectations.

Another difficulty pertains to the definition of *authority system*. In spite of the variable language used, there is an agreement in the literature that this construct includes two elements. One is *group legitimacy* and the other is *regime legitimacy*.[71]

Group legitimacy involves the set of concepts which define the boundary of a group. This boundary is normally defined in terms of membership and territory. The criteria for legitimising membership are based on what Lewin called 'feelings of interdependence'[72], which include, among other things, sharing of a historical time perspective. Other social psychologists stress similarities such as kinship, language, culture and religious traits. These traits are incorporated into the social subidentities of the individual and it is through them that the group membership is perpetuated. The criteria for legitimising territorial expanses can range from the very instrumental to the sentimental-normative. Research in ecological sociology indicates that the former is based on perception of the territorial tract as property, resource or military asset, whereas the latter perceives the expanse as the centre of the moral-religious order of the group.[73]

External groups play a major role in legitimising a group's membership and territory but one which is difficult to determine. Coser and other sociologists of conflict pointed out that conflict with external forces over membership or territory may increase the cohesion and hence the self-legitimacy of the group[74], but others argued that withdrawal of external legitimacy may negatively affect the group.[75] Neither does external acceptance lead to an automatic increase in the discharge of group legitimacy. Multiethnic or multinational empires, which have been accorded high legitimacy by the international system, have often failed to generate enough internal legitimacy among their members.

The boundaries of membership have fluctuated widely throughout history. Legitimisation of more inclusive forms of membership has led from primordial kinship groups to larger multigroup entities, of which the nation state is the most contemporary form. The group membership of a nation state is legitimised on the basis of a collective national identity which subsumes or supersedes more primordial types of association.

Territorial boundaries, a habitual contesting ground between competing authority systems, have also fluctuated widely, producing a whole range of territorial/membership discrepancies. Some groups, such as the Jews prior to 1948, were left without territory, whereas some territorial states are composed of groups which refuse to legitimise their membership in the central authority system. Among stateless societies, the Palestinians are a more recent example of this discrepancy. Self-refusal of membership has taken many forms. The most common are demands for special membership status, i.e. autonomy; voluntary group exit, i.e. emigration; irredentism, i.e. a demand by a group (inclusive of its territory) to change membership by joining another state; and secession, i.e. a demand for full self-determination.

Regime legitimacy is a composite construct which includes two interrelated components. One pertains to the legal base of the authority system and the other focuses on the conceptualisation of the problem of distributive justice. This distinction corresponds to what was traditionally called authority legitimation and interest articulation.

Most typologies which deal with the legal base of authority incorporated to some extent Weber's distinction between three types of authority: rational-legal, traditional, and charismatic.[76] More recent treatment dichotomised these categories into a *numinous* and a *civic* authority system. Numinous legitimacy is based on claims of divine origin or externally-derived rights of the group members.[77] A democratic type of contractual legitimacy requires the group to institute procedures for an ongoing reaffirmation of legitimacy. Seen in this way, democratic elections are not only a means of staffing the decision-making structure of the authority system, but also a constant 'legitimisation referendum'.

In non-democratic settings, the process of legitimisation of the civic authority system is more diffuse. The variety of regimes which are included in this category normally rely on what may be called 'mobilisatory legitimisation'. Mobilisation structures and processes which are focused on monopolistic parties provide means of discharging popular legitimacy for the authorities. Forums for populistic participation like mass rallies and plebiscites provide additional ways of reaffirming legitimacy. Quite often, the process of legitimisation is targeted on an individual leader and stimulated by a leadership cult. Alternatively, it can be focused on a collective leadership recruited from the social stratum which is perceived as most salient in sustaining the authority system and thus most closely identified with it in the public eye. Some contemporary examples of such leadership are military juntas and collective revolutionary coteries.

The dichotomous presentation of the numinous and civic types obscures the fact that legitimisations of the authority system are and do include elements of both. In fact, because of the uneven process of modernisation, there are an abundance of regimes in which select elements of numinous authority were not delegitimised in spite of the onset of more civic norms. Constitutional monarchies, semi-theocratic democracies and civil religion-oriented modernising regimes are all cases in point.

The conceptualisation of distributive justice constitutes the second component of regime legitimacy. Derived from the general category of *principles of justice* which Galston defined as reasons or criteria for assigning particular things to particular individuals, distributive justice pertains to the pattern in which a group divides goods and resources among its members.[78]

Each social group legitimises the type and range of resources which are perceived as instrumental in facilitating its corporate existence. Scholars generally agree that resources can range from the very symbolic to the very material. Material resources, both public and private, include economic opportunities and rewards. In most cases, symbolic and material resources are interchangeable at both the individual and the collective level. To satisfy the requirements of distributive justice, the criteria for distributing resources are invariably based on validity claims. In the most simplified manner, three types of validity claims can be identified: ascriptive-traditional, utilitarian-productive, and equalitarian.

Ascriptive-traditional validity claims are based on a mixture of economic and non-economic principles. Ascriptive claims, such as birth rights, or divine rights, are crystallised into a class or caste order, and used as a basis for a disproportional division of resources, including production factors such as land, capital and command of entrepreneurship. Conversely, the absence of ascriptive rights, as in the case of slavery or serfdom, could lead to a nearly total 'expropriation' of members from the distributive process.

The utilitarian-productive validity claim is derived from the market principle. In a free market economy, the price system determines the quantity of material resources each member of the society will receive. An individual who possesses scarce factors of production such as capital or labour skills will get a higher share of resources than his counterpart who possesses production factors which are in relative abundance. Adam Smith's theoretical treatment of capitalism and the English utilitarian philosophy contributed enormously to the legitimisation of validity claims based upon meritocracy in contemporary models of distributive justice.

The equalitarian validity claim, conceptualised by Marx, is based on the notion that members of the community are entitled to an equal share of the collective material resources. Thus, an individual's share of the resources is not related to his ascriptive status or to his command of productive capacity, but is the quotient of the collective resources divided by the number of members. With the exception of small groups, modern societies have not managed to legitimise any of the pure types of validity claims. Even the communist regimes seem to be regressing towards some of the free market validity claims rather than progressing towards what Marx envisaged as an ultimate stage in distributive justice, that is, distribution according to individual needs.

The process of legitimisation of a political belief system takes place within the framework of what is known as the 'discursive practice' of a society, that is, 'interpretation or narrative presentation of validity claims or norms'.[79] Scholars seem to agree that the ideological discourse of a group is not generated by a simple equitable model of participation. Rather, it is dominated by *crucial elites* which specialise in 'defining the situation', that is, symbolically interpreting the world. Such elites are drawn from the political, economic and religious sectors of the society, but also include free-floating intellectuals or intelligentsia. Intellectuals have been important in 'objectifying' conflict, that is, transmuting a conflict of interests into a conflict of ideas.[80]

Recent research on changing communication in modern societies seems to challenge some of these generalisations. Scholars have pointed out that the advent of communication and advertising has resulted in the 'merchandising' of social reality. Young, a major proponent of the 'dramaturgical society' theory, argues that 'legitimacy itself is as a commodity for sale'.[81] But it may also be argued that mass dissemination of the legitimacy discourse has contributed to a more sophisticated public understanding of the issues involved.

Incremental Changes in the Political Belief System: The Process of Delegitimisation.

Efforts to discern evolving changes in a belief system are inherently difficult. These changes are normally incremental and spread out over long stretches of time. Even when political change is dramatically 'telescoped' into a short revolutionary period or is revealed in a realigning election, it has been preceded by a largely undetected or subtle change in the dominant political belief system. Broadly speaking, political change is caused when elements of the dominant belief system become delegitimised. *Delegitimisation* is an aggregate result of personal psychological states. Individuals may discard their beliefs and values if they clash with new realities. When enough individuals in a society go through the same dissonant process, they eventually delegitimise the old beliefs.

The process of delegitimisation is even less understood in political science than its corollary, legitimisation. Eldridge, who surveyed the literature on political alienation, which is a major form of delegitimisation, commented that scholars are not interested in identifying the sources of an alienated perception. Alienation sets in when 'people perceive that the values of the government differ from and conflict with their own political values. What causes this perception is not clear.'[82] Other scholars treat the process of legitimisation and delegitimisation as a 'black box'. For instance, the authors of a recent article on delegitimisation in the dominant party system of Israel simply stated that this process is 'a construction of periods of crisis and transformation or both'.[83]

Unfortunately, there is no single theory which can explain the extremely complex way in which individuals and macrosystems interact in delegitimising the political belief system. At the systemic level of discussion, it is possible to relate changes in belief systems to the notion of *equilibrium* and *disequilibrium*. System theories indicate that political change is minimal when the polity is in equilibrium. Disequilibrium may result from a disalignment between inputs and outputs in the system.

One of the major problems in the analysis of the phenomenon of disequilibrium is to identify the threshold conditions, i.e. the causes which may trip the equilibrium. Johnson's typology of possible 'triggers' is by far the most sophisticated treatment of the sources of change. The four types include exogenous value changing, e.g., external reference groups; endogenous value changing, e.g., religious innovation; exogenous environment changing, e.g., war and foreign conquest; and endogenous environment changing, e.g., technological innovation.[84]

The major shortcoming of this typology stems from the difficulty of classifying some types of triggers. One of them is demographic change in the racial, ethnic, and religious composition of the population. In countries like Israel, where ethnic groups are marked by differential fertility rates, continuous uneven growth can change the demographic distribution. The emergence of a new group can be included in the endogenous value-changing category, but it may also be classified as an endogenous environment trigger. Another problematic variable is the rise of new classes. In some ways, changing class structure is an outcome of technological innovation, that is, the endogenous environment-changing category. But new classes, by creating different norms, also bear on the endogenous value change of a society. Such problems, though, should not detract from the usefulness of this typology, especially as one may assume that 'triggers' can interact across dimensions.

The analysis of the process of delegitimisation at the individual level is even more complex. A perusal of social science literature reveals that there are three explanatory perspectives. The first perspective is loosely based on Durkheim's notion of anomie. Anomie develops when progress in the division of labour upsets the traditional belief system and threatens the delicate normatively established balance between the needs and demands of the society, and the idiosyncratic needs of the individual.[85]

In an anomic social state, the meaning of normatively defined legitimate expectations and the prescribed behaviour to achieve them becomes ambiguous. Social work theorists demonstrated that by generating *stress*, anomie affects individual psychological states. Stress is conceptualised as malfunctioning in the emotional *homeostasis* of the individual. Homeostasis is defined as successful coping with the 'demands of life which constantly confront the individual'.[86] Since individuals perceive the society as the source of need-satisfaction and gratification, or, in Parson's terms, as the 'optimation of gratification',[87] successful coping hinges upon satisfying normatively perceived needs. While in every society there are individuals who fail to cope because of idiosyncratic reasons, anomic states, by creating ambiguities in perceiving what is a legitimate need-satisfaction, produce group stress. When such group stress sets in, the affected group, class or society will proceed to delegitimise elements in the authority system.

The second explanatory perspective is derived from what can be broadly described as the sociological tradition of normative and value strain analysis. These studies deal with the structure of stratification in social systems and its contingent hierarchy of roles. The ranking of roles in a society is derived from *determinants* which are based on the 'social value' of roles. 'Social value' is a perceived property of the role that is normally dictated by *expediency*. Expediency is highly variable, for, as Stinchcombe pointed out, societies do differ over time and space with regard to their needs.[88]

It is easy to see how such a densely patterned role structure in a society can produce normative strain at the individual level. This occurs most often when social expediencies change, but the role is not 'demoted' accordingly. In European history, normative stress developed between the newly expedient middle classes and the socially 'redundant' aristocracy which refused to relinquish its social and political position. In many newly created states, including Israel, normative strain between new social strata and the old pioneering elite helped to delegitimise the founding ideology.

The third explanatory perspective is derived from cognitive psychology, more specifically the theories of cognitive consistency that have dominated the field for more than two decades. To put it simply, cognitive dissonance theories assume that individuals feel uncomfortable when they are faced with two cognitive elements which are dissonant, i.e. contradictory. An individual may develop the same uneasiness when there is dissonance between the cognitive and affective elements in his attitude. In order to reduce the psychological discomfort, the individual will eliminate the source of dissonance. Reduction of dissonance should not be equated with 'scientific rationality'. Some individuals, faced with cognitive evidence which contradicts their beliefs or affects, may readjust them to absorb the new reality; others may 'write off' the new information to protect their consonant state.[89]

Cognitive dissonance theories have come under increasing criticism in recent years. Billig, in his excellent critique, argues that the major weakness of these theories is the difficulty of determining what constitutes a dissonant cognitive element in an individual's belief system. Since there is no universal logic which 'dictates whether two cognitions will be perceived as being consistent or inconsistent', his conclusion is that consistency is defined by the 'social context'.[90] The more recently popular attribution theory demonstrates that people can tolerate dissonance and cognitive ambiguity because of errors in causal inference.[91] Converse, in his seminal work on mass belief systems, found empirical evidence that most people harbour contradictory or dissonant attitudes towards politics.[92] Finally, anthropologists and social theorists have long argued that ambiguity and contradictions are functional to both the individual and the societies.

The discussion of consistency theory and its intellectual rivals which emphasise human capacity to cope with ambiguity and dissonance makes difficult reading for the understanding of the process of delegitimisation. If people can misinterpret information in order to protect their beliefs and affects, or because they can tolerate dissonance and ambiguity, how then do they change their beliefs and delegitimise traditional values? Worse still, the normative system can 'block' the elimination of such inconsistencies by continuous socialisation. Indeed, the existence of such defence mechanisms can explain why political changes can be agonisingly slow and convoluted.

It is possible to provide a more adequate explanation of the process of delegitimisation by combining the insights of all three explanatory perspectives. The point of departure for our synthesis is based on the widespread notion in cognitive psychology that humans engage in *validation* of their beliefs with the behavioural outcomes of these beliefs, i.e. actions. The concept of validation, or rather construct validation, is derived from scientific research methods. It involves hypothesising some theoretical construct, linking it with some other causes, devising a method for measuring the hypothesised construct, and deciding whether the measured construct is consistent with the theoretical expectations.[93]

Of course, individuals do not act in a strictly scientific manner when they engage in validation. Rather, they reproduce in a very imprecise way parts of this process or act as 'intuitive scientists'. No matter how normatively skewed individual perceptions may be, or how faulty their inferential process is, some amount of 'reality testing' is involved in the process of thinking. In the process of coping, that is, obtaining need-gratification, individuals validate their beliefs and the normative claims of their collective belief system. If the behavioural outcomes of the normative structure fail to meet their expectations, they eventually change their beliefs and thus delegitimise the collective belief system.

Cognitive validation is a crucial but not sufficient condition for generating delegitimisation. A closely related prerequisite involves changes in the affective components of individual attitudes. In order to eliminate resistance to cognitive changes, an individual has to align his affect with the new cognition. He can achieve this by decreasing the *centrality* or salience of a belief and by depreciating its positive *valence*. Beliefs of high centrality, i.e. located in the central and more intimate personal spaces, and positive valence, i.e. high attractiveness, are more resistant to cognitively induced change.[94]

Crucial elites may accelerate the perception of dissonance which underlies the process of delegitimisation. It is a commonplace in social research that elites have a more consonant attitude structure and thus are more sensitive to emerging incongruities. Elites are also more skillful in successfully validating their claims, which are then disseminated to the mass public through the 'demonstration effect'.

A good illustration of how such dissonant states can lead to a delegitimisation of some traditional beliefs pertains to distributive justice. We have previously argued that the criteria of distributive justice are articulated in the process of the legitimisation discourse. The emergence of new groups, with a different view of what should constitute a legitimate criterion, may prompt them to validate the normative claims of the authority system by using these particularist expectations. For instance, emerging ethnic groups in a Western type of society may delegitimise a meritorious and universalist set of criteria, in favour of an ethnically based ascriptiveness and particularism. Demands for affirmative action, in order to close the gaps between various groups in the United States, are a prime example of such a process. In Israel, where the Oriental group became a majority, such a process has led to the delegitimisation of the Ashkenazi-dominated criteria of distributive justice.

The Shaping of a New Belief System: The Process of Transvaluation

Transvaluation is the companion process to delegitimisation, whereby new and more consonant values are sanctioned to replace the beliefs which were discarded. As with legitimisation, this process takes place both at the individual and the collective level. There are two difficulties in discussing the process of transvaluation.

The first difficulty derives from the fact that transvaluation can be separated from delegitimisation only analytically. Empirically, the formulation of new values takes place in the course of the same discourse which undermines the old values. The interaction between delegitimisation and transvaluation is so dynamic that no clear 'end periods' exist. Apter, in his study of modernisation, touched upon this difficulty when discussing the concept of *retraditionalisation*. In retraditionalisation, 'a new coherence of values, institutions and organization' has to be established toward the end of the development period. But he also admits that the 'urge to cohere' may not necessarily materialise successfully, leaving the system in a 'perpetual flux'.[95]

The second problem involves estimating the direction of transvaluation. Smith, in his work on religion and political development, argued that secularisation is the most important form of transvaluation. His rigorous analysis of the process of transvaluation involves structural, functional and cultural elements:[96]

(1) the separation of the polity from religious ideologies and ecclesiastical structures; (2) the expansion of the polity to perform regulatory functions in the socioeconomic spheres which were formerly performed by the religious structures; (3) the transvaluation of the political culture to emphasize nontranscendent temporal goals and rational, pragmatic means, that is secular political values.

This direction of transvaluation is neither universal nor irreversible. Borthwick pointed out that, in Islamic countries, transvaluation often takes the form of *polity-expansion secularisation*. The State's expansion does not involve a full structural or functional separation from the ecclesiastical realm, but bolsters the religious establishment. The political culture is a mixture of religious transcendental values and secular pragmatic values. In spite of considerable differences, Borthwick found that the mixture of Judaism and secular elements in Israel is in some ways akin to the pattern of polity-expansion secularisation in Islamic countries. The historical bond between religion, nation and land in Judaism was inherited and perpetuated by the State of Israel.[97]

Even when the transvaluation of the society achieves a certain degree of secularisation of the political culture and a matching infrastructure, this process can be reversed. The fundamentalist revolution in Iran is one of the more recent examples of such a trend. The progressive expansion of the religious realm in Israel is an even more interesting phenomenon in view of the fact that the country achieved a high degree of secularisation in its initial period.

Any empirical analysis of the process of transvaluation has to take these problems into account. We can solve some of the difficulties by studying a number of dimensions in the political process which are potentially most revealing of the ongoing transvaluation. First, it is possible to look at the patterns of mobilisation and political culture. This dimension can provide us with a sense of direction in the process of transvaluation. Second, we can identify the 'crucial discourse' of the society. Since crucial elites are instrumental in legitimising and delegitimising the dominant belief system, the thrust and theme of the public discourse can provide us with an early indication of the transvaluation which is taking place. For instance, the militarisation of the public debate in Israel is a reflection of the high status attained by the military.

Third, the analysis should account for the changing structure of interest groups in a society. In democratic or semidemocratic societies, a dominant belief system is sustained by an array of interest groups. Changes in the political coloration of these groups are early indicators of the impending transvaluation of the belief system.

This analytical framework should be adapted to the specific conditions of the society under investigation. In foreign policy analysis it is also essential to identify those parts of the collective belief system which have the most bearing on the *foreign policy decisions* of the country. We have argued throughout this introduction that the boundaries of the different dimensions are porous; thus, a broad-gauged definition of the foreign policy discourse and of the relevant dimensions of the political culture are in order.

The major methodological difficulty of such an approach to foreign policy stems from the fact that a broadly defined belief system does not delineate sharply enough the contours of the foreign policy system. This type of analysis also requires a mixture of traditional and behavioural techniques in order to achieve a more balanced picture of the reality under investigation. More specifically, we propose to study the foreign policy systems as an interaction of the macrosociological and the microsociological level of beliefs.

Analysing a Societal Belief System Under Conditions of Complexity: A Decision-making Approach

A most suitable way to achieve such an approach is to adopt a decision-oriented definition of the collective belief system. Derived from the anthropological concept of culture pattern, it was defined by Linton as the 'limited range of behavior within which the response of a society's members to a particular situation will normally fall'.[98] Elkins and Simeon define a belief system as the 'range of acceptable possible alternatives from which groups and individuals may choose a course of action, other circumstances permitting'.[99] Handel describes it as a 'formulation of a preferred course of action for a specific class of actors in a specific class of situations'.[100] Such a conceptualisation of a belief system has a number of advantages:

(1) It introduces the notion of probability into the explanation. The alternatives within the range (or set) are treated as permissive rather than deterministic events. Each individual event does not have to happen, but it has a certain probability of occurring. Such a definition is most appropriate for complex political systems in which personalities, social and political structures, role definitions, and external circumstances mediate the relationship between the range of belief options and policy decisions and behaviour.

(2) The notion of a range or set of alternatives, i.e. A, B, C or X, Y, Z, may instruct us as to the range of choices which the policy elite may pursue in response to certain given contingencies. In spite of personal idiosyncrasies, elites are rarely known to exceed the permissible range of alternatives for any given contingency.

(3) The notion of a range can help us to identify and compare the degree of variance among belief systems, either between nations or within one country. This is especially crucial when analysing incrementally changing belief systems within one polity. The

comparison of the old and new sets of alternatives will reveal whether there is a complete discontinuity, i.e. A, B, C, D, E, F or whether there is a degree of overlap between the sets, i.e. A, B, C, B, C, D or A, B, C ¯, C, D, E.

(4) The identification of a set can also help us to analyse the degree of salience (an increase in probability of occurrence) which the system attaches to a given alternative. It is often the case that two belief systems contain the same options, but accord them each a different salience. Options which carry high salience would be acted upon more readily by the elite.

(5) It is possible to identify assorted groups in terms of what subset of alternatives they occupy within the range. It is particularly important to identify the options of the power elite, because their preferred alternatives have a higher probability of turning into policy choices. Moreover, the position of ethnic, religious, pressure or challenge groups should be located. In coalition governments, their preferences may receive disproportionate weight and increase the probability that the alternatives in their subset will turn into policies. Also, policy makers would normally defer to the views of groups that invoke the spectre of *Kulturkampf*.

(6) The range can be used to estimate the empirical fit between elite and mass beliefs. One way to consider such a relation between elite beliefs and decision making is in power terms. Whenever there is massive popular support for elite beliefs, there is a high probability that the elite will act upon these beliefs.

Another way is to look at the same relationship through the psychological concept of 'anticipated reaction'. Elites frequently screen alternatives in anticipation of a positive or negative popular reaction. The effect of anticipated reaction on elite behaviour is difficult to determine empirically, because the process of screening may be at least partially subconscious. The knowledge of the distribution of mass attitudes within the range can provide an empirical substitute in investigating the effect of anticipated reaction.

A Research Design for Analysing the Foreign Policy System of Israel

The research design proposed here is based on a systematic effort to apply theoretical considerations to the study of the changing foreign policy system of Israel. The scheme consists of three parts which correspond to the three major themes: the historical change in the Jewish and Israeli collective belief system from Socialist Zionism to New Zionism; the psychopolitical dynamics which have underpinned the delegitimisation of Socialist Zionism and its trans-valuation into New Zionism; the application of New Zionism to the conduct of foreign policy under the Likud Government.

Part I traces the ideological changes throughout Jewish history in Diaspora and Israel. Chapter 2 reconstructs the psychopolitical predicaments caused by the marginal status of Jews in the host societies of the Diaspora and the traditional ideological responses to this predicament. Chapter 3 discusses the emergence of New Zionism from its Revisionist roots in the Diaspora and through new ideological formulations in Israel which include neo-Revisionism, National-Religious Zionism and the historiosophical evaluation of the phenomenon of anti-Semitism and the Holocaust.

Part II analyses the psychopolitical process through which Socialist Zionism was delegitimised and transvalued into New Zionism. Chapter 4 discusses the areas of dissonance which con-tributed to the delegitimisation of Socialist Zionism: the tension between a pioneering ideology and statism and the emergence of ethnic and religious groups which did not share the definition of group identity and distributive justice of the dominant ideology. Chapter 5 discusses the activation of latent contradictions between the relatively secular and universal elements in Socialist Zionism and the religious and particularist tendencies which were brought to the fore by the Six-Day War.

Chapter 6 identifies a number of factors which contributed to the transvaluation into New Zionism. One is the changing pattern of political mobilisation and the matching changes in the political culture. Another is the emergence of foreign policy as the crucial discourse in the society and its subsequent militarisation. The third is the changing political coloration of the pressure groups in Israeli society.

Part III relates the New Zionist belief system to the actual conduct of foreign policy under the Likud Government. Chapter 7 provides an overview of the impact of New Zionism in shaping the idealistic-initiating model of foreign policy and its actual application in the war in Lebanon. Chapter 8 discusses modifications of the New Zionist belief systems in the aftermath of the war.

The concluding section tries to integrate the three parts into a meaningful theoretical discussion. In a way, each of these parts can be treated as independent units. The integrating theme is derived from our view of a foreign policy system which relates the macrosociological and microsociological levels of analysis over an extended time period. Although this is a single country study, it is hoped that the conclusion will provide some comparative insights into the structure and process of foreign policy systems in general.

The Appendix provides a chronology of the developments which led to the Israeli decision to invade Lebanon.

Notes

1. For a good example see M. Brecher, *The Foreign Policy System of Israel*, (Oxford University Press, London, 1972).
2. K. N. Boulding, 'National Images and International Systems', *Journal of Conflict Resolution*, vol. 3, no. 2 (1959), pp. 120–37 and *The Image: Knowledge in Life and Society*, (University of Michigan Press, Ann Arbor, MI, 1963); H. Sprout and M. Sprout, 'Environmental Factors in the Study of International Politics' in J. N. Rosenau (ed.), *International Politics and Foreign Policy* (The Free Press of Glencoe, IL, 1961), pp. 106–19.
3. Boulding, 'National Images', p. 128.
4. *Ibid.*, pp. 120–37.
5. For some representative treatment, see N. Abercombie and S. B. Turner, 'The Dominent Ideology Thesis', *The British Journal of Sociology*, vol. 29, no. 2 (1978), pp. 149–67; T. Asad, 'Anthropology and the Analysis of Ideology', *Man*, vol. 14, no. 4 (1979), pp. 607–27; R. Ashcroft, 'Political Theory and the Problem of Ideology', *The Journal of Politics*, vol. 42, no. 3 (1980), pp. 687–721; H. Schmid, 'On the Origin of Ideology', *Acta Sociologica*, vol. 24, no. 1 (1981), pp. 57–73; M. Seliger, 'Fundamental and Operative Ideology: The Two Principal Dimensions of Political Argumentation', *Policy Sciences*, vol. 1, no. 4 (1970), pp. 325–38; L. B. Szalay, R. M. Kelly and T. W. Moon, 'Ideology: Its Meaning and Measurement', *Comparative Political Studies*, vol. 35, no. 2 (1972), pp. 151–73; R. Wuthnow, 'Comparative Ideology', *International Journal of Comparative Sociology*, vol. 22, no. 3–4 (1981), pp. 121–40.
6. K. Mannheim, *Ideology and Utopia* (Harvest HBJ Books, New York and London, 1955).
7. For a survey see L. B. Szalay and R. M. Kelly, 'Political Ideology and Subjective Culture: Conceptualization and Empirical Assessment', *The American Political Science Review*, vol. 76, no. 4 (1982), pp. 585–602.
8. T. W. Adorno, E. Frenkel-Brunswick, D. J. Levinson and N. Sanford, *The Authoritarian Personality*, (Harper and Row, New York, 1965).
9. For a good review see Schmid, 'On the Origin'.
10. Mannheim is the most emphatic advocate of this theory, *Ideology*, pp. 264–311.
11. Ashcroft, 'Political Theory,' pp. 687–721.
12. For a review see D. J. Elkins and R. E. B. Simeon, 'A Cause in Search of its Effects or What Does Political Culture Explain', *Comparative Politics*, vol. 11, no. 2 (1979), pp. 127–46.
13. G. A. Almond and S. Verba, *Civic Culture*, (Little, Brown and Company, Boston, 1965), p. 13.

14. M. Billig, *Social Psychology and Intergroup Relations*, (Academic Press, London, 1976), pp. 45, 220.

15. P. Elliot and P. Schlesinger, 'On the Stratification of Political Knowledge. Studying Eurocommunism, an Unfolding Ideology', *Sociological Review*, vol. 27, no. 1 (1979), pp. 55–81.

16. J. Habermas, *Legitimation Crisis*, (Beacon Press, Boston, 1975), p. 105.

17. Elliot and Schlesinger, 'On the Stratification'.

18. E. Goffman, *The Presentation of Self in Everyday Life*, (Doubleday Anchor, Garden City, NY, 1959).

19. J. D. Frank, 'Nature and Function of Belief Systems: Humanism and Transcendental Religion', *American Psychologist*, vol. 32, no. 7 (1977), pp. 555–9.

20. T. R. Gurr, *Why Men Rebel*, (Princeton University Press, Princeton, NJ, 1970); C. Tilly, *From Mobilization to Revolution*, (Addison Wesley Publishing, Reading, MA, 1978); J. J. Spengler, 'Rising Expectations: Frustration' in H. D. Laswell, D. Lerner and H. Speier (eds), *A Pluralizing World in Formation*, vol. 3, *Propaganda and Communication in World History*, (University of Hawaii Press, Honolulu, HI, 1980), pp. 37–93.

21. G. W. Allport, *The Nature of Prejudice*, (Addison Wesley, New York, 1979); T. F. Pettigrew, 'Personality and Sociocultural Factors in Intergroup Attitudes: A Cross-National Comparison' in R. S. Sigel (ed.), *Learning About Politics: A Reader in Political Socialization* (Random House, New York, 1970), pp. 491–8; T. F. Pettigrew, G. W. Allport and E. O. Barnett, 'Binocular Resolution and Perception of Race in South Africa', *British Journal of Psychology*, vol. 49, no. 2 (1958), pp. 265–79.

22. A. Rolle, 'The Historic Past of the Unconscious' in Laswell, Lerner and Speier, *Propaganda*, pp. 403–60.

23. *Ibid.*, p. 404.

24. J. A. Arlow, 'Ego Psychology and the Study of Mythology', *Journal of American Psychoanalytical Association*, vol. 9, no. 3 (1967), pp. 371–93.

25. S. Diamond, 'Kibbutz and Shtetl: The History of an Idea', *Social Problems*, vol. 5, no. 2 (1957), pp. 71–99.

26. R. C. Tucker, *Stalin as a Revolutionary*, (Norton, New York, 1973).

27. P. Converse, 'The Nature of Belief Systems in Mass Publics,' in D. E. Apter (ed.), *Ideology and Discontent*, (The Free Press, New York, 1964), pp. 206–61.

28. M. Rokeach, *The Open and Closed Mind*, (Basic Books, New York, 1960).

29. R. E. Lane, *Political Thinking and Consciousness*, (Markham Publishing Company, Chicago, 1969), p. 315.

30. K. Booth, *Strategy and Ethnocentrism*, (Holmes and Meir Publishers, New York, 1979), p. 15.

31. B. R. Wilson, 'A Sociologist's Introduction' in B. R. Wilson (ed.), *Rationality*, (Harper and Row, Evanston and New York, 1970), pp. viii–ix.

32. A. Przeworsk and M. Teune, *The Logic of Comparative Social Inquiry*, (Wiley, New York, 1970).

33. S. Lukes, 'Some Problems About Rationality' in Wilson *Rationality*, p. 207.

34. A. Rapoport, *Strategy and Consciences*, (Shaven Books, New York, 1969), p. 9.

35. S. K. Langer, *An Introduction to Symbolic Logic*, 3rd Revised Edition, (Dover Publications, New York, 1967).

36. T. S. Kuhn, *The Structure of Scientific Revolution*, (University of Chicago Press, Chicago and London, 1962).

37. J. Von Neumann and V. Morgenstern, *The Theory of Games and Economic Behavior*, 2nd edition, (Princeton University Press, Princeton, NJ, 1947).

38. Billig, *Social Psychology*.

39. For a good review see J. Gross Stein and R. Tanter, *Rational Decision Making, Israel's Security Choices 1967*, (Ohio State University Press, Columbus, OH, 1976), pp. 3–87.

40. L. I. Janis, *Victims of Groupthink: A Psychological Study of Foreign Policy Decisions and Fiascos*, (Houghton Mifflin, Boston, MA, 1972); A. Vinokur and E. Burstein, 'Effects of Partially Shared Persuasive Arguments on Group Induced Shifts: A Group Problem-Solving Approach', *Journal of Personality and Social Psychology*, vol. 29, no. 3 (1974), pp. 305–15.
41. I. C. Jarvie, 'Explaining Cargo Cults' in Wilson, *Rationality*, pp. 50–61.
42. Elkins and Simeon, 'A Cause in Search,' pp. 127–46.
43. Lane, *Political Thinking*, p. 205.
44. N. Sivin, 'Chinese Conception of Time,' *The Ertham Review*, vol. 1, no. 1 (1966), pp. 82–92.
45. O. Seliktar, 'New Zionism,' *Foreign Policy*, no. 51 (1983), pp. 118–38.
46. Lane, *Political Thinking*, p. 315; see also P. Frassie, *The Psychology of Time*, (Harper and Row, New York, 1963).
47. Mannheim, *Ideology*, p. 57.
48. F. Heider, 'Social Perception and Phenomenal Causality,' *Psychological Review*, vol. 51, no. 3 (1944), pp. 358–76.
49. J. N. Rosenau, *Linkage Politics*, (The Free Press, New York, 1969).
50. M. Brecher, 'Towards a Theory of International Crisis Behavior', *International Studies Quarterly*, vol. 21, no. 1 (1977), pp. 39–74.
51. R. Jervis, *Perceptions and Misperceptions in International Politics*, (Princeton University Press, Princeton, NJ, 1976), p. 62.
52. J. N. Rosenau, 'Foreign Policy as an Issue Area', in J. N. Rosenau (ed.), *Domestic Sources of Foreign Policy*, (The Free Press, New York, 1967), pp. 11–50.
53. H. McClosky, 'Personality and Attitude Correlates of Foreign Policy Orientation' in Rosenau, *Domestic Sources*, pp. 51–107.
54. R. Axelrod, 'Structure of Public Opinion on Policy Issues', *Public Opinion Quarterly*, vol. 35, no. 2 (1967), pp. 51–60. G. Almond, *The Appeals of Communism*, (Princeton University Press, Princeton, NJ, 1965); D. Bell, 'The Depressed' in D. Bell (ed.), *The Radical Right*, (Anchor Books, New York, 1964), pp. 1–45; and L. H. Melikian, 'Authoritarianism and its Correlates in the Egyptian Culture and in the United States', *Journal of Social Issues*, vol. 15, no. 1 (1959), pp. 58–69.
55. G. Turkel, 'Privatism and Orientation Towards Political Action', *Urban Life*, vol. 9, no. 2 (1980), pp. 217–35.
56. R. P. Abelson, 'Script Processing in Attitude Formation and Decision Making' in J. S. Carrol and J. W. Payne (eds), *Cognitive and Social Behavior*, (John Wiley & Sons, New York, 1976), pp. 33–45.
57. J. N. Rosenau and O. R. Holsti, 'U.S. Leadership in a Shrinking World: The Breakdown of Consensus and the Emergence of Conflicting Belief Systems', *World Politics*, vol. 35, no. 3 (1983), pp. 368–92.
58. F. Greenstein, 'The Impact of Personality and Politics: An Attempt to Clear Away the Underbrush,' *American Political Science Review*, vol. 61, no. 4 (1967), pp. 629–41; P. Rosenblatt, 'Origins and Effects of Group Ethnocentrism and Nationalism,' *World Politics*, vol. 16, no. 1 (1964), pp. 146–81.
59. A. Lijphart, *The Politics of Accommodation: The Dutch and West New Guinea*, (Yale University Press, New Haven, CT, 1966).
60. R. Stagner, *Psychological Aspects of International Conflict*, (Brooks Cole, Belmont, CA, 1967); A. Stratchey, *The Unconscious Motives of War*, (International Universities Press, New York, 1957).
61. H. McClosky, 'Personality and Attitude Correlates' in Rosenau, *Domestic Sources*.
62. Szalay and Kelly, 'Political Ideology'.
63. H. Tajfel, 'The Structure of Our Views About Society' in H. Tajfel and C. Fraser (eds), *Introducing Social Psychology*, (Penguin Books, Harmondsworth, Middx., 1978), p. 308.

64. Mannheim, *Ideology*, p. 21.

65. R. F. Benedict, *Patterns of Culture*, (Penguin Books, New York, 1946), p. 237.

66. D. R. Miller, 'The Study of Social Relationship: Situation, Identity and Social Interaction' in S. Koch (ed.), *Psychology: A Study of a Science*, vol. 5, (McGraw Hill, New York, 1963), p. 674.

67. E. H. Spicer, 'Persistent Cultural Systems', *Science*, vol. 174, no. 4011 (1971), pp. 795–830.

68. D. E. Apter, *The Politics of Modernization*, (University of Chicago Press, Chicago and London, 1965), p. 391.

69. J. H. Hertz, 'Legitimacy, Can We Retrieve it?' *Comparative Politics*, vol. 10, no. 3 (1978), pp. 317–44.

70. J. Fraser, 'Validating a Measure of National Political Legitimacy', *American Journal of Political Science*, vol. 18, no. 2 (1974), pp. 117–34.

71. Hertz, 'Legitimacy'.

72. K. Lewin, *Field Theory in Social Science*, edited by D. Cartwright, (Harper and Row, New York, 1951), p. 148.

73. F. Toennis, *Community and Association*, (Routledge and Kegan Paul, London, 1955).

74. L. A. Coser, *The Function of Social Conflict*, (The Free Press of Glencoe, New York, 1964), p. 88.

75. H. Adams, 'Survival Politics: Afrikanerdom in Search of a New Ideology', *The Journal of Modern African Studies*, vol. 16, no. 4 (1978), pp. 657–69.

76. M. Weber, *The Theory of Social and Economic Organization*, (The Free Press of Glencoe, IL, 1957), Part III.

77. Hertz, 'Legitimacy'.

78. W. A. Galtson, *Justice and the Human Good*, (University of Chicago Press, Chicago, 1980), p. 5.

79. Habermas, *Legitimation Crisis*, p. 112.

80. Elliot and Schlesinger, 'On the Stratification'; Coser, *The Function*, p. 69.

81. T. R. Young, 'The Division of Labor in the Construction of Social Reality', *Urban Life*, vol. 9, no. 2, (1980), p. 143.

82. A. F. Eldridge, *Images of Conflict*, (St. Martin's Press, New York, 1979), p. 114.

83. A. Levite and S. Tarrow, 'The Legitimization of Excluded Parties in Dominant Party Systems: A Comparison of Israel and Italy', *Comparative Politics*, vol. 15, no. 3 (1983), pp. 295–327.

84. C. Johnson, *Revolutionary Change*, (Little Brown, Boston and Toronto, 1966), p. 106.

85. For a cogent review of Durkheim's concept of anomia see Tilly, *From Mobilization to Revolution*, p. 19.

86. Z. Ben-Sira, *Interethnic Cleavage, Stress, Coping and Compensatory Mechanism: The Case of Israel*, (The Israel Institute of Applied Social Research, Jerusalem, 1983).

87. T. Parsons, *The Social System*, (Free Press of Glencoe, IL, 1964), pp. 3–4.

88. A. L. Stinchcombe, 'Some Empirical Consequences of the Davis-Moore Theory of Stratification,' *American Sociological Review*, vol. 28, no. 5 (1963), pp. 805–90.

89. The work on cognitive dissonance is mostly associated with E. Festinger, *A Theory of Cognitive Dissonance*, (Stanford University Press, Stanford, CA, 1957).

90. Billig, *Social Psychology*, pp. 142–3.

91. R. Nisbett and L. Ross, *Human Inference: Strategies and Shortcomings of Social Judgment*, (Prentice Hall, Englewood Cliffs, NJ, 1980), pp. 169–92.

92. Converse, 'The Nature of Belief Systems'.

93. D. T. Campbell and D. Fiske, 'Convergent and Discriminant Validation by

Multitrait Multimethod Matrix', *Psychological Bulletin*, vol. 56, no. 2 (1959), pp. 81–104.

94. K. Lewin, *Resolving Social Conflict*, (Harper and Row, New York, 1948), p. 20 and *A Dynamic Theory of Personality*, (McGraw Hill, New York, 1935), p. 51.

95. Apter, Modernization, pp. 65–6.

96. D. E. Smith, *Religion and Political Development*, (Little Brown, Boston, MA, 1970), p. 85.

97. B. M. Borthwick, 'Religion and Politics in Israel and Egypt,' *The Middle East Journal*, vol. 33, no. 2 (1979), pp. 145–63.

98. R. Linton, *The Cultural Background of Personality*, (Prentice Hall, London, 1945), p. 45.

99. Elkins and Simeon, 'A Cause in Search'.

100. W. Handel, 'Normative Expectations and the Emergence of Meanings as Solution to Problems: Convergence of Structural and Interactionist Views', *American Journal of Sociology*, vol. 84, no. 4 (1979), pp. 855–81.

PART ONE

2   JEWISH BELIEF SYSTEMS IN PERSPECTIVE: TRADITIONAL AND ZIONIST IDEOLOGIES

The task of identifying the psychological underpinning of broad ideological traditions is not easy. Historical modes of thought are the product of their period and should be related to their historical context. Yet conveying the subjective meaning of historical action involves what the distinguished historian Bernard Bailyn described as 'relating latent events . . . to events that register in the awareness of the contemporaries'.[1] Such a reconstruction poses many methodological problems. One problem pertains to the existence of multiple, often conflicting and politicised accounts. Identifying the reasons behind this diversity and a comparison between the accounts can help, but cannot guarantee a 'true' representation of the subjective context.

Another major problem in analysing belief systems over extended historical periods stems from identifying the elites who were crucial in articulating the ideology. A related issue involves the need to discern perceptual changes among the elites in response to changing reality. A broad analysis of collective belief systems must focus on the complex task of charting these changing perceptions across the life history of the leadership and the movement.

Perhaps the most serious problem pertains to the interaction of universal psychological processes and the historically specific context. Quite often, social psychologists, who consider political ideology, emphasise psychological generalities at the expense of the historical, political and economic setting. Political theorists tend to reverse this emphasis, by paying only scant attention to psychological states.

This book, in line with the theoretical introduction, will try to emphasise the interrelationship of these elements, in the relatively well-elaborated Zionist trends of the nineteenth and twentieth centuries. It is not the intention to present a complete intellectual history of the Zionist movement: a variety of good accounts of this period are available. Rather, we shall try to delineate the psychopolitical predicament of Jewish existence in the Diaspora and illustrate how different intellectual trends were shaped in response to these conditions.

41

The Diaspora Jew as a Marginal Man: The Psychological Predicament

The nearly two thousand year-old history of dispersion has seen many, and often dramatic, changes in the geographical and sociopolitical condition of Jewish existence. Historically, the Oriental Jews, who lived in the Middle East and North Africa under Islam, were the leading community in the Diaspora. In the eleventh century, the Oriental Jews lost their hegemony to the Sephardi Jews who lived in Spain, where they achieved their political and sociocultural prominence under the Moors.

The Christian reconquest of Spain, which started in the fourteenth century, led to a Europeanisation of the Sephardi Jews. Beginning with the sixteenth century, the Ashkenazi (European) Jews have gradually progressed towards both cultural and numerical hegemony among the Jewish Diaspora. At the end of the nineteenth century there were some ten million Jews in the world; almost 80 per cent of them lived in Europe. A vast majority of the Ashkenazi Jews — about 75 per cent — were *Ostjuden*, East European Jews who lived in Poland, in Galicia in the Hapsburg Empire and in the Pale of Settlement of the Russian Empire.

The Ostjuden had been subjected for many generations to increasingly harsh religious, cultural and economic restrictions. Within the extensive territorial ghetto of the Pale of Settlement, their livelihood was legally restricted to a few artisan, trading and middlemen professions. Their subsistence economy gave rise to a numerous class of lumpenproletariat, which was symbolised in Jewish lore by the sociological archetype of the *Luftmensch*.

Their precarious position was made even more difficult by a Gentile society whose popular culture was characterised by hostility towards the outgroup. The largely illiterate native peasantry and, to a lesser extent, the middle class and the aristocracy, harboured stock medieval stereotypes of the Jews; they were perceived as Christ-killers and often accused of well-poisoning, witchcraft and ritual murder of Christian children. The position of Jews as traders and middlemen, which gave rise to economic grievances, further aggravated these images. With few civil rights to protect them, the Jews were often subject to physical persecutions. The legitimacy of aggression towards an outgroup in the host societies culminated in periodical pogroms, in which Jews were brutally murdered and their dwellings ransacked and set on fire. The fate of Jews in Western and Central Europe was much better, but even they suffered enough social and political restriction to demarcate the group as a minority.

There is little doubt that this backdrop of Diaspora life has shaped psychological parameters of Jewish marginality. Stonquist, drawing on the work of Park, developed the concept of marginality in his seminal work, *The Marginal Man: A Study in Personality and Cultural Conflict.*[2] It was subsequently elaborated by Erikson, Miller and Horney who discussed aspects of identity formation under marginal conditions. Lewin and Allport broadened the analysis to include the various defence mechanisms which minorities use.[3]

Stonquist's concept of contextual dissonance can be readily applied to the Jews in the Diaspora, who lived in two antagonistic cultures, Gentile and Jewish. Under normal circumstances, a person builds his identity through the constructive integration of a body of social norms derived from his parents, immediate environment, ethnic group and ultimately from the society at large. Because of the contextual dissonance, the Jews have apparently developed elements of negative identity. Negative identity is based on attitudes and roles, which are presented to the person as most undesirable, but also as the most real.

The dominance of negative identity will cause a person to lose self-esteem, a phenomenon which is common among minorities. If self-esteem is absent over time, a person may experience a strong urge to disrupt the sense of his ethnic sameness, as a way of avoiding identification with negatively valued norms and behaviour. For instance, Jews who converted voluntarily have apparently tried to recover self-esteem by opting for a new ethno-religious identity.

The amount of negative identity of a marginal individual depends on a number of macrosociological factors, and especially the social order of the group. Douglas, who adopted Durkheim's perspective on solidarity, argued that the most important elements are the strength of the boundaries of the social unit and the density of the grid, i.e., the extent to which normative rules are clearly articulated.[4] Indeed, it has been a commonplace to argue that, historically, strong religious commitment and social cohesion protected the Jewish collective from most of the negative consequences of psychological marginality.

There is some disagreement, though, as to when the disintegration of the community started. Traditional research emphasises that this process coincided with the onset of modernisation during the period of Enlightenment in the nineteenth century. More recent sociopsychologically oriented research has identified important strains in the Diaspora existence, which pre-date the Enlightenment. The following discussion provides a necessarily concise analysis of the broad trends of Jewish response to the psychopolitical predicament of Diaspora existence.

Traditional Religious Belief System

So long as the Jews were confined to a ghetto-type existence, which spelled out a rigid social and cultural division between the Jewish and Gentile world, the psychological problem of marginality was not overwhelming. Enforced and voluntary segregation enhanced the vigour of the religious and communal commitment of the individuals, and generated a positive valuation of their ethnic identity. The Talmudic definition of the Jews as a moral-religious community might have actually created feelings of superiority over the Gentiles, who were perceived as lacking in spiritual, scholarly and intellectual values.

The corporate structure of the feudal society, which legitimised separatist existence and afforded a modicum of legal protection and a limited structure of economic opportunity, facilitated the group's existence.[5] Physical suffering, caused by either the structured persecution of the Church or sporadic outbreaks of mob violence, was theologically explained. The religious notion of exile was in line with outbursts of anti-Semitism, because suffering was intimately associated with the notion of a divine mission of the Jews. This theodicy, that is an attempt to explain the meaning of an 'ultimate problem', might have ameliorated the psychological problem of coping with both personal and collective-historical suffering.[6]

Apparently, a particularly powerful psychological shelter was provided by the messianic theodicy, a belief in the millennial idea of Redemption and return to the Land of Israel. In an almost unique manner among the monotheistic creeds, the Jewish religion was intimately bound up with the land in which it achieved its initial expression. The Jewish liturgy, the traditional rituals and festivities have preserved the consciousness of the Land of Zion, both as a collective memory and as a messianic promise.

This rather schematic representation of the psychological reality of the Jewish existence in the Diaspora obscures the fact that contextual dissonance has occasionally surfaced at both the individual and collective levels. Cohen, who surveyed the traditional Jewish response to the question of suffering, found that there were numerous fissures in the supernatural explanation of suffering. Both Ibn Virga and Maimonides emphasised natural causes for Jewish suffering, such as passivity and neglect of military skills.[7] Patai discerned the same theme in Luzzatto's description of Jews as a timid and unmanly society.[8] Shmueli, the author of a systematic study on the readjustment of the Jewish culture to evolving reality, found instances of dissatisfaction with official Talmudic rabbinical views of passivity.[9]

The extent of this dissatisfaction is difficult to estimate. Moritz Lazarus, a Jewish philosopher and the founder of the discipline of *Volkenpsychologie* (folk psychology), argued that the Jews accepted suffering as part of the theological interpretation of the Diaspora.[10] Salo Baron and other historians emphasised that some Jewish accounts written in the pre-modernisation period were 'lacrimonious,' i.e. they deliberately emphasised Jewish misery in order to obtain emancipation.[11]

The periodical outbursts of millennial messianism are perhaps the most significant indication of mass psychological unrest. The most famous such outburst was the Sabbatian movement. Sabbatai Zvi (1626–76) was a self-appointed Messiah who had an extraordinary influence on Jewish communities in Eastern Europe and the Middle East. The hope for the realisation of a messianic millennium was so widespread that whole communities sold their possessions and waited to be transferred physically to the Land of Zion.

Gershon Sholem, by attributing Sabbatianism to the spread of cabalistic practices, has influenced classic scholarly interpretation of the movement.[12] Sharot, following the psychological tradition of Festinger and his associates in *When Prophecy Fails*, makes a credible case for viewing the millennial movement as an outcome of dissonant psychological states. Sabbatianism was prevalent among Jews whose families had been forcibly converted to Christianity in previous centuries, and in communities which were exposed to cross-cultural currents.[13]

The catastrophic collapse of the false Messiah's movement had a profound effect on the psychological defences of the Jewish collective. Although a tiny minority persisted in clinging to mystical beliefs, the demise of Sabbatianism brought to a close a long period in Jewish history in which religion alone would provide an adequate means for dealing with adverse political and social reality.

The attendant disillusionment was so widespread and lasting that it led to a theological 'purging' of the popular messianic yearnings. The official Orthodox establishment, which has always viewed messianic movements as a challenge to its authority, became even more rigid in resisting any attempts to bring Redemption. This disillusionment transformed messianism into dependence upon a halcyonic era, which alone would mark the final Redemption of the Land of Israel. The official theology held that Redemption could be accelerated only by acts of individual piety — suffering and praying — and not through organised collective action.[14]

The post-Sabbatian period, by depriving the Jews of the 'cognitive and affective grounding' derived from religious-messianic beliefs, set the stage for the secularisation of the Jewish community. In losing some of their faith in a divine beginning and an ultimate culmination in history, the Jews had to come to terms with their psychological predicament as both individuals and as a collective.

The Enlightenment (Haskala) Movement

These developments in the Jewish community coincided with the move in Western and Central Europe to emancipate the Jews, which was one of the hallmarks of the Age of Reason. Emancipation exposed the Jews for the first time to modern philosophical and scientific ideas and to the secularisation which had already begun to transform the Christian society.

The impact of emancipation on the Jews has normally been discussed in legal, political or economic terms. The psychological cost of emancipation is less clear. Most generally, modernisation involved a decrease in the centrality and valence of the religious subidentity and a concomitant emphasis on the civic and national subidentity. For the Jews, this process was highly problematic because their religious subidentity overlapped with their ethnic and other subidenties. Achieving psychological concordance with the outgroup, i.e. the host societies, meant a normative depreciation of the Jewish subidentity. Moreover, it undermined what Lewin called 'the interdependence of fate', a major psychological defence mechanism which bolstered the cohesiveness of the group.[15]

There are indications that the process of Jewish modernisation triggered a number of responses, along the lines discussed by Allport and other social psychologists who deal with intergroup relations. One prevalent reaction was an increase in social comparison, which led to a negative self-perception of Jewish identity.[16] For the first time, the Jews clearly saw themselves through the eyes of the Gentiles. In the words of Pinsker in his book, *Autoemancipation*: 'To the living, the Jew is a corpse, to the native a foreigner, to the homesteader a vagrant, to the proprietor a man without a country, to all a hated rival.'[17]

Another reaction resulted in a growing ambivalence in the perception of Gentiles. Traditional Jewish equanimity or even superiority gave way to feelings of inferiority, because of constant humiliation, persecution, and rootlessness. Talmudic piety was criticised for the failure of Jews to display physical stamina and manly behaviour in facing the aggressor.

The growth of these feelings is perhaps best documented by Chaim Bialik, the great national poet. In a poem *Bair Haharega* (in the Slaughter City), written after the 1903 pogrom in Kishiniev, Bialik chastised the Jews for not resisting the violence of the oppressor. It is interesting that Nahum Horowitz, a member of the first Jewish defence organisation, *Hashomer*, subsequently criticised Bialik for misrepresenting the Jews and failing to mention that there was a defence unit in Kishiniev.[18] However, Bialik's poem captured what was apparently a widespread subjective perception of Jewish reality.

More difficult to analyse is the Jewish phenomenon of 'self-hatred'. The term has often been used in a generic sense, to refer to all forms of Jewish self-criticism, which are based on Gentile arguments. Allport made a distinction between self-criticism which underlies the assimilationist strivings of a minority, and its more pathological form, when an ethnic individual is barred from assimilation but is identified with the practices of the outgroup.[19]

There is no doubt that some of the thinking of the emancipation period reflects highly disparaging criticisms of Jewish society. Avineri documented that Marx's treatise of 1884 'On the Jewish Question' might have been influenced by the young Moshe Hess. Hess, who later became a major figure in the Zionist movement, sent Marx his book 'On Money,' in which he accused the Jews of worshipping *Mamon* (Money).[20] Max Nordau's theme of *Muskeljudentum* (muscle Jewry), and Berdychevsky's identification with the Aryan *Uebermensch*, are additional cases in point. Nevertheless, given the fact that Jews were not prevented from assimilation, pathological self-hatred was hardly a mainstream phenomenon.

The *Englightenment* (Heskala) movement provided an answer to the quest for a new assimilated Jewish identity. The Enlightenment movement was started by Moshe Mendelssohn (1829–86), a German-Jewish philosopher and man of letters. In keeping with the Age of Reason, the movement was based on a number of rational assumptions: 1) that Jews should become as normal, free and equal as possible compared to the Gentile society, i.e. assimilated; 2) that Jews are not a people, that Jewish nationhood ceased to exist after the destruction of the Second Temple and hence Jews are equal citizens in their countries of birth; 3) that the new Judaism should be purged of medieval obscurantism, including its messianic and folk nationalistic elements.

The underlying rationale for these assumptions was the belief that anti-Semitism was caused by the vestiges of the medieval character of the minority. In other words, the Enlightenment advocates believed that anti-Semitism was a remnant of the Middle Ages which, with the spread of education, would gradually be laid to rest. They believed that by developing a civic identity, i.e. being exemplary citizens, they would convince the anti-Semites of the erroneousness of the latter's views. They argued that if they had some 'Jewish weaknesses', that is underdevelopment, these were the residues of centuries of oppression and economic deprivation. Given time for education and peaceful development, the Jews would prove to the world that they 'fit into civil society'.[21]

Although the German Enlightenment did not preach the abandonment of Judaism, free-thinking attitudes and conversion to Christianity were widespread. Moreover, in their quest to emphasise their new civic identity, many of the German Jews went so far as to assert a high degree of patriotism. Riesser, one of Mendelssohn's chief followers, articulated this approach: We have one father in heaven and one mother — God the father of all beings, Germany our mother on earth.[22]

In adopting such a high degree of patriotism, the Enlightenment Jews drifted away from rationalism and into the German Romantic Age with its emphasis on faith, mystery and race-based *Volksgeist*. It is precisely this conceptual mix which was subsequently destined to provide the philosophical underpinning of the Nazi movement. These developments highlighted the limits of the new civic identity of the Jews. Such an identity was contingent upon the existence of a civically defined polity and national and liberal political culture. The transvaluation of this culture into Romanticism, coupled with the continuous lack of civil liberties in Eastern Europe, prompted the Jewish collective to look for an alternative solution.

Political Zionism

By the early 1870s the relatively liberal climate, which the Jews in Germany, France and central Europe enjoyed, was turning more conservative. The financial crisis in Germany, coupled with the high tide of Romanticism, resulted in a new severe outbreak of anti-Semitism. Treitschke, a leading German historian and a forerunner of Nazism, coined the phrase 'the Jews are our enemies'. Numerous German thinkers echoed William Marr's accusation that the Jews 'enslaved' Germany.

Some of these anti-Semitic sentiments were a reaction to the social and economic progress which the Jews had achieved after the emancipation. But a more ominous note was sounded by the new racial elements in the Romantic belief system. Billig, in his excellent study of the psychological underpinning of ideological thinking, traces its origin to the growth of eugenics. The eugenic trend in nineteenth-century European philosophy was initiated by Francis Gulton. Inspired by Darwin's *Origin of Species*, Gulton emphasised racial and hereditary elements in human development.[23] The racial theory of eugenics, which was subsequently incorporated in Romantic thinking, emphasised the racial and hence *immutable* differences between human groups.

The implications of eugenics for anti-Semitism and the perception of the Jews cannot be overemphasised. The Jewish problem was no longer viewed in religious or social terms, but as a racial one. According to this doctrine, the Jew had different racial characteristics which could not be changed, even if he changed his religious or ethnic subidentity. A change in religion did not make a Jew into a German any more than an apple can be transformed into an orange.[24] The logic of racial anti-Semitism cast doubt on the Jewish efforts to assimilate.

The Dreyfus Affair in France in the early 1880s was the most symbolic representation of the new wave of anti-Semitism. Perceptually, France was then the centre of the civilised world, and the home of the most liberal and revolutionary ideas and experiments in human relations. Dreyfus was not a 'medieval Jew' in traditional cloth and sidelocks, but a highly assimilated Jew and an officer in the French Army.

The trial of Dreyfus for treason attracted the attention of Theodor Herzl, an assimilated Austrian Jew, who in 1891 went to Paris as correspondent of the Viennese *Neue Freie Press* to cover the affair. The symbolism of the Dreyfus trial led Herzl to reconsider the basic assumptions of the Enlightenment belief system. Although Herzl was the focal figure in Zionism, there are indications that the Dreyfus trial affected a whole generation of Jewish intelligentsia in Europe.[25]

Even before Herzl, people like Hess and Pinsker contributed to a deeply pessimistic prognosis for the Jewish existence in the Diaspora. Herzl, like Hess and Pinsker, came to view Gentile society as implacably and immutably hostile towards the Diaspora Jews. According to this image, anti-Semitism was not a rational Gentile reaction to a specific condition of Jewish existence or even Jewish character, but rather a deep, instinctive, almost mystical force. Transcribed into the terms of cognitive psychology, Gentile attitudes towards the Jews were dominated by a deeply ingrained affective reaction which was not anchored in any tangible reality.

The logical corollary of this image was the conclusion that the modern Jew could not hide behind philosophical abstractions, civic reforms or assimilation. He could change his name, religion or otherwise mask himself, yet he would always be recognised as a Jew. 'The Jew might become a naturalized citizen, but he would always be separated from the Gentiles. The Gentiles will always regard his existence among the nations of Europe as an anomaly.'[26]

To Herzl and other Zionist advocates, the Jewish problem and the concomitant anti-Semitism were not related to any particular historical period, to differences in class structure of a given society, or to differences in cultural attributes. In his later years, influenced by the bloody pogroms in Eastern Europe, Herzl's vision of anti-Semitism darkened even further. Hannah Arendt criticised Herzl for what she interpreted to be his irrational view of anti-Semitism, which amounted to 'unchanging bodies of people viewed as biological organisms which . . . breathed hostility towards the Jews'.[27]

Arendt's criticism raises the intriguing possibility that early political Zionism, in reacting to what it perceived as a racial and irrational ideology, might have adopted some of its conclusions. More generally, the Zionist reaction might have been indicative of the predicament of any reasonably rational belief system which is faced with a racially flavoured and intolerant ideology.

Whatever the case, psychologically Herzl, Hess, and Pinsker came to view the efforts of the Enlightenment to turn *individual* Jews into normal, free and equal citizens of the Diaspora as futile. The Zionist response was to redefine the negative self-identity by making the Jews normal, free and equal as a *collective*. Only within the framework of a Jewish state would the Jews become a 'nation like all other nations'.

Pinsker, in his major work *Autoemancipation*, gave a full exposition of this theory. Although his use of sociological concepts is somewhat archaic, the psychological dimension of Zionism, which adds to the Jewish self by enabling the Jew to meet the Gentile on the basis of equality, is clearly evident. According to Pinsker, Jewish existence in the Diaspora was a social anomaly which had always inspired anti-Semitism. Human relations are founded on mutual respect, not love; the Jews could not achieve respect because they lacked its foremost prerequisite, national equality. The lack of territory turned them into a 'phantom people' which inspired fear among the Gentiles, and this fear bred hatred. The prejudice of the Gentiles against the Jews rested on these principles, which were like 'natural laws — innate and ineradicable'. The anomaly could be corrected only by becoming a 'nation like all other nations'.[28]

Herzl, in his books *Der Judenstaat* (the Jewish State) and *Altneuland*, developed more fully the idea of normalisation of the Jewish people. In his quest to turn the Jews into a 'nation like all other nations', Herzl advocated the creation of a new Jewish man. An almost exact antithesis of the *Ostjude* image of the ghetto Jew, the new Jewish man carried most of the characteristics of the 'enlightened Gentile' — presumably modelled on the 'ideal type' of the Age of Reason. The new Jewish archetype was a man of physical strength, politically liberal, culturally progressive and technologically advanced. Herzl expected the citizens of the new Jewish state to abandon their traditional economic pursuits of small merchants, middlemen and lumpenproletariat.

Altneuland focuses on the integration of the Jews into European politics on the basis of their new social and cultural identity. It is of interest that the Jewish state of *Altneuland* almost completely lacks any ethnic Jewish characteristics. It is not even clear what language the new Jew speaks. Scholars pointed out that *Altneuland* might have included some images of 'Gentile Zionists', a longstanding but limited Christian Romantic tradition which envisaged the restoration of Zion. These images were expressed in millennial form in the works of Byron, Sir Walter Scott and George Eliot, among others.[29] The 'Gentile Zionists' had also been instrumental in helping the Zionist movement to obtain the Balfour Declaration which paved the way for a Jewish National Home in Palestine.

Cultural Zionism

Herzl's image of full normalisation of the Jewish people as equal partners in the international system was not unanimously accepted. It encountered resistance among most European Zionists. The *Ostjuden*, who were less assimilated than their West European brethren, had more ambivalent feelings about normalisation. Although they cognitively rebelled against the negative Jewish image, they were effectively attached to the religious and cultural tradition of Judaism.

The most articulated theory in this rather amorphous and often subtle opposition to Herzl came to be known as Cultural Zionism. This trend was most intimately associated with Ahad Ha'am, the pen name of Asher Ginsburg (1856–1927), a Jewish writer and publicist. In pursuing his brand of nationalism, Ahad Ha'am, not unlike Masaryk, emphasised the emotional and moral aspects of national rebirth.

Ahad Ha'am outlined his ideas in the article *Lo Zu Haderech* (Not This is the Way) and in other works. The founder of Cultural

Zionism rejected the basic premises of political Zionism which called for the normalisation of the Jewish people through national sovereignty and national power. He was deeply apprehensive that a normal Jewish state would eventually spell the end of the Jewish people; the Jews would imitate the habits of the Gentiles in order to prove that they could be 'normal and valiant'. He criticised political Zionism for wanting to 'emancipate the physical life of the Jews from its subservience to the limiting force of the spirit'.

In Ahad Ha'am's conception of history, the Jews had survived, where all the other ancient nations had perished, because of the prophetic vision of Israel which abstained from material power and political domination. To the prophets who lived in the Land of Israel, national sovereignty could derive its meaning only from the spirit. The existence of the state was valued only as an embodiment of that spirit. The essence of this spirit was based on Jewish ethics which were irreconcilable with Christian ethics. According to Ahad Ha'am the moral bases of Christianity and Judiasm have different premises: in the former, morality is based on subjective altruism, in the latter, on objective justice.

These considerations prompted Ahad Ha'am to advocate the idea of a small Jewish state in Palestine. Rather than normalise the Jewish people, such a state should become a spiritual centre for the Jews, who would, by and large, live in the Diaspora. Moreover, the Jewish state, by becoming *Or Le'Goim* (Light unto the Gentiles), would reflect the fact that the Jews are the Chosen People, that is, that they have a special moral function to fulfill in the international system.

Ahad Ha'am's interpretation of the 'essential Judaism' of the prophets included a set of normative prescriptions which would prevent the Diaspora Jew from assimilation. At the same time, he advocated a change in some of the Jewish traits, such as lack of discipline, unity and public spirit as well as excessive stubbornness and sophistry. Ahad Ha'am viewed such an 'attitudinal reform' as a precondition for achieving the highest human standards. Unlike the political Zionists, Ahad Ha'am did not believe that behavioural changes or the establishment of a Jewish state would eliminate anti-Semitism. In the essays *Slavery in Freedom* and *Two Masters*, he explained that anti-Semitism is an outcome of the 'mentality of early ages' of humanity, to which civilised men can revert at will.[30]

Cultural Zionism did not have a mass following or a formal

organisation, but Ahad Ha'am's ideas were extremely influential. Various configurations of his ideas were adopted by both traditional and contemporary strands of Zionism.

Socialist Zionism

Political Zionism, which led in 1887 to the First Zionist Congress in Basle, was largely articulated by the liberal, middle-class intelligentsia of Central Europe and the transplanted East European Jews. But at the same time, socialism became a dominant political force among the *Ostjuden*.

The early attraction of Jews to socialism and subsequently to the revolutionary vision of Marxism stemmed from its *universalism*, the negation of all inequalities of birth, race, and creed. Socialism provided the Jews with an alternative to the Enlightenment's option of assimilation into another culture, which had failed to provide political or psychological equality. The Jewish image of socialism envisaged a new type of society which would divest itself of national identity, and accept the Jew on equal terms.

This vision of socialism was particularly attractive to the Jews because it promised to replace the divisiveness of the existing religions with a new universalistic creed, a religion of mankind based on a social gospel. The unarticulated but fervently held assumption was that only such a universalistic creed could liberate the Jew from the tribal exclusiveness of Judaism. This creed was perceived as the dialectical antithesis to Christian universality; however, even though embracing a Christian antithesis, the Jew would be more a part of the Christian world than by adhering to the dialectically unrelated world of Judaism.

Another powerful impetus for embracing socialism stemmed from its vision of productivisation and normalisation for a Jewish people. The Bund Party was the major advocate of these views; nevertheless, the praxis of general and Bundist socialism fell short of solving the psychosocial predicament of the Jewish socialist.

Ber Borchov, who became the leading socialist Zionist ideologue, soon realised that the Jews would not be able to become more productive as long as they competed within the industrial structure of the Diaspora. The socialist Jewish intelligentsia also became disillusioned with the anti-Jewish sentiments of the revolutionary movement, and especially with the Russian revolutionaries. Some disappointed Jewish socialists openly complained about the fact that the Russian socialists made no class distinction between the Jews; they regarded all of them as harmful. Like the German Jewish advocates of the Enlightenment, the Jewish socialists discovered that a change in the belief system of a group did not guarantee a radical breakthrough that could eradicate ethnic prejudice. A small minority of the Jewish socialists responded to this double concern by fusing nationalism with socialism. Socialist Zionism, subsequently consolidated under the leadership of David Ben-Gurion, became the most decisive force in the Zionist movement.[31]

The Socialist Zionists shared with the Political Zionists the vision of the social and economic normalisation of the Jewish people. However, their ideological premises and operational plan were much more radical. The ideational roots of Socialist Zionist thinking are extremely complex. Stated briefly, in addition to the core beliefs of Marxist materialism three secondary elements can be surmised.

First, they either accepted or subconsciously internalised the anti-Jewish socio-economic critique of some early Socialists like Proudhon and Toussenel. The crux of this critique was that the Jew is 'by temperament an anti-producer', an 'intermediary' and a 'parasite'. Second, through the strongly populist *Narodniaa Volia* (a populist-revolutionary Russian party), they apparently inherited the Tolstoyan notion of redemption through agrarianism. Third, it is also possible that the Socialist Zionists were influenced by Bakunin's anarchism which sought to escape from the psychological anonymity of industrial society through an agrarian utopia.

The Socialist Zionist belief system was much more clear in elaborating the programme for normalisation. The hallmark of this programme was the *social redemption* of the Diaspora Jew through manual, agricultural labour. To use contemporary social science terminology, the Socialist Zionists proposed to restructure the socio-economic environment of the Jews in order to produce normative and behavioural changes in the society.

In order to achieve such a total transvaluation of Jewish society, the Socialist Zionists adopted the collectivist-equalitarian model of social action which required total commitment of the individual. Gerber-Talmon, in a seminal analysis of secular asceticism, argued that the Socialist Zionist model of behaviour amounted to a collective version of the Protestant ethic of individual salvation. In addition to voluntary de-urbanisation and proletarianisation, the pioneering creed emphasised personal poverty and ascetic restraint.[32]

Given the economic conditions of the Jewish *Yishuv* in Palestine, the collective-agrarian model might have had some economic rationale. According to Kimmerling, who analysed the economic practice of Zionism, the Socialist Zionist did not *a priori* reject economic rentability. Yet the *Wirtschaftsethik* (normative background of the economy) was dominated by the social imperative.[33]

This impression is borne out by the repeated emphasis on the psychosocial value of work in Socialist Zionist ideology. Gordon, the philosopher-labourer of the movement, stressed the importance of agricultural work as a means of 'regaining sanity', and Ben-Gurlon emphasised the need to invert the social pyramid of the Diaspora Jews in order to create a more productive and self-reliant individual. The psychosocial restructuring was also perceived as a necessary requirement for turning the Jews into a nation 'like all other nations'. Bendycrewski went so far as to make such a transformation contingent on the Jew becoming the 'New Goy' (new Gentile).[34]

The Socialist Zionists were equally adamant in their efforts to secularise the traditional Diaspora Jewish culture. In rejecting Talmudic piety, they turned most harshly against the image of the *Ostjude* and especially his physical weakness and lack of military valour. This image was best captured in the poem which Bialik wrote after the pogrom in Kishiniev: 'The grandsons of the Maccabeans, they ran like mice, they hid themselves like bedbugs and died the death of dogs whenever found.'

To offset this image, the Socialist Zionists focused on Biblical Judaism for new cultural symbols and a normative interpretation of history. One important behavioural archetype was the Maccabeans. The Maccabean dynasty fought the Greek Empire in the second century BC and won independence against extreme odds. According to the mystical-romantic lore of the Socialist Zionist belief system, there was a mysterious thread between Modiin, the home of the Maccabeans, and the new Jewish settlements in Palestine. Massada, where the Jews fought and committed collective suicide rather than surrender to the Romans, became another important symbol in the belief system. The choice of national Biblical symbols illustrates the dilemma of the Socialist

Zionists in their quest to secularise the evolving culture. Since Biblical values were religious, they had to be redefined in the light of what was regarded by the Socialist Zionists as a secular line. Liebman and Don-Yehiya argued that the transvaluation of the religious heritage amounted to creating a 'civil religion'. The most comprehensive effort was Bialik's transcription of the non-Talmudic literature.[35] Borthwick, however, argued that the transvaluation was only partial. He pointed out that the Socialist Zionist system contained an inordinate number of references to redemption and other religious symbolism.[36]

The heavy emphasis on social redemption raises the question of the extent to which the Socialist Zionists were committed to national sovereignty. Because of the many divisions within the movement, the conception of sovereignty in the early stages of ideological development is difficult to discern. As a rule, national movements which fight foreign domination focus primarily on national sovereignty. But the international complexities, and the fact that the Jewish presence in Palestine was minute, made an immediate quest for sovereignty dubious. Instead, the Socialist Zionists adopted the strategy of 'practical Zionism'.

Sociologically, 'practical Zionism' implied a definition of a society based on membership units without any explicit reference to their territorial dimension.[37] Such a definition fitted well with the prevalent Socialist Zionist perception that normalisation could best be achieved socially rather than through national collectivism.[38] This interpretation is borne out by Ben-Gurion's persistent refusal to follow the plea for a mass Jewish immigration to Palestine. Ben-Gurion cited international considerations such as the British and Arab objections to a large immigration, but he and other Socialist Zionist leaders like Berl Katzenelson were also concerned that a non-selective immigration would interfere with the efforts to reshape the Jewish society.

The emphasis on sovereignty has gradually increased, mainly in response to pressures from other strands in the Zionist movement, and the international and domestic contingencies in Palestine. The new formula of 'synthetic Zionism', which was adopted in the 1930s, implied that the goal of social redemption and the quest for self-determination were accorded a more or less equal priority.

The Zionist Belief System and the Arab Problem

When the first Zionists proposed to recreate a Jewish state in Palestine, they were motivated by the need to find a solution to the Jewish problem in Europe. The implementation of the Zionist vision brought the movement into direct conflict with the Palestinians and their national aspirations — a conflict which has lasted most of this century.

The continuous tragedy of the Arab-Israeli conflict has raised the question of whether the founders of the Zionist movement were aware of the Arabs in Palestine. Traditional Israeli historiography, preoccupied with the Jewish question, created a widespread perception that, by and large, the Zionist movement did not take the Arabs into account. This perspective is bolstered by the widely quoted slogan coined by Israel Zangwill, a British Zionist and a close collaborator of Herzl: 'the country without people to the people without country'. In this contention, the Zionist movement missed a historical opportunity to settle the conflict.

Arab and especially Palestinian historiography has evolved the colonial theory of the Zionist movement. According to this view, the Zionists did not differ from other European colonisers in Africa and Asia. They set out to establish a colonial society in Palestine in conjunction with the traditional colonial empires, notably Germany and Great Britain. The colonial theory routinely emphasises that the Jewish settlers used colonial instruments of nation-building such as the Jewish Colonial Trust, the 'colonisation committee' and the Palestine Land Development Fund.[39]

Recent Israeli historiography, largely in response to this trend, has tried to refute the contention that the Zionist movement ignored the Arabs. The major theme of this research is that the Zionists misperceived the Arab question. As a result, most of the Zionist strands underestimated the aspirations of Arab nationalism and the extent of Arab opposition to Zionist plans.[40]

The difficulties in dealing with the question of the history of Zionist perceptions of the Palestinians are overwhelming. Jervis, in his pioneering study on perceptions and misperceptions in international relations, pointed out that any discussion of the subject inevitably runs into problems of historical evidence, intentional or subconscious autobiographical misrepresentation, and the assessment of the amount of information available to the actors.[41]

The study of Arab-Israeli relations poses two additional difficulties. First, the conflict has produced an inordinate number of politicised accounts — some corresponding to the Arab-Israeli lines of the conflict and others reflecting the internal divisions within the Zionist camp. Even when the account is not overtly political, there are problems in sorting out what constitutes the perception of the actors as opposed to the author's perception of the actors. Secondly, the research has to be constantly updated to accommodate newly released documents, and the publication of autobiographies. For instance, the publication of the Sharett diaries some years ago and the most recently released diary of Ben-Gurion have already changed some of the traditional interpretations.

The only study which is methodologically designed to analyse Israeli perceptions of the Arabs is Brecher's seminal work on the foreign policy system of Israel.[42] Unfortunately, this does not include the early Zionist period. In the absence of a definitive study of the subject, we can only offer a tentative discussion of the formation of Zionist perceptions of the Arab problem.

When Herzl set out to find a homeland for the Jews in Palestine, he must have shared the cognitive perspectives on nationalism which were prevalent in his day. One perspective was based on the Romantic notion of the national revolutions in Europe; national liberation was viewed as an almost pre-ordained event, a natural fulfilment of 'organic' universal rules. The other perspective was based on the prevalent mode of nineteenth-century colonialism. The rule of the white man over the native races seemed equally pre-ordained and 'organic', especially as the white minority could boast a moral superiority derived from what was perceived as an advanced political and social order.

These cognitive perspectives would be considered dissonant by contemporary standards, but we have already indicated in the previous chapter that collective belief systems and individuals who are socialised into them are tolerant of a fair amount of dissonant belief. Such a frame of reference may explain the psychological prism through which Herzl and his associates viewed the Arab problem. The historian Elon compiled a long list of evidence which indicates that Herzl was aware of the Arab problem during his brief visit to Palestine and throughout his activities. Herzl exchanged letters with Yussuf Ziah el-Khalidi, a former mayor of Jerusalem, and was even warned by the eminent sociologist of his day, Gumplowitz, that no state can be created without conflict and bloodshed. The Irish nationalist, Michael Davitt, in a book published in 1900, similarly predicted that the Arabs would object by force.[43]

Yet Elon and other scholars of Herzl note that he did not mention the Arab problem in his diaries. Our source for Herzl's image of the Arabs comes mostly from the novel *Altneuland*. The Palestinians, who were symbolised in the figure of Rashiol Bey, were depicted as eager to join the Jewish State, because of its superior social and economic system. To the extent that *Altneuland* is representative, it indicates that Herzl had what Deutch called a *co-operative* i.e. a variable zero-sum game perception of Arab-Jewish relations as opposed to a *competitive*, i.e. zero-sum game perception.[44]

This assumption is enhanced by the fact that the international beliefs prevailing in the nineteenth century were influenced by the concept of Manifest Destiny and a host of other theories that did not envisage any dissonance between the superordinate whites and the native populations which could benefit materially from colonial rule.[45] Moreover, the Political Zionists perceived their own social and political order as superior to the Ottoman rule under which the Palestinians had lived for centuries.

Another psychological perspective in early Zionism was derived from the application of the Romantic movement to the Middle East. Not unlike the later British Romanticists of the Levant, St John Philby or T. E. Lawrence, some early Zionists viewed the East as superior to what they described as the decadent and corrupt Western civilisation. In this image, the Jews were held to be the People of the East; they were strangers in the lands of Europe and were urged to return to the Levant. According to this view, which was expressed by Lilinblum, Ben Eliezer and Israel Belkind, among others, the Arabs who lived in Palestine were descendants of the early Hebrews. This theory was given prominence in Belkind's book *The Origins of the Fellahin* published in 1919 and was even discussed by Ben-Gurion and his close collaborator Yitzhak Ben-Tzvi. The Bedouin in particular were viewed as close to the ancient Hebrews; their lifestyle was greatly admired and sometimes emulated by the settlers.[46]

The Romantic Levant perspective implied a highly co-operative

perception of Jewish-Arab relations. According to the theories of
settler societies, such a perception was synonymous with the concept of an inclusive frontier. Frontiers of exclusion and inclusion
describe the pattern of interaction between immigrant settlers and
the native inhabitants. Indeed, one theme advocated in this group
envisaged a radical form of inclusivity based on 'miscegenation',
i.e. mixed marriages.[47] The inclusive frontier trend in early
Zionism was rather marginal, but was subsequently crystallised in
the influential Canaanite movement. The Canaanites negated the
Jewish Diaspora and advocated the union of Hebrew and other
Semitic people in the region.[48]

The co-operative image of relations with the Arabs was not
unanimously shared by the Zionist movement. Occasional
warnings about the impending clash were published in Zionist
publications and delivered at the Zionist Congress. Kollat and
Rubinstein documented numerous such instances including the
1907 article by Yitzhak Epstein in *Hashilo'ah*, in which he accused
the Zionist leadership of avoiding the Arab problem.[49]

Ahad Ha'am was the only major Zionist figure to develop what
may be defined as a competitive, i.e. zero-sum game perception of
the conflict. He was also the only one who articulated it quite
consistently. It is interesting that Ahad Ha'am was almost alone in
having what is known as a perception of low *'frontierity'*, i.e. a
subjective estimate of how much territory was available for
settlement. Already in 1881 Ahad Ha'am warned that it was
difficult to find 'untitled soil in Palestine', except on hills or dunes.

The founder of Cultural Zionism was equally pessimistic about
the presumed Arab willingness to accept the Jewish co-operative
solution. 'We think that the Arabs are all savages who live like
animals and do not understand what is happening around them.'
This line of reasoning led him to articulate one of the sharpest
internal rebuffs to Zionism. 'The Arab people regarded by us as
non-existent ever since the beginning of the colonisation of
Palestine, heard and believed that the Jews were coming to drive
them from their soil and deal with them at their own will.'[50]

It is difficult to explain why Ahad Ha'am diverged so sharply
from his contemporaries. Simon, his biographer, points out that he
was didactic and a moralist. He was also a scrupulous observer of
the local scene during his visits to Palestine. His vision of Cultural
Zionism, which called for a small moral and religious Jewish
centre in Palestine, did not go well with the subjugation and

expropriation of the Arabs.[51] It is also entirely conceivable that Ahad Ha'am emphasised the negative arguments in order to 'bolster' his advocacy of a spiritual centre. Whatever the cognitive sources, Ahad Ha'am's zero-sum image was a forerunner of the more conflictual articulation of the problem by the Revisionists.

The Socialist Zionists had a much clearer perception of the Arab problem than the Political Zionists. Beginning with the Second Aliyah (immigration) (1906–14), the Socialists had settled in Palestine in increasing numbers. All together, in 1914 there were some 85,000 Jews and about 700,000 Arabs in Palestine. Almost from the very beginning of modern Jewish immigration, there was tension and occasionally bloody clashes between the settlers and the Arabs.

An analysis of the Socialist Zionist image of the Arabs is necessarily dominated by the perspective of Ben-Gurion and his associates in the movement. A comparison of a number of historical accounts which draw on interviews and written materials reveals that the leader of Socialist Zionism had a rather ambivalent attitude towards Arab-Jewish relations. According to Elon, Ben-Gurion had become aware of the basic Arab enmity already in 1915 when he took cognisance of the Arab reaction to his imprisonment by the Turks.[52] By 1919 he had apparently developed the zero-sum game perception of the conflict: 'But not everyone sees that there is no solution to this question. No solution! I do not know what Arab will agree that Palestine should belong to the Jews — even if the Jews learn Arabic.'[53] Yet there are numerous records that Ben-Gurion and other members of the elite felt that the conflict could be resolved by a direct approach to the Arab masses. Indeed, there is a widespread historical contention that, at least initially, Ben-Gurion perceived the Arab-Jewish conflict in class terms.

The question of ambivalent and changing attitudes is so difficult to resolve partly because attitudes can be based on misperceptions and partly because an individual can change his attitudes in the course of validating beliefs, whether misperceived or not. We can assume that both elements affected Socialist Zionist thinking on the Arab problem.

All the published records and scholarly interpretations point out that the process of communication between the Jewish settlers and the Arabs was full of misperceptions. They were caused by cultural differences, and bolstered by geographical and social separation.

One popular thesis in the historiography of the Oriental community today even claims that the initial frictions deteriorated into a full-fledged conflict because the Zionist movement was dominated by the Ashkenazim, who did not understand the Arabs as well as the Oriental Jews did.[54] Such an interpretation may be far-fetched, in view of the objective divergence of interests between the two communities, but it is true that lack of mutual knowledge compounded the communication problem. For instance, few of the early Zionists were familiar with the writings on Arab nationalism. When the *Hashiloa'h* reprinted excerpts from Nagib Azuri's *Le Reveil de la Nation Arabe*, they were largely ignored.[55]

A major source of misperception stemmed from the Marxist materialistic interpretation of conflicts to which the Socialist Zionists adhered. Following classic Marxist logic, the elite Labour movement attributed at least some of the tension to a class conflict between the Jews and the Arab *effendis* (landlords), with the Arab equivalent of the proletariat, the *fellahin* (peasants), caught in the middle. Once the Jewish proletariat and the *fellahin* united against the *effendis*, the conflict would be over.

Like Lenin and the Russian Bolsheviks, the Socialist Zionists came from East European countries. In granting legitimacy to national movements, their psychological prism might also have been influenced by the yardsticks of the Italian *Risorgimento*, the liberal nationalism of Masaryk in Czechoslovakia, or the massive nationalist outpouring of the Spring of Nations of 1848. It was inconceivable to them that what they perceived as fanaticism and the reactionary ideology of the Arab masses could join forces with the small middle class to produce a national movement in a backward country. In the view of Berl Katzenelson, the official ideologue of Mapai, the Arab national movement was not truly mobilisatory; it lacked social support, was conservative or even xenophobic and stemmed from the desire of the middle class to perpetuate the exploitation of the toiling Arab masses.[56]

This underestimation of the national sentiments of the Arabs was undoubtedly enhanced by the fact that Palestinian nationalism was not well articulated at the time. Emerging Arab nationalism was Pan-Arab in orientation and confined to small elites. Although a Pan-Arab orientation should not have made it less legitimate — the Palestinians could define their group membership in either inclusive or exclusive terms, without affecting the legitimacy of their territorial claim — the diffuse expressions of Palestinian nationalism made the Jewish attribution process more difficult.

A perusal of the sources reveals that initially the Socialist Zionists attributed Arab resistance to numerous causes, ranging from common banditry to the alleged desire of the Arab *effendis* to drive up the price of land. Indeed, in the first few decades, sporadic Arab attacks on Jewish settlements were quite common. One of the most popular theories at that time was that Arab nationalism was instigated by the British who were perceived to be applying their colonial 'divide and rule' practices to Palestine. In choosing some of the attribution themes, the Socialist Zionists might have been trying to delegitimise Arab nationalism. Mutual delegitimisation is extremely common in inter-group conflict, and has been a dominant feature in the Arab-Israeli conflict.

A less articulated but rather pervasive early misperception was related to the peculiarities of Jewish existence in the Diaspora. In their interpretation of the initial stirrings of Arab resistance, the Jews often used the cognitive analogy of anti-Semitism. For instance, when the first Arab riots broke out in Jaffa in 1908, these were described as pogroms. Initially, Zionist leaders quite often equated the *fellahin* with the Russian peasants.[57]

Ben-Ezer, a literary scholar and critic, points out that many of the writings in this period indicate such an analogous perspective on Arab resistance. Haim Brenner, a literary figure and one of the ideologues of the Socialist Zionist camp, was even criticised by some of his contemporaries for failing to distinguish between Arab hatred and Gentile anti-Semitism.[58] Yet in spite of this conscious striving to achieve a differentiated perspective, there is an impression that the anti-Semitic analogies prevented the Jews from discerning the national motives in Arab resistance.

The initial Socialist Zionist perception of the Arab problem had begun to change by the early 1930s. The parameters of the impending conflict were crystallised by the time of the Arab revolt in 1936. Two elements contributed to the growing Jewish realisation that the Arabs had evolved a national movement which was based on a total rejection of the Jewish national aspirations.

One element pertained to the ideological articulation and organisational consolidation of the Palestinian national movement. The focal points of this resistance were the Hebron massacre of 1929 and the massive revolt in 1936, in which the

Arabs demonstrated reasonable unity. The Socialist Zionists, as indeed the whole of the Zionist movement, were also aware of the growing international legitimacy of the Arab cause in Palestine. British mandatory policy, which indicated an increasingly constrained interpretation of the 1917 Balfour Declaration of the Jewish National Home in Palestine, bore witness to this trend. The hallmark of this policy was contained in the Peel Commission Report of 1937 which limited Jewish immigration and land purchase.

The other element was related to the failure to validate the initial Socialist Zionist beliefs about the conflict. A stock notion in the traditional historiography of the Middle East conflict holds that the clash was at least partially generated by the lack of contacts between Jews and Arabs. More recent research, including Caplan's work on the history of negotiations, reveals a rather extensive bargaining pattern.

Caplan and other scholars documented a number of instances in which the Arabs dismissed the offers of Zionist leaders to furnish large-scale economic aid. Even the moderate Palestinian leader Musa Alami turned down Ben-Gurion's offer of help in 1936. Of course, a major problem in the negotiation process was the structure of Arab decision-making. The Zionist leaders apparently had difficulty in deciding who, among the local and regional Arab leaders, could 'deliver the goods', that is, make the necessary political commitments.[59]

The Socialist Zionists were equally unsuccessful in validating their belief that the Arab proletariat would not follow their leaders. The pattern of Arab unrest which culminated in the 1936 revolt was quite clearly a mass phenomenon; there is considerable evidence that it was evaluated as such by the Socialist Zionist elite.[60]

Moreover, in the early 1930s the Socialist Zionists did not entirely dominate what the sociologists of knowledge call the 'definition of the situation'. They were under increasing attack from the right wing of the Zionist movement. The Revisionists, although a small minority in Palestine, were extremely vocal in interpreting the Arab-Jewish conflict in terms of a zero-sum game. They had routinely used the failure of the Socialist Zionists to win Arab co-operation in order to legitimise their own arguments. The Arab unrest and the Revisionist criticism forced the Socialist Zionist elite to make some major adjustments at the operational level. They expanded and modernised the Jewish self-defence organisation, the Hagana, which was established in 1910.

The modifications in the image of the Arab problem did not lead the Socialist Zionists to adopt the Revisionist perception of the conflict as a zero-sum game. Instead, Ben-Gurion and his colleagues redefined some of the conditions for a co-operative solution. The crux of the new thinking was based on the assumption that the Arabs would agree to a territorial compromise in face of the increasingly feasible option of Jewish sovereignty. Ben-Gurion also came to appreciate the function of military power. The embryonic deterrence theory was constructed around the premise that military strength would prevent the Arabs from physically destroying the Yishuv (the Jewish community in Palestine) and force them into a territorial compromise. Brecher, who extensively researched the outlook of the Socialist Zionist elite, has emphasised that Ben-Gurion's attitude towards the Arabs was probabilistic rather than deterministic. Ben-Gurion assumed that, given the proper conditions, the Arabs would come to accept a co-operative outcome to the conflict.[61]

Two additional reasons may explain the continuous Socialist Zionist adherence to a variable-sum game perspective. One was inherent in the pacifist and universalistic perceptive of the early Socialist Zionists, and especially in the powerful semiutopian influence of Gordon. A major ideologue of the Labour movement, Gordon preached the values of redemption through a return to all agricultural and pacifist society. Although the executive elite was not fully identified with Gordonism, the pacifist and cosmopolitan residue, combined with traditional Jewish notions of morality, was apparently strong enough to create a rather painful dissonance when the movement faced the power realities of the situation.

One telling indicator of this dissonant perception was the widespread debate on the morality of the Zionist act in Palestine. Although the Socialist Zionists accepted Ben-Gurion's dictum of 1917 that in a 'historical and moral sense' Palestine belonged to the Jews, they were clearly aware of the 'injustice to another people', the Arabs. For instance, during the debate about a possible transfer of the Arab population in the 1920s, Ben-Gurion paraphrased Dostoyevsky, when he maintained that 'Zionism did not have the moral right to harm one single Arab child, even if it could realize all its aspirations at that price'.[62]

The moral dilemma was particularly emphasised by the small

number of intellectuals who joined the philosopher Martin Buber to form the *Brit Shalom*, the Peace Pact. Contrary to some popular notions, Buber did not deny the moral claim of the Jews to the Holy Land. On the contrary, in his perception, the Jews are not like 'all other nations', but a *res sui generis*, a unique national entity. This uniqueness derives from their mission to bring Judaic morality into the international system. The conclusion of *Brit Shalom* at the operational level was to establish a bi-national state.[63] *Kedmah Mizrachia* and *Ihud*, the *Brit*'s successors, also advocated this line.

The bi-national solution was only marginally popular among the Jews, and was not acceptable to the Arabs. But the mainstream Zionist movement kept on searching for a solution to the moral dilemma. Such a formulation was also imperative because the question of Arab rights had increasing international ramifications. Chaim Weitzmann, the leader of the World Zionist Congress, provided the most interesting insight into this problem. In his testimony to the United Palestine Committee Weitzmann admitted that equal justice for both sides was not possible. The problem of the Jewish presence in Palestine could only be solved along the lines of least injustice, namely, partition.[64]

The dissonance between the pacifist ideas of Socialist Zionism and the imperatives of power politics were particularly evident in the defence organisation, the *Hagana*. The Jewish underground adopted the principle of *Tohar Haneshek* (purity of arms). Weapons were to be used only in self-defence and reprisals against Arab populations were ruled out. Luttwak and Horowitz, in their research on Israel's military history, found that the moral question was often debated at the tactical level. In particular, there was uncertainty as to whether the policy of *havlaga*, self-restraint, would allow the ambush of Arabs in certain operations.[65]

The other reason which argued against a zero-sum game perspective of the conflict stemmed from problems of self-legitimacy and political mobilisation. Contrary to the Revisionists, the Socialist Zionist elite felt that an emphasis on Arab intransigence, coupled with the moral dilemma, would create doubt among the Jewish settlers and undermine the territorial legitimacy of the group. Both Berl Katzenelson and Yacov Golomb, who were involved in the mobilisation process, admitted in private and public forums that such a perception could create self-doubt among the younger generation and the new immigrants.

Katzenelson, a chief ideologue of the movement, was also apprehensive that, by accepting the Revisionist definition of the conflict, the Socialist Zionists would legitimise the opposition.[66]

The mix of normative convictions and tactical considerations prompted the Socialist Zionists to accept the United Nations Partition Plan of 1947. Under the terms of the plan, Palestine was to be divided into a small Jewish state and a larger Palestinian entity. However, Arab refusal to accept the UN Resolution, and the subsequent Arab-Israeli war, led to yet another modification of the Socialist Zionist perspective. It is not clear to what extent Ben-Gurion and the associated elite adhered to the theory of territorial compromise during the 1948 war. Kimmerling, who has carried out the most detailed study on the perception of territory in Zionist thinking, admits that an objective analysis is difficult because the subject has been politicised and is fraught with emotions. The Zionist leaders were convinced that the Arab states would try to destroy the Yishuv; failing that, they would try to limit the Partition Plan boundaries of the Jewish state. To counter this threat, the General Staff of the *Hagana* prepared a strategic outline, known as Plan D, which called for a defence of the partition borders and clusters of Jewish settlements outside the boundaries.[67]

This outline changed during the actual fighting, which increasingly demonstrated the military superiority of the *Hagana*. Manor's detailed work on the military feedback into the political decision-making during the war creates the impression that the territorial shape of the State of Israel followed the outcome of the military operation. Moreover, the communication process between the political leadership and the General Staff was only sporadic. The internal frictions in the *Hagana*, which was composed of different political factions, and the regional divisions at the front further fragmented any central planning. The initiative of local command units, acting on their own, was behind some major territorial gains and especially the March 1949 decision to conquer Eilat and secure the Negev for Israel.[68]

The question of an Arab population was closely related to the problem of territory. The Socialist Zionists had a highly exclusive perception of frontiers. They wanted to establish a homogeneous Jewish entity. Due to their concern with social redemption, they even objected to the use of Arab labour. Ruling out the option of population transfer, they tried to increase homogeneity by settling

in relatively sparsely populated areas. Thus, the Galilee was preferred for settlements to Judea and Samaria, which, though constituting the Biblical core of the Jewish state, were densely
populated by Arabs.

It is difficult to estimate to what extent the leadership of the
Yishuv deliberately planned to expel the Arabs during the war.
Numerous accounts seem to indicate that the Arab exodus in
1947–8 was a combined outcome of psychological states and
coercion. As in other acute military conflicts, the Jews and the
Arabs had a 'mirror image' perception of each other.[69] Both sides
were exposed to events which illustrated the potential for cruel
mistreatment of the enemy.

On the Jewish side, this included the murder of the Jewish
community in Hebron, the slaughter of the Jews of Safad, and the
murder of the captured professors and medical staff in the Hebrew
University convoy to Mount Scopus. On the Arab side, there was
the April 1948 slaughter of the inhabitants of Deir Yassin by the
Revisionist splinter, the Lehi group.

Although the Deir Yassin killings were denounced by the
Hagana, in the generally chaotic communications of the war the
Arabs could hardly be expected to distinguish between the various
Hagana groups. The Deir Yassin effect might have been actually
magnified by the 'mirror image' phenomenon; since the Arabs
engaged in attrocities against the Jews, they came to expect the
same treatment from the Jews. The preceding Hagana offensive
and the Deir Yassin incident were used by the local leadership to
mobilise the Arab community. This strategy backfired, because it
apparently intensified the flight of the Arabs after the British left
Palestine in May 1948.

The coercive character of some of the Hagana operations was an
additional factor in the de-Arabisation of the territory. Plan D
explicitly permitted the expulsion of 'resistant populations' during
the course of the military action. This provision was often loosely
interpreted to cover a wholesale expulsion of the population.
Although there is no detailed study on the subject, the expulsion
pattern seemed to follow the political and personal convictions of
the regional and local commanders. It is virtually impossible to
estimate how many of the more than half a million refugees were
expelled and how many fled.

Regardless of the reasons, the Israeli leadership welcomed the
fact that only about 150,000 Arabs were left in the new State of

Israel. The Provisional Council of the State moved quickly to consolidate its legal control over abandoned Arab property. Ben-Gurion and subsequent Israeli leaders have always objected to any provision for the return of the refugees.

The war and the foundation of the State of Israel in May 1948 modified once more the Socialist Zionist perception. However, because of the institutionalisation of the major advocacy groups, the image of the Arab-Israeli conflict became fragmented. Brecher identified three major images and their concomitant lines of policy. One was *Ben-Gurionism*, reconciliation with the Arabs resulting from Israel's superior power. This outlook was expressed in the policy of retaliation which culminated in the 1956 Sinai campaign. The second was *Weitzmannism*, reconciliation through a search for moderate solutions. The major exponent of this view in the Cabinet was Moshe Sharett, Ben-Gurion's Foreign Minister and subsequent Prime Minister. The third image was *Buberism*, which emphasised concessions in exchange for peace. Buberism was confined to a small left-wing circle which was located outside the executive domain.[70]

There is some disagreement as to Ben-Gurion's image of the Arab-Israeli conflict. Brecher, Ben-Gurion's biographer, Ben-Zoher and other interpreters maintained that the first leader of Israel upgraded the power imperative, but did not change his basically co-operative outlook. Sharett, Ben-Gurion's chief rival, revealed in his posthumously published diaries, that Ben-Gurion adopted a confrontational position.[71]

It is interesting that, towards the end of his career, Ben-Gurion came to adopt a conciliatory image. In the wake of the Six-Day War, he was one of the few Israeli leaders of stature to call for a territorial compromise in exchange for peace. However, as we shall demonstrate in the next chapter, by this time, the societal belief system was increasingly deviating from the traditional Socialist Zionist perceptions.

Notes

1. Quoted in M. P. Kammen (ed.), *The Past Before Us: Contemporary Writings in America* (Cornell University Press, Ithaca, NY, 1980) p. 38.

2. E. V. Stonquist, *The Marginal Man: A Study of Personality and Cultural Conflict* (Charles Scribner & Sons, New York, 1937).

3. E. H. Erikson, *Childhood and Society* (Norton, New York, 1950); D. R.

Miller, 'The Study of Social Relationship: Situation, Identity and Social Inter-action' in S. Koch (ed.), *Psychology: A Study of a Science*, vol. 5, (McGraw Hill, New York, 1963); K. Horney, *Neuroses and Human Growth: The Struggle Toward Self-Realization* (Norton, New York, 1950); K. Lewin, *Field Theory in Social Science* edited by D. Cartwright, (Harper and Row, New York, 1951); G. Allport, *The Nature of Prejudice* (Addison Wesley, New York, 1979).

4. M. Douglas, 'Social Preconditions of Enthusiasm and Heterodoxy' in R. F. Spencer (ed.), *Forms of Symbolic Action* (University of Washington Press, Seattle, WA, 1969), pp. 69–80.

5. For an interesting discussion on Jewish-Gentile relations in medieval times see J. Katz, *Exclusiveness and Tolerance* (Schocken, New York, 1962).

6. For a discussion of the concept of theodicy see M. Weber, *Economy and Society*, edited by G. Roth and C. Wittich, (Bedminster Press, New York, 1968).

7. A. A. Cohen, *The Natural and Supernatural Jew. A Historical and Theological Introduction* (Pantheon Books, New York, 1962), pp. 12–19.

8. R. Patai, *The Jewish Mind* (Charles Scribner & Sons, New York, 1977), p. 223.

9. E. Shmueli, *Seven Jewish Cultures. A Reinterpretation of Jewish History and Thought* (Yahdav, Tel Aviv, 1980), p. 272 (Hebrew).

10. Patai, *The Jewish Mind*, p. 461.

11. Shmueli traces the appearance of the 'lacrimony history' theory to an article by Salo Baron, 'Ghetto and Emancipation' which appeared in the June 1928 issue of the *Menorah Journal*. See *Seven Jewish Cultures*, pp. 315, 322.

12. G. Sholem, *Sabbatai Sevi: The Mystical Messiah 1626–1679* (Princeton University Press, Princeton, NJ, 1973). For a traditional example of the cabbalah influence see Max I. Dimont, *Jews, God and History* (Simon and Schuster, New York, 1962), p. 271.

13. S. Sharot, *Messianism, Mysticism and Magic: A Sociological Analysis of Jewish Religious Movements* (University of North Carolina Press, Chapel Hill, NC, 1982), pp. 86–129.

14. For a detailed study of the official orthodoxy see E. Marmorstein, *Heaven at Bay: Kulturkampf in the Holy Land* (Oxford University Press, London, 1969).

15. Lewin, 'Field Theory', p. 148.

16. For a review of research on social comparison and ethnic identity see M. Billig, *Social Psychology and Intergroup Relations* (Academic Press, London, 1976), pp. 348–54.

17. Quoted in W. Laqueur, *A History of Zionism* (Weidenfeld and Nicolson, London, 1972), p. 72.

18. Horowitz demanded a Commission of Inquiry into Bialik's allegations, *Haaretz*, 18 August 1983.

19. Allport, *The Nature*, pp. 150–1.

20. S. Avineri, *Essays on Zionism and Politics* (Sifrei Mebat, Tel Aviv, 1977), p. 70 (Hebrew).

21. J. Guttman, *Philosophies of Judaism* (Schocken Books, New York, 1973), pp. 330–44.

22. Quoted in Laqueur, *A History*, p. 8.

23. M. Billig, *Ideology and Social Psychology, Extremism, Moderation and Contradiction* (St. Martin's Press, New York, 1982), p. 72.

24. The eugenic school of thought was transferred to German Romanticism through the works of Chamberlain and the activities of the German Eugenic Society, *Archiv für Rassen und Gesellschaftsbiologie*. It culminated in the writings of the Nazi psychologist E. R. Janesch. In one of his books, *Der Gegentypus*, Janesch made a distinction between the genetic J-type personality of the Aryans and the S-type, weak-willed Jewish personality. Billig, *Ideology*, pp. 79, 124–5.

25. The psychologist, S. N. Herman, who specialises in research on Jewish

identity, maintains that Zionist conversion has often resulted from unexpected encounters with anti-Semitism, such as the Dreyfus affair. *Zionism and Pro-Israelism: A Social Psychological Analysis* (The Institute of Contemporary Jewry, The Hebrew University of Jerusalem, 1976), p. 18.

26. The English translation of *Autoemancipation* is included in Y. L. Pinsker, *The Road to Freedom*, edited by B. Netanyahu (Scopus Publishing Company, New York, 1944).

27. H. Arendt, 'The Jewish State: Fifty Years After — Where have Herzl's Politics Led?' in G. V. Smith (ed.), *Zionism, The Dream and Reality* (David and Charles, Newton Abbot, London, and New York 1974), pp. 67–80, especially p. 75.

28. Pinsker, *Autoemancipation*.

29. N. A. Rose, *The Gentile Zionists* (Frank Cass, London, 1973).

30. For a discussion of Ahad Ha'am's thinking see L. Simon, *Ahad ha-Am (Asher Ginsburg) A Biography* (Jewish Publication Society, Philadelphia, 1960) and D. Vital, *The Origins of Zionism* (At the Clarendon Press, Oxford, 1975), pp. 187–200.

31. P. Merhav, *The Israeli Left. History, Problems, Documents* (A. S. Barnes & Company, San Diego and New York, 1980), pp. 13–30.

32. Y. Gerber-Talmon and Z. Stup, 'Secular Asceticism: Patterns of Ideological Change' in S. N. Eisenstadt, R. Bar-Yosef and C. Adler (eds), *Integration and Development in Israel* (Pall Mall, New York, 1970), pp. 469–504.

33. B. Kimmerling, *Zionism and Economy* (Schenkman Publishing Company, Cambridge, MA, 1983), pp. 6, 13.

34. Simon, *Ahad ha-Am*, p. 159.

35. C. Liebman and E. Don-Yehiya, *The Civil Religion in Israel: Traditional Judaism and Political Culture in the Jewish State* (University of California Press, Berkely, CA, 1983).

36. B. M. Borthwick, 'Religion and Politics in Israel and Egypt', *The Middle East Journal*, vol. 33, no. 2 (1979), pp. 144–63.

37. D. Wilner, *National Building and Community in Israel* (Princeton University Press, Princeton, NJ, 1969), p. 37.

38. D. Horowitz and M. Lissak, *The Origins of the Israeli Polity. The Political System of the Jewish Community in Palestine under the Mandate* (Am Oved, Tel Aviv, 1977), p. 190 (Hebrew).

39. For a representative work see A. W. Kayyali, 'The Historical Roots of the Imperialist-Zionist Alliance' in A. W. Kayyali (ed.), *Zionism, Imperialism and Racism* (Croom Helm, London, 1979).

40. S. Almog (ed.), *Zionism and the Arabs* (The Historical Society of Israel and the Zalman Shazar Center, Jerusalem, 1983), p. vii.

41. R. Jervis, *Perceptions and Misperceptions in International Politics* (Princeton University Press, Princeton, NJ, 1976), pp. 3–10.

42. M. Brecher, *The Foreign Policy System of Israel* (Oxford University Press, London, 1972).

43. A. Elon, *The Israelis* (Sphere Books Ltd, London, 1971), pp. 156–67.

44. M. Deutsch, *The Resolution of Conflict: Constructive and Destructive Processes* (Yale University Press, New Haven, CT, 1973).

45. For instance, the philosophy of Manifest Destiny was behind American expansionism in the nineteenth century. R. Dallak, *The American Style of Foreign Policy* (Alfred A. Knopf, New York, 1983).

46. Y. Shavit, *From Hebrew to Canaanite* (The Domino Press, Tel Aviv, 1984), pp. 54–63, (Hebrew).

47. B. Kimmerling, *Zionism and Territory. The Socio-Territorial Dimension of Zionist Politics* (University of California, Institute of International Relations Studies, Berkeley, CA, 1983).

48. Shavit, *From Hebrew*, pp. 114–38.

49. I. Kolatt, 'The Zionist Movement and the Arabs', and E. Rubenstein, 'Zionist Attitudes on the Jewish Arab Conflict Until 1936' in Almog, *Zionism*, pp. 35–72 and 1–34 respectively.

50. *Ahad Ha'am, All Writings of Ahad Ha'am*, (Hebrew Publishing, Jerusalem, 1956).

51. Simon, *Ahad Ha'am*.

52. Elon, *The Israelis*, p. 161.

53. Quoted in N. Caplan, 'Negotiations and the Arab Israeli Conflict', *The Jerusalem Quarterly*, no. 6 (1978), pp. 3–19.

54. N. Menahem, *Ethnic Tension and Discrimination in Israel, Sociohistorical Perspective* (Rubin Publishing, Ramat Gan, 1983), p. 355 (Hebrew).

55. Elon, *The Israelis*, p. 159.

56. A. Shapiro, *Berl Katzenelson: A Biography*, vol. 1, (Am Oved, Tel Aviv, 1981), pp. 302–9 (Hebrew).

57. Elon, *The Israelis*, p. 179; Katzenelson was particularly apt to view the Arab peasants through the prism of anti-Semitism in his native Russia, Shapiro, *Berl*, p. 308.

58. E. Ben-Ezer, 'War and Siege in Hebrew Literature After 1967', *The Jerusalem Quarterly*, no. 9 (1978), pp. 20–37.

59. Caplan, 'Negotiations'.

60. Horowitz and Lissak argue that, after the 1936 riots, the Zionist elite reacted by overestimating the strength of the Arab opposition. *The Origins*, pp. 65.

61. Brecher, *The Foreign Policy*, p. 281.

62. Elon, *The Israelis*, p. 162.

63. M. Buber, 'Nationalism' in Smith, *Zionism*, pp. 56–66.

64. F. Zweig, *Israel: The Sword and the Harp* (Farleigh Dickinson University Press, Rutherford, NJ, 1969), p. 244.

65. E. N. Luttwak and D. Horowitz, *The Israeli Army 1948–1973* (Abt Books, Cambridge, MA, 1983), p. 12.

66. Y. Wagner and E. Kaphafi, *The Sources of the Dispute. The Historical Quarrel Between the Labor Movement and the Revisionists* (Am Oved, Tel Aviv, 1982), p. 202 (Hebrew).

67. Kimmerling, *Zionism*, p. 133.

68. R. Manor, 'Perceptions, Decision-Making and Feedback in Israeli Foreign Policy: The Forming of the Israeli Border Map During the War of Independence', *State Government and International Relations*, no. 13 (1979), pp. 17–51 (Hebrew); see also footnote 29 in Chapter 3.

69. R. K. White, 'Misperceptions in the Arab Israeli Conflict', *Journal of Social Issues*, vol. 33, no. 1 (1977).

70. Brecher, *The Foreign Policy*, pp. 280–2.

71. For a discussion of the divergent approaches to Israeli foreign policy see A. Shlaim, 'Conflicting Approaches to Israel's Relations with the Arabs: Ben-Gurion and Sharett, 1953–1956', *Middle East Journal*, vol. 37, no. 2 (1983), pp. 180–201; G. Sheffer, 'The Confrontation Between Moshe Sharett and D. Ben-Gurion' in Almog, *Zionism*, pp. 95–147.

3 THE EVOLUTION OF NEW ZIONISM

The preceding chapter might have suggested a straightforward pattern in the historical development of the Jewish belief system which culminated in Socialist Zionism. Yet all along the way, Socialist Zionism had to compete with other ideological strands, which it could neither assimilate nor ignore. The most powerful challenge came from Revisionism, or New Zionism. The term was made official when the Revisionists left the World Zionist Organisation, and established the rival New Zionist Organisation in 1935.

Even before the split, Revisionism emerged as a separate subculture among Diaspora Jewry and its followers in the Yishuv. The Revisionist belief system had a distinctive interpretation of history, and a different notion of group legitimacy and distributive justice. This chapter will examine the phenomenological underpinning of this distinctive Revisionist 'definition of the situation' and the operational solution to the Jewish problem which it offered.

The analysis will trace the evolution of Revisionism into New Zionism, which eclipsed Socialist Zionism and paved the way for the Likud victory in 1977. Contemporary New Zionism is a rather loosely-knit belief system which combines secular and religious elements. In addition, it contains some broad historiographical strands which deal with the meaning of anti-Semitism and the Holocaust.

Revisionism

The Revisionist movement has usually been identified with Vladimir (Zeev) Jabotinsky (1880–1944), a journalist and publicist from Odessa in Russia. Like many of his contemporaries Jabotinsky's early Russophilia was shattered by the wave of pogroms of 1904–5 which the Tzarist regime condoned. He became an enthusiastic follower of Herzl's political Zionism. Jabotinsky's intellectual prominence attracted an increasing following and led him to establish the Revisionist organ, *Rassviet*.

Although historians of Revisionism credit the collective thinking of *Rassviet* with developing the Revisionist creed, Jabotinsky's prolific output clearly overshadowed the movement.

Almost from the very beginning, Jabotinsky deviated from the Socialist Zionists with whom he collaborated upon his arrival in Palestine in the early 1920s. In fact, Jabotinsky's demand for a revision of the Socialist Zionist ideology gave his name to the movement. Historians emphasise that these differences are related to his background. Unlike the Jewish Socialists, Jabotinsky spent his formative years in the West. His exposure to Italian Socialism, Austrian liberal-populism and Central European nationalism are all credited with shaping his Zionist thinking. Other scholars note the influence of Polish nationalism on Jabotinsky's belief system.[1]

Jabotinsky's most serious disagreement with Labour Zionism focused on his perception of anti-Semitism and the Jewish national character. He believed that anti-Semitism in Europe was based on two elements: 'the anti-Semitism of men' and the 'anti-Semitism of things'. The former corresponded to the psychological expression of ethnic prejudice towards the Jewish minority. The latter was caused by the objective socio-economic realities of Central and Eastern Europe, where the Jews lived in overpopulated and impoverished rural societies. In other words, to Jabotinsky, anti-Semitism was a *particular* but not a unique expression of anti-minority prejudice. The predicament could be solved by a massive Jewish immigration to Palestine.

Jabotinsky's analysis of the Jewish character indicates that he accepted the then prevalent critique of the *Ostjude*. The founder of Revisionism singled out for special criticism the lack of physical stamina, discipline and military prowess of the Diaspora Jew. The ideal type of new Jewish man can be discerned from his educational philosophy of *Hadar*. The concept of *Hadar* was embodied in the Revisionist youth movement *Betar*, which drew on the German youth movement's Bund, the Italian Balli and the Czeck Sokol. The term *Hadar* implies a number of attitudes and qualities: respect, politeness, loyalty, chivalry, physical cleanliness, proper social manners, and above all, self-esteem.

Instead of social redemption, however, Jabotinsky advocated *national redemption*, that is, the need to attain sovereignty. The extent of social transvaluation, which was required to achieve what Jabotinsky envisaged as the New Jewish society, is not entirely clear. Shavit, a leading authority on the Revisionist movement, has pointed out that the Revisionist ideal type was socio-economically akin to a European bourgeois.[2] Although Jabotinsky's contemporaries and historians alike have commented on the absence of Jewish traits in his personality and writing, he was circumscribed in criticising the religious character of Judaism. From the early 1930s, there has been a tacit agreement between the Revisionist movement and the national religious circles of Rabbi Abraham Kook. The platform of the New Zionist Organisation vowed to implement the traditional values of Judaism in the future state.[3]

Jabotinsky was much more elaborate in discussing his concept of national redemption. According to this, the national dimension organises the social dimension, because of the heightened salience of national symbols and roles. The military struggle for national liberation is the most important mobilisatory role. The full psychosocial transformation of a group can be achieved only in a sovereign state and not, as the Labour Zionists assumed, through a gradual and small-scale process of social redemption. Jabotinsky's emphasis on national and military symbols has often been interpreted in psychoanalytical terms; to wit, his personal fascination with military power and its paraphernalia.[4] Regardless of his egotistical motives, Jabotinsky's choice of national themes, symbols and operational goals reflects a quite coherent philosophy of national integration.

First, he emphasised the central role of military struggle in the genesis of the state. His perception was undoubtedly shaped by study of the national revolutionary movements in Europe and especially the Italian *Risorgimento*. Jabotinsky and his followers were equally impressed by the Polish national movement. The Revisionists considered the Polish model — the attainment of independence against considerable odds — a particularly appropriate example for the Zionist cause. It is not known whether Jabotinsky was familiar with the work of the eminent sociologists of conflict, Ludwig Gumplowicz, Gustav Ratzhenhofer and Franz Oppenheimer, who all stressed the role of war in the evolution of the state.[5] But his novel *Simson* is a literary expression of the concept that all great states have been founded by the sword.

Second, Jabotinsky viewed military struggle in the nation-building stage as crucial to the psychological transformation of a people from passivity to activity. He deemed such a transformation particularly necessary for the Jews, who were accustomed to perceive powerlessness as part of their cultural ethnic heritage. This perspective was part of a broader philosophy common to the Revisionists and the national revolutionary movements in Europe. Described once as a 'Sorelian who may have never read Sorel', Jabotinsky apparently came to believe that only through struggle, suffering and violence can a people prove themselves worthy of becoming a nation. Avineri found that Jabotinsky was concerned with the paucity of active and military role models in modern Jewish literature. He commended the translation into Hebrew of *Ogniem i Mieczem* (By Fire and the Sword), the Polish military epic, written by Henryk Sienkiewicz.[7] The Revisionists also adopted the motto of *Hashomer*, the first Jewish defence organisation: 'In blood and fire Judea fell; in blood and fire she will rise again'.

It is interesting that the Sorelian tradition as exemplified by Jabotinsky was subsequently adopted by Third World nationalism. The author-psychiatrist, Frantz Fanon, in his most popular book, *The Wretched of the Earth*, written against the background of the war in Algeria, claimed that the struggle for independence provides the channel for the psychological redemption of the individual. Fanon's use of the term disalienation, the achievement of self-respect through struggle, and his view of violence as a means of transference from passivity to activity are strikingly similar to Jabotinsky's arguments.[8]

Third, Jabotinsky appreciated national and military symbols as a means of achieving internal legitimacy. Zionism suffered from what the mobilisation literature calls 'a low specificity threshold', i.e. the absence of a specifically identified enemy, such as a foreign coloniser.[9] Moreover, being a settler society in the midst of a native population, the Zionist movement had some problems in generating self-legitimacy for its territorial aspirations. The Socialist Zionists responded to this predicament by emphasising historical rights and socio-economic achievements in Palestine. As in other settler societies, the 'blooming of the desert' ideology served both to increase individual mobilisation and to legitimise territorial claims. The Revisionist model of mobilisatory legitimacy can be most usefully described as an effort to create a mass national consciousness in a relative vacuum. The claim of national rights takes on validity and concreteness only when it is stridently emphasised. This model is somewhat akin to the populist mobilisation of agrarian discontent in eighteenth and nineteenth century Europe and America, which was summed up in the famous slogan, 'Raise more hell and less corn'.[10]

Jabotinsky, in claiming the primacy of a national solution, was also influenced by the historiosophical-naturalistic school of H. T. Buckle. Buckle, a nineteenth-century historian, emphasised the geopsychological boundaries of society. Jabotinsky used this approach to argue that the collective psychology of the Jews had been shaped by the geography of the Land of Israel. Any national revival of the Jewish collective would have to be based on re-creating the Biblical statehood of Israel, that is, a national entity on both banks of the Jordan River.[11]

These premises led Jabotinsky to oppose most of the policies of the Socialist Zionist leadership of the Yishuv. Serving as the head of Hagana in the early 1920s, he pressed for the establishment of a large Jewish military force in Palestine. He disputed the argument that a military body would provoke the Arabs and aggravate the Jewish position vis à vis the British. In the Revisionist image, a large Jewish military force would deter the Arabs from repeated attacks on Jewish settlements and symbolise the evolving sovereignty of the Yishuv.

Jabotinsky demanded even more emphatically the creation of a Jewish entity on both sides of the Jordan River. Writing in 1926, the Revisionist leader asserted that this should be made the chief and openly proclaimed aim of the Zionist movement. It is not clear whether, at this early stage, he envisaged full sovereignty for the proposed state or some sort of self-government, but there can be no disputing that he advocated a Jewish majority. Even so, the strategy of *Enziel*, i.e. a discussion of the final aim of Zionism, was antithetical to the gradualist diplomacy pursued by the established Zionist elite.

The Revisionist movement reserved its most bitter criticism for the social and economic hegemony of the Socialist Zionists in the Yishuv. Jabotinsky's exposure to the Italian Socialism of Antonio Laberiola and Enrico Peri was enough to ensure a Socialist perspective in his early socio-economic writings. His subsequent advocacy of a national solution led him to a growing perception of the incompatibility between the Socialist class struggle and the goal of nation-building. This dissonance brought the Revisionists to adopt the dictum of *monism*, known in Hebrew as *had ness* (literally, one flag).

One way of interpreting the idea of monism is through the

analogue of coalition-formation in the pre-independence stage of nation-building. Since ethnic or class issues are divisive, and can undercut the collective effort, an emphasis on national struggle seems more efficient than a simultaneous class and national struggle. Some scholars have interpreted monism in terms of national coalition-building.[12] Such a monistic coalition was in line with what Canover defined as a populist style of mobilisation; an appeal to 'the people' in order to cancel existing divisions and create a realignment against the traditional politicians.[13]

An alternative way of viewing Jabotinsky's monism is in terms of integralist nationalism. Avineri argued that *had ness* was an expression of national hegemony over the freedom of the individual and particularist associations such as class. Instead of class struggle, the Revisionists proposed mandatory arbitration. As a consequence, they leaned towards a view of leadership as a main motivational force in society.[14]

Whether such a monistic perspective could have led Jabotinsky to dictatorship is not clear. Shavit claimed that, because of internal challenges, Jabotinsky was forced to reassert his dominance over the Revisionist movement, but he did not belief in a dictatorial style.[15] Perhaps he was psychologically closer to the type of leadership known as *negotorium gesto*. This derives from a Roman legal concept, which enables an agent or gestor to conduct the affairs of a person who, for some reason, cannot negotiate his own affairs. Herzl, who was fairly authoritative in conducting Zionist affairs, first entertained such a concept of leadership, but he had apparently been troubled by its anti-democratic implications.[16]

Jabotinsky's critique of the socio-economic model of Labour Zionism was also related to his vision of mass immigration and impending sovereignty. The Revisionists criticised the limited and largely voluntary public financing of the Jewish settlement in Palestine and the discrimination against private initiative in all sectors. Jabotinsky claimed that private capital was necessary for large-scale land acquisition. He was particularly scornful of the 'dunam here dunam there' policy, that is, small and patchwork land acquisition. The Revisionists were also concerned that the pioneering Socialist Zionist economy was particularly unsuitable for the middle and lower middle class potential immigrants from Eastern Europe.

To counter the Labour order in the Yishuv, Jabotinsky developed his own socio-economic creed. A number of intellectual sources apparently influenced his thinking. One was Josef Popper Lynkeus, an Austrian engineer turned social thinker, who advocated an ideal economy based on a mixture of free enterprise and minimum welfare for all. Another was the Jewish historian, Yosef Klausner, who developed a Biblically-based version of moral economy. Jabotinsky's own 1934 socio-economic essay indicates that he adopted some of the anti-Marxist critique, which emphasised the dominance of the psychological rather than the materialistic principles in human development.

Put briefly, the Revisionist socio-economic belief envisaged an equalitarian distribution of resources at the level of basic human needs, or a limited welfare state. Beyond that, they believed in free enterprise based on meritorious concepts. Above all, the programme advocated an immediate systematic regime of colonisation, which would be able to create the conditions for a mass settlement of Jews in Palestine. Its core was a demand for land reform which would place all the uncultivated land on both sides of the Jordan River at the disposal of the mandatory authorities. The colonisation programme was also aimed at the 1930 British White Paper of Lord Passfield. Passfield's report limited Jewish immigration to Palestine on the grounds that the country had limited land and water resources.

The colonisation programme was indicative of the sharp division between the Revisionists and mainstream Zionism on two issues. One was the question of external legitimacy, and the other the scope of permissible strategies in the conduct of foreign policy. Brecher distinguished between two major strands of external self-legitimacy among the Socialist Zionists: the *declaratory subjective* and the *constitutive objective*. The former was based on self-proclaimed historical rights and the accomplishments of the drive for Jewish settlement. The latter strove for recognition by the international system and its various representatives, including the mandatory power.[17]

A perusal of Jabotinsky's writing indicates that he had a *declaratory constitutive* view of external legitimacy. Historical rights were elevated to a constitutive level and served as the basis for seeking international recognition. Jabotinsky's stringent insistence on the indivisibility of historical rights is most forcefully related to this image. A longstanding Revisionist tenet holds that giving up part of *Eretz Israel* (Land of Israel) will undermine the legal principle behind the external legitimacy of the Jewish state.

Jabotinsky did not negate achievement-oriented legitimisation *per se*, but maintained that the Socialist-Zionist model of gradual settlement was too incremental to generate international legitimacy. He advocated mass immigration as a much faster way of gaining external recognition.

Jabotinsky's perception of the global system was subject to periodical changes and seems less clearly defined. His 1910 essay, *Homo Homini Lupus*, used Hobbes's motif of all-out struggle and seemed to reflect a Hobbesian perception of the international order. Jabotinsky's observations about the inevitability of struggle for national liberation and his own experience with the multi-ethnic conflicts in Eastern Europe were undoubtedly in line with such an interpretation.[18]

Following World War I and the Balfour Declaration, Jabotinsky's perception of the international order became more differentiated. An analysis of his argument reveals three perceptual elements. One was based on the assumption that the international order is responsive to declaratory politics backed by power. This perception was apparently behind Jabotinsky's growing demand for the creation of a Jewish army and the seeking of full sovereignty. The second one was anchored in his interpretation of *Realpolitik*, which led him to believe that Britain ought to be interested in creating a large Jewish entity in Palestine in spite of Arab objections. The Revisionist leader emphasised an early political Zionist theme of a Jewish state which would serve as a Western outpost in the Middle East.

The third perception was based on what might be described as a public-moralist concept of the international order. In forming this view, Jabotinsky was undoubtedly inspired by the age of open diplomacy ushered in by President Wilson after World War I, and the general sensitivity to ethnic pressures in the post-war period. To cash in on such sentiments, Jabotinsky urged the Zionist elite to change its secretive and low-key diplomatic tactics, which he described as the worst example of *schtadlanut. Schtadlan*, or the Court Jew, was the old-style Jewish leader, who pleaded by interceding with Gentiles in positions of authority on behalf of the Jews.[19] In 1933, the Revisionists organised a petition drive by East European Jews, to influence the British Government. Jabotinsky regularly used the analogy of the Court Jew to emphasise that the Jews, who had no experience of sovereignty, were too deferential in conducting foreign affairs.

The Revisionists were in turn sharply condemned by the mainstream Zionist elite. Jabotinsky was personally accused of dilettantism, lack of political realism, naiveté and even dangerous delusions of grandeur. His critics pointed out that Jewish immigration to Palestine was slow to come, and that even Herzl failed to procure large-scale financing for the Yishuv. The executive elite was particularly alarmed that the militant style and maximalist demands of the Revisionists would provoke more Arab unrest and British retaliation.

Traditional Israeli historiography has normally upheld the Socialist Zionist critique of Revisionist politics. More recent work is divided in its assessment of the feasibility of these plans. Undoubtedly, Jabotinsky's belief system, like historical conservative thought everywhere, was reflective of what Mannheim called an awareness of the 'irrational realm in the life of the state'.[20] Jabotinsky was an ardent follower of certain popular psychosocial theories of his period which emphasised the dominance of the 'play principle', i.e. the superiority of human will and drive over the material environment.[21] The founder of Revisionism was also given to oversimplified formulations of complex problems, which often earned him the name of *simplificateur terrible*.

On the other hand, scholars point out that Jabotinsky's criticism of the Socialist Zionist economic model was not totally unfounded. Without taking a normative stand, Kimmerling's research on the Yishuv economy implies that private transfer of capital and a more liberal structure of the market could have resulted in a faster pace of economic development.[22] Jabotinsky might not have been familiar with the migration theory, which was first formulated by the British demographer-statistician Roverstein in 1889.[23] However, as Shavit has argued, Jabotinsky's analysis of the prospects for Jewish emigration from the progressively fascist regimes of Eastern Europe reflects fairly well the 'push and pull' rules of this migration theory.[24]

More generally, the differences between Labour Zionism and the Revisionists derived from divergent perceptions of foreign policy management. The Socialist Zionist model was based on a means-ends type of rationality, whereby an actor chooses ends which roughly correspond to his perceived means. The Revisionist model sought active changes in the international environment to accommodate an internally focused set of goals. The Revisionists claimed that the process of implementing these goals would create a sufficiently dynamic momentum to change the international conditions. In other words, the means-ends calculus should be applied to the end point of the process rather than to the initial search for options. To improve their odds, the Revisionists advocated initiatives which went beyond the legally prescribed rules of the international system.

These diverging perceptions underlay the final split in the Zionist movement. The immediate cause of the clash was Jabotinsky's efforts to evacuate the East European Jews before the onset of fascism. The Revisionist petition appeal, which carried 600,000 signatures, failed to convince Britain, which, under Arab pressure, further limited the number of entry permits to Palestine. The Socialist Zionist leadership and the Jewish Agency refused to concede the Revisionist demand for illegal immigration. When, in October 1933, the leadership of the Revisionist Betar advised its members to seek immigration outside the official channels, the Jewish Agency refused to authorise entry permits for Revisionists. After the subsequent clash over the partition proposals, the Revisionists left the World Zionist Organisation. The New Zionist Organisation which they established in 1935 claimed some 700,000 members.

As Chairman of the NZO, Jabotinsky devoted considerable time to his population transfer schemes. In 1936, the Revisionists outlined a plan for settling one and a half million Jews in Palestine. Jabotinsky met with the heads of state of Poland, Rumania, Czechoslovakia, Lithuania and Latvia. These countries, which had large Jewish populations, were sympathetic to the scheme but had no influence on British politics. The Revisionist activities were also criticised by the Socialist Zionist elite which, until 1938, refused to consider illegal immigration.

Jabotinsky was equally unsuccessful in his other foreign policy endeavours. After the failure of his British design, his thinking seems to have become stressful and erratic. He tried to enlist the help of Ireland, the United States, and a host of other countries. There are also allegations that he entertained the idea of offering the mandate to the Mussolini Government in Italy. After the Nazi takeover of Austria and Czechoslovakia, Jabotinsky became deeply pessimistic. In August 1939 he proposed a plan modelled on the 1916 Easter rising in Ireland. A boatload of Betar members, in co-operation with the Revisionist underground in Palestine, was to occupy Government House in Jerusalem and proclaim a provisional Jewish government. Jabotinsky emphasised that the plan could not save East European Jewry; it was envisaged as setting up a role model of active resistance in face of the impending catastrophe.[25]

Jabotinsky's manoeuvres in his later years also reflected a power struggle within the Revisionist movement. For all his formative influence, Jabotinsky's leadership was increasingly criticised in the 1930s. One type of challenge came from a number of peripheral groups in Palestine. The best-known is the *Brit Habyrionim*, which was founded in 1924 by Aba Ahimeir and other former Socialists, including the poet Uri Zvi Greenberg, Chaim Altman and Y. Yevin.

The ideational roots of the Brit were extremely complex and often contradictory. Ahimeir was influenced by the morphological historiosophy of Oswald Spengler and his thesis of the decline of the West. He saw in the Jewish return to the Land of Israel an expression of authentic 'culture' as opposed to the cosmopolitan elements of 'civilisation'. The founder of the Brit adopted part of the Canaanite ideology of Yonatan Ratosh, and especially the mystique of violence of the ancient Hebrews. Ratosh perceived violence as part of the process of progress and redemption. The Brit's ideology was territorially maximalist and intensely anti-Arab. The Arabs were accused of endangering the sense of spiritual-territorial integrity of the Jews in the Land of Israel.

The social creed of the Brit was closely modelled on the Italian fascism of Mussolini and his corporatist state. The Revisionist philosophy of *Hadar* was translated by the Brit into a cult of leadership, discipline and the psychology of 'conquer or die'. Jabotinsky, who became uneasy about the fascist tendencies of the Brit, was subsequently forced to denounce the organisation for being sympathetic to Nazi Germany.

Functionally, Brit Habyrionim can be classified as a special type of challenge group. A challenge group operates against the existing authority system by frequently infringing the law and order of society.[26] The Brit was a 'putschist' sub-category, which opted for a direct 'explosive collision with history' rather than a gradual evolutionary change.[27] At an operational level, the Brit preferred direct confrontational-symbolic actions, such as brawls with pacifists and Socialist Zionists, or the boycott of the 1931 British census in Palestine. The organisation disintegrated after

Ahimeir was implicated in the murder of the prominent Socialist Zionist leader, Chaim Arlosoroff, in 1933.

A much more serious challenge to Jabotinsky's leadership came from the Revisionist military organisation in Palestine, *Irgun Zvai Leumi* (the National Military Organisation). Popularly known as the *Irgun*, it seceded in 1931 from the Hagana over the policy of *havlaga* (restraint vis à vis the Arabs). Partly because of the normative belief in 'purity of arms' and partly because of operational considerations, the Socialist Zionist-controlled Hagana decided not to react to Arab resistance. The Irgun advocated retaliation, including attacks on civilian Arabs. In spite of Jabotinsky's protests, the Irgun continued its terrorist activities against the Arab population.

In addition, it took a stringent anti-British line. This policy was, by and large, supported by the Revisionist youth movement Betar, which was headed by Menachem Begin. In its March 1938 conference, the combined Irgun-Betar leadership implicitly criticised Jabotinsky for what it saw as his pro-British stand. In September 1938, Jabotinsky retaliated by describing Begin's proposal for an immediate conquest of Palestine as absolutely unfeasible. The 2,000-strong Irgun was too weak to face the British forces and the Hagana, which was at that time fighting Irgun members.

The power struggle in the Revisionist movement was to some extent generational; it also reflected the growing weight of the Palestinian branch. The younger Revisionist leaders, who were socialised in the Betar movement, were more radical than their ideological mentor. The Palestinian leadership of the Irgun, which regarded Britain as a major impediment to Jewish national aspirations, was already engaged in active resistance to the mandatory power. Nevertheless, after the outbreak of World War II, the Irgun accepted Jabotinsky's request to cease hostilities against the British and joined the war effort against the Axis powers.

This decision prompted Abraham Stern (Yair) to split the ranks of the Irgun and establish in 1940 a rival organisation *Lehi*, an acronym for *Lohami Herut Israel* (Israel Freedom Fighters). Known also as the Stern Gang, it had only a few hundred followers. Lehi's doctrine, shaped by Stern, was a mixture of rather disparate elements. It inherited the mystique of violence from its Brit Habyrienim predecessor but it later acquired a socialist colouring. At one time Lehi sought the help of Soviet officials to establish a Jewish state in Palestine. Although Lehi adhered to maximalist territorial demands, it also considered the Arabs as allies in the anti-colonial struggle. Since Lehi perceived the British, rather than Germany and Italy, as its chief enemy, the organisation continued attacks on British troops in Palestine. During World War II, one of Stern's emissaries approached a Nazi diplomat in Beirut to seek help against Britain. After Stern was shot by the British in 1942, Lehi was run by a collective leadership which included, among others, Natan Yelin-Mor, Israel Eldad and Yitzhak Shamir. Lehi gained subsequent publicity for the murder of Lord Moyne, the British minister in Cairo, in 1944 and the murder of the UN mediator, Count Folke Bernadotte, in 1948.

In spite of the fact that the Revisionist movement and its military organisations, Irgun and Lehi, collaborated with the Hagana during the War of Independence, the ideological schism between Revisionism and Social Zionism remained unbridgeable. Two issues in particular evolved into what is known as the 'historical conflict' between the rival belief systems.

One issue pertained to the territorial integrity of *Eretz Israel*. The Revisionists were highly critical of the Hagana because it failed to secure the West Bank during the 1948 war. Irgun and Lehi units refused to accept the ceasefire, and planned to fight on in order to establish a 'Free Judea' outside the State of Israel.[28] There is limited but persuasive evidence that this criticism was either shared, or subsequently accepted, by other segments of the Labour movement including the military. Yigal Allon, Moshe Dayan and a host of lesser Labour elite were among the critics.[29] The question of whether the Yishuv leadership could or should have achieved a different territorial outcome is, of course, impossible to separate from the larger issue of the two contending ideologies. Nevertheless, the fact that some of the Revisionist critique was accepted undoubtedly legitimised the latter's belief system.

The second issue stemmed from the refusal of the Yishuv leadership to support mass immigration. Almost immediately after the Holocaust, the Revisionists accused the Socialist Zionists of failing to rescue the Jews. This charge became highly publicised during the Kastner trial in the early 1950s. Kastner, who was affiliated with Labour, was accused of collaborating with the Nazis in occupied Hungary. Similar accusations have been repeated over the years in numerous political and journalistic publications.[30]

Academic research into this highly sensitive and politically explosive issue is not conclusive. According to one interpretation, the Socialist Zionists stalled on the question of mass immigration because of their commitment to a socially selective and pioneering society. Sharett described these potential immigrants as *Stam Yehudim* ('just Jews'), or even 'riff-raff'. The Socialist Zionists were also apprehensive that a mass immigration would upset their political supremacy in the Yishuv.[31] Shavit's study of the political demography of East European Jewry bears out this point. The Revisionist supporters were heavily concentrated in Poland and the Baltic states, which were targeted for the proposed transfer.[32]

None of these studies imply that the Labour leadership deliberately chose selective immigration in preference to the option of rescue. A more plausible hypothesis is that the two sides had a markedly divergent perception of the danger to the European Jews. Such a divergence can arise because of the cognitive phenomenon of the 'evoked set'. In complex political situations, an actor will draw inferences from bits of evidence according to the types of images to which he is exposed.[33]

The general impression is that, due to geographical remoteness and local concerns, the Labour elite in the Yishuv was less sensitive to developments in pre-war Europe. On the other hand, Jabotinsky is credited with being more attuned to the impending danger. Already in March 1933 he wrote about the danger of a Nazi Germany, and at the August 1933 World Zionist Congress he tried to organise a world-wide anti-Nazi boycott. His mass immigration plans were all permeated by what Sharot called the prophecy of a 'coming apocalyptic catastrophe for European Jewry'.[34]

Although Jabotinsky was not the only one to warn against Nazi Germany, he was apparently the first to equate the fate of the Jews with the destiny of the free world. The pattern of what Shils calls placing the conflict within a world order which is universally legible,[35] was already evident in Jabotinsky's writing in 1933. It culminated in an article in 1940 entitled *Kadish* (Mourning Prayer):[36]

Let a Jew come and say: I demand justice and equal rights for myself. Where I am a king among other kings there progress will be solid and well. If my fate is to be thrust outside the pale . . . there is no redemption for a world if I have no part in it.

In terms of belief validation, the crucial fact was that Jabotinsky was proved right in his debate with the Socialist Zionists. Even though the Revisionist leader was not altogether consistent in his vision — he did not think the war would break out after all — his views came to dominate the public discussion after the Holocaust. The question of whether the Yishuv leadership could have done more (even if it did appreciate the danger) was overshadowed by the criticism that the Socialist Zionists did not show proper sensitivity. Perhaps the most interesting reflection on the vindication of Jabotinsky came from Judah Magnes. Writing in 1948, Magnes, who was a close associate of Buber and a founding member of *Brit Shalom*, described Jabotinsky as a prophet of the Jewish state. 'Jabotinsky was ostracized and condemned and ex-communicated, and we see now that almost the whole Zionist camp has adopted his point of view.'[37]

The Revisionists and the Arab Question

Jabotinsky's belief system had important implications for the Revisionist perception of the Arab question. Jabotinsky was the only major Zionist leader who, from the very beginning, viewed the Jewish-Arab conflict as an inevitable zero-sum game. He was also the only leader to have developed a consistent attitude towards the problem. This can be explained by the fact that there was little dissonance between his general views on society and the power politics of the conflict.

Jabotinsky's 'definition of the situation' was based on two inter-related elements. The first stemmed from his perception of the Western and Eastern civilisations. He acknowledged that the Islamic Orient was a unique civilising entity, but one which was inferior to the Western culture. There is some scholarly debate whether he attributed these differences to racial characteristics prevalent in the 'white supremacy' theory, or applied a Marxist-type analysis which focused on the socio-economic backwardness of the region.[38] He criticised the Zionist school of thought, which romanticised the Levant, and in turn was criticised by Brit Habyrionim and Lehi, which adhered to the Canaanite ideology of the supremacy of the East.

The second element was related to Jabotinsky's conviction that the Jewish settlement in Palestine constituted a broad European colonising effort. By contemporary standards, the concept of colonisation was not congruent with the notion of a Jewish return to restore *Malchut Israel* (Kingdom of Israel). However, Jabotinsky, who always emphasised the historical legitimacy of Malchut Israel, often argued that the European countries should back the establishment of a Jewish state. Such a country would be the only indigenous European outpost in the Middle East.

This 'definition of a situation' dictated the Revisionist views on the Arab-Jewish conflict. They were spelled out in two widely publicised articles, 'The Iron Wall' and the 'Ethics of the Iron Wall', which Jabotinsky wrote in 1923. There are three major assumptions in these articles. First, the Arabs in Palestine are a distinctive national group; they are neither a British invention nor 'props' used by other Arab nations in the region. Second, the Arabs in Palestine have a historical and common consciousness of their national identity. National consciousness is not necessarily synonymous with class sophistication, nor should it be equated with 'rabble rousing', as the Socialist Zionists had held it to be. Third, the Arabs will not be deceived by the low-profile approach to settlements nor will they consent to a territorial compromise. Neither will they be bought off by the economic benefits generated by the Jewish presence in Palestine. 'There is no precedent in history of a native population accepting a colonization project by foreigners . . . the local people will fight always, everywhere and without exception.'[39]

'The Iron Wall' also contained the strategic assumptions about this inevitable conflict. For our purpose, we shall consider only its meaning as the main deterrence theory of the Revisionists. In this view, Jewish weakness would prompt the Arabs towards a more conflictual posture. If the Yishuv were to continue its territorial and military restraint, it would not only compromise the most important values at stake, but also encourage a harder Arab line in the future. To avoid such a development the Jews must deter the Arabs by continuous military resolve. The Arabs would never accept the situation, unless they lost all hope that they could prevent — 'either by force, constitutional method or God's miracle' — the Jewish presence in Palestine.

In Jabotinsky's view, once the Arabs acquired such a perception, the Jews could move on to create a majority in Palestine. Since Jabotinsky opposed a population transfer, the Revisionist movement became resigned to having a substantial Arab minority in the Jewish state. At various instances, the Revisionists proposed a limited autonomy for the Arabs which was

allegedly influenced by the principles of personal autonomy proposed in the Helsinford programme of 1900 on minorities in
Europe. Revisionist thinking on the future status of the Arabs was
not fully articulated. The general impression is that Jabotinsky,
unlike the Labour leaders, supported the integration of the Arabs
into the Jewish economy. At one time, he even advocated the
lowering of Jewish wages, in order to compete with Arab labour,[40]
but he never defined the civic status of the Arabs.[41]

By outlining a completely competitive theory of the
Arab-Jewish problem, Jabotinsky hoped to respond to the
Socialist Zionist concerns for internal and external legitimacy. He
argued that a clear declaration of the ultimate goal of Zionism, the
creation of a Jewish state in the whole of Palestine, and the
readiness to support this claim by military struggle, would increase
internal self-legitimacy. Although there is no empirical research of
public opinion in this period, there are some indications that the
younger generation in the Yishuv tended to press for a more
military stand. For instance, during the period of restraint, the
number of defections from the Hagana to the Irgun increased.
Younger Hagana commanders, such as Allon, pressed for the
expression of a policy of deterrence because they assumed that
Arabs were accustomed to force in their intra-group relations.[42]

In terms of external legitimacy, Jabotinsky felt that the Iron
Wall theory amounted to a case of self-protection. According to
his logic, the Zionist endeavour was both historically justified and
legally guaranteed by the Mandate and it was morally right to
protect it. As the Jewish situation in Europe worsened, Jabotinsky
redefined his concept of morality. In his 1937 testimony to the Peel
Commission, which considered a partition plan for Palestine, he
came up with the principle of 'relative morality'. He compared the
needs of the Jews who faced disaster to the 'claim of starvation', as
opposed to the 'claim of appetite' of the Arabs who possessed
several states.[43] This argument received wide circulation after the
Holocaust.

Jabotinsky's Iron Wall theory was extensively criticised by his
political contemporaries and by Labour historiographers. To use a
current term in the theory of international relations, he was
accused of having a *dominant strategy*, i.e. one which the actor
regards to be best, no matter what the other side does.[44] Such a
perception is related to deterministic thinking and premature
cognitive closure. There is little doubt that Jabotinsky, like other

actors who have rigid deterrence views, underestimated the impact
of such a policy on the Arabs and their resolve to adopt a similar
policy.

However, the Revisionists were only marginally involved in
conducting the affairs of the Yishuv. Towards the end of this
period, they become ostracised and did very little to undermine
the co-operative approach of the Socialist Zionists. They could
subsequently claim that the Arabs, who rejected the UN Partition
Plan, were not ready to accept a co-operative solution to the
conflict. Indeed, following the 1948 war, the Revisionist argument
about the inevitability of the conflict came to play a major part in
the delegitimisation of the Socialist Zionist belief system.

Neo-Revisionism

After the creation of the State of Israel in 1948, the Socialist
Zionist belief system continued to pervade the society through the
dominant *Mapai* Party. The Revisionist movement, which lost its
power base in the Holocaust and was forced to disband its military
organisations, re-emerged as the *Herut* (Freedom) movement.
The party which was established in June 1948 was led by
Menachem Begin, the former commander of the Irgun. In the first
parliamentary election in 1949, Herut won 14 seats in the 120-seat
Knesset and in the 1959 election it increased its representation to
17 seats. Although Mapai, with an average of 44 seats in the
1949–1961 period outdistanced all the other parties, Herut became
the second largest party in 1955.

Herut's political platform reflected the classic Revisionist theme
of restoring *Malchut Israel* (Kingdom of Israel) in the whole of
Mandatory Palestine. The party approved the 1949 Armistice
Agreement with Egypt and Syria, but argued that Jordan had
acquired the West Bank illegally and her borders should therefore
not be legitimised. Because Herut did not press for military action,
its irredentism seemed to be largely declaratory. Herut also repeated the Revisionist tenet that peace overtures to the Arab
states had proved fruitless. The party's 1961 platform warned that
appeals for peace would be interpreted by the Arabs as a sign of
weakness and would invite aggression.

Ben-Gurion's efforts to delegitimise Herut, and the fact that the
party's following did not expand at a constant rate, prompted

Begin to seek unification with the Liberal Party (General Zionists), whose electoral fortunes had declined since the early 1950s. There is a historical disagreement over the question as to whether during the merger Herut was still committed to its irredentist platform. Elimelech Rimalt, who led the Liberal team during the negotiations, maintained that Herut's position was largely ritualistic.[45] The parliamentary bloc *Gahal*, created by the two parties in 1965, produced a vaguely worded political platform which paid dues to the divergent views of both parties.

Most observers credited the establishment of Gahal with legitimising the Herut party. Even if this process did take place, foreign policy issues did not figure prominently in Gahal's appeal. According to a longitudinal analysis of electoral advertisements in the Israeli press, there was little change in the appeal pattern of the parties. In 1959, foreign policy issues accounted for 10.3 per cent of the total electoral advertising of the General Zionists and 7.8 per cent of Herut's. In 1961, the numbers were 7.7 and 21.8 respectively, but in the 1965 election Gahal's foreign policy appeals constituted 6.9 per cent of the total number of issues.[46]

A more serious increase in the legitimacy of the Revisionist belief system took place when Gahal joined a National Unity Cabinet during the 1967 war. This process accelerated dramatically after the formation in September 1967 of the Greater Land of Israel Movement (*Hatnuah Lemaan Eretz Israel Hashlemah*). The founding Manifesto of the Movement, which reflected traditional Revisionist concerns, was almost entirely supported by prominent members of the Labour establishment.

Among the fifty-seven initial sponsors of the Manifesto, there were distinguished men of letters, including the Nobel Laureate Ṣ. Y. Agnon, the poet Natan Alterman, and the writers Moshe Shamir and Haim Hazaz. The widow of the former President of Israel, and a known Labour leader in her own right, Rachel Yanait Ben-Zvi, signed the Manifesto, along with some half a dozen generals and commanders in the Hagana. Among the latter was the first Air Force Commander, Dan Tolkovsky, the distinguished field commander, Abraham Yaffe, and the veteran Hagana commanders, Eliezer Livneh and Beni Marshak. Also among the sponsors were the two surviving leaders of the Warsaw ghetto uprising, Yitzhak (Antek) Zukerman and Zviah (Lubatkin) Zukerman, the veteran Labour leaders Yosef and Moshe Tabenkin, and a host of intellectuals.

The emergence of the Greater Land of Israel Movement is not easy to explain in conventional sociological terms. The group did not constitute a generational phenomenon, nor was it generated by the internal struggle in the Labour movement, which Shapiro related to the blocked mobility of the native-born elite.[47] Perhaps the most plausible hypothesis is that the Movement reflected a hitherto little noticed crisis in Socialist Zionism which was galvanised by the Six-Day War.

Segre, in a perceptive study on the ideological crisis in Israel, has argued that historically there has been a certain value disalignment among the constituent elements of Zionism. Not unlike the case of African self-colonisation, this disalignment produced a dissonance between the Western and universal values of the official culture and the efforts to create a genuine native identity.[48] The nativist critique in the Labour movement which surfaced in the 1960s adopted many Revisionist ideas. This critique became institutionalised when Zvi Shiloah, Eliezer Livneh, Abraham Yaffe, Moshe Shamir and Dov Yosefi, among others, organised the Labour Movement for Greater Israel. Subsequently, the Labour contingent became a section within the Greater Land of Israel Movement.

Eliezer Livneh, the former co-founder of the Hagana, became the chief ideologue of Neo-Revisionism. In his book, *Israel and the Crisis of Western Civilisation*, and other writings, he criticised the Western assimilation of Israel. Livneh accepted the thesis of the Austrian historian Friedrich Heer that the Holocaust was the 'central truth' of European history. He claimed that the destruction of the Jews was facilitated by the complicity of almost all the Western nations, regardless of their political regime. Livneh, who saw behaviour towards the Jews as the yardstick of Western civilisation, believed that the philo-Semitic period after World War II would constitute only a short interlude, to be followed by a more severe anti-Semitic backlash.

Reflecting the shifting emphasis on the religious-Jewish rather than the secular-Israeli identity, Livneh argued that the Six-Day War infused Zionism with a new meaning. The establishment of the State of Israel normalised the Jewish people by giving them sovereignty, whereas the Six-Day War exposed the Israelis to their religious traditions. This exposure reversed the process of identification with the Gentile cultural values of the West. Livneh proposed to set up a new type of community in the Holy Land, i.e.

the occupied territories, which would implement traditional Jewish values and act against the alienation of Jewish society. According to his view, Zionism, which reflects these traditional values, is not comparable to any other national movement of liberation, because it expresses the process of redemption. As such, Jewish rights to Judea and Samaria are *sui generis*, and should not be judged by conventional international standards.[49]

This formulation, which was shared by other founding members of the Greater Land of Israel Movement, reveals some subtle but important changes in the definition of the major goals of Zionism. Traditional Zionism was concerned with the ingathering of the exiles and providing them with sovereignty, physical security and a normal existence. New Zionism claims that the 1967 war dramatised the New Zionist goal of fully reunifying the Jewish people with the Land of Israel. In other words, the Six-Day War indicated to the New Zionists that Israel should assume the mission of securing a Jewish state within its proper Biblical border. Physical safety, normalisation in international relations, and even the yearning for peace should be subordinated to this goal. Livneh argued that neither peace nor war are absolute Biblical Judaic values. They complement each other in the words of the prophet Isaiah: 'They shall beat their swords into ploughshares' and in the words of Joel the prophet of Return: 'They shall beat their ploughshares into swords'.[50]

Jewish control of the occupied territories had also purely instrumental dimensions. One of them was Israel's quest for space. Some of the land, and especially areas which were not settled by the Arabs, were perceived as valuable for agricultural settlement and the absorption of new immigrants. This argument was voiced by the *Ein Vered* circle, which represented the Labour agricultural settlements in the movement. The claim to space was originally voiced by the maximalist camp in Socialist Zionism led by Yitzak Tabenkin who joined the movement.[51]

The various spokesmen of Greater Israel have also advocated the strategic and the deterrent importance of the occupied territories. According to this view, the ease with which Egypt recovered the Sinai Desert after the 1956 Suez campaign was a major factor in the Arab belligerency of 1967. Since the Arabs were expected to fight Israel, regardless of the shape of its borders, the painful loss of the territories in 1967 would deter them from future wars. Needless to say, the movement adopted the classic Revisionist assumption about the deterministic nature of the Arab-Israeli conflict. Yuval Neeman, who became the leader of the radical right-wing Tehiya Party, fully reflected this view when he claimed that the Middle East conflict was analogous to the centuries-old national struggles in Europe.[52]

In spite of the fact that the Greater Land of Israel Movement had a limited mass following, it was extremely influential in contributing to New Zionism. After the movement disintegrated, some of its ideas were adopted by the Tehiya Party, a 1980 splinter from Likud. Other ideas surfaced in the agenda of the New Israeli Right. The New Right is a loosely-knit conservative group which espouses a mystical missionary interpretation of the role of Israel and has rejected democracy as a sign of Jewish subservience to Western ideas.

The Religious Influence: From Talmudic to National-Religious Judaism

The religious influence in New Zionism is normally associated with the activities of Gush Emunim. A focus on the structure and function of the Gush is warranted because of the group's key position in shaping Israel's perception of the West Bank. Yet such an emphasis obscures the fact that the Gush emerged as a consequence of a much broader historical process of adjusting religious orthodoxy to contemporary political developments. This process can be best understood by reviewing the re-interpretation of two major tenets of Talmudic Judaism: the meaning of Redemption and the meaning of political action.

The Re-interpretation of the Talmudic Meaning of Redemption

Although the Talmud's teachings are rarely straightforward, the approach to Redemption is based on what may be called a fused notion of time — the fusion of past, present and future. Talmon, Zweig and Gonen have emphasised that the traditional Talmudic notion of Redemption is the epitome of fusion: Redemption is consigned to the remote future, though it will restore the glory of the past.[53] Redemption involves the coming of the Messiah and the ingathering of the exiles, and will be preceded by Hevlei Mashiah — a period of suffering Jews must endure to pay for Redemption, which some New Zionists interpret as a prophecy of the Holocaust.

Unlike the secular Western notion of time, which postulates a linear progression from one time event to another, the Judaic fused notion of time has influenced religious thinking on foreign policy. First, like other religious notions of time, fused time is a cyclical concept. It gives a certain timeless quality to Jewish history and explains why Jews have always felt so close to their remote past. Conversely, the notion of fused time renders meaningless to a religious Jew the argument that the Arabs deserve some claim to Palestine, since they lived there more recently than the Jews, because this claim is based on a linear concept of time.

Second, the notion of fused time holds a major moral significance because it organises events as a moral sequence leading to Redemption. Helping to bring about the Redemption is a *mitzvah* (moral imperative) of the highest order in Judaism. However, Orthodox Jewry has never agreed upon the appropriate ways for effecting the Redemption. When political Zionism first appeared, it was bitterly denounced by most of the Orthodox camp. With the exception of Rabbis Zvi Hirsh Kalisher (1795–1874) and Judah Alkalai (1798–1878) who, in their advocacy of Return, predated modern Zionism, the official Orthodox dictum was that Jews should pray and hope for the return to Zion. But any political activity was considered a most dangerous pseudo-messianic or even Satanic attempt to accelerate the Redemption.

The Holocaust and the foundation of the State of Israel have caused profound confusion in the Orthodox camp. Rabbi Pinches Peli, who analysed the various theological attempts to understand the Holocaust, found a number of explanatory models. At least one of the theological explanations views the Holocaust as a sin for opposing Zionism.[54] Although the creation of Israel has been increasingly accepted as a sign of divine intervention, not a Satanic contrivance, official Orthodoxy is still most reluctant to deliver a formal verdict. For instance, the Chief Rabbinate formulated special prayers for Independence Day, but the holiday was not accorded the same *halacha* (religious law) status as other religious holidays.

It was left to an initially limited circle of national rabbinical authorities to evolve the religious theory of Zionism. The main proponents of Religious Zionism were Rabbi Abraham Y. Kook (1865–1935) and his son Rabbi Zvi Y. Kook (1891–1982), who succeeded his father as head of *Merkaz Harav Yeshiva* in

Jerusalem - the spiritual centre of Gush Emunim. Zvi Kook, who was regarded as having a mystical bent, was the teacher of many of the Gush leaders.

Rabbi Abraham Kook was the first to confront the incongruity between the secular character of Zionism and the fact that the movement was building the Holy Land. In a most important theological innovation, he shifted from what Yonina Talmon-Gerber called *mythical* to *historical interpretation of the Redemption*. In this 'rational form of millenarianism', the Redemption is not perceived as a mythical-apocalyptical event but takes place within a historical framework.[55] National-Religious Zionism does not view the foundation of the State of Israel as a triumph of national liberation, but as the beginning of a divinely inspired process of Redemption. One of the most important elements in this process is the territorial integrity of *Eretz Israel* (Land of Israel).

The historical-contemporary perception of Redemption was greatly enhanced by the 1967 war. The *Menkaz Harav* circles regarded the speedy victory of the Israeli army, against tremendous odds, as an act of divine intervention, rather than a manifestation of Israel's military prowess. The occupation of the West Bank and Jerusalem came to be interpreted as a most important step in the process of Redemption, because it restored the intrinsic wholeness of *Eretz Israel*. Morever, since the God of Israel promised the whole country to the sons of Israel, this divine title deed pre-empts any other claim to either bank of the Jordan River. Giving up Judea and Samaria would constitute a mortal sin by interfering with the unfolding process of Redemption.

The Religious Zionist theology has been supported by part of the official Orthodoxy. In 1967, the Sephardic Chief Rabbi of Israel, Yitzhak Nissim, issued a *psak halacha* (a ruling comparable to a papal bull in Roman Catholicism) which prohibits the evacuation of Judea and Samaria.[56] However, other *halachic* authorities, and especially the powerful Council of Sages which runs the ultra-orthodox *Agudat Israel* Party, objected to the retention of the occupied territories on the grounds of *pikuah nefesh*, i.e. the bloodshed it can generate. At the other end of the religious spectrum, liberal religious circles in the National Religious Party like the *Oz Veshalom* group argued for a territorial compromise in the name of traditional Jewish values of justice and peace.[57]

The Re-interpretation of the Talmudic View Regarding the Moral Validity of the Political Act

Talmudic Judaism was deeply preoccupied with the morality of the political act. In an imaginative treatment of politics and perfectability in Judaism, Selzer used a Weberian classification of perceptions of the political act. The political realist considers the political act to be intrinsically evil because it requires a Kantian-style manipulation of human beings and yet views political activity as unavoidable. The political idealist perceives the political act as neither intrinsically good nor intrinsically evil. Rather, he judges it on the basis of its results. The pacifist-anarchist regards the political act as intrinsically evil, and refrains from political activity because he is unwilling to do evil.

Selzer argued that the classic Talmudic conception of political action closely resembles the pacifist-anarchist view. One *midrash* (Talmudic commentary) compares the Jews to the dust of earth 'made for kingdoms to trample' — the implication being that dust survives and kingdoms perish. Another *midrash* provides a most eloquent exposition of the pacifist-anarchist theory: 'Because you have drowned others, they have drowned you, and in the end those who drowned you will also be drowned.' Phrased in the language of politics: 'Every victory must be defended and every defence carries the seed of defeat.' Thus security cannot be won by action: it can only be achieved by refraining from action — a prescription, Selzer observes, that grew out of the Jews' powerlessness in exile.[58]

The pacifism of Talmudic Judaism was, of course, a reaction to one of the greatest historical disasters in Jewish history. Following an unsuccessful rebellion led by Simeon Bar-Kochba and Rabbi Akibba in 69 AD, Rome destroyed the second Temple in Jerusalem and exiled the Jews. Talmudic Judaism emerged when Rabbi Yochanan Ben-Zakkai, who disputed the wisdom of the military rebellion, fled from Jerusalem and established the first academy in Yavneh. Ben-Zakkai's message, which condemned power politics and emphasised the spiritual function of Judaism, became an overriding command of Talmudic Judaism.

The Holocaust challenged the Talmudic view that renunciation of power and its instruments — sovereignty, territory and military might — could best guarantee Jewish survival. For the Nazi policy of genocide demonstrated that Jewry could be utterly destroyed by the physical elimination of every single Jew.

The power and survival demands created by statehood strengthened the challenge to Talmudic attitudes, and led the most
nationalistically-oriented religious circles to re-interpret the
Talmudic concept of action. They abandoned the pacifist-anarchist
approach in favour of the Biblical concept of political idealism.
This shift was most strikingly shown in the belief system of the
Gush Emunim and its followers in the National Religious Party.

National Religious Zionism contends that political action is
imperative in order to accelerate the process of Redemption, and
it can only be judged by this standard. Among the activities
legitimised by the new approach has been the Gush Emunim
settlement drive in the West Bank. The Gush, officially created in
1974, holds that the boundaries of the state are defined by the
holiness of the land. The belief in the sacred ties of the Jews to the
Land of Israel legitimises the expropriation of land from the
Palestinians. The process of settlement in Judea and Samaria is
viewed as analogous to the Biblical conquest of the Land of Israel
from the native Canaanites.

This political idealism has also led the Gush Emunim to
legitimise a militant approach towards the Palestinians. The
radical particularist orientation of the Gush towards non-Jews has
enhanced this attitude. A number of authors and prominent civil
libertarians in Israel documented instances in which rabbinical
authorities justified killing civilians — including women and
children — in wartime. According to a Biblically-oriented interpretation of religious Jewish law, such killings are justified, even if
they contradict Israeli military policy.[59]

Even some of the Gush's deadly vigilante activities against
Palestinian civilians on the West Bank, which culminated in the
Jewish terrorist underground, have been so justified in the past.
For the settlement drive has been viewed as a military campaign,
and anyone who impedes it is considered an enemy. Rabbi Israel
Hess has further argued that the struggle between the Jews and the
Arabs is not an ordinary international conflict but a holy war. The
Arabs have declared a *jihad* (holy war) against the Jews, and it is a
Jewish duty to destroy them, just as God commanded Joshua to
destroy the hostile Amalekites in Biblical times.[60]

The sacredness of *Eretz Israel*, and the political activities aimed
at creating it, are the most popularised part of National Religious
Zionism. Yet this is only a part of a more comprehensive
eschatology that purports to explain social developments in Israel

and its isolation in the world. Broadly defined as the theory of Coming, it has permeated National Religious writings.

The theory of Coming was best described by the religious thinker Chaim Peles. Using a Hegelian dialectical style, he equated the works of religious Zionists like Rabbis Alkalai and Kalisher with the original Zionist thesis. The antithesis was the secular Zionist movement which failed to infuse the State of Israel with Jewish substance. This fatal deviation from the values of religious Judaism led to the spiritual decline of the society and culminated in the almost fatal October War of 1973. The ideal synthesis is Religious Zionism which has been reflected in the national religious revival since the Yom Kippur War and is symbolised by the activities of the national-religious camp.[61]

In this vision, Israel was not created to normalise the Jewish people so that they would become 'a nation like all other nations'. According to a representative statement of Rabbi Amital of the *Gush Elzion Yeshiva*, the proper aim of Zionism is to prepare the Jews in Israel to become the Chosen People.[62] This argument departs from the original secular vision of Revisionist Zionism, but bears a resemblance to the formulations of Livneh and other Neo-Revisionists, who emphasised Israel's anti-Western uniqueness.

The imperative of the Chosen People calls for a radical revision of Israel's perception of the international system. Its current isolation has been the outcome of an everlasting hatred of Gentiles towards the Chosen People. Rabbi Ephraim Zemmel, reflecting a broad trend, has argued that this hatred has little to do with ordinary human envy. Rather, it is an expression of the eternal confrontation between Good and Evil and of Satan's desire to eradicate the Holy Torah.[63] Peles, using a Biblical analogy, claimed that Israel's isolation is the fulfilment of Balaam's 'curse' in Numbers 23:9: 'Lo, it is a people that shall dwell alone, and shall not be reckoned among the nations'.[64]

The most eloquent exposition of this theory was provided by Yaacov Herzog in a collection of his writings entitled *A People that Dwells Alone*. Herzog, the son of the former chief Ashkenazi Rabbi and a high Foreign Ministry official under Labour, preceded National Religious Zionism, when he argued that Balaam's prophecy is second only to that of Moses in importance. The phenomenon of 'a people that dwells alone' is not an abnormality, as early Zionists argued, or a Biblical curse. It is the sign of a Jewish spiritual mission, which should be regarded as a blessing, a paramount moral imperative and the *raison d'être* of Israel's international existence.[65]

This vision of the international order has important implications for the perception of peace in National Religious thought. At the most general level of analysis, this ideology adopted the notion of *shlom emet* (true peace), which is equivalent to the concept of the eternal peace which will follow the Redemption.[66] Operationally, the concept of 'true peace' was interpreted to mean a stage in the Arab-Israeli conflict, when the Arabs would come to accept the historical and moral rights of the Jews to the Holy Land.[67] However, as Eliakim Haetzni, one of the chief spokesmen of the Gush, noted, the probability of *shlom emet* in the Middle East is virtually non-existent. As in Biblical times, when the longest period of peace lasted some forty years, contemporary international relations in the region are dominated by conflict.[68]

The *millenarian rationality* which permeates National Religious Zionism raises the question of its concordance with the secular, and thus more utilitarian, national elements in New Zionism. Rubinstein reported that, at a 1975 conference in Gush Etzion, the national religious movement openly discussed the routinisation of Redemption and its impact on Israeli foreign policy.[69] Sharot, however, argued that the Gush was careful to de-emphasise its millenarian aspects in order to attract secular support.[70]

Whatever the strategy of the Gush Emunim was, the concordance of religious and secular nationalism can be plausibly explained through Weber's concept of elective affinity.[71] Such an affinity to religious beliefs has been evident in Neo-Revisionist thought and was further enhanced by the historiographical treatment of the phenomenon of anti-Semitism and the Holocaust.

Anti-Semitism and the Holocaust in the Contemporary Israeli Belief System

The process of re-interpretation of some of the basic assumptions about the relationship between Jews and Gentiles has been gradual and often unnoticed. It is methodologically difficult to discern such a process because of its diffusiveness. Unlike the more focused partisan ideologies, such a trend is broadly historiographical and historiosophical. Academic and literary accounts, personal experience, journalistic interpretations, and elite perceptions have all interacted to change Israeli beliefs about Jewish-Gentile relations. We can analyse this process in two dimensions: re-interpretation of the meaning of anti-Semitism and evaluation of the meaning of the Holocaust.

The Re-interpretation of the Meaning of anti-Semitism

It has already been mentioned that most of the Zionist movement, including the Revisionists, believed that, after the creation of the State, the Jews will become 'a nation like other nations'. This belief was based on the assumption that Israel would be received as an equal partner in the international system and that anti-Semitism would cease to exist.

Almost from the country's birth, this assumption was progressively undermined. Israel remained isolated at the regional level and confronted by seemingly implacable Arab enmity, reminiscent of the Christian hostility of the Diaspora. Objectively, there were substantial differences between Christian rejection of the Jews and the Arab reaction to what they regarded as Israel's occupation of Palestine. Yet centuries of psychological conditioning to classic images of anti-Semitism have made it difficult for Israeli Jews to make this distinction.

Furthermore, from the very beginning of the conflict, the Arabs used traditional Christian modes to express anti-Israeli sentiments. Already during the Mandate, Arab newspapers regularly reprinted articles from European anti-Semitic publications. Since 1948, the Arab countries have increased the publication of anti-Semitic literature, including the *Protocols of the Elders of Zion*, considered by the Jews the hallmark of anti-Semitism. Egyptian propaganda material captured after the 1967 war included Nazi-type cartoons depicting Aryan-like Arab soldiers vanquishing Semitic-looking Israelis.[72]

Following the lead of Bernard Lewis, most historians have argued that the Arabs imported Christian anti-Semitic literature because they were initially unfamiliar with the European Jews. Other scholars noted that anti-Semitic symbols were disseminated by Christian Arabs, who were at the forefront of the Arab national movement in the early twentieth century.

Yet some Israeli observers emphasised that the Palestinian Arabs were ready to participate in Hitler's final solution. Haviv Kanaan, in his book *Two Hundred Days of Anxiety*, documented that the Mufti of Jerusalem, Haj Mohammed Amin el-Husseini, planned to build concentration camps for Jews in the Middle East, in case of a German victory in Africa. These findings, and the fact that Palestinian units served with the Gestapo in Europe, are well publicised in Israel.[73] During the Eichmann trial in Jerusalem, Arab newspapers expressed regret that the Germans had failed to complete the process of extermination.[74]

Israel's steady transformation into an international pariah further challenged the assumptions about Jewish-Gentile equality. Although this trend stemmed, no doubt, from a number of causes, many Israelis attributed it to the traditional anti-Semitic isolation of the Jews. Instead of being directed toward individual Jews, this anti-Semitism has been focused on the Jewish collective, the State of Israel.

The perceptual linkage between anti-Semitism and anti-Zionism has been periodically reinforced by the international system. In what seems to be a first major instance in creating such a linkage, President Charles de Gaulle said in 1967 that Israel displayed the characteristic Jewish traits of an elitist, conceited and domineering people. The UN resolution equating Zionism with racism had an even more powerful effect. The weeks preceding the Six-Day War provided Israelis with an unprecedented insight into the traditional Jewish sense of isolation and helplessness. Subsequent psychological research and popular impressions tend to confirm that the prevalent image among Israelis was that of Israel, the eternal Jewish collective in mortal danger, while the Gentile world watched, at best with indifference.[75]

Although it is difficult to pinpoint dates, these cumulative impressions have invalidated the early optimistic beliefs about Jewish-Gentile relations. Moreover, they have led the Israelis to equate criticism of Israel with anti-Semitism. The theory of *transference between anti-Semitism and anti-Zionism* is not unanimously accepted. Some of the most prominent members of the political and intellectual elite have repeatedly warned against assuming that all criticism of Israel is anti-Semitic in origin.[76] Yet the transference theory has been widely propagated in both academic and popular writing. Yankelevich, the French Jewish philosopher, developed a systematic treatment of this theory. He assumed that the process of transference is underlaid by a human search for new symbolic expressions of hatred and provides the anti-Semite with a legitimacy for persecuting Jews in their collective form, Israel.[77] The distinguished Israeli historian, Shmuel Ettinger, likewise argued that 'anti-Zionism is a direct historical and psychological extension of anti-Semitism'.[78]

The cognitive readiness of Israelis to accept the transference theory might have been facilitated by the particular nature of anti-Semitism. Allport and other leading social psychologists have emphasised that anti-Semitism is the most persistent of all known social prejudices. Jews have come closest to an 'all-duty' scapegoat . . . 'the evil can be viewed . . . as a permanently threatening character continuing from generation to generation'.[79] Because of such an ingrained historical perspective, Israelis have apparently underestimated the rather widespread phenomenon of philo-Semitism and support for the Jewish state in the contemporary international system.

The Likud elite which came to power in 1977 enhanced the popular perceptions of anti-Semitism as an unchanging, almost mystical phenomenon. Begin, in a series of well-publicised incidents, forcefully equated any criticism of Israel with international anti-Semitism. His follower as Prime Minister, Yitzhak Shamir, has similarly emphasised that 'anti-Semitism and anti-Zionism are the same thing'. The Likud leadership has often been accused of using this analogy as a rhetorical strategy in political mobilisation.

Nevertheless, even before the Likud era, 'anti-Semitism' was quite commonly used as a generic term to refer to all forms of criticism of Israel. Herman, a leading Israeli authority on public attitudes towards anti-Semitism and the Holocaust, found that between 1965 and 1974 the tendency to see the Gentile world as anti-Semitic had increased among Israelis. Herman and other researchers have pointed out that these perceptions were indirectly influenced by the historiography of the Holocaust and especially by the growing knowledge that Western countries did virtually nothing to help the Jews.[80]

The Evaluation of the Meaning of the Holocaust

The perception that the Jews are destined to be set apart has been strengthened by the interpretation of the meaning of the Holocaust. The Nazi atrocities have had a profound and increasingly well-documented impact on the Israelis. Initially, Israel was too preoccupied with its survival to dwell on the meaning of the tragedy. The Socialist Zionist elite lacked first-hand experience of the Holocaust and felt uncomfortable in emphasising its uniqueness. Gershon Shoken, the distinguished Israeli publisher, claimed that Ben-Gurion, after viewing the first documentaries on the Holocaust, refused to accept the fact that the Jews were singled out for genocide.[81]

The Eichmann trial in 1962 provided the stimulus to evaluate the meaning of the tragedy. Herman and his associates, who conducted a survey of public attitudes during the trial, found that the event increased the psychological correlation of involvement in the Holocaust among the respondents.[82] This correlation bolstered the salience and centrality of the tragedy among the second generation and altered its time perspective, i.e. it produced an intergenerational closeness to the events which comprised the Holocaust. Subsequent studies have amply demonstrated that the massive psychic traumatisation caused by the Holocaust was transmitted to the next generation of Israelis.[83]

Confronting the Holocaust presented the Israelis with two cognitive problems. One stemmed from the efforts to explain Jewish quiescence during World War II. According to some estimates only about 20 per cent — mostly in Western Europe — escaped. Even a smaller fraction, between five and seven per cent, engaged in active resistance.[84] There are two major explanatory strategies used to analyse Jewish behaviour. One is based on universal psychological principles, such as Maslow's hierarchy of needs. According to this, individuals who are denied basic physiological needs cannot engage in higher-ranking activities such as resistance. This mechanism, along with such phenomena as mass delusion and the psychological trauma of incarceration, explains why millions of people, including at least two million Russian prisoners of war, died in concentration camps without resisting.

Patterns of cognitive calculation are another universally oriented explanation. In a well reasoned piece of research, Zuckerman demonstrated that because the probability of a Holocaust occurring was deemed to be very low, most Jews calculated that their best strategy for survival was to stay put and quiet. The author argued that the same calculus of survival strategy was used by the victims of the Stalinist purges, which were widely perceived by the Russians as a similarly low-probability event.[85]

The alternative approach is to view Jewish quiescence as a uniquely Jewish response caused by what Hilberg described as attitudinal conditioning during centuries of Diaspora existence. Jewish passivity in the Holocaust was enhanced by attitudes of anticipatory compliance with the demands of the aggressor, evasion of flight based on awareness that all places were equally hostile, and paralysis during the last stages of extermination.[86] In line with the traditional analysis of Jewish behaviour in the Diaspora, popular interpretation in Israel has been dominated by the perspective of Jewish uniqueness. The image of the Jews as 'sheep led to the slaughter' was particularly acute in the initial stages of the State. Yet, in spite of a major educational effort aimed at changing this perception, Farago, in his replication in 1982 of Herman's research, found that 33 per cent of the respondents emphasised Jewish passivity and only 23 per cent graded the behaviour as activist. The rest, who had an ambivalent attitude, i.e. chose the middle categories between passive and active, constituted 44 per cent of the sample.[87]

The second problem pertains to the difficulty in explaining the causes of the Holocaust. The enormous scientific and popular literature on this phenomenon is not conclusive. The two most structured efforts to understand the German behaviour towards the Jews — Horkheimer's Frankfurt School and Adorno's authoritarian personality — have been extensively criticised. A major tenor of this critique is that the Holocaust is difficult to explain in conventional psychological terms.[88] Billig, who reviewed most of this literature, found that neither the individual psychological explanation nor the systemic perspective is satisfactory; their interaction, which produced the Holocaust, is difficult to generalise upon.[89]

Friedlander, a noted Israeli historian and a Holocaust survivor, defined the problem well when he raised the question as to whether the Holocaust was a unique event outside normal historical interpretation. Though, like Hannah Arendt and other scholars, he tried to identify the discrete historical processes which culminated in the Holocaust, he has admitted that it is difficult to explain in a 'rational context events which cannot be encompassed in rational terms'.[90] Moreover, the Israelis tend to perceive the Holocaust not only as a German atrocity committed against the Jews, but as the culmination of centuries-long Gentile persecution of the Jews. Elie Wiesel, one of the most forceful spokesmen of the Holocaust, and Emil Fackheinheim, a philosopher of the Holocaust and a theologian, are among those who view the

Holocaust as an evil of metaphysical proportion.[91] The literary scholar and critic Gertz pointed out that the theme of the persecuted Jew, in which past disasters must repeat themselves in the future, was prevalent in the Israeli existential literature of the 1960s, and could have enhanced the perception of the Holocaust as an inexplicable metaphysical evil.[92]

The public belief system is permeated by these notions. In the original Herman survey, 22 per cent of the respondents thought that a future Holocaust was possible in all countries, and 58 per cent felt that it could occur in some countries. In the 1982 Farago study the distribution was 18 per cent and 52 per cent respectively.[93]

These interpretations of anti-Semitism and the Holocaust have helped to secularise the theological notion of the Chosen People. The idea that the Jews have been chosen by their unchanging suffering, because of the mystical hatred of the Gentiles, has received what seemed to be irrefutable proof. Moreover, because of the perceptual linkage between anti-Semitism, anti-Zionism and criticism of Israel, there has been a tendency to view the condemnation received from the global system as the outcome of anti-Semitic hostility rather than as a specific reaction to a given policy act on the part of Israel.

Together with the Neo-Revisionist and especially the National Religious Zionist beliefs, the re-interpretation of anti-Semitism and the Holocaust contributed to a highly Hobbesian perception of international order in Israel. The act of power has often been regarded as 'intrinsically evil'. International relations, the arena *par excellence* of the political action, have been viewed as a series of competitions which are resolved through the exercise of power. Compromise is effected only when the adversary lacks the power to secure another outcome.

In this Hobbesian view of the global environment, justice and moral commitment rarely exist. The actors act only upon their material interests, without allowing for moral considerations. It has been quite common for the Israelis, New Zionists and others, to view past American policy in the Middle East as a 'selling out of Israel for the sake of Arab oil'. Western European countries have been routinely condemned for going back on their moral commitment to Israel. The Venice Declaration in which the Western European countries pledged support to the Palestine Liberation Organisation was seen as a particularly blatant example of a 'sellout'.

Perception of international reality as power-governed competition is not unique to New Zionism. But the pariah dimension of Israel's international isolation made the Hobbesian perspective especially poignant. We shall demonstrate in later chapters how these images contributed to the delegitimisation of the Socialist Zionist belief system, and subsequently came to dominate the operative level of Israel's foreign policy.

Notes

1. Y. Shavit, *Revisionism in Zionism: The Revisionist Movement: The Plan for Colonizatory Regime and Social Ideas, 1915–1935*, 2nd Edition (Hadar Publishers, Tel Aviv, 1983), pp. 152–4, (Hebrew); W. Laqueur, *A History of Zionism*, (Weidenfeld and Nicolson, London, 1972), pp. 346–8; S. Avineri, 'The Political Thought of Vladimir Jabotinsky', *The Jerusalem Quarterly*, no. 16 (1980), pp. 3–26.
2. Shavit, *Revisionism in Zionism*, p. 176.
3. Rabbi Abraham Kook, the founder of National Religious Zionism, defended the Revisionist organisation, *Brit Habyrionim*, when it was implicated in the murder of Chaim Arlosoroff, a prominent Socialist leader, in 1933.
4. It is difficult to estimate to what extent political rivalry was responsible for this interpretation. Jabotinsky was profoundly disliked by most of the Socialist Zionist camp, but some, like Levy Eshkol, found him extremely impressive. M. Brecher, *The Foreign Policy System of Israel*, (Oxford University Press, London, 1972), p. 293.
5. For a discussion of the sociological school of conflict see L. A. Coser, *The Function of Social Conflict*, (Free Press of Glencoe, NY, 1964), p. 88.
6. Laqueur, *A History*, p. 360.
7. Avineri, 'The Political Thought', p. 360.
8. For a discussion of the psychological function of military struggle in Fanon's writings, see L. M. Killion, 'The Respect Revolution: Freedom and Equality' in H. D. Laswell, D. Lerner and H. Speier (eds), *A Pluralizing World in Formation, Propaganda and Communication in World History*, vol. 3, (University of Hawaii Press, Honolulu, HI, 1980), pp. 43–147.
9. J. P. Nettle, *Political Mobilization*, (Faber and Faber, London, 1967), p. 251.
10. *Ibid*, p. 248.
11. Y. Shavit, *From Hebrew to Canaanite* (The Domino Press, Tel Aviv, 1984), p. 109 (Hebrew).
12. D. Horowitz and M. Lissak, *Origins of the Israeli Polity: The Political System of the Jewish Community in Palestine under the Mandate*. (Am Oved, Tel Aviv, 1977), p. 192 (Hebrew); also, Y. Wagner and E. Kaphafi, *The Sources of the Dispute. The Historical Quarrel between the Labor Movement and the Revisionists* (Am Oved, Tel Aviv, 1982), p. 25 (Hebrew).
13. M. Canover, *Populism* (Harcourt, Brace Jovanovitch, New York and London, 1981), p. 261.
14. Avineri, 'The Political Thought', p. 14.
15. Shavit, *Revisionism in Zionism*, pp. 101–103.
16. J. Y. Gonen, *A Psychohistory of Zionism*, (Meridian Books, New York, 1975), p. 53.
17. Brecher, *The Foreign Policy*, p. 275.
18. Avineri, 'The Political Thought', pp. 7–8.

19. For a discussion of the role of intercession in Jewish life in the Diaspora see D. Vital, *The Origins of Zionism*, (At the Clarendon Press, Oxford, 1975), p. 68.

20. K. Mannheim, *Ideology and Utopia* (Harvest HBJ Books, New York, 1955), p. 120.

21. This was the tenor of the psychohistorical school which was antithetical to Marxist materialism. Shavit, *Revisionism in Zionism*, p. 292.

22. B. Kimmerling, *Zionism and Economy*, (Schenkman Publishing Company, Cambridge, MA, 1983), pp. 19–39.

23. E. S. Lee, 'A Theory of Migration', *Demography*, vol. 3, no. 1 (1966), pp. 47–57.

24. Shavit, *Revisionism in Zionism*, pp. 67–80.

25. L. Brenner, *Zionism in the Age of the Dictators*, (Croom Helm, London, 1983), p. 133.

26. H. Daaldar, 'The Netherlands: Opposition in a Segmented Society' in Robert Dahl (ed.), *Political Opposition in Western Democracies*, (Yale University Press, New Haven, CT, 1966), pp. 232–3.

27. Mannheim, *Ideology*, p. 141.

28. Y. Peri, *Between Battles and Ballots, Israeli Military in Politics*, (Cambridge University Press, Cambridge, 1983).

29. For instance, in 1954 Moshe Dayan and a group of senior officers created a considerable upheaval by complaining about the shape of the 1948 borders. Peri, *Between Battles*, p. 237. Ben-Gurion's position is difficult to determine. According to Sharett, Ben-Gurion accused him of hindering the military operations in Judea and Samaria in 1948, thus creating a situation which, in Ben-Gurion's words, 'would be mourned for generations to come'. G. Sheffer, 'The Confrontation Between Moshe Sharett and David Ben-Gurion' in S. Almog (ed.), *Zionism and the Arabs. Essays* (The Historical Society of Israel and the Zalman Shazar Centre, Jerusalem, 1983), pp. 95–148. On the other hand, S. Sandler and H. Frisch claim that Ben-Gurion ordered the cessation of the offensive in the West Bank, because the territory was heavily populated by Arabs, and out of concern for future peace negotiations. *Israel, the Palestinians and the West Bank: A Study in Intercommunal Conflict*, (Lexington Heath, New York, 1984), p. 108. See also S. Aronson, *Conflict and Bargaining in the Middle East*, (Johns Hopkins University Press, Baltimore, MD, 1978), p. 7.

30. The most recent round in this historical discussion was provoked by a pamphlet of the young circles in the *Agudat Israel* Party which accused the Zionist movement at large of sacrificing the East European Jews. In response to this accusation, Israel Eldad claimed that the Socialist Zionists prevented the Revisionist rescue effort, 'The Protocols of the Anti-Zion Young', *Haaretz*, 17 May 1984.

31. Wagner and Kaphafi, *The Source of Dispute*, pp. 128–9, Horowitz and Lissak, *Origins of the Israeli Polity*, p. 262.

32. Shavit, *From Hebrew*, p. 187.

33. R. Jervis, *Perceptions and Misperceptions in International Politics* (Princeton University Press, Princeton, NJ, 1976), p. 203.

34. S. Sharot, *Messianism, Mysticism and Magic. A Sociological Analysis of Jewish Religious Movements*, (University of North Carolina Press, Chapel Hill, NC, 1982), p. 223.

35. E. Shils, 'Charisma, Order and Status', *American Sociological Review*, vol. 30, no. 2 (1965), pp. 199–213.

36. Quoted in R. J. Isaac, *Party Politics in Israel* (Longman, New York, 1981), p. 138.

37. J. L. Magnes, 'A Solution Through Force?' in G. V. Smith (ed.) *Zionism: the Dream and the Reality: A Jewish Critique*, (David and Charles, Newton Abbot, London, and New York, 1974), p. 112.

38. Avineri, 'The Political Thought', pp. 3–26, supports the racial argument theory.

39. For a detailed discussion of Jabotinsky's deterrence theory see I. Eldad, 'Jabotinsky Distorted', *The Jerusalem Quarterly*, no. 16, Summer 1980, pp. 27–39, Y. Shavit, 'Revisionism's View of the Arab National Movement' in Almog, *Zionism and the Arabs*, pp. 73–94.

40. Shavit, *Revisionism in Zionism*, p. 187.

41. There is some confusion in Revisionist argument on this subject. Some observers believe that after the situation of the Jews in Eastern Europe worsened, Jabotinsky changed his mind on autonomy. In *The War Front* and the *Jewish People*, written in 1940 shortly before his death, he discussed a voluntary Arab population transfer. Likewise, Israel Eldad from *Lehi* advocated a population transfer. Isaac, *Party Politics*, p. 141. Shmuel Katz, another Revisionist leader, argued that the movement has been always committed to autonomy for the Palestinians. *No Daring and No Glory* (Dvir, Tel Aviv, 1981), p. 143 (Hebrew).

42. Wagner and Kaphafi, *The Source of the Dispute*, pp. 104, 102.

43. Quoted in Gonen, *A Psychohistory*, p. 185.

44. Jervis, *Perceptions and Misperceptions*, p. 134.

45. *Haaretz*, 22 March 1965.

46. J. Mendilow, 'The Transformation of the Israeli Multi-Party System 1965–1981' in A. Arian (ed.), *The Elections in Israel 1981*, (Ramot Publishing Co, Tel Aviv, 1983), pp. 15–37.

47. Y. Shapiro, 'Generational Units and Inter-Generational Relations in Israeli Politics' in A. Arian (ed.), *Israel — A Developing Society*, (Van Gorcum, Assen, 1980), pp. 161–80.

48. Dan V. Segre, *A Crisis of Identity: Israel and Zionism*, (Oxford University Press, Oxford, 1980), pp. 34–50.

49. E. Livneh, *Israel and the Crisis of Western Civilization* (Schocken Publishing, Tel Aviv, 1972), (Hebrew); E. Livneh and S. Katz, *Land of Israel and its Borders*, (The Greater Land of Israel Movement, Tel Aviv, 1968), (Hebrew).

50. E. Livneh, 'The Spiritual Meanings of the Six Day War' in A. Ben Ami (ed.), *The Greater Land of Israel Book*, (The Greater Land of Israel Movement and Freedman Publishers, Tel Aviv, 1977), pp. 22–6 (Hebrew).

51. For a representative summary of the space argument see O. Shem-Ur, *The Challenges of Israel*, (Shengold Publishers, Inc., New York, 1980).

52. Y. Neeman, 'Sovereignty and Territories' in Ben Ami, *The Greater Land*, p. 185.

53. F. Zweig, *Israel; the Sword and the Harp*, (Fairleigh Dickinson University Press, Rutherford, NJ, 1969), pp. 61–2; Gonen, *A Psychohistory*, pp. 4–5; J. L. Talmon, *Political Messianism: The Romantic Phase*, (Praeger, New York, 1960).

54. This model is presented in *Happy is the Mother of Sons* by Rabbi Isachar Solomon Teichtel. P. Peli, 'Where Was God During the Holocaust?' *The Jerusalem Post*, 17–23 and 24–30 April 1983.

55. Sharot applied Talmon-Gerber's distinction between historical and mythical perception in millenarian movements in Gush Emunim, *Messianism*, p. 230.

56. A. Elon, *The Israelis*, (Sphere Books Ltd, London, 1971), p. 343.

57. Rabbi Eliezer Shach, associated with *Agudat Israel*, who is a major opponent of National Religious Zionism, accused the Gush of false interpretation of the *halacha*, the Talmudic law. D. Rubinstein, *On the Lord's Side: Gush Emunim*, (Hakibuttz Hameuhad Publishing House, Tel Aviv, 1982), pp. 105, 152 (Hebrew). For a review of religious attitudes towards the West Bank see C. Liebman and E. Don-Yehiya. *Religion and Politics in Israel*, (Indiana University Press, Bloomington, IN, 1984), Chap. 5.

58. M. Selzer, 'Politics and Human Perfectability: A Jewish Perspective', in Smith, *Zionism*, pp. 285–303.

59. A. Rubinstein, *From Herzl to Gush Emunim and Back*, (Schocken Publishing House, Tel Aviv, 1980) pp. 124–5 (Hebrew).

60. Rabbi Israel Hess, 'On the Duty of Genocide in the Bible', *Bat Kol*, The Journal of Students of Bar Ilan University, February 1980; quoted in Rubinstein, *From Herzl*, p. 125.

61. C. Peles, 'The Dialectical Development of the Zionist Ideas', *Deot*, The Journal of Religious Academics, 1977, p. 333; quoted in Rubinstein, *From Herzl*, pp. 118–20.

62. Rabbi Yehuda Amital, *Hama'alot Mema'amakim*, *(Jerusalem, Alon More, 1974)*, pp. 42–3; quoted in Rubinstein, *From Herzl*, p. 112.

63. Rabbi Ephraim Zemmel, *Mahshavot*, 1975, pp. 6–8; quoted in Rubinstein, *From Herzl*, p. 122.

64. Peles, *Deot*, pp. 119–20.

65. Y. Herzog, *A People That Dwells Alone*, (Maariv Publishing, Tel Aviv, 1976), especially pp. 140–9 (Hebrew).

66. E. Schweid, *Homeland and A Land of Promise*, (Am Oved Publishers, Tel Aviv, 1979), p. 32 (Hebrew).

67. Rabbi Moshe Levinger, the spiritual leader of Gush Emunim, developed the theory that the Arabs should accept the link between the Jews and the Land of Israel which is the highest order of morality. The Palestinians should regard their second-rate citizenship as part of participating in this moral scheme. An interview in *Haaretz*, 15 July 1983.

68. D. Rubinstein, *On the Lord's*, p. 148.

69. *Ibid.*, p. 162.

70. Sharot, *Messianism*, p. 231.

71. M. Weber, *Economy and Society*. Edited by Guenther Roth and Claus Wittich, (Bedminster Press, New York, 1968), pp. 442–99.

72. *National Security of the Hebrew People*, (Tsaizer Studio, Tel Aviv, 1974), pp. 178–81.

73. Arab involvement in the Final Solution is normally discussed in the media at the annual Holocaust Memorial Day. For the most recent discussion of the Kanaan book, see *The Jerusalem Post*, 24–30 April 1983. See also M. S. Arnoni, *Rights and Wrongs in the Arab-Israeli Conflict*, (The Minority of One Press, Passaic, NJ, 1968), pp. 59–91.

74. H. Arendt, *Eichmann in Jerusalem. A Report on the Banality of Evil* (Viking Press, New York, 1963), p. 10.

75. S. N. Herman, 'In the Shadow of the Holocaust', *The Jerusalem Quarterly*, no. 3, (1977), pp. 85–97.

76. For instance, see A. Rubinstein, *To Be A Free Nation*, (Schocken Publishing House, Jerusalem and Tel Aviv 1977), pp. 147–56; S. Avineri, *Essays on Zionism and Politics*, (Sifrei Mabat, Tel Aviv, 1977), pp. 44–5, (Hebrew); N. Rotenstreich, *Examining Zionism Today*, (The Zionist Library, Jerusalem, 1977), pp. 71–8, (Hebrew). Yitzhak Navon, the former President of Israel in a speech to the Zionist Congress criticised the automatic equation of anti-Semitism and anti-Zionism, *Haaretz*, 8 December 1982.

77. Segre, *The Crisis of Identiy*, p. 8.

78. S. Ettinger, 'Anti-Semitism in Our Time', *The Jerusalem Quarterly*, no. 23 (1983), pp. 95–113. This view has been shared by personalities who are not identified with the Likud and is widely reflected in the media. For instance, see the interview with Moshe Rosen, the Chief Rabbi of Rumania, *Maariv*, 6 May 1983, and the Conference of the International Association of Jewish Reports, *Haaretz*, 5 December 1982.

79. G. Allport, *The Nature of Prejudice*, (Addison Wesley, New York, 1979), p. 246.

80. Herman, 'In the Shadow', p. 86.

112 *The Evolution of New Zionism*

81. This story was related by Shoken to Rubinstein, *To Be a Free Nation*, pp. 143–4.

82. S. N. Herman, Y. Peres and E. Yuchtman, 'Reaction to the Eichmann Trial in Israel: A Study in High Involvement', *Scripta Hierosolymitana*, vol. 14 (1965), pp. 98–119.

83. Approximately 20 per cent of the Israeli population in 1980 were Holocaust survivors. The Holocaust acts as a major source of psychological stress for the survivors' generation and has been intergenerationally transferred. S. F. Landau and B. Bet-Hallahmi, 'Israel: Aggression in Psychohistorical Perspective' in A. P. Goldstein and Marshall H. Segall (eds), *Aggression in Global Perspective* (Pergamon Press, New York, 1983), pp. 261–3. S. Kav-Venaki and A. Nadler, 'Trans-Generational Effects of Massive Psychic Traumatization: Psychological Characteristics of Children of Holocaust Survivors', paper presented at the annual conference of the International Society of Political Psychology, Mannheim, West Germany, June 1981.

84. A. S. Zuckerman, 'The Limits of Political Behavior: Individual Calculations and Survival During the Holocaust', *Political Psychology*, vol. 5, no. 1 (1984), pp. 37–52.

85. *Ibid.*, p. 49–51.

86. R. Hilberg, *The Destruction of the European Jews* (Quadrangle Press, Chicago, 1967).

87. U. Farogo, 'The Perception of the Holocaust Among Israeli Students — 1983' in *Dapim Le Mehkar Hasho'ah*, (November 1983), pp. 117–28, (Hebrew).

88. M. Billig, *Social Psychology and Intergroup Relations* (Academic Press, London, 1976), pp. 104–12.

89. M. Billig, *Ideology and Social Psychology. Extremism Moderation and Contradiction*, (St. Martin's Press, New York, 1982), pp. 61–134.

90. S. Friedlander, 'Some Aspects of the Historical Significance of the Holocaust', *The Jerusalem Quarterly*, no. 1 (1976), pp. 36–59.

91. For instance, see E. Wiesel, 'The Death of My Father' in Jack Riener (ed.), *Jewish Reflection on Death*, (Schocken Books, New York, 1976), pp. 35–9. Emil Fackheinheim's thesis is summed up in his latest book, *To Mend the World*; see also an interview with Fackheinheim, *The Jerusalem Post*, 11–17 September 1983.

92. N. Gertz, 'Israeli Novelists', *The Jerusalem Quarterly*, no. 17 (1980), pp. 66–77.

93. Herman, 'In the Shadow', pp. 85–97; Farago, 'The Perception of the Holocaust', pp. 117–28.

PART TWO

4 THE DELEGITIMISATION OF SOCIALIST ZIONISM: THE DOMESTIC POLITICS OF A NATION IN THE MAKING

Independence presented the Socialist Zionist belief system with two new developments. First, the foundation of the State caused a major alteration in the institutional and social patterns of the society. There was an increase in bureaucratisation and the formalisation of social roles. The centralisation of political, social and economic activities was enhanced by a rapid shift towards industrialisation and urbanisation. Second, the huge immigration brought to the new state diverse groups, whose value systems differed sharply from the Socialist Zionist creed. The first of these developments evolved into statism, that is, efforts to adapt the Socialist Zionist ideology to the requirements of positive government. The second development led to cultural pluralism, which came to give expression to the rising religious and Oriental groups in Israeli society. The interaction of these two developments caused the delegitimisation of Socialist Zionism. During this lengthy process Labour's dominance was eroded and the Israeli electorate legitimised New Zionism.

The Political Dimension: Pioneering Ideology and the Requirements of Statism

The core of the Socialist Zionist belief system was based on a pioneering concept of social behaviour, which involved personal asceticism, voluntarism, collective orientation, and egalitarianism. Central to this approach was the twin emphasis on *idealism* and *collective materialism* — self-abnegation which disregards personal, sectoral, and particularist interests in order to achieve collective material ends. The primacy of agriculture in material production underlined the early Socialist Zionist concern with the reform of the society's structure. This value system was embodied in the kibbutz — an elite social institution, which provided the pioneering role model for the society. The *Histadrut*, a comprehensive trade union organisation that ran substantial parts of the economy, was charged with overseeing egalitarian principles in the system of distributive justice.

Even before independence, the majority of the Yishuv were neither strictly pioneering nor egalitarian. Yet the supremacy of the kibbutz in the receipt of scarce economic resources and the control of the Histadrut over the economy had been widely accepted and bolstered by the organisational dominance of the Labour movement.

The influx of immigrants which turned Israel into a mass society and the industrialisation drive created what Merton called a disassociation 'between culturally prescribed values and roles and socially structured avenues for realizing these values'.[1] This disassociation was evident in the shift from the future-oriented collectivist goals of the Socialist Zionists to the temporally defined individualism of the Israelis. The coercive institutionalisation of roles, and, especially, military service, have undermined the pioneering spirit of voluntarism. The emphasis on industrialisation clashed with the traditional legitimacy of agriculture in the productive scheme of the society. Technological modernisation led to a greater role differentiation and required the use of utilitarian-meritorious principles of remuneration, which put a special pressure on the egalitarian notions of distributive justice.

Attempts to redefine the pioneering ideology to meet the new challenges were only partially successful. Eisenstadt, who labelled the Labour response 'dynamic conservatism', has argued that some of the key socio-economic structures — the agricultural settlements and the Histadrut — have been flexible enough to adapt to mass immigration and industrialisation, even though this initial success bred future discontent.[2]

In other dimensions, the Labour elite was unwilling or unable to face the discrepancy between the dominant belief system and the new realities. *Mapai*, like movements in other developing societies, was an inheritance type of party. It was plagued by intergenerational power struggles and conflict over the extent of permissible ideological changes. As a result, the belief system developed a number of tension points which served to delegitimise Socialist Zionism. Some of them were based on a readily manifest clash of material interests; others were derived from more subtle and time-lagged changes in popular values.

The most immediate manifestation of stress developed around the growing economic and social differentation of the society and the government's attempts to counter meritorious wage claims. The principles of egalitarianism, which the government and the Histadrut implemented through a policy of minimal wage differentials, met with resistance from a variety of professional groups. Derber, who studied early labour unrest in Israel, found that in the public sector the differential between the highest and lowest salary grades was 3:1, only half the ratio in the United States. The egalitarian wage policies, although enhanced by cost of living indexation and other compensations, were also imposed on the small private sector. Since the first major doctors' strike in 1954, these policies had generated protest among professionals, who demanded adequate compensation for special skills.

However, attempts to meet these demands invariably provoked other groups to counterclaims in the name of the egalitarian principle of the interrelatedness of wages. Derber pointed out that, in spite of some ingenious compromises by the government and the Histadrut, this policy resulted in widespread alienation among both professionals and the rank and file.[3] One direct measure of this dissatisfaction was the large number of strikes which were not approved by the Histadrut. For instance, in the 1960–64 period, unapproved strikes constituted an average of 56.4 per cent of all work stoppages, and in some years they reached 90 per cent.[4]

A more serious stress point evolved out of the contradiction between the commanding control of the government and the Histadrut over the Israeli economy and Mapai's leftist ideology, which was predicated upon the existence of a class cleavage in the European tradition. As the biggest employer in a country where the private sector was small and dependent upon the government, Mapai's socialist theme of the 'inequality of workers versus employers' was particularly hard to accommodate, given the fact that Mapai had to reconcile its roles as both an employer and the articulator of working-class interests.

A somewhat more diffuse discrepancy stemmed from the difficulty of implementing the concept of pioneering behaviour in the progressively modernised and statist-oriented society. Empirical research demonstrates that the trend towards Western middle-class values, which had already been evident in the Yishuv, was greatly enhanced after independence. Table 4.1, which sums up the most relevant research in the 1948–67 period, is arranged in chronological order and graded according to its hypothesised delegitimisation value. This arrangement helps to specify the areas in which popular values diverged most from official ideology. Undoubtedly, the two most delegitimising changes occurred in the belief system of the kibbutz and the younger cohorts of the Israeli population.

Table 4.1: Changes in Public Belief System 1949–70

Year	Title	Summary Conclusions	Degree of Legitimisation
1949	Public Opinion Towards Mass Immigration	82% of respondents felt that some restrictions should be applied to the mass immigration[a]	− −
1949	Public Attitudes Towards Salaries of High Officials	A majority (64%) of respondents supported reasonably high salaries. Only 50% approved of the salaries of Knesset members[a]	− −
1949	Public Support for Austerity Programme	About half the Israeli population supported austerity programme. Higher professional groups and residents of large cities supported it least[a]	+/−
1950	Public Attitudes Towards Government Anti-inflation Policy	Unskilled workers and new immigrants were least supportive of the wage cuts[a]	− − −
1953	Tension and Affinity in a New Immigrant Housing Community	Tension between the Ashkenazi and Oriental groups is underpinned by socio-economic factors[a]	− −
1954	Youth's Attitudes Towards Social Responsibility	There was no generalised notion of 'good citizenship'[a]	− − −
1954	Public Attitudes Towards Income Tax	A relatively positive attitude towards taxes. 30% felt that taxes are too high and should be opposed[a]	+/−
1955	Attitudes of High Officials in *Mapai*	The originally ideological group was transformed into a professional group. Professionalism led to a decrease in contacts with the rank and file and a decline in personal and ideological dynamism[a]	− − −
1958	Listening to the International Bible Quiz Final	66% of the Jewish population listened to the quiz[a]	− − −

1959	Occupational Trends Among Urban Youth in Israel	The perceived prestige hierarchy is based on Western type of education and professional ranking. There is an erosion of perceived prestige in occupations which relate to 'collective enterprise'[b]	– – –
1962	The Political Ideologies of Israelis	A moderate correspondence between the ideological position of an individual and his voting. The highest concentration of 'non-ideological' voters was among the lower class[a]	– – –
1963	Public Attitudes to Voluntary Contribution	About 97% contributed, but only 27% did so voluntarily[a]	– – –
1963	Public Attitudes Towards *Histadrut*	Only 28% of the respondents joined the *Histadrut* for ideological reasons[c]	– – –
1965	Youth Organization in Israel	Decline in voluntarism and a concomitant increase in Western type of middle-class values[d]	– – –
1966–7	Youth Culture in Israel	Decline in collectivists and an emphasis on individualistic values[e]	– – –
1970	Social Relations in the Kibbutz	The major problem of kibbutz members was the lack of a firm belief in the institution of the kibbutz	– – –

Notes:
  a Israel Institute of Applied Social Research. All the surveys of the IIASR available as internal publications. A description of the sample and a short executive summary are provided in H. Gretch (ed.), *25 Years of Social Research in Israel,* (Jerusalem Academic Press, Jerusalem, 1973).
  b M. Lissak, Unpublished Ph.D. dissertation, Hebrew University in Jerusalem, 1963.
  c A. Rubinstein, *To Be A Free People,* (Schocken Publishing House, Tel Aviv, 1977), p. 48.
  d J.W. Eaton and M. Chen, *Influencing the Youth Culture: A Study of Youth Organization in Israel,* (Sage Publications, Berverly Hills, CA, 1970).
  e C. Alder and Y. Peres, 'Youth Movements and Salon Societies', *Youth and Society,* vol. 1, no.2 (1970), pp. 309-32.

Two complementary conclusions can be derived from the data on the attitudes of kibbutz members. One is that there was a decrease in the overall degree of ideological commitment, and the other that there was a shift from ascetic-collective goals towards consumer-individual values. The industrialisation of the kibbutz, which necessitated the employment of outside labour, accelerated this value transformation. The percentage of employers in all types of kibbutz enterprises went up from 20 per cent in the 1950s to an average of 65 per cent in the late 1970s.

The kibbutz served as a key role model in the pioneering Socialist Zionist belief system. Based on its pre-independence importance, the kibbutz movement has also continued to receive a disproportionately high share of state resources. Most observers have attributed the decline in the popularity of the kibbutz to Likud's efforts to discredit the movement in the 1981 election. Nevertheless, more than half of a representative sample of Israelis polled in 1976 and 1978 thought that the kibbutz was not paying enough taxes and 66 per cent felt that the kibbutz failed to help the lower groups in society.[5] The latter finding implies that the public expected the kibbutz movement to redefine its pioneering role in the post-independence period in order to contribute to social integration. Because the kibbutz remained an exclusive society, its perceived social value has been eroded, leading to public delegitimisation of the institution.

Numerous studies which probed the attitudes of the younger generation reveal equally serious deviations from the Socialist Zionist belief system. Most important, the popular status hierarchy became increasingly based on utilitarian and meritorious concepts, such as education and occupation. Lissak's study of the *perceived hierarchy* of occupation among a sample of young Israelis is particularly indicative of this trend. The upper portion of the perceived prestige hierarchy included occupations based on formal education. The bottom range was made up of manual labour occupations. Such a hierarchy was in contradiction to the official practice of hiring under Mapai. Most often, occupational recruitment and mobility were based on ascriptive considerations such as length of residence in the country or political affiliation with the ruling party.

Research on the cultural values of the younger generation, most notably the work of Eaton and Chen, demonstrates that, since the mid-1950s, Israeli youth have increasingly developed individualistic and Western consumption-oriented values. Since commitment to collectivity became almost isomorphous with military service, which had been institutionalised and compulsory since 1948, the Socialist Zionist ideology lost credibility because of its continuous emphasis on the voluntary nature of social services to the country.

Rubinstein's survey on the decline in voluntary behaviour and the decrease in voluntary associations is equally indicative of this trend. Most important, a 1963 opinion poll found that only 28 per cent of Histadrut members joined the organisation for ideological reasons. This figure is particularly indicative of the existing dissonance, because voting behaviour studies found that, in the late 1960s, membership of the Histadrut was the best predictor of support for the Labour party.[6]

Perhaps the most striking evidence about the degree of disparity between the popular belief system and the official ideology comes from Arian's study on ideological change in Israel. The study revealed that, already in the 1960s, the general voting public was much more right-wing than the political elite. There was therefore only a slight correspondence between an individual's ideological position and his party affiliation. The most discrepant attitudes were found among a sample of the general public (students), followed by civil servants. Only the *Knesset* members in the survey closely resembled the political position of their party.[7]

Etzioni-Halevy, who analysed a number of public opinion surveys dating from 1969 to the mid-1970s, found that the gap between the rightist shift in the popular belief system and the Socialist Zionist ideology had increased in this period. A particularly interesting conclusion to emerge from her study is that, during this period, the left-right cleavage lost its class meaning. Individuals who identified with the leftist belief system and voted for the Labour Party (formerly Mapai), largely belonged to the better educated middle class. The less educated and blue collar voters predominated among those who identified themselves as rightists and tended to vote for Likud (formerly *Gahal*).[8] Of course, these changes have been heavily underlaid by the delegitimisation of the Socialist Zionist belief system among two emerging groups in Israel, the religious and the Oriental Jews.

The Demographic Dimension of Delegitimisation: The Rise of Religious and Oriental Groups in Israel

It is a truism in social research that demographic changes in a society influence the extant belief system. We have already indicated in Chapter 1 that emergent groups may delegitimise some of the criteria used to define the group identity or the validity claims of distributive justice or both. In Israel, the two groups which challenged the Socialist Zionist belief system were the religious and the Oriental communities.

The Religious Community

The size of the religious community is difficult to estimate, because it is not entirely clear how to define a religious Jew in Israel. Judaism, like Islam, is an organic religion which is highly penetrative of the sociocultural sphere. Since it is also a state religion, for some people Judaism is only nominal. The degree of religious orthodoxy is more indicative of religious commitment. But, among Jews, there are no universal standards of observance with regard to the commands and prohibitions of the rabbinical code of laws, known as the *halacha*.

A common classification used in surveys is based on a three-fold typology of orthodox, traditional, and secular Jews. The orthodox Jews observe all or most of the halacha rules, the traditional Jews observe some halacha commandments such as the Sabbath and visits to the synagogue, and the secular Jews are completely non-observant. Liebman refined the category of orthodoxy by introducing two subcategories, the neo-traditionalists and the modern orthodox.[9] Deshen proposed a classification into orthodox, neo-orthodox, traditional-secularising, and secular.[10]

Because of the different critiera used to measure orthodoxy, estimates of the size of the religious community have varied considerably. The rate of growth of the community since independence is even more difficult to estimate. A 1963 survey found that about 30 per cent of respondents defined themselves as orthodox, 46 per cent as traditionalist, and 24 per cent as secularist.[11] Smooha, who evaluated religious trends in the 1970s, found little change in this pattern.[12] The various projections for the 1980s assume that there may be an increase in the trend towards orthodoxy, because of the higher fertility rates of the religious group and the structure of immigration to Israel. Yehuda Dominitz, the head of the Immigration Department in the Jewish Agency, has pointed out that in the past decade there has been a large religious contingent among the immigrants, especially from the United States.[13]

Apparently, even the secular group is not totally non-observant. Ben-Meir and Kedem, who used a detailed scale to measure religiosity, found that between 80 and 90 per cent of the total population observed some of the religious commands, and the celebration of the High Holidays, *Pessah* and *Yom Kippur*, is almost universal.[14]

The most obvious dissonance between Socialist Zionism and the religious community has stemmed from the different definition of collective identity. There is overwhelming empirical evidence to indicate that religious Israelis tend to define themselves as Jews, whereas secular Israelis choose the Israeli identity. In the 1964–5 Herman study, 55 per cent of religious Israeli parents and 60 per cent of their children chose the Jewish identity. In the secular group, only 16 per cent of the parents and 4 per cent of the children identified themselves as Jews. Among traditional parents and students, 20 and 22 per cent respectively chose the Jewish identity rather than the Israeli one.[15]

The preference for Jewish identity among the younger generation of religious Israelis, already evident in the Herman study, has increased over the years. In a 1972 survey, Zuckerman-Bareli found that 86 per cent of orthodox students opted for a Jewish self-identity versus 16 per cent of secular students. In the traditional group, 45 per cent chose Jewish identity. When both the Jewish and Israeli choices of identity were offered, 89 per cent of the religious group and 81 per cent of the traditional identified themselves in co-joint terms. Among the seculars, 53 per cent chose to describe themselves as both Jews and Israelis.[16]

The religious community has also clashed with Socialist Zionism over the degree of universalism in the definition of national identity. Herman, Zuckerman-Bareli and other researchers demonstrated that the degree of religiosity is negatively correlated with universalism. For instance, in the Zuckerman-Bareli study, none of the religious students chose to identify themselves as 'humans in a world society', as opposed to 19 per cent of the secular students who did so. The polarising impact of religiosity was especially evident in the question about the desired culture in Israel. Sixty-seven per cent of religious students expressed the opinion that Israel should have a national culture with minimal Western influence. Eighty-two per cent of secular students wanted Western influence in the Israeli culture. The traditionalists were almost equally split on this issue.[17]

The issue of legitimising a certain type of group identity has important behavioural consequences. Since, in Judaism, national identity is inexorably linked with religious identity, there has been a constant pressure from the religious camp to impose the rule of the halacha on the public domain. The organic nature of the Jewish religion has never allowed a full separation between state and religion. Yet on a continuum ranging from complete separation to full theocracy, the pre-state Socialist Zionism system was quite close to the secular pole. The religious camp was not homogeneous in its attitudes towards the issue of theocracy. The ultra-orthodox group, which was represented by the *Agudat Israel* Party, called for a full theocracy. The moderate orthodox in the National Religious Party were prepared to accept a selective implementation of the halacha, through the legislative apparatus of the state.

The dissonance between the Socialist Zionist belief system and the beliefs of the orthodox communities has compelled the Labour elite to redefine its attitudes towards Jewish national identity and Jewish religion. Although observers normally emphasise that Mapai accepted the religious dictum because of the danger of a *Kulturkampf*, there were additional reasons.

One of them was the growing impression that a secular Israeli identity was not enough to secure the spatial dimension in Zionism, that is, the continuous link with Diaspora Jewry. A totally secular identity could not attract immigration and prevent emigration from Israel. Dela Pergola, a leading authority on Jewish demography, pointed out that Zionism could not compete with the normal 'pull and push' processes of migration. In order to gain demographically, Israel, which was materially behind the Western countries, had to strengthen the Jewish elements in the collective identity.[18]

Most important, Socialist Zionism had to make an adjustment because of the Holocaust. At the symbolic level, the destruction of European Jewry made the critique of orthodox Judaism and the Diaspora redundant, if not harmful to Labour. At the demographic-institutional level, the Holocaust prompted the remnants of the great ultra-orthodox centres of Eastern Europe to relocate in Israel. Even though most of the ultra-orthodox camp did not recognise the State of Israel, the Labour elite felt compelled to accede to religious demands. Ben-Gurion, following his famous meeting with the revered representative of ultra-orthodox Jewry, Hazon Ish, gave the Holocaust as his main reason for exempting the ultra-orthodox from military service.[19] In other words, the perception of Israel as a refuge for all Jews came to dominate the more traditional notions of social redemption and even the vision of a civic-secular Jewish state.

These perceptions generated two major policy changes. One was the 1955 decision to implement the Ministry of Education proposal for a 'Jewish consciousness' programme in schools. It is significant that a majority of the non-religious members of the Knesset who debated this proposal felt that students should become familiar with religious beliefs and practices within the curriculum of the general (secular) schools. The 1959 directive of the Ministry of Education stipulated that instruction in religious subjects and celebration of religious holidays in school should make students more receptive to the Jewish religious heritage. Adar, who reviewed the educational system in Israel, found that the study of the Bible and Jewish history has been more successfully implemented than that of oral law (Talmud).[20]

The other policy outcome pertained to the compromise between Mapai and the religious parties over a selective imposition of the halacha on the public domain. Known as the *Status Quo* arrangement, it stipulated that some halachic principles, such as the observance of the Sabbath and dietary law, should be mandatory in all state institutions. Following some early disputes over the interpretation of who is a Jew in the Law of Return, which grants automatic citizenship to all Jewish immigrants, the definition was tightened. According to a subsequent amendment, a Jew was defined as a person born to a Jewish mother or converted to Judaism.[21]

The enormous literature on the state-religious issue in Israel has documented that the *Status Quo* arrangement has been plagued by continuous strife. The recurrent demand of the religious groups for amendment of the Law of Return, in order to make conversion to Judaism conform to the halacha, was the focal point of this struggle, but other issues were equally stressful.

The policy adjustments neither eliminated the dissonance nor arrested the strife between Socialist Zionism and the religious belief system. These changes may have served to delegitimise the secular values in the Labour ideology. The effectiveness of the 'Jewish consciousness' programme was never fully evaluated. But some subsequent studies demonstrated that the programme enhanced the convergence between religious and non-religious students. In a representative sample of high school students in 1974–6, 87 per cent of the religious and 61 per cent of the secular students felt that the Jewish religion was an important part of their Jewish identity.[22] Moreover, along with the fact that the dominant belief system has been growing more traditional, the relative gap between Labour and the religious camp has increased. This gap was apparently generated by some subtle and often little noticed changes in the structure of the religious belief system.

In his pioneering work on religious beliefs in Israel, Liebman identified two major 'ideal type' categories of religious reaction to the process of modernisation. One is *neo-traditionalism*, which seeks to preserve the orthodox way of life through a total rejection of modern values. The other is *modern orthodoxy*, which tries to preserve the halacha, while accommodating it to some aspects of modernisation. There are three subcategories in modern orthodoxy: (i) *adaptation*, i.e. changes in the halacha; (ii) *compartmentalisation*, i.e. isolation of a number of dimensions in which to preserve the halacha; and (iii) *expansionism*, i.e. acceptance of modernity by re-interpreting it according to Jewish tradition.[23] The neo-traditional type roughly corresponds to the ultra-orthodox *Agudat Israel* political persuasion: accommodationism, in modern orthodoxy primarily compartmentalisation, can be identified with the National Religious Party.

Empirical evidence on the distribution of these behavioural categories across time is scanty, but there is a general impression that two attitudinal changes took place. First, there was an increase in the number of neo-traditionals in the religious camp. Zelniker and Kahan, who studied changes in religious attitudes in the 1962–3 period, found that, by 1973, 82 per cent of religious voters identified themselves as theocrats (neo-traditionalists).[24] The Antonovsky survey in the 1960s revealed that 23 per cent of respondents definitely agreed with the statement that public life should be conducted according to Jewish tradition and 20 per cent were partially supportive of the idea. A Gallup Poll in Israel in August 1971 indicated that 55 per cent of respondents opposed the separation of religion from the state.[25]

Aviad pointed out that the increase in neo-traditionalists was fed by a number of sources: the high fertility rates of the ultra-orthodox population; the concentrated efforts to rebuild the Hassidic and other ultra-orthodox centres in Israel; and the substantial process of *teshuva* (return to Judaism) or 'born again' Jews. There are no estimates of the numbers involved, but 'born again' Jews tend to join the ultra-orthodox community.[26] The numerical balance between neo-traditionalists and modern orthodox has also been related to generational and ethnic changes. Zelniker and Kahan calculated that, among Israeli-born religious respondents, 72 per cent were theocrats as opposed to 67 per cent of the group born in Europe or America; the Asian-African group was 75 per cent theocratic.[27]

Second, a major transformation was caused in the modern orthodox camp when the older generation of accommodationists was replaced by the younger cohort of expansionists. The previous chapter indicated that the hallmark of expansionist modern orthodoxy was the National Religious Zionism of Rabbi Kook, which interpreted the establishment of the State of Israel as the beginning of the process of Redemption. According to some experts, during the past two decades the educational system of the National Religious Party has come under the dual influence of National Religious Zionism and the ultra-orthodox elements.[28] Since the mid-1960s *Bnei Akiba*, the youth movement of the National Religious Party, and the Young Circles leadership in the party, have been closely associated with the *Merkaz Harav Yeshiva* of Rabbi Kook. The modern orthodox expansionist movement also gained public legitimacy by pioneering the *Yeshivat Hesder*, the rabbinical colleges whose students did military service. The effects of these developments became felt politically in the early 1970s, when the younger leadership of the NRP adopted a more nationalistic and theocratic stand.

The restructuring of the religious belief system also led to a change in the *modus operandi* of the community. The early, largely *responsive* style of the political leadership was replaced by an *initiating* posture which sought active changes in the *Status Quo*. The style of the new leaders in the NRP contributed to a growing discord between Socialist Zionism and the religious camp. The clash came when the NRP demanded a more theocratic interpretation of relations between religion and the state and put forward binding claims to the West Bank; the subsequent crisis resulted in the collapse of the Labour Government in 1976.

Following the Likud victory in 1977, Agudat Israel and the NRP, which joined the coalition, managed to change the important sections of the *Status Quo*. They broadened the domain of Sabbath observance in the public sectors, changed the Anatomy and Pathology Law to prohibit post-mortem examinations without the written permission of the family, and effected an amendment in the Abortion law which would prevent state aid for socially motivated abortions. Agudat Israel also achieved a relaxation of the regulation under which women could obtain exemption from military service on religious grounds.

These multidimensional modifications in the religious belief system have been reflected in the electoral strength of the religious parties. Because the vote for religious parties represents only about half of the potential religious constitutency, conclusions based on electoral results are only tentative. Yet it is interesting that, since the 1947–9 period, the two neo-traditionalist parties, Agudat Israel and *Poalei Agudat Israel,* have together held an average 5 per cent of the Knesset vote. The NRP, the modern orthodox accommodating party, has had an average 9.2 per cent of the vote.

In the 1984 elections, the 5 per cent of the neo-traditionalist vote was split between the 2 seats of the Ashkenazi Agudat Israel and its Oriental counterpart, the 4-seat *Shas* Party (Sephardi Torah Guardians). The accommodating sector of the modern orthodoxy shrank to the 3.3 per cent (4 seats) gained by the NRP. The Gush Emunim's party *Morasha,* which got 1.6 per cent of the vote (2 seats), represents the modern orthodox expansionist camp. The remaining vote in this category, especially among the 86,000 Jewish electors in the West Bank, went to the radical nationalist-religious *Kach* of Rabbi Kahane, Likud and Tehiya.

Given the similarities between National Religious Zionism and Neo-Revisionism, the transfer of the religious vote to the right-wing parties is not surprising. Empirical findings confirm that this affinity has dated at least from the late 1960s. Using a 1969 representative sample, Tockatli found that religious voters over-whelmingly picked Gahal (forerunner of Likud) as their second choice. Second choice is considered to be a measure of the psycho-logical proximity between two parties.[29] Other studies have reg-ularly revealed that the traditional, mainly Oriental, voters tend to support the secular right-wing parties.

These modifications in the religious belief system illustrate the difficulties of the alliance between the Socialist Zionists and the religious camp. If the shift towards neo-traditionalism and the increase of the expansionists among the modern orthodox are permanent, the distance between Labour and the religious parties will exceed the range permissible for coalition formation. To the extent that this religious transvaluation involves the most fundamental political issues, it would affect the entire context of the Israeli policy.

The Oriental Community

The definition of group membership in the Oriental community is based on Asian-African country of origin. The disposition of the second, Israeli-born generation is a socio-ethnic convention, whereby sons of Oriental fathers are assigned to the Oriental category. Orientals constituted 23 per cent of the population at independence. Due to their preponderance in the immigration to Israel and their high fertility rates, the Orientals reached parity with the Ashkenazim in 1963. They currently constitute some 60 per cent of the population and are expected to reach 75 per cent in the late 1980s.

The dominance of the Ashkenazim in the Yishuv period dictated a Western orientation in the evolving society. The Socialist Zionists enhanced this trend by opting for what Horowitz defined as an incorporative type of ethnic assimilation. Incorporation follows the $A+B=A$ pattern, that is, one group assumes the identity of the other as opposed to amalgamation in which two groups form a third identity along the $A+B=C$ pattern.[30] Invariably, incorporation involves the comprehensive assimilation of the subordinate group.

The Western-Ashkenazi definition of the Israeli group identity did not change in spite of the influx of Oriental Jews after independence. In the first wave of the migration, between May 1948 and December 1951, 330,400 or 48.2 per cent of the 684,201 immigrants, came from Asia-Africa. All together, between 1948 and 1972, when the major immigration ended, out of the 1,496,928 newcomers, 48.7 per cent, that is 729,230, were classified as Asian-African.[31]

The decision to admit the Asian-African Jews was taken within the framework of a broader policy to turn Israel into a 'haven' for all Jewish refugees. In addition, security needs demanded a large population to forestall the Arab threat. Yet the Labour elite was apprehensive about the impact of the Oriental immigrants on the Western character of the emerging polity. This issue is a highly politicised and controversial one, but some recently disclosed documents indicate that in certain Zionist quarters there was a preference for Ashkenazi immigrants.[32]

Although Ben-Gurion and other Labour leaders defended the

decision to admit Oriental Jews, they were highly vocal in expressing their fear of 'creeping Levantinism'. Ben-Gurion often described in contemptuous and derogatory terms the 'primitive Arab mentality' of the Oriental Jews, and expressed apprehension that even the children of these immigrants 'whose forebears have been uneducated for generations will sink to the level of Arab peasant children'.[33] Abba Eban, the then Minister of Education, was equally uneasy that the newcomers would drag Israel into an 'unnatural Orientalism', and Golda Meir wondered whether they could be brought to a 'suitable level of civilisation'.[34]

Invidious distinctions were particularly pervasive in military thinking. There was widespread apprehension in the Israel Defence Force that the Oriental immigrants and their children would not be able to sustain the human quality needed to offset Arab numerical superiority. A number of Chiefs of Staff, including Yaakov Dori, Moshe Dayan, and Mordechai Gur, publicly expressed their doubts about the performance of Oriental soldiers.[35] Misgivings about Oriental military capability surfaced more recently when a *Ha'aretz* editorial revealed that in the past few years the IDF had had a higher than average percentage of recruits with low IQ and low motivational levels.[36] Roumani, an authority on Oriental and military sociology, pointed out that 80–90 per cent of recruits who score below the minimum average are Orientals, mostly slum dwellers. He concluded that, although the military has contributed to the integration of the Oriental soldiers, there are pockets of ethnic alienation in the IDF.[37]

Stringent adherence to the incorporationist model of assimilation posed serious problems for the group identity of the Oriental immigrants. In line with the then prevailing modernisation school in sociological thinking, the official view was that, in order to become successfully acculturated, the Oriental Jews would have to transvalue their attitude structure completely. Among other changes, they were expected to dispose of what were perceived as Arab mental characteristics, such as laziness, lack of motivation and drive, and excessive individualism.[38]

Anthropological studies of Israel's first two decades document the widespread contempt for the habits and culture of Oriental Jews, who were often labelled as 'primitive'. There is abundant evidence of the existence of extremely strong *opprobium controls*, that is, societal mechanisms of disapproval, ridicule or ostracism, directed against any display of Arab characteristics by the Oriental immigrants and especially by their offspring.[39] For instance, a comprehensive survey of Israeli literature for children reveals that there was a paucity of Oriental heroes, but there were frequent disparaging descriptions of Oriental parents and children.[40]

In shaping their new identity, the Orientals faced an even more insurmountable problem when they tried to conform to the ideal personality type of the dominant belief system. This type was embodied in the image of the Sabra, the native-born Israeli, implicitly of Ashkenazi parentage. This model personality was developed by early Ashkenazi pioneers, in response to their own identity predicament in Eastern Europe. The Sabra type included a set of attitudinal and behavioural traits, such as physical strength, contempt for excessive intellectualism, lack of outward emotionalism, and emphasis on honesty and courage. It also involved a partiality for a particular set of *somatic* (physical) characteristics which idealised tall, blue-eyed Nordic-type features.[41]

The dissonance between the definition of group identity in the Socialist Zionist belief system and the identity of the Oriental immigrants was further aggravated because of the issue of religious traditionalism. The Jewish identity of the Orientals included a strong religious component which earned them the name of the 'messianic immigration'. Shama and Iris, who drew up a typology of the Oriental newcomers, noted that traditional Judaism was prevalent at the individual-attitudinal level and institutionalised in the structure of the Oriental communities, where rabbis often served as sociopolitical leaders.[42] The secular and egalitarian Socialist Zionist culture also clashed with the social structure of the Oriental community, which was based on an extended traditional family and where woman and the young were subordinated to the patriarch.

There is some confusion about the extent to which the Oriental community retained its religious commitment. Early studies normally indicated that the process of secularisation among the Orientals was extremely fast. In a 1962 survey, 53 per cent of immigrants from North Africa and 44 per cent of immigrants from Asia claimed that they observed all the religious duties. The comparable number for the whole population was 33 per cent.[43] Intergenerational comparisons showed a decrease in Oriental religiosity. A 1974 study found that 56 per cent of Oriental students considered themselves less religious than their parents and only 7 per cent more religious; 37 per cent reported the same degree of religiosity.[44]

More sophisticated research design, however, revealed that the extent of religiosity among the Orientals might have been under-estimated, because of the Ashkenazi-Talmudic criteria which were used to measure the degree of orthodoxy. Deshen and other anthropologists urged the adoption of a separate category of Oriental religiosity. This can be roughly translated into the traditional category used in most surveys.[45] In fact, an ethnic analysis of the traditional category in voting surveys consistently reveals that most of the traditionalists are Oriental Jews. The traditionalists are less likely to score on behavioural aspects of observance, but are high in personal religious belief and support many theocratic concepts.

The serious subcultural differences between the group identity of the Orientals and the dominant Socialist Zionist belief system have apparently created an historical tension. Because of the paucity of empirical studies on the early stages of Oriental alienation, only a partial observation can be offered. The accounts of the 1950s by social psychologists, sociologists and anthropologists are divided. Some scholars found that the Oriental immigrants accepted and even internalised some of the values of the Socialist-Zionist group identity. For instance, Patai, who re-viewed the empirical data of the early 1950s, concluded that some Oriental groups, most notably the Yemenites, internalised the dominant values of the group identity.[46] Eisenstadt indicated that the predisposition to change among the new immigrants was linked to a number of psychological and situational charac-teristics.[47] The extensive research of Shuval demonstrated that there had been some strain in ethnic relations, but there was no evidence that the Orientals rejected the Western value system.[48]

Anthropologists who carried out detailed field observations in the 1950s found evidence of Oriental alienation. Zenner documented instances of ambivalence in the self-image among Oriental Jews, and Wilner described the difficulties in applying the Socialist Zionist ethos to the Oriental Jews in the development towns and co-operative agricultural settlements. She argued that kibbutz members and other Labour officials, who were assigned to key roles in immigration absorption, compounded the problem by lack of professional skills, insensitivity to the cultural and social structure of the Oriental community, and ideological zeal.[49] Des-hen admitted that part of the problem might have been perceptual. Even in cases where Mapai officials and kibbutz veterans showed good intentions, the Oriental immigrant perceived them as paternalistic and snobbish.[50] Spiro, however, found that there was active hostility on the part of kibbutz members towards their Oriental neighbours.[51]

The difficulties which the first generation of Orientals faced in transvaluating their identity have created a second-generation problem of ethnic alienation. Alienation is defined as the affective distance between an individual and other members of his society.[52] The most important indicator of such alienation is the continuous salience of ethnic divisions in the polity.

Common observations and empirical evidence overwhelmingly indicate that the ethnic division has not disappeared among the Israeli-born offspring of immigrants. Because of the asymmetrical self-perception of the two groups, this alienation is felt more by Orientals than by the Ashkenazim. A number of studies in the 1960s demonstrated that Ashkenazi respondents evaluated the Ashkenazi group more positively than the Oriental community. The Orientals, on the other hand, tended to evaluate their own group less positively than they evaluated the Ashkenazim.[53] This asymmetrical relationship is also revealed in visual evaluation of ethnic stereotypes. Rim's 1968 survey and his and Aloni's research of 1969 found that both Ashkenazi and Oriental respondents attributed more positive characteristics to pictures of Ashkenazi-looking Israelis.[54] Yinon, Avnad and Heirar, who replicated this study in the early 1970s, found similar results.[55]

Ethnic alienation has not meant the automatic rejection of the symbols of the state. Ben-Sira, who studied the pattern of Oriental integration in the 1980s, demonstrated that Oriental Jews have been identified, albeit to a lesser extent than the Ashkenazim, with the State of Israel. He argued that this pattern can be defined as *alienated identification*. In a representative sample of the Jewish population in Israel, 50 per cent of North African Jews were classified as alienated identifiers, followed by 46 per cent of Asian-origin Jews and 34 per cent of Jews of Balkan descent. Significantly, there were 34 per cent of alienated identifiers among the second generation of Israelis.[56]

The phenomenon of alienated identification is helpful in illustrating the precise psychological mechanism which delegitimised the group identity inherent in Socialist Zionism. Since Western and Ashkenazi values were intimately associated with the dominant ideology, Oriental alienated identifiers could vent their frustration against Labour, without undermining their commitment to the state. This assumption is supported by the finding that education, which is associated with a more Westernised and modernised identity, tends to decrease alienation. In the Ben-Sira sample, 54 per cent of Orientals in the lower educational bracket were classified as alienated identifiers, compared to 39 per cent with high school education. It is known that support for the Labour Alignment among the Orientals increases with the level of education.

The dissonance created by the definition of group identity was compounded by the dissatisfaction of Orientals with what we defined as the rules of distributive justice. The two major dimensions of distributive justice are symbolic-political rewards and material remuneration. Discussion of the political dimension is especially complicated in an immigrant society. Normally, in immigrant democracies, there exists what Caspi has called 'timelagged political absorption'. There is no expectation that the demographic composition of the population will be immediately mirrored in political representation.[57] In the American, Canadian, and Australian model, lengthy periods have been allowed to pass before immigrant cohorts have penetrated the political system. However, because of the strong egalitarian ethos of Socialist Zionism, the immigrants were enfranchised upon arrival, and expectations of 'mirror image' political representation were created in the evolving political culture.

In practice, the representation of Orientals in the executive and parliamentary bodies of Mapai was time-lagged. Smooha found that, in the 1950s, the number of Orientals did not exceed an average of 10.4 per cent in the party's bureau, 10.7 per cent in the secretariat, and 11.4 per cent in the Central Committee. In the 1960s the comparable numbers were 11.8 per cent, 15 per cent, and 23.1 per cent respectively. In the early 1970s the average Oriental representation stood at 8.2 per cent in the bureau, 11.8 per cent in the political committee, 17.3 per cent in the secretariat, and 27.4 per cent of the Central Committee.[58]

The representation of the Orientals in *Herut* was higher. In the 1950s they constituted on average 17.5 per cent of the executive committee and 11.1 per cent in the Central Committee. In the 1960s, these numbers went up to 22.7 per cent and 20.2 per cent respectively. In the early 1970s the Oriental representation stood at an average of 13.6 per cent of the executive committee and 27.4 per cent of the Central Committee.[59]

In order to cope with the disparity between the official ideology and its recruitment practice, Mapai resorted to 'symbolic' or 'pseudo' representation. Czudnowski defined this pattern as recruitment of members of a specific demographic group who were picked by the party in order to gain the support of the group, although such candidates were not designated by the group. Eighty per cent, or 12 out of the 15 Knesset members of Oriental origin in this period, were 'pseudo-representatives', mostly in Mapai.[59] Goldberg and Hoffman, who reviewed the nominating procedures in the parties before the 1981 election, found that most of the Orientals nominated by the Labour Alignment for the Knesset were still 'pseudo-representatives'. On the other hand, the Oriental candidates in the Likud were perceived as truly representative of the community.[60]

There is no empirical evidence to assess the impact of 'pseudo-representation' on the delegitimisation. of Socialist Zionism. Academic accounts and popular observation give the impression that the dissonance between the fundamental and the operative levels in the Labour belief system was harmful to the party's credibility among Oriental immigrants. Some of the anthropological accounts cited earlier in this chapter demonstrate that these 'pseudo-representatives' in Mapai were not popular in the Oriental community. Lissak and Horowitz pointed out that Herut, which attracted a larger proportion of Oriental members to its pre-independence *Irgun* and *Lehi* underground movements, had always been perceived as more genuinely representative of the community.[61]

Even more serious discord was created by what the Orientals perceived as lack of distributive justice in material remuneration. The first case invalidating the egalitarian claims of Socialist Zionism involved the immigration of Yemenite Jews in the early 1900s. The Jews from Yemen were brought to Palestine by *Poalei Zion*, the predecessor of Mapai, in order to compete with cheap Arab labour. The Yemenite Jews received lower wages and land allotments than their Ashkenazi counterparts. These discriminatory practices provoked a bitter debate in the Socialist Zionist camp and were criticised by Ben-Gurion personally. The immigration of Yemenite Jews was stopped shortly afterwards, in preference for European Jews, and was completed only after 1948.[62]

Virtually ignored by Israeli historiography, the case of the early

Yemenite immigration has become widely publicised only in the
1980s. The claim that the Yemenites or, indeed, all Oriental Jews
were brought to Israel by the Ashkenazi Labour establishment in
order to supply unskilled workers has become a stock argument in
the Oriental protest movement.[63] The influx of mass immigration
from North Africa and Asia increased the demands on egalitarian
ideology. The Oriental immigrants faced a number of handicaps in
the process of absorption. They had few of the occupational skills
which were required in a modernising economy. No initial
statistics are available, but the general impression is that the
Orientals were concentrated on the lower rungs of the educational
and professional hierarchy. Oriental families were typically much
larger than the average Ashkenazi family, putting a special strain
on family income.

The arrival of the immigrants, which coincided with major expenditures on security and the need to restructure the economy,
imposed a heavy burden on the absorptive capacity of the country.
Inflation, budget deficits and food shortages forced the government to impose an austerity programme in the 1949–52 period.
In 1952, it was replaced by the New Economic Policy, which
sought to curb inflation and improve the balance of payments
through a freeze on wages and compulsory development loans.

According to the official view, these constraints necessitated a
uniform absorption policy with regard to all immigrants. Lissak,
who conducted the earliest research on occupational mobility in
Israel, showed that in 1954 there was little differentiation in the
employment patterns of the Ashkenazi and Oriental immigrants.
The bulk of the Asian-African newcomers, 42.5 per cent, were
employed in the construction industry and trade, compared to 42.2
per cent of Ashkenazi immigrants. Agriculture claimed 27.4 per
cent of Oriental employees versus 20.7 per cent of Ashkenazim.
The biggest difference was registered in the professions and the
bureaucracy (9.7 vs. 21.9 per cent) but business and services were
roughly equal (7.1 and 11.8 per cent of Orientals as opposed to
11.4 and 10.0 per cent of Ashkenazim). The major occupational
disparities were between the newcomers and the veteran
Ashkenazim, who dominated the bureaucracy and the liberal professions.

Lissak's statistics demonstrated that the gap between the immigrants had grown considerably in the mid-1960s. In 1965, the
percentage of Orientals employed in agriculture and the con-

struction industry was 20.9 per cent and 45.1 per cent respectively. The comparable numbers for Ashkenazi employees went down to 7.3 per cent and 34.8 per cent. In the liberal professions and the bureaucracy, there were 14.7 per cent of Orientals and 31.5 per cent of Ashkenazim. The ethnic breakdown in business and services was 5.8 per cent and 16.1 per cent Oriental and 10.8 per cent and 12.4 per cent Ashkenazi.[64] At that time, it was already clear that the coalescence between ethnic and social stratification had a significance which went beyond the market-place. Known in popular sociology as the 'Two Israels', it implied that Israeli society was divided into two ethnocultural blocs, the Westerners and the Easterners.[65]

Subsequent research indicates that the Oriental-Ashkenazi cleavage has been exacerbated in the native-born second generation. In his excellent study on integration, Smooha compiled a detailed account of the socio-economic gaps in the 1970s. He found that, compared to the Ashkenazim, the Orientals were disadvantaged in occupational status at a ratio of 1:2. The greatest disparities were registered in scientific and academic occupations.[66]

This trend has continued into the 1980s. A 1983 statistic reveals that 42.1 per cent of foreign-born and 42.4 per cent of Israeli-born Orientals are blue-collar workers. Only 11.8 per cent and 12.5 per cent are classified in scientific and academic occupations. The clerical and commercial sector employs 41.2 per cent of the foreign-born and 41.0 per cent of Israeli-born Orientals. Among the Ashkenazim, 25.5 per cent of foreign-born and 17.4 per cent of Israeli-born have blue-collar occupations, as opposed to 32.4 per cent and 42.0 per cent who are in the scientific, academic, and managerial professions. 36.7 per cent of foreign-born and 33.3 per cent of Israeli-born Ashkenazim were in clerical and service professions.[67]

This occupational distribution has been underpinned by the disparities in the educational process. According to various estimates, only 18 per cent of Orientals are among the number of students who matriculate from high school. The proportion of Oriental students in institutions of higher education reaches some 18 per cent, although their share in the entire age cohort amounts to 60 per cent. The gap in the second generation is particularly large. In 1980, only 2.5 per cent of Israeli-born Orientals had a college education, compared to 16.6 per cent of native-born Ashkenazim.[68]

Educational failure has spilled over to other prestigious fields of endeavour, including the military. There are no official statistics but some private estimates in the late 1970s and 1980s show this disparity. Orientals constituted only 30 per cent of cadets, in spite of the fact that their cohort at the conscript level reached 60 per cent. In 1980, there were 3 per cent of Oriental officers at the rank of lieutenant-colonel and above.[69]

It is beyond the scope of this study to review the enormous literature that has tried to explain the persistence of the socio-ethnic gaps between the Ashkenazi and Oriental communities. Broadly speaking, some studies emphasised the personal-motivational factors, whereas others dwelt on structural-institutional variables. Shuval found the Oriental immigrants lacking in motivation, future-orientation, and other attitudinal prerequisites of success in a modernised economy.[70] Motivational and value variables are often invoked to explain the educational failure of Oriental students.[71]

Another type of explanation focuses on the disparity between the status ranking and the power basis of the Orientals. Kimmerling pointed out that, not unlike some Italians in the United States, some strata among the Oriental immigrants accumulated capital in illegal ways or in ways which society considered illegitimate.[72] Converting such material acquisitions into socio-economic status and political power is inherently difficult.

Still another avenue of research used both perceptual and socio-economic variables in forming some sophisticated explanatory hypotheses. Utilising the expectation-state theory, Yuchtman-Yaar and Semyonov demonstrated that subtle and often subconscious processes of discrimination combined with more objective factors to inhibit Oriental achievement in the Ashkenazi-dominated society.[73] Fishelson and his colleagues, among others, found that income differentials have increased among the Israeli-born generation of the two ethnic groups and that some 20 per cent of these differentials cannot be explained in terms of any measurable attributes of the groups.[74] The methodological debate as to whether this lower income is attributable to indirect discrimination has left the sociologists and economists divided.

The more recent revisionist school of sociology in Israel has argued that the persistent socio-ethnic stratification was created by deliberate economic exploitation of the newly arrived Oriental immigrants. Swirsky and Bernstein, who re-examined some of the early records on immigration absorption, found that Oriental newcomers served primarily as an unskilled and low-paid pool in a labour-intensive economy. This economy was dominated by a number of privileged centres, most notably the kibbutz and the Histadrut.

The *maabarot* (transit camps) and the development towns, where Oriental immigrants predominated, provided a source of cheap labour for the kibbutzim. Moreover, the kibbutzim received a disproportionately high share of land, water, and other capital investment resources compared to the Oriental settlements in their localities. The Oriental immigrants also benefited the Histadrut enterprises, especially the construction company *Selel Boneh*, and citrus production. Revisionist sociologists do not accept the argument that low wages were essential because of the difficulty of creating jobs for mass immigration.[75]

Objectively, all these interpretations constitute partial explanations of the consolidation of socio-ethnic stratification in Israel. Yet the subjective perception of the Oriental group has been predominantly focused on the discrimination perspective. The dissonance created over the definition of collective identity, coupled with what was seen as a serious deviation from the egalitarian notion of distributive justice of the Labour ideology, has prompted the Orientals to adopt the rival New Zionist belief system. The behavioural outcome of the delegitimisation of Socialist Zionism demonstrated itself in an increased Oriental vote for Herut.

In the absence of early opinion polls, it is difficult to analyse the pattern of Oriental voting behaviour. Using an ecological analysis of voting, Matra found that already in the early 1950s there was a positive correlation between the vote for Herut and Oriental concentrations in urban and rural settlements.[76] Lissak calculated that between the second and sixth Knesset (1951–1965), the average vote for Herut in immigrant towns went up from 4.9 per cent to 22.7 per cent, and in development towns it increased from 9.3 per cent to 17.0 per cent. Mapai's average vote in immigrant towns went down from 45.9 per cent to 34.4 per cent, and in development towns it decreased from 45.2 per cent to 35.9 per cent.[77] Immigrant and development towns have large Oriental populations.

Arian, a leading authority on voting behaviour in Israel, has conducted electoral surveys since 1969. He found that, between

1963 and 1981, the share of the Labour Alignment's portion of the Oriental vote given to the two large parties shrank considerably — from 79 per cent to 35 per cent among foreign-born Orientals and from 77 per cent to 27 per cent among native-born Orientals. The support for the Labour Alignment in the second generation of Israeli-born voters, who are designated as ethnically neutral, declined from 70 per cent to 43 per cent in this period.[78]

Etzioni-Halevy, in her study of political culture in Israel, provides some of the most interesting evidence on the extent to which the Orientals have delegitimised the Socialist Zionist distributive justice beliefs. In a 1973 survey, the lower-class Oriental respondents tended to associate *rightism* with a concern for social equality. The better-educated Westerners held an opposite association; they argued that leftism was more concerned with eradicating inequality. Acknowledging that such an association goes against conventional political wisdom, Etzioni-Halevy inferred that the less-favoured Oriental groups, who were affected by these inequalities, turned to the right in order to protest their own disadvantage. The better-off Westerners turn to the left to protest in the abstract the inequalities of others.[79] In other words, Orientals turned to the right-wing Herut because of the discrepancy between official ideology and official policies. Arian and Shamir pointed out that right-left labelling in political communication in Israel has often served to denote the popular legitimacy of a party.[80]

Finally, Ben-Sira devoted several studies to the different perceptions of distributive justice among Easterners and Westerners in Israel. A number of his findings are relevant to our concerns. First, there is a considerable ethnic difference in the validity claims which underlie the legitimisation of distributive justice. Oriental Jews tend to legitimise, though not necessarily consciously, ascriptive and particularist criteria, that is, they demand affirmative action rewards. Western Jews, on the other hand, are more likely to legitimise achievement-oriented and meritorious criteria. However, socio-economic mobility in Israel is based on achievement-oriented criteria, such as education and formal skills, in which Oriental Jews tend to do less well than the Ashkenazim. Thus, Easterners tend to accuse the Western group of deliberately distorting the rules of distributive justice.[81]

Second, the Oriental Jews tend to blame Socialist Zionism for creating the socio-ethnic gap. Twenty-two per cent of the Israeli-born Orientals and 17 per cent of the foreign-born generation agreed with the statement that 'kibbutz members are millionaires who exploit the Orientals as a source of cheap labour'. Thirty-three per cent and 28 per cent respectively agreed with the statement that the labour movement caused the socio-ethnic gap because it wanted to create a relationship of dependence. The statement 'absorption of immigration created the socio-ethnic gap' received the support of 56 per cent of foreign-born and 43 per cent of Israeli-born Orientals. The first two items have a .41 and .47 correlation with the overall score of Oriental alienation.[82]

Third, welfare and affirmative types of action serve only to increase the perception of distortions in distributive justice among the Easterners. Ben-Sira related this non-obvious result to the fact that individuals tend to associate this type of remuneration with an external locus of control in their lives and dependence on the dominant group. This conclusion is supported by a number of studies which found that Orientals who benefited from affirmative action in education and other fields have become even more critical of what they perceive as the Ashkenazi-dominated rules of the system. Moreover, Ben-Sira found that even those who cope successfully are overriden by the 'shadow of the cleavage', namely, the belief 'that they could do much better were it not for the distortion of the rules of distributive justice'.[83]

The perceptual characteristics of the socio-ethnic cleavage in Israel have some long-term partisan implications. The historical association of the Labour movement with ethnic grievances has made Likud more attractive to those Orientals who tend to blame the Ashkenazim for the gap. The continuous perception of the cleavage has increased the support of second-generation Orientals for Likud, even among those individuals who are objectively successful. If, as Ben-Sira's research seems to indicate, the Orientals continue to accuse the Ashkenazim of blocking their avenues of mobility, the New Zionism of Likud may prove continuously popular among this ethnic group. The delegitimisation of Socialist Zionism and the contingent change in voting behaviour has had a crucial impact on the party system in Israel.

Decline of Socialist Zionism and the Change of the Party System in Israel

Although the empirical evidence which we reviewed indicates that, from the early days of the State, there had been a consider-

Table 4.2: Distribution of Knesset Seats 1944–84 (%)

Party	1st Knesset 1949	2nd Knesset 1951	3rd Knesset 1955	4th Knesset 1959	5th Knesset 1961
(1) Communists					
Maki	3.3	4.2	5.0	2.5	4.2
Hadash (Rakah)					
(2) Labour parties					
Mapam	15.8	12.5	7.5	7.5	7.5
Achdut Ha'avoda			8.3	5.8	6.6
Rafi					
Mapai (Labour)[a]	38.3	37.5	33.3	39.2	35.0
Labour Alignment[b]					
(3) Centre parties					
Progressives (Independent Liberals)	4.2	3.3	4.2	5.0	
General Zionists (Liberals)	5.8	16.7	10.8	6.6	14.2
Shinui (Movement for Change)					
Ratz (Movement for Citizen's Rights and Peace)					
Yahaad					
(4) Right-wing parties					
Herut	11.7	6.7	12.5	14.2	14.2
Gahal					
Likud					
Tehiya					
Kach					
(5) Religious parties					
Torah Religious Front	13.4				
Agudat Israel		2.5	5.5	5.0	3.3
Poalei Agudat Israel		1.7			1.7
National Religious Party		8.2	9.2	10.0	10.0
Matzad					
Morasha					
Shas (Sephardi Torah Guardians)					3.3
(6) Others	7.5	6.7	3.7	4.7	3.3
(Minorities and Ethnic Lists)					

	6th Knesset 1965	7th Knesset 1969	8th Knesset 1973	9th Knesset 1977	10th Knesset 1981	11th Knesset 1984
(1) Communists						
Maki	1.1	0.8	0.8			
Rakah (Hadash)	2.5	2.5	3.3	4.6	3.3	3.3
The Progressive List for Peace						1.6

	(1)	(2)	(3)	(4)	(5)	(6)
(2) Labour parties						
Mapam	6.7					
Achdut Ha'avoda						
Rafi	8.3					
Mapai (Labour)	37.5					
Labour Alignment		46.7	42.5	24.6	39.1	36.6
(3) Centre parties						
Progressives (Independent Liberals)	4.2	3.3	3.3	1.2		
General Zionists (Liberals)						
Shinui (Movement for Change)				11.6	1.6	3.3
Ratz (Movement for Citizen's Rights and Peace)			2.5	1.2	0.8	3.3
State List	3.3	3.3				
Free Centre	1.7	1.7				
Democratic Movement for Change				11.6		
Telem					1.6	
Yahaad						2.5
Ometz						0.8
(4) Right-wing parties						
Herut	21.3					
Gahal[c]		21.7				
Likud[d]			32.3	33.4	40.0	34.1
Tehiya-Tzomet					2.5	4.1
Kach						0.8
(5) Religious parties						
Torah Religious Front						
Agudat Israel	3.3	3.3	4.2	3.4	3.3	1.6
Poalei Agudat Israel	1.8	1.8		1.4		
National Religious Party	9.2	10.0	8.3	9.2	5.0	3.3
Matzad					0.8	
Morasha						1.6
Shas (Sephardi Torah Guardians)						3.3
(6) Ethnic parties						
Tami					2.5	0.8
Others	3.3	3.3				

Notes: (a) Labour is a merger of Mapai, Rafi and Achdut Ha'avoda. (b) Labour Alignment is a parliamentary bloc of Labour and Mapam. (c) Gahal is a parliamentary bloc of Herut and Liberal parties. (d) Likud is a parliamentary bloc of Herut, the Liberal Party and other small factions. Following the creation of the National Unity Government in 1984, the 6-member Mapam party left the Labour Alignment and one Labour MP defected to Ratz. Labour's strength is 30.6 per cent.

Source: O. Seliktar, 'Israel: Fragile Coalitions in a New Nation' in E.C. Browne and J. Dreijmanis (eds), *Government Coalitions in Western Democracies*, (Longman, New York and London, 1982), p. 286 and *The New York Times*, 1 August 1984.

able discrepancy between popular sentiments and the Socialist Zionist ideology, the spreading public delegitimisation of Socialist Zionism had still not led to an immediate change in voting behaviour. Writing in the 1950s and 1960s, observers have often commented on the remarkable stability of the political system. In spite of the tremendous socio-economic, cultural and demographic changes, the Labour camp retained its dominance of the party system for nearly three decades. Table 4.2 illustrates that only in the early 1970s did Labour decline in power, paving the way for the 1977 electoral victory of Likud.

There are a number of hypotheses which can explain the delayed effect of delegitimisation on voting behaviour. One is that Mapai was identified with independence and nation-building and thus symbolised the national elements in the collective identity system. The charismatic style of Ben-Gurion's political mobilisation, which appealed to the more effective elements in an individual's value system, enhanced this symbolism. Comparative electoral research indicates that it is not uncommon for a person to cast his vote for a party because of affective considerations. Such a pattern of partisan preference is more likely to occur among the lower strata of a society.

Surveys of voting behaviour are normally not designed to reveal whether an individual casts his vote because of cognitive or affective considerations. The amount of 'split ticket' voting, that is, individuals who vote for one party at the national level and for a different party at the local level, can be used as an indirect measure. An analysis of partisan preference in the 1965 and 1969 elections found that more Easterners than Westerners tended to split their vote. The prevalent pattern among the Easterners — a vote for Mapai at the national level and a different choice at the local level — is apparently indicative of their cognitive-affective dissonance.[84]

An additional explanation is that the dominant Mapai party secured voting allegiance through an extensive network of patronage. The large amount of literature on patronage politics in Israel demonstrates that the actual and perceived economic dependence on the government had created a vast 'clientele' vote for the dominant party. Such a way of soliciting support was directed in particular towards the mostly Oriental new immigrants who settled in the development towns and agricultural co-operatives. Studies which probed the impact of patronage on voting revealed the advantages enjoyed by the incumbent Mapai.[85]

Yet, as Rosenblum and Richardson indicated in their model of *expedient* political socialisation, clientelism can produce very narrow and highly functional support for a party.[86] When patronage politics started to decline in the 1960s, such super-ficially-inducted Mapai partisans increasingly abandoned the party. Because of their perfunctory commitments, 'client' parents are especially ineffective in transferring partisan loyalties to their children. A 1974 survey by the present author demonstrated that children of 'client' Mapai voters displayed a higher rate of support for Likud than their peers in 'non-client' Mapai families.The 'de-fection rate' of the younger Oriental voters from development towns to Likud was exceptionally high.[87]

It is also possible that some of the early observations about the stability of the support for Mapai were misleadingly derived from aggregate election results. Since the increase of the electorate in the 1950s and early 1960s was due mainly to the influx of new immigrants rather than to natural growth, the dominant Mapai could sustain electoral support by mobilising the new arrivals. Also, in multi-party systems there are numerous ways in which voters can move between any pair of elections without necessarily upsetting the general parliamentary basis. Analysis of electoral behaviour in the 1960s found a considerable floating vote among the electorate. The first academic research of electorate behaviour by Arian in 1969 cast further doubt on the extent of successful intergenerational transference of Labour partisanship. A major conclusion of this and his subsequent studies of voting behaviour is that the younger generation has tended disproportionately to support Likud.

Research on voting behaviour in Israel demonstrates that the two largest parties have become increasingly homogeneous in ethnic terms. The Ashkenazi character of Labour and the Oriental coloration of Likud was already evident by 1973. Oriental support gave Likud its electoral victory in 1977. In the 1981 elec-tion, the ethnic consolidation of the two large parties was almost complete and symmetrical; some 70 per cent of the Labour vote was Ashkenazi and about 70 per cent of Likud supporters were Orientals.[88] According to Sarah Shemer, who conducted the opinion polls for Likud, the same ethnic breakdown obtained in the 1984 elections.[89]

There is consensus that the 1977 elections were a realignment in the systemic sense, that is, they marked the transference of the party system from a dominant to a competitive one. There has been less clarity as to how permanent the new socio-ethnic basis of the partisan realignment is. A major reason for the confusion stems from the fact that the Oriental 'defection' from the Labour Alignment has been normally described as a protest vote.

A perusal of the literature on electoral behaviour reveals that there is a certain ambiguity in defining a protest vote. One interpretation views the protest vote as a variant of strategic voting. In such a case, an individual would vote for one party in order to block another party from coming to power. This type of partisan preference is basically negative, in the sense that the voter has not formed a positive identification with the new party of his choice. Undoubtedly, among the 60 per cent of the voters who left the Labour Alignment between the 1973 and 1977 elections, there was a considerable protest vote. The Democratic Movement of Change which took 18 per cent of the Labour vote in 1977 is a case in point. Predictably, the DMC did not manage to establish itself in the subsequent elections.[90]

It is much more difficult to apply the concept of a protest vote to the partisan preference of the Oriental and younger cohorts of the Israeli electorate. Protest voting implies that this phenomenon is somewhat temporary, and that it constitutes a certain 'aberration' of the socio-economic rationale in partisan choice. Early popular and academic discussions of the voting pattern of Oriental Jews have normally echoed the theme of 'abberation'. Goldberg was entirely representative of this view when he claimed that this vote reflected a protest 'rather than a considered critique of the ruling Labour Party's policies, or agreement with the social and economic platform of Herut'.[91]

Other observers assumed that the Oriental preference was basically an anti-establishment vote which would dissipate itself after Likud's tenure in power. Still others have pointed out that the political culture of the Oriental voters has made them particularly susceptible to Begin's populist methods of mobilisation, or that they were lured by the promise of the economic prosperity under Likud. These assumptions were largely undermined by the 1984 election which was conducted in Begin's absence and in an orderly manner. Although the Oriental voters fragmented their support between Likud, Tehiya, and the orthodox *Shas* party, they did not return to the Labour Alignment.

The voting pattern which began in the 1973–7 period lends

credence to the assumption that the Oriental Israelis, rather than 'protesting' against Labour, have become positively identified with Likud. New Zionism, with its vague anti-Western appeal and positive emphasis on traditional and authentic values, has been more consonant with the Oriental concept of the collective Israeli identity. The group identity inherent in New Zionism is half-way between the Western secular and civic definition of Socialist Zionism and the notion of a totally separate Oriental ethnic identity. The persistent failure of the ethnic parties supports the assumption that the Orientals, who share all the core-culture elements with the Ashkenazim, have rejected ethnic separatism in their group definition.

The New Zionism belief system is also closer to the Oriental perception of distributive justice. Two important dimensions underlie this perception. First, as the preceding chapter indicated, the socio-economic parts of the Revisionist creed were a mixture of a *laissez faire* economy and populist welfare principles. This creed was inherited by Herut and partially implemented after Likud came to power. Likud's management of the economy led to a 400 per cent annual inflation rate and an external debt of more than $20 billion by 1984. Political and academic observers alike have extensively criticised the Likud coalition for jeopardising the economy in order to maximise its electoral support.

Yet the considerable literature on the sociology of inflation demonstrates that countries like Israel, which suffer from 'Latin inflation', i.e. up to 1,000 per cent annually, have been going through a comprehensive change in distributive justice. Like contemporary Latin America and France in the 1920s, this process entails a major redistributive effort on behalf of the lower social stratum without affecting the resources of the middle and upper classes.[92] In Israel, the closing of the distributive gap between the Ashkenazi population and the Oriental supporters of Likud was accomplished through a combination of welfare legislation and manipulation of subsidies. Although the socio-economic cleavage did not diminish, the Likud tenure has created a more equitable standard of living in the entire population.

The second dimension derives from the structure of social mobility in Israel. In fully crystallised societies, education, income, and occupation are highly related in the status attainment process. Nachmias, who studies the patterns of social mobility in Israel, found that, in the 1970s, Israel had only a moderately crystallised status attainment system. A major implication of her research was that, in such systems, models of social mobility are so complex that they require analysis of the antecedents for the attainment of each status component.[93]

In a pioneering research effort, Yuchtman-Yaar argues that the normal practice of unidimensional comparison between the occupational status or earnings of the Ashkenazim and the Orientals may obscure alternative models of status attainment. He demonstrates that the social mobility of Oriental Jews tends to by-pass schooling by channelling the incumbents into occupations which generate relatively high income, without the requirement for formal education or skills. As salaried employees, Orientals are underrepresented in the managerial category and overrepresented in the workers' stratum. In the self-employed, small entrepreneurial sector, though, Orientals are overrepresented as compared to the Ashkenazi group.

Yuchtman-Yaar concludes that this pattern of social mobility may have an important impact on ethnic relations in Israel. Since the Orientals tend to congregate in the less prestigious small-business sector rather than to penetrate the educational-professional hierarchy, they may be negatively disposed towards the value system of the better-educated Ashkenazim.[94] Politically, the combination of the traditional lifestyle of the Orientals and their tendency to enterpreneurship may alienate them from Socialists and Zionists and impel them into a long-term support for New Zionism.

So far, we have discussed the delegitimisation of Socialist Zionism in terms of group identity and distributive justice. However, observers are almost unanimous in pointing out that the foreign policy debate in Israel has come to dominate the political cleavage in the country. In the next chapter, we shall turn to the analysis of the Israeli foreign policy dilemma created by the Six-Day War and its contribution to the delegitimisation of the Labour ideology.

Notes

1. R. K. Merton, *Social Theory and Social Structure: Towards the Codification of Theory and Research* (Free Press, Glencoe, IL, 1949), p. 43.

2. S. N. Eisenstadt, 'Change and Continuity in Israeli Society. II Dynamic Conservatism vs. Innovation', *The Jerusalem Quarterly*, no. 2 (1977), pp. 3–11.

3. M. Derber, 'Israel's Wage Differential: A Persisting Problem' in S. N. Eisenstadt, R. Bar-Yosef and C. Adler (eds), *Integration and Development in Israel* (Praeger and Pall Mall, New York and London, 1970), pp. 185–201.

4. Calculated on the basis of Table 34 in S. N. Eisenstadt, *Israeli Society* (Weidenfeld and Nicolson, London, 1967), p. 193.

5. U. Leviatan, 'The Attitudes of the Jewish Public Towards the Kibbutz Movement and the Possibility of Living in a Kibbutz', *Megamot*, vol. 26, no. 2 (1980), pp. 232–7 (Hebrew).

6. A 1969 survey showed that 77 per cent of Histadrut members voted for Labour as opposed to 40.6 per cent of non-members. A. Arian, *The Choosing People*, (Massada, Ramat-Gan, 1973), pp. 54–5 (Hebrew). A Tree Analysis of the 1969 survey demonstrated that *Histadrut* membership explained 5.3 per cent of the variance in voting. The next variable of observance explained only 2.2 per cent of the variance. O. Seliktar, 'Israel: Electoral Cleavages in a Nation in the Making' in R. Rose (ed.), *Electoral Participation: A Comparative Analysis* (Sage Publications, Beverly Hills and London, 1980), p. 231.

7. A. Arian, *Ideological Change in Israel* (Case Western Reserve University Press, Cleveland, OH, 1968), especially pp. 23–57.

8. E. Etzioni-Halevy with R. Shapiro, *Political Culture in Israel; Cleavage and Integration Among Israeli Jews* (Praeger, New York and London, 1977), pp. 64–6.

9. C. Liebman, 'The Development of Neo-Traditionalism Among the Orthodox Jews in Israel', *Megamot*, vol. 27, no. 3 (1982), pp. 231–51.

10. S. A. Deshen, 'Israeli Judaism: Introduction to the Major Patterns', *International Journal of Middle East Studies*, vol. 9, no. 2 (1978), pp. 141–69.

11. A. Antonovsky, 'Israeli Political-Social Attitudes,' *Amot*, vol. 1, no. 16 (1963), pp. 11–22, (Hebrew).

12. S. Smooha, *Israeli: Pluralism and Conflict*. (University of California Press, Berkely and Los Angeles, 1978), p. 82.

13. An interview in *Haaretz*, 3 March 1984.

14. Y. Ben-Meir and P. Kedem, 'A Measure of Religiosity for the Jewish Population in Israel', *Megamot*, vol. 24. no. 3 (1978), pp. 353–62, (Hebrew).

15. S. N. Herman, *Israelis and Jews: the Continuity of an Identity* (The Jewish Publication Society of America, Philadelphia, 1970), p. 57.

16. C. Zuckerman-Bareli, 'The Religious Factor and its Impact on Consensus and Polarity among Israeli Youth', *Megamot*, vol. 22, no. 1 (1975), pp. 62–80, (Hebrew).

17. *Ibid*, p. 67.

18. S. Dela Pergoia, 'Immigration, Emigration and other Demographic Problems' in A. Hareven, *On the Difficulty of Being an Israeli* (The Van Leer Foundation, Jerusalem, 1983), pp. 225–56, (Hebrew).

19. Hazon Ish ('Man of Vision'), Rabbi Abraham Yeshayahu Karelitz (1878–1953), was a great authority on Jewish Law. Related by A. Oz, *A Journey in Israel Autumn 1982*, (Am Oved Publishers, Tel Aviv, 1983), p. 19 (Hebrew).

20. Z. Adar, *Jewish Education in Israel and the United States*, (The School of Education and the Institute of Contemporary Jewry of the Hebrew University, Jerusalem, 1977), pp. 55–84.

21. For a concise treatment see N. L. Zucker, *The Coming Crisis in Israel: Private Faith and Public Policy*, (MIT Press, Cambridge, MA, 1973).

22. S. Levy and E. L. Guttman, *The Values and Attitudes of the Israeli Students*, vol. 2, (The Institute for Applied Research, Jerusalem, 1976), p. 185 (Hebrew).

23. Liebman, 'The Development', pp. 231–7.

24. S. Zelniker and M. Kahan, 'Religion and Nascent Cleavages: The Case of Israel's National Religious Party', *Comparative Politics*, vol. 9, no. 2 (1976), pp. 21–48.

25. Quoted in Zucker, *The Coming Crisis*, pp. 59, 236.

26. J. Aviad, 'From Protest to Return: Contemporary Teshuvah', *The Jerusalem Quarterly*, no. 16 (1980), pp. 71–86.

27. Zelniker and Kahan, 'Religion and Nascent Cleavages', p. 61.

28. N. Mendler, 'The Wild Outcrop of the Religious Education,' *Haaretz*, 8 August 1984.

29. R. Tockatli, 'Party Distances in Israel, 1969,' *Megamot*, vol. 20, no. 22 (1974), pp. 136–54, (Hebrew).

30. D. L. Horowitz, 'Ethnic Identity' in D. Glazer and D. P. Moynihan (eds), *Ethnicity Theory and Experience*. (Harvard University Press, Cambridge. MA, 1975), pp. 111–40.

31. Calculated on the basis of Tables 2 and 4 in Israel Pocket Library, *Immigration and Settlement* (Keter Books, Jerusalem, 1973), pp. 54, 64.

32. The Jewish Agency was apparently pivotal in demanding preference for Ashkenazi immigrants. According to the journalist Tom Segev, author of the book *1949 — The First Israelis*, records of the Jewish Agency meetings in 1949 indicate that secret funds were transferred to a special 'public committee' in order to absorb the immigrants from Poland. Ben-Gurion and Levi Eshkol objected to this decision but were defeated in a vote, *Haaretz*, 6 May 1984. Shaul Ben-Simchon documented that in 1952 Nahum Goldmann, then Chairman of the World Zionist Congress, asked Ben-Gurion to send back 100,000 Morrocan and Iraqi Jews, but this was turned down. *Haaretz*, 2 August 1983.

33. Quoted in S. Avigal, 'Morrocan Dybbuk?' *The Jerusalem Quarterly*, no. 2 (1981), pp. 48–54.

34. Summarised in S. Smooha, 'Ethnic Stratification and Allegiance in Israel: Where Do Oriental Jews Belong?', *Il Politico*, vol. 41, no. 4 (1975), pp. 635–57.

35. S. Smooha, 'Ashkenazi Hegemony,' *New Outlook*, July-August, 1981, pp. 17–21.

36. *Haaretz*, 3 February 1983. Another article revealed that 95 per cent of the soldiers who participate in the supplementary education programme of the IDF — Hinuch Daviol are Oriental recruits, *Haaretz*, 13 September, 1983.

37 M. M. Roumani, *The Contribution of the Army to National Integration in Israel*, (Foundation for the Study of Pluralistic Societies, the Hague, 1979), p. 39; 'An Effort to Advance and Integrate the Underprivileged Population in IDF and Israeli Society', unpublished report, n.d.

38. The emphasis on extensive transvaluation was derived from the then prevalent model of modernisation. Most of the leading Israeli sociologists, such as Shmuel Eisensdadt, Judith Shuval and Rivka Bar-Yosef, were associated with the modernisation approach. More recently, this model has been criticised by the revisionist sociologists for creating ethnic alienation. D. Bernstein, 'Immigrants and Society. A Critical View of the Dominant School of Israeli Sociology,' *British Journal of Sociology*, vol. 31, no. 1 (1980), pp. 246–64.

39. W. P. Zenner, 'Ambivalence and Self Image Among Oriental Jews in Israel', *Jewish Journal of Sociology*, vol. 5, no. 2 (1963), pp. 214–23. L. Gordon, 'Reflections on Inter- and Intragroup Relations in Israeli Society', *Jewish Social Studies*, vol. 36, no. 3–4 (1974), pp. 262–70.

40. A. Stahl, *The Cultural Integration in Israel* (Am Oved, Tel Aviv, 1976), (Hebrew).

41. G. P. Tamarin, *The Israeli Dilemma: Essays on a Warfare State*, (Rotterdam University Press, Rotterdam, 1973), p. 131; F. Zweig, *Israel: The Sword and the Harp*, (Fairleigh Dickinson University Press, Rutherford, NJ, 1969), p. 3; R. Patai, *Israel Between East and West* (Greenwood Publishing Corporation, Westport, CT, 1970), p. 177.

42. A. Shama and M. Iris, *Immigration Without Integration*, (Schenkman Publishing Company, Cambridge, MA, 1977), p. 43.

43. Antonovosky, 'Israeli Political-Social'.

44. S. Herman, U. Farago and Y. Harel, *Continuity and Change in the Jewish Identity of High School Youth in Israel 1965–1974*, (Eshkol Institute, Hebrew University, Jerusalem, 1976), (Hebrew).

45. Deshen, 'Israeli Judaism' and 'The Judaism of Middle Eastern Immigrants', *The Jerusalem Quarterly*, no. 13 (1979), pp. 48–109.

46. Patai, *Israel Between*, p. 109.

47. S. N. Eisenstadt, 'The Process of Absorption of New Immigrants in Israel', *Human Relations*, vol. 5, no. 2 (1952), pp. 223–46; 'Communication Process Among Immigrants in Israel', *Public Opinion Quarterly*, vol. 16, no. 1 (1952), pp. 42–58; 'The Place of Elites and Primary Groups in the Absorption of New Immigrants in Israel', *American Journal of Sociology*, vol. 57, no. 3 (1951), pp. 222–31.

48. J. T. Shuval, 'Patterns of Inter Group Tension and Affinity', *International Social Science Bulletin*, vol. 8, no. 1 (1956), pp. 75–103 and 'Emerging Patterns of Ethnic Strain in Israel,' *Social Forces*, vol. 40, no. 4 (1962), pp. 323–8.

49. Zenner, 'Ambivalence', pp. 214–23; D. Wilner, *Nation-Building and Community in Israel* (Princeton University Press, Princeton, NJ, 1969), pp. 130–9.

50. S. A. Deshen, *Immigrant Voters in Israel*, (Manchester University Press, Manchester, 1970), p. 18.

51. M. E. Spiro, 'The Sabras and Zionism: A Study in Personality and Ideology,' *Social Problems*, vol. 5, no. 2 (1957), pp. 100–10.

52. M. E. Olsen, 'Alienation and Political Opinion', *Public Opinion Quarterly*, vol. 29, no. 2 (1965), pp. 200–12.

53. For a thorough discussion see Y. Peres, *Ethnic Relations in Israel*, (Sifriat Hapoalim, Tel Aviv, 1977), pp. 83–97, (Hebrew). See also Y. Shwartzwald and Y. Yanon, 'Symmetry and Asymmetry in Ethnic Perceptions', *Megamot*, vol. 24, no. 1 (1978), pp. 45–52, (Hebrew).

54. Y. Rim, 'National Stereotypes in Children', *Megamot*, vol. 16, no. 1 (1968), pp. 45–51, (Hebrew); Y. Rim and R. Aloni, 'Stereotypes according to Ethnic Origin, Social Class and Sex', *Acta Psychologica*, vol. 31, no. 4 (1969), pp. 312–25.

55. Y. Yanon, A. Avnad and A. Heirar, 'Indirect Measurement of Ethnic Prejudice Among Young Western Israelis towards Oriental Jews,' *Megamot*, vol. 21, no. 3 (1975), pp. 314–23, (Hebrew).

56. Z. Ben-Sira, *The Jewish Society in Israel, Ethnic Relations* (The Israel Institute of Applied Social Research, Jerusalem, 1983), pp. 13, 15, (Hebrew).

57. D. Caspi, 'How Representative is the Knesset', *The Jerusalem Quarterly*, no. 14 (1980), pp. 68–81.

58. Calculated from Tables 61 and 65 in Smooha, *Israel*, p. 324, p. 329.

59. M. M. Czudnowski, 'Legislative Recruitment Under Proportional Representation in Israel: A Model and a Case Study' in M. Lissak and E. Gutmann (eds), *Political Institutions and Processes in Israel* (Akademon, Jerusalem, 1975), pp. 348–82.

60. G. Goldberg and S. A. Hoffmann, 'Nominations in Israel: The Politics of Institutionalization' in A. Arian (ed.), *The Elections in Israel — 1981* (Ramot Publishing Co, Tel Aviv, 1983), pp. 61–87.

61. D. Horowitz and M. Lissak, *The Origins of the Israeli Polity: The Political System of the Jewish Community in Palestine Under the Mandate*, (Am Oved, Tel Aviv, 1977), pp. 177–8, (Hebrew).

62. Y. Nini, 'Immigration and Assimilation: The Yemenite Jews', *The Jerusalem Quarterly*, no. 2 (1981), pp. 85–98.

63. For instance, see N. Menachem, *Ethnic Tension and Discrimination in Israel, Sociohistorical Perspective* (Rubin Publishing, Ramat Gan, 1983), pp. 105–7 (Hebrew); Oz, *A Journey*, p. 32.

64. M. Lissak, *Social Mobility in Israel Society*, (Israel University Press, Jerusalem, 1969), pp. 10–11.

65. A. Weingrod traced the appearance of this label to the 1959 Oriental riots in Wadi Salib, 'The Two Israels', *Commentary*, vol. 33, no. 4 (1962), pp. 313–19.
66. Smooha, *Israel* pp. 157–8.
67. Middle East Research Institute, *MERI Report: Israel*, (Croom Helm, London, 1985).
68. *Haaretz*, 23 May and *Maariv*, 2 November 1983.
69. Compiled on the basis of Y. Peri, *Between Battles and Ballots, Israeli Military in Politics* (Cambridge University Press, Cambridge, 1983) and I. Zamir, 'IDF Attacks the Educational Gap', *Al Hamishmar*, 1 January 1981.
70. J. Shuval, 'Value Orientations of Immigrants to Israel', *Sociometry*, vol. 26, no. 1 (1963), pp. 247–59.
71. For the application of motivational variables to education see A. Yogev and H. Ayalon, 'The Impact of Sex and Ethnic Origin on Expectations for Higher Education in Israel', *Megamot*, vol. 27, no. 4 (1982), pp. 349–69, (Hebrew).
72. B. Kimmerling, *Zionism and Economy* (Schenkman Publishing Company, Cambridge, MA, 1983), p. 110.
73. E. Yuchtman-Yaar and M. Semyonov, 'Ethnic Inequality in Israeli Schools and Sports — An Expectation State Approach', *American Journal of Sociology*, vol. 85, no. 3 (1979), pp. 576–90.
74. G. Fishelson, Y. Weiss and N. Mark, 'Ethnic Origin and Income Differentials Among Israeli Males, 1969–1976' in A. Arian (ed.), *Israel — A Developing Society* (Van Gorcum, Assen, 1980), pp. 253–77.
75. S. Swirski, *Orientals and Ashkenazim in Israel: the Ethnic Division of Labor* (Machbarot Le'mechkar u'Lebikoret, Haifa, 1981), pp. 1–73 (Hebrew); D. Bernstein, 'Immigrant Transit Camps — The Formation of Dependent Relations in Israeli Society', *Ethnic and Racial Studies*, vol. 4, no. 1 (1981), pp. 26–43.
76. J. Matras, *Social Change in Israel*, (Aldine, Chicago, 1965), p. 115.
77. Lissak, *Social Mobility*, p. 78.
78. M. Shamir and A. Arian, 'The Ethnic Vote in Israel's 1981 Elections', in Arian, *The Elections*, p. 96.
79. Etzioni-Halevy with R. Shapiro, *Political Culture*, p. 39.
80. A. Arian and M. Shamir, 'The Primary Political Function of the Left-Right Continuum', in Arian, *The Elections*, pp 259–79.
81. Z. Ben-Sira, *Interethnic Cleavage, Stress, Coping and Compensatory Mechanism* (The Israel Institute of Applied Social Research, Jerusalem, 1983), p. 30.
82. Ben-Sira, *The Jewish Society*, p. 64.
83. Ben-Sira, *Interethnic Cleavage*, p. 37.
84. O. Seliktar and L. E. Dutter, 'Israel as a Latent Plural Society' in W. C. McCready (ed.), *Culture, Ethnicity, and Identity*, (Academic Press, New York and London, 1983), pp. 301–26.
85. P. Burnstein, 'Social Network and Voting: Some Israeli Data', *Social Forces*, vol. 54, no. 4 (1976), pp. 833–47 and 'Political Patronage and Party Choice Among Israeli Voters', *The Journal of Politics*, vol. 38, no. 4 (1976), pp. 1024–32.
86. G. Rosenblum, *Immigrant Workers: Their Impact on American Labor Radicalism* (Basic Books, New York, 1970); B. M. Richardson, 'Party Loyalties and Party Saliency in Japan', *Comparative Political Studies*, vol. 8, no. 1 (1975), pp. 32–57.
87. O. Seliktar, 'Acquiring Preferences in a Plural Society: The Case of Israel', *Plural Societies*, vol. 11, no. 4 (1980), pp. 3–19.
88. Y. Peres and S. Shemer, 'The Ethnic Factor in Elections to the Tenth Knesset', in D. Caspi, A. Diskin and E. L. Gutmann (eds), *The Sources of Begin's Success*, (Croom Helm, London, 1984), pp. 89–112.
89. An interview in *Maariv*, 13 July 1984.
90. S. Levy and E. L. Gutmann, *Towards A Prediction of Election to the Next*

Knesset, (Israel Institute for Applied Social Research, Jerusalem, 1979), p. 8, (Hebrew).

91. H. Goldberg, 'Ethnic Groups in Israeli Society', *Ethnic Groups*, vol. 1, no. 3 (1977), pp. 163–86.

92. C. S. Maier, 'The Politics of Inflation in the Twentieth Century' in F. Hirsch and J. H. Goldthorpe (eds), *The Political Economy of Inflation*, (Martin Robertson, London, 1978), pp. 37–72.

93. C. Nachmias, 'The Status Attainment Process: A Test of a Model in Two Stratification Systems', *The Sociological Quarterly*, vol. 18, no. 4 (1977), pp. 589–607.

94. E. Yuchtman-Yaar, 'Differences in Ethnic Patterns of Socio-economic Achievement in Israel — A Neglected Aspect of Structured Inequality', *International Review of Modern Sociology*, forthcoming.

5 FOREIGN POLICY AND DELEGITIMISATION: SOCIALIST ZIONISM IN THE AFTERMATH OF THE SIX-DAY WAR

Socialist Zionist foreign policy enjoyed relatively broad support in the 1948–67 period. Although security was a central concern during this time, it involved considerations mostly at the strategic and tactical level. The public consensus which surrounded the foreign policy of Mapai had not been tested by the issue of territorial integrity, which plagued the Zionist movement in the Yishuv period.

The Six-Day War, in which Israel occupied substantial territories from three Arab states, created a growing dissonance between official ideology and public beliefs. As in the case of the internal delegitimisation, there were a number of interactive foreign policy processes which worked against Socialist Zionism. Perhaps the most important change focused on the transition from an *instrumental* to a *normative* perception of the occupied territories. This change was bolstered by a radicalisation of the image of the Arabs and Palestinians among the public in general, and, in particular, among the up and coming demographic groups, the religious and Oriental communities. Cumulatively, these developments led to the delegitimisation of Labour's foreign policy and the breakdown of the national consensus.

From Spatial to Temporal Zionism: The Emergence of Normative Approaches to the Occupied Territories

We have already argued that Zionism is more complex than many other ideologies of national independence. It evolved outside a territorial base, and aimed to mobilise the Jewish Diaspora which was geographically dispersed and divided in terms of religious orthodoxy. These initial conditions shaped the fundamental level of Zionist ideology, which emphasised the co-equality of its *temporal* and *spatial* dimensions. The temporal concept involved the perception of the State of Israel as the legitimate embodiment of the Jewish state. The spatial concept focused on the unity of

Jewish people across geographical boundaries. In operational terms, Zionism advocated *hitnahlut* (settlement), which was designed to secure the territorial base for the state, and *aliyah* (immigration), which underlined the concept of the ingathering of the exiles.

In defining the boundaries of the settlements, Socialist Zionism stirred a middle course between a number of imperatives: the historical concept of the Land of Israel, the demographic balance between Palestinians and Jews, and the perceived need of a territorial trade-off for peace with the Arab states. The temporal dimension in Zionism was used in order to legitimise the settlement drive and the subsequent foundation of a state, but the perception of boundaries remained uncrystallised. Gonen, who surveyed the various definitions of 'border' in the Yishuv period, found that the concept had no fixed meaning: there were 'security borders', 'historical borders', 'Biblical borders', and 'borders of destiny' (*gvulot he'ieud*).[1]

However, Socialist Zionism made it clear that the historical religious borders were politically not practical. During the War of Independence the Hagana tried to achieve a territorial continuity for Jewish settlement; it also seized relatively sparsely populated areas. It has already been indicated in Chapter 2 that the leadership of the Yishuv apparently did not try to occupy the densely populated West Bank region, given the perception of power disparity between Israel and the Arab states. The Green Line borders which were negotiated at the 1949 Armistice Agreement with the Arab states were accepted as a favourable outcome. Initially, the Israeli Government expected that these borders would be finalised in a peace treaty with the Arab states.

The subsequent influx of immigrants naturally shifted the focus from the temporal to the spatial dimension of the ingathering of the exiles. At the same time, the temporal dimension in continuity between the ancient Jewish state and Israel was relegated to the area of collective symbols. *Eretz Israel* (The Land of Israel) was perceived as an important geo-religious concept, which legitimised the state of Israel but did not overlap with its international boundaries. Because of the newly acquired sovereignty, the act of settlement which was formerly conceived temporally, i.e. redeeming Eretz Israel, was re-interpreted in spatial terms, i.e. creating an infrastructure for the absorption of the new immigrants. The act of settlement lost its pioneering status when, in the wake of the mass immigration, it was routinized and taken over by the new immigrants. In fact, settlement activity acquired a negative connotation because the new arrivals often refused to engage in agriculture, earning them the label of 'reluctant pioneers'.

During the nineteen years which preceded the Six-Day War, there was a seeming consensus about Labour's foreign policy. Even Herut, which objected to legitimising the border with Jordan, did not advocate a conquest of Arab territory. There is also substantial evidence to indicate that, in spite of dissatisfaction with the strategic quality of the 1949 boundaries, the Labour elite opposed major border changes through annexation. For instance, Ben-Gurion and Sharett voted down a plan by Moshe Dayan, the then Chief of Staff, to annex the Gaza Strip when it served as a base for terrorist attacks in the early 1950s.[2] On another occasion, Labour leaders sharply censured Ezer Weitzmann who, in his capacity as Chief of the Air Force, called for border rectification.[3] Israel also, under American pressure, returned the whole of the Sinai Peninsula, which it had occupied during the 1956 Suez campaign.

The outcome of the 1967 war which Israel did not anticipate was the activation of the temporal conception of Zionism. The occupation of some 26,000 square miles of territory, which included the Sinai Desert, the Golan Heights, and the West Bank, reopened the pre-independence debate on the desirable boundaries of the Jewish state. The territorial debate, which has dominated the legitimisation discussion in the society, has challenged the Labour vision of temporal Zionism. The underlying causes of the gradual delegitimisation of the Socialist Zionist belief system can be best analysed in terms of a perceptual shift from an *instrumental* to a *normative* attachment to the administered territories.

Using the approach of ecological sociologists like Toennis and Eliade, Kimmerling developed a typology of Zionist approaches to territory. At one end of the continuum was the instrumental approach, which considers a particular territorial tract as an economic resource or a strategic asset. At the opposite end of the continuum was the moral-religious orientation which perceived the territorial expanse to be the normative centre of the society.[4] The categories have not been mutually exclusive; different tracts were legitimised in terms of one or more categories, or redesignated to keep in tune with the changing belief system.

The circumstances surrounding the Six-Day War evoked both the instrumental and the normative salience of the territories. Cognitive psychology suggests that salience determinants — factors which increase or decrease the salience of one set of determinants relative to another — are related to regions in the perceptual field that are made vivid by major sociopolitical events. There is little doubt that the outcome of the war evoked the instrumental salience of the territories. At one level, the territories were perceived as a strategic asset; at another level they were considered useful in bargaining for peace. On the other hand, the normative-religious perception of the territories was evoked by the central role of the Land of Israel in the collective symbols of Zionism.[5] Numerous lay observers and academic studies have documented the depth of public feeling in Israel which was aroused by the renewed contact with East Jerusalem, Judea and Samaria. It is interesting that religious sentiments were spontaneously expressed by some of the staunchest secularists. Moshe Dayan's theme that 'we have returned to our people's holy places' was echoed by many in the Socialist camp, including the highly influential *Sdemot*, a literary magazine of the kibbutz movement.[6]

The initial policy of the National Unity Government reflected both instrumental and normative considerations. The government annexed East Jerusalem, but considered all other territories as a combined strategic-bargaining asset. In a meeting on 19 June 1967, the Cabinet decided that it would return the Golan Heights and the Sinai Desert, subject to demilitarisation, in exchange for a peace treaty with Syria and Egypt. This proposal was transmitted to the Arab states through the US State Department. The Allon Plan dealt with the disposition of the territories occupied from Jordan. Submitted to the Cabinet in July 1967 by Yigal Allon, the Deputy Prime Minister, the plan called for the retention of the strategic Jordan Rift Valley and Gush Etzion and the return of the populated areas of Judea and Samaria to Jordan. Although the Cabinet did not reach formal agreement on the Allon Plan, it was submitted to King Hussein in the course of secret negotiations following the war.[7]

However, subsequent developments have eroded some of the instrumental considerations. Most critically, following the Khartoum Conference of 1967, where the Arab countries decided against dealing with Israel, the perception of the territories as a bargaining asset declined. It is difficult to speculate on the Arab motives, but the three famous 'Nos' of Khartoum — no peace, no recognition, and no negotiations with Israel — discredited the moderate wing of the Labour movement, which was identified with the 'bargaining' conception. The Cabinet, reflecting a shift of power towards those who advocated a strategic use of the territories, annulled its June decision in August 1967.

Table 5.1:   Type of Perception

Time Period	Instrumental-Bargaining	Instrumental-Strategic	Normative (moral-religious)
July 1967	Golan Heights Sinai Desert Most of West Bank	Jordan Rift Valley[b] Gush Etzion Latrun region	East Jerusalem[a]
August 1967-1973	Sinai Desert Most of West Bank	Golan Heights Jordan Rift Valley[c] Gush Etzion Latrun Rapha Salient Gaza Strip	East Jerusalem Kiryat Arba
1973-1977	Sinai Desert	Golan Heights Jordan Rift Valley Gush Etzion Rapha Salient Gaza Strip	East Jerusalem West Bank
1977–1984	Sinai Desert[d] Rapha Salient[d]	Golan Heights[e] Gaza Strip	East Jerusalem West Bank

Notes:
(a) Annexed in 1967
(b) Allon Plan
(c) Galili Plan
(d) Returned to Egypt
(e) Annexed in 1980

Labour's administration of the occupied territories between 1967 and 1977 demonstrated these conceptual transformations. Table 5.1 provides a schematic representation of the changing perception of the territories. Following the August decision, the Golan Heights and the Rapha Salient were designated as instrumental-strategic. Forty-eight of the 76 settlements which Labour built between 1967 and 1977 were located there. The strategic Jordan Rift Valley and Gush Etzion were bolstered with 17 and 5 settlements each. One settlement was built in the Latrun region, as part of the minor territorial adjustments around Jerusalem.[8] But Labour refrained from settling territories which were designated as bargaining assets.

The most important perceptual change involved the gradual spread of the normative view, which emphasised the moral and religious significance of the West Bank. Developed by the Religious National circles associated with *Merkaz Harav*, this approach stated that settling the territories was a religious imperative, which superseded any strategic considerations. The normative view was applied principally to Judea and Samaria. Acting under pressure from Rabbi Levinger, the Labour Government approved the Kiryat Arba settlement near Hebron in 1970.

The foundation of the Gush Emunim in 1974 greatly enhanced the normative perceptions. Partly in response to Gush Emunim pressure, and partly because of a gradual modification of their own attitudes, the Labour leaders took the first steps towards settling the heartland of the West Bank. In 1975, after a prolonged struggle with Gush settlers, the Cabinet approved the settlement of Ofra and Kedumim in Samaria as well as Maale Adumim east of Jerusalem. The Galili Plan, named after Israel Galili who served as adviser to Golda Meir, broadened the strategic strip of the Jordan Rift Valley to include the eastern slopes of the Samarian Mountains.

In spite of these measures, the Labour movement could not match the extent to which the public had legitimised the normative approach to the West Bank. Although it is difficult to pinpoint dates, sometime in the 1970s the vision of restoring the state of Israel to the Biblical boundaries of the Land of Israel apparently superseded instrumental considerations as regards the West Bank.

Some of this transference was part of a broader public shift towards religious values. A 1973 study of attitudes towards Independence Day festivities found that this holiday was increasingly perceived in religious terms. While only 8 per cent of the respondents celebrated Independence Day by going to a synagogue or lighting candles, 55 per cent thought that religious activities would contribute significantly to the holiday.[9] The new round of changes in the educational system also contributed to deepening public attachment to the Land of Israel. Peri documented that after the 1973 war, the Ministry of Education reacted to questions of legitimisation among soldiers and civilians, by introducing more national and religious values into the curriculum.[10]

The clearest proclamation of the normative claim occurred when the Gush Emunim refused to use strategic arguments in order to justify the seizure of land for the Elon Moreh settlement. Although the Supreme Court refused to legalise the settlement in its decision of 1976, the Elon Moreh case came to symbolise the normative view that retention of the territories is the first necessary step to Redemption of the Land of Israel. It is equally interesting that the traditional theme of spatial Zionism, the ingathering of the exiles, was turned round. Rather than viewing the absorption of immigrants as the *raison d'être* of Israel, immigration was increasingly perceived as necessary to settle the Land of Israel. Indeed, some of the settlement plans in the densely populated West Bank were explicitly contingent upon the renewal of mass immigration. The alternative argument was that, without the additional space provided by the occupied territories, no large-scale immigration would be possible.

Major methodological difficulties are encountered in using the available empirical evidence to analyse the depth of normative sentiment towards the occupied territories. The problem stems from confusion surrounding the question of whether public support for retention of the territories was based on instrumental-strategic or normative perceptions. Political critics of Israel and some academic observers have often argued that religious values were used in order to legitimise the continuous occupation of Arab land. Beit-Hallahmi, in a fairly representative statement, argued that religious sentiments were more acceptable to the international community and were therefore used by the Israeli Government to cover up the aggression.[11] Leibovitz, one of the most distinguished religious critics, has consistently argued that the events surrounding the Six-Day War have no religious meaning, and he has even warned that the transference of the absolute religious values of *Kedusha* (holiness) to the secular entity of the state smacks of false Messianism.[12]

Other observers have been inclined to accept moral-religious sentiments at their face value. Verblovsky, a noted authority on comparative religion, pointed out that an overlap between religious and national values is common in other cultures, such as those of Mexico, Spain and Poland.[13] Gellner theorised that, even in advanced societies, religious beliefs may be socially effective. Such beliefs can exhort conduct which is not rational by utilitarian standards, because there are 'undercurrents of willingness' to credit religious concepts with suprarational power.[14]

It is significant that the spread of normative religious perceptions followed the Six-Day War and the Yom Kippur War. In terms of cognitive theories of religion, both wars qualify as events capable of inducing *cognitive quest*. Such quests can expose individuals to ambiguities in their belief system, and generate a search for new principles to re-interpret present experience. Even without going through a formal conversion in faith or practice, individuals may adopt selected religious beliefs.[15]

An additional explanation can be derived from Simmel's theory of symbolic interaction. According to this, it is entirely possible that psychological trade-offs can be formed between the religious and strategic arguments. The process may not necessarily be deliberate or conscious; however, the repeated mutual bolstering of the arguments will eventually weld them into an indistinguishable symbolic mixture in the collective belief system.[16]

Unfortunately, early empirical studies of the Israeli elite and public were not designed to test the distribution of instrumental as opposed to normative approaches to the occupied territories. However, some indirect observations can be derived from the extant evidence. Kaplowitz, in a 1971 survey of the elite, found that there was an annexationist group largely associated with Likud and the National Religious Party. This group wanted to annex the West Bank, regardless of any considerations of peace or security.[17] Heradstveit, who interviewed a sample of the elite in May 1972, concluded that general attitudes towards territorial expansion were diffuse and split, but the majority of the right-wing elite was normatively committed to annexation. Caspi and Yaniv and Pascal, who analysed the attitudes of Knesset members in the 1970s, found similar sentiments.[18]

The most comprehensive public opinion survey has been conducted by the Israel Institute of Applied Social Research. Table 5.2 illustrates the extent of public support for the retention of the various territories during Labour's tenure. It can be assumed that those respondents who object to any concessions possess a normative perception or have developed a symbolic interaction between the instrumental-strategic and normative view. The group which supports partial concessions may be described as broadly instrumental: it perceives parts of the territories as strategic assets and would use others for peace bargaining. The only purely instrumental bargainers are those respondents who are willing to give up all the territories in exchange for peace.

Table 5.2: Public Support for Territorial Concessions in Return for Peace 1968–77 (%)

	Golan Heights			West Bank			Gaza Strip			Sinai Desert		
Date	None	Part	All	None	Part	All	None	Part	All	None	Part	All
Feb. 1968	94	3	3	72	21	6	75	13	12	42	30	28
Apr. 1971	92	6	2	58	37	5	75	10	15	32	58	10
Jan. 1972	90	7	3	45	46	9	70	18	12	35	46	19
Sept. 1973	92	6	2	74	18	8	75	15	10	55	35	10
Oct. 1973	90	7	3	65	25	10	55	30	15	30	40	30
Nov. 1973	80	15	5	45	35	20	55	25	20	30	40	30
June 1974	65	25	10	40	45	15	40	30	30	20	55	25
Jan. 1975	65	25	10	30	40	30	25	40	35	10	45	45
Sept. 1976	63	28	9	55	30	15	57	18	25	27	48	25
Jan. 1977	66	26	8	48	42	10	45	30	25	–*	–*	–*
Nov. 1977	62	31	7	48	37	15	38	28	34	7	34	59
x̄ (mean)	78.1	16.3	5.6	52.7	34.2	13.0	55.5	23.4	21.2	28.8	43.1	28.1
S (standard deviation)	13.8	10.8	3.2	13.6	9.2	7.2	17.1	9.2	9.1	14.2	9.1	14.9

* not asked

Source: Adapted from, A. Stone, *Social Change in Israeli Attitudes and Events 1967–1979*, (Praeger Special Studies, New York, 1983), Figure 1.4, p.41.

The distribution of responses indicates that the Golan Heights, the West Bank and the Gaza Strip have been viewed by a fairly high average of Israelis in either normative or instrumental-strategic terms. Only the Sinai Desert had a substantially instrumental-bargaining image among the population. There is also relatively little variance with regard to the various perceptions. The only significant drop in the 'none' category coincided with the 1974–5 agreements between Israel, Syria and Egypt on partial disengagement.

The theory that Israelis have tended to perceive the territories in either normative or instrumental-strategic terms is indirectly borne out by another finding of the Israel institute of Applied Social Research. Kiess, who re-reviewed the 1969–73 statistics, emphasised that only a minority of Israelis were ready to give up territories in exchange for peace.[19] Stone found that in the 1973–9 period an average of 18.5 per cent of respondents believed that territorial concessions would lead to peace.[20] The Israelis' pessimistic outlook, which underlay the emergence of normative approaches to the occupied territories, can be best understood by analysing their collective image of the Arab enemy.

Radicalisation of the Image of the Enemy: Popular Perceptions of Arabs and the Palestinians

The proposition that external conflict tends to generate and reinforce negative images of the enemy is central in social psychology. The negative image of the enemy is derived from the threat involved in any external conflict. Frank, drawing on the work of Tomkins and Izard, defined this process as 'circular incremental magnification'. Such a process ensues when a threat-defence-threat sequence develops. Each defence is overcome by a stronger threat and the successive breakdown of each defence magnifies the threat and the negative image of the enemy.[21]

There is no doubt that the Arab-Israeli conflict constitutes a classic expression of such a sequence. Although the core of the conflict was realistic and objective, it generated an enormous feeling of threat in both Israel and the Arab countries. In order to appreciate the depth of this phenomenon, it is imperative to note that, at the psychological level, 'threat' is not an objective attribute of the stimulus situation. Lazarus argued that perceptions of threat vary according to activity, i.e. active-passive; potency, i.e. strong-weak; and affect, i.e. central-peripheral.[22]

From the Israeli perspective, the Arab threat was extremely active and strong; above all, it affected the central, that is the *physical*, dimension of the society's existence. Two factors interacted in producing such a high perception of threat. First, over the years the Arabs have repeatedly indicated their intention to destroy the State of Israel. Harkabi, in his comprehensive book *Arab Attitudes Towards Israel*, has documented in great detail the profound nature of Arab hostility.[23] One of the most threatening themes was the 'crusader theory', i.e. the Arab claim that the State of Israel is bound to disappear from the Middle East, like the medieval state of the Crusaders. Abraham, who reviewed Arab literary themes of the conflict, found frequent references to a holy war (*jihad*), and blood vengence.[24]

Using this extensive evidence, Harkabi was among the first to develop the concept of *politicide*, a reference to Arab desires to annihilate the State of Israel. In his view, politicide could be carried out either as a wholesale act or incrementally through a number of wars. Harkabi and the theory of politicide were criticised by a number of other scholars. For instance, Shamir maintained that studying the verbal expressions of a society at conflict can distort reality, and Cohen pointed out that Arab statements do not automatically lead to bellicose behaviour.[25] Patai felt that Arab verbal threats are part of their cultural heritage but not necessarily an indication of intention.[26]

However, as White admitted, the question 'do they mean what they say?' is not merely an abstract methodological problem.[27] Jervis noted that the interpretation of the message is influenced by first-hand experience with the enemy or salient transgenerational events which serve as analogues.[28] In the case of the Holocaust, the aims of Jewish genocide were clearly spelled out by Hitler and pursued by Germany. Hence an empirical precedent existed among Israeli Jews for accepting verbal threats as indications of behavioural intent. In fact, Harkabi's early statement that 'where the Arab-Israeli conflict is concerned, there may be no absolute distinction between politicide and genocide'[29] was widely accepted by the public. It was translated into the ideology of survival, known in Israel as *ein-breira*, i.e. a dichotomous perception that an Arab victory would lead to the physical extinction of the society.

This view was greatly enhanced in the anxious weeks before the Six-Day War. Even such liberals as former Prime Minister Levi Eshkol and Abba Eban could not escape the Holocaust analogy when they described the atmosphere of foreboding in the case of an Arab victory. Eshkol felt that 'Hitler's six millions would have been joined by another two and a half million victims of the Arab lust for destruction', and Eban argued that '. . . there would be a ghastly sequel, leaving nothing to be discussed . . . ending with no renewal and no consolation'.[30] Empirical surveys indicate that such sentiments were shared by the public. For instance, in the Herman study on attitudes towards the Holocaust, most of the 56 per cent of respondents who indicated that another Holocaust could happen felt that it would happen in Arab countries.[31]

Second, the perceptions of verbal threat were bolstered by frequent military conflicts. Perhaps the most potent factor in threat perception in Israel was the terrorist activity which gained momentum after 1967. Moshe Arens, the former Minister of Defence, has claimed that, since Arafat took over the PLO, there have been 7,000 terrorist actions; more than 600 Israelis have been killed and some 4,000 wounded.[32] Thornton and other psychologists of guerrilla and terrorist movements have argued that terror is a psychological weapon designed to produce anxiety, withdrawal and fear. Targets are often selected for their symbolic content which ensures a 'high return' for the guerrilla or terrorist. Yet, as Waltzer observed, such symbols can communicate brutal and extreme messages to the target population.[33]

There is ample empirical evidence to illustrate the fact that Israel has developed the psychological syndrome of a highly threatened nation. Table 5.3 indicates that a consistently high percentage of Israelis believes the real aim of the Arabs is to destroy the State of Israel. There is also a widespread belief in the inevitability of war. The perceived median estimated number of years to the next war has normally fluctuated around five.

Table 5.3: Israeli Evaluation of Arab Interest in Peace (%)

Date	Arabs (in general)	Egypt	Syria	Number of Years till next war (average of medians)
1967	45.0	*	*	*
1969	10.0	*	*	*
1970	16.6	30.0	*	*
1971	23.3	31.5	*	*
1972	23.3	*	*	*
1973	44.3	47.2	*	4.3
1974	30.6	50.5	*	4.1
1975	27.5	39.5	*	2.4
1976	27.0	49.0	13.0	4.3
1977	49.5	76.1	20.0	6.2
1978	49.0	61.8	13.5	5.7
1979	43.0	64.0	12.0	5.7

* Question Not Included in Survey

Source: Adapted from Stone, *Social Change* Figures 1.1 and 1.2, pp. 21 and 35.

A number of researchers who deal with the impact of terror have found a significant correlation between terrorism and perception of threat. For instance, both Peled and Levy and Guttman found that terrorism after 1967 increased the Israelis' worry score. The latter reported that the median worry score for acts of terrorism in Israel was 1.67 and for terrorism against Israeli targets abroad 1.35. Symbolically-oriented terror, such as the massacre of the Israeli sportsmen in Munich, is more central to the structure of worry than other types of terrorism. Fifty-nine per cent of respondents claimed that they were worried about terrorism abroad as opposed to 45 per cent who were worried about internal terrorism. The overall correlation between symbolic terrorism and worry among respondents was 0.42.[34]

The more recent 1979 survey on the subject reveals a significant increase in the pattern. Eighty-eight per cent of respondents were worried about terrorism abroad, 93 per cent were worried about terrorism in Israel and 73 per cent expressed a worry that they or their families might be hurt. In this study the rates of worry seemed to be constant, rather than related to any specific event.[35]

The perception of threat has led to a gradual radicalisation of the image of the Arab enemy in general, and of Palestinians in particular, among Israelis. Drawing from the enormous literature on prejudice, stereotyping and hostile labelling, it is possible to generalise that images of an enemy involve a deviation from three basic norms: the norm of justice which requires equal treatment of all individuals, the norm of humanism which requires that every individual should be treated in human terms, and the norm of rationalism which requires that rational thinking and information-gathering should be employed. Even short-term international crisis can rapidly change the picture of the out-group.[36] Prolonged conflicts which decrease differentiated thinking may lead to gross distortions of these basic norms.

Early research on Israeli attitudes towards the Arabs revealed hard-line positions. For instance, a 1948 opinion poll found that a majority of Israelis were opposed to the return of Arab refugees.[37] A 1959 international study found that Israeli children expressed more negative judgments about Arabs than about any other nationality.[38] Benjamini, who compared Israeli images of the Arabs between 1965 and 1968, found that the Six-Day War produced twelve negative and only one positive change in the image of Arabs.[39] Peres and Yuval-Davis have found similar results.[40]

The terrorist attacks have had a particular impact on the hardening of the image of the enemy. Peled found that after each major terrorist attack the percentage of negative responses about the Arabs went up significantly. Merari and Friedland concluded that terrorism had led Israelis to support extreme hard-line treatment of the PLO. An average 86 per cent of the representative sample of respondents were in favour of such measures as expulsion of PLO supporters, destruction of their houses, and bombing of PLO houses outside Israel.[41]

Contrary to some assumptions, empirical evidence does not indicate that the actual existence of Palestinians or the PLO threatens Israeli perceptions of Israel's legitimacy. The Israel Institute of Applied Social Research, which conducted a detailed study after Arafat's appearance at the UN in November 1974, revealed that 94 per cent of Israelis thought that the existence of the State of Israel was justified, even though 33 per cent believed that Arafat and the PLO represented the Palestinian quest for nationhood. However, 95 per cent argued that, because of terrorist activity, the PLO and the Palestinians should not obtain an independent state.[42]

A hardening image of the enemy exacerbates all the normal problems of misperceptions in acute international conflicts. White, who pioneered the study of misperception in conflict, found that the Arab-Israeli struggle produced all the normal syndromes, such as a mirror image of the enemy, a black and white image of the enemy, selective intention, bolstering one's own position, selective interpretation of information, and double moral standards for evaluating actions.[43] The Israelis, like other societies in conflict, protected their moral position by using a number of mechanisms such as the 'just self-image', or the 'false consensus effect'. The latter occurs when a society develops a highly consensual perception of its behaviour in order to convince itself of the appropriateness of its acts. Even the average 'decent' person, who does not necessarily share all of the society's attitudes towards the enemy, is caught up in a situation where breaking the consensus may be perceived as a threat to the security of his society.[44]

The radicalisation of the image of the enemy had two major effects on foreign policy thinking in Israel. The first is known as the 'vicious circle of fear'. Rakover and Yaniv found that fear aroused by war has been associated with the tendency to give priority to security based on *physical force*. In particular, individuals who suffered physical injury tended to emphasise security above all other considerations. For instance, 37 per cent of respondents who suffered physical injury during the 1973 war listed security as their first consideration in voting for a party in a Knesset election. Only 20 per cent of those who were not hurt ranked security first.[45] This finding explains why Israelis in general tend to have little faith in contractual security, such as international guarantees or alliances. This research also contributes to the understanding of Israeli voting behaviour. Soldiers, whose chances of getting hurt are quite high, routinely vote for the security-oriented right-wing parties.

The second effect pertains to the changes in the balance between deterministic and probabilistic thinking on the part of the Israeli collective. Probabilistic thinking refers to the tendency to view the environment in terms of uncertainty and the ability to express this 'uncertainty either verbally or as a numerical probability'.[46] In situations of high threat, probabilistic thinking is replaced by determinism, that is, cognitive certainty that the enemy is bound to annihilate the society. When a society's survival is at stake, or is perceived to be at stake, determinism is at a maximum and risk-taking or experimentation in foreign policy is at a minimum. Moreover, the image of the conflict situation becomes *non-interactive*, meaning that the Israelis do not tend to see any of their actions as contributing to Arab hostility.

Such modes of perception had a particularly detrimental effect on the foreign policy of the Labour movement. Harkabi, in his excellent work on Israeli responses to Arab attitudes, outlined three master conceptions, the 'hawkish-hawkish,' the 'hawkish-dovish,' and the 'dovish-dovish.'[47] The 'hawkish-hawkish' conception is based on the premise that the Arabs are intent on either wholesale or incremental politicide, which should be met with a hard-line Israeli response. This conception has been constantly emphasised by the Israeli right. The model has been publicly popular because of its internal consistency and its consonance with the perceived image of the enemy.

The 'hawkish-dovish' model corresponded to the Labour foreign policy. It is based on a hawkish evaluation of Arab intentions but advocates a relatively dovish Israeli response. Harkabi, who has been personally identified with this policy, was aware of the dissonance of the model, but justified it on the basis of international requirements. However, because of the low level of public tolerance of ambiguity and dissonance, the Labour 'hawkish-dovish' foreign policy model was delegitimised as the image of the enemy became progressively negative.

The 'dovish-dovish' model, which was characteristic of the left wing of the Labour movement and the Israeli left, was based on a positive evaluation of Arab intentions and advocacy of a liberal Israeli foreign policy. Although the model was internally consonant, it has been highly dissonant with the public perception of Arab intentions and behaviour. It was particularly discredited at the popular level, because the Israeli left has repeatedly failed to validate its claim that Arabs in general, and the PLO in particular, are intent on peace. The 'cold peace' with Egypt has not eradicated the image of Arab hostility.[48]

The Israel Council for Israel-Palestine Peace and other organisations, which have propagated the idea that there are PLO moderates like Sa'id Hammami, Sabri Jiryis and Issam Sartawi, were rebuffed by the argument that PLO moderation constitutes a tactical adjustment rather than a genuine change in intention.[49] Needless to say, incidents such as the murder of Issam Sartawi, apparently by PLO extremists, have contributed to a further delegitimisation of the small group of PLO sympathisers in Israel.

In spite of the fact that the 'dovish-dovish' model has been popular among intellectuals and the media, its dissonance with public perception of the enemy has hurt the Israeli left. Bar-Tal, who did a detailed epistemological analysis of the Palestinian and Israeli belief systems, found an extreme level of *cognitive discrepancy*. The accounts and interpretations of events produced by mainstream Palestinians and Israelis are so contradictory that they have led to a permanent 'freezing' of the beliefs.[50] Apparently, because of this 'freezing', the Israeli left has failed to change virtually any of the beliefs of the Jewish society so as to make the 'dovish-dovish' model more attractive.

At this point, it should be noted that we have discussed the radicalisation of public opinion towards the Arabs as a relatively uniform phenomenon. Yet, as was mentioned in the preceding chapters, the general belief system in Israel has changed mostly because of a radical demographic transformation in the population. Since the religious and Oriental Jews have become pivotal in Israeli society, their attitudes towards the conflict will now be examined.

Religious and Ethnic Stratification and Foreign Policy

Extensive academic research and commercial opinion polls have been unanimous in demonstrating that, by and large, the orthodox and Oriental Israelis take a much harder anti-Arab stand than the secular and Ashkenazi Jews.

Orthodox Jews

Empirical evidence indicates very clearly that orthodoxy is the most polarising factor in the overall structure of attitudes and opinions among Israelis. This polarisation is most pronounced in attitudes towards the Arabs and the Arab-Israeli conflict. The surveys of the Israel Institute of Applied Social Research regularly show that orthodox Jews legitimise Israel's retention of the territories because of the Bible. Zuckerman-Bareli found that 71 per cent of orthodox students objected to any territorial concessions as opposed to 38 per cent of secular students.[51]

Orthodox Jews seem also to be more prejudiced against the Arabs than their secular counterparts. Academic and lay observers have reported that orthodox Jews tend towards extremely negative perceptions of Arabs. Such negative stereotyping is particularly common among the National Religious circles of Gush Emunim; it is reflected in the Gush publication *Nekuda* and has been documented by a number of authors.[52]

There are two reasons for the religious hard line towards the Arabs. First, religion can become a focus of prejudice because it is easily contaminated by ethnocentric attitudes. This danger is great in Judaism because of the overlap between religious and ethnic elements. Smooha, calling the Jewish-Arab division in Israel a quasi-caste, argued that religious Jews view the Arabs as Gentiles; that Jews should intermingle with Arabs is regarded as anathema by the orthodox. Although liberal religious circles do not share this sentiment, orthodox Jews normally display a fair amount of animosity towards the Arabs.[53]

Second, the attachment of religious Jews to the Land of Israel generates hostility to all Arabs. In neither case is the lack of tolerance for Arabs mitigated by civic considerations, because the religious groups have a different political culture. Their political and behavioural norms are dominated by religious precepts which are expected to be implemented regardless of the civic norms of the Israeli polity.

Oriental Jews

Research demonstrates that the Orientals take a much harder anti-Arab line than the Ashkenazi Israelis. Orientals exceed the Ashkenazim in negative stereotyping of Arabs and in ranking them in a least-preferred category.[54] Orientals also have a statistically significant lead over the Ashkenazim in advocating hard-line policy options. In particular, Orientals oppose any territorial compromise and rule out political and humanitarian concessions to the Palestinians.[55]

This hard line is consistent across time. In 1969, the first comprehensive study of public opinion revealed that more than half of the Orientals, as opposed to only one-third of the Ashkenazim, supported an aggressive policy towards the Arabs.[56] Moreover, recent opinion polls indicate that the war in Lebanon, the massacre in the refugee camps, and the publication of the Kahn Report of the Commission of Inquiry have not modified hard-line Oriental sentiments. The consistency of Oriental anti-Arab attitudes stands out even when the socio-economic status and education of the respondents are considered. Studies which control for both reveal that within each social and educational category the Orientals are more hawkish than the Ashkenazim.[57]

It is the members of the Oriental lower classes, however, who display the most hostile attitudes towards the Arabs. Lower stratum Orientals have been occasionally observed man-handling Arab passers-by and demanding strong retaliatory measures in the wake of terrorist attacks.[58] Some have been implicated in the murder of a Peace Now activist and a number of terrorist attacks against the Arabs.

The empirical evidence is conclusive in establishing that the Orientals as a group display a more extreme posture than the Ashkenazim. However, it is far less clear why the Orientals have such distinctive anti-Arab attitudes. The answer to this question is not only important academically, but has significant foreign policy implications in view of the fact that Orientals constitute a majority of the electorate. The pervasiveness and consistency of these anti-Arab sentiments indicate that they do not arise from pragmatic concerns with run-of-the-mill foreign policy issues. Rather, they seem to have psychological and socio-cultural roots which touch upon the core problem of Oriental integration in Israel.

There are two methodological problems involved in analysing the psychological sources of Oriental attitudes. Most of the voluminous research done to date was not specifically designed to probe psychological questions. The limited number of studies which address themselves directly to the latter issue vary widely in their sample bases, methodology and discipline, thus limiting comparative inference. The second problem which besets psychological research in general stems from the fact that the impacts of ethnicity, education and low socio-economic status are highly interactive and reinforce each other. Some of the most common symptoms of social distancing, such as stereotyping and 'scapegoating', are characteristic of both lower socio-economic groups and low-status ethnic groups.

In order to overcome these methodological problems, four broad psychological perspectives are presented. The additional advantage of this approach is that it provides a number of explanations, rather than focusing on one narrow perspective which is too limited to analyse the problem. In exhibiting a distinctive pattern of hostility, the Orientals are acting under a number of psychological stimuli.

The Mino-Majority Perspective.   The post-1948 immigrants to Israel have been transformed over time from a minority into a majority. As in similar instances, however, this change was not immediately accompanied by a psychological transformation. In such cases, a member of the new majority still harbours a set of attitudes which he acquired during membership of a minority. We already indicated in Chapter 2 that these attitudes are related to the 'marginal man' phenomenon and include feelings of inferiority, insecurity, anxiety and ethnocentricity. In facing the Arab minority in Israel and coping with the general Arab hostility emanating from the Middle East conflict, these mino-majority immigrants have developed a variety of responses, ranging from a sense of guilt and anxiety about subjugating the Arabs to the need to act in self-confidence and self-approbation in order to fortify their new status.

Guilt and anxiety may translate into sympathy and identification with the Arabs, whereas the need for self-approbation may result in an attitude described by one social psychologist as: 'now (that) we are in a position of a dominant majority, let the others know how it feels to be a minority'.[59] This compensatory reaction is not totally dissimilar to the attitudes of lower middle-class white settlers which Mannoni identified in his classic study of colonialism.[60]

While both Ashkenazi and Oriental immigrants have shared the mino-majority problem, the latter have apparently been more disposed to adopt an aggressive attitude. Such a stand is often explained by the historic experience of the Jews under Islam. Although objectively less persecuted than the European Jews, their existence as *dhimmis* — people who are allowed to retain their religion — was perceived as difficult. Occupational opportunities were felt to be rigidly prescribed. Oriental Jews perceived themselves to be subject to humiliating practices and verbal abuse, making them at best second-class citizens.

Whatever the true extent of the persecution of Jews under Islam, recent revisionist literature asserts that it was actually underestimated in early research, because of the tendency to idealise the Jewish experience in Muslim Spain.[61] It is also interesting that the theme of subjugation and persecution has been particularly emphasised by Orientals associated with the Likud. Writing in the *Greater Land of Israel Book*, a leading collection of Revisionist and New Zionist writings, Moshe Sharon points out that the Yellow Patch and the Yellow Star of David were invented by the Muslims in the ninth century, and Shlomo Ben Shoshan argues that the Revisionist Right has always objected to the thesis that Jews under Islam enjoyed better conditions than their brethren in Christian countries.[62]

The historical experience of living with the Arabs, whether personal or socialised into the second generation, has also produced what Tamarin calls a 'wisdom based on life experience' approach to the Arab-Israeli conflict. A dominant theme in this context is the frequently expressed belief that the Arabs respect and submit only to power: 'I know the Arabs well, they are all cowards and treacherous. A kick in the teeth is the only language they understand.' Hence, a hard-line approach to foreign policy is advocated.[63]

The Relative Deprivation Perspective. The relative deprivation perspective is derived from the classical frustration theory as modified by Berkowitz. Objective socio-economic conditions can produce perceptions of relative deprivation and cause aggressive feelings. Presumably, aggressive impulses become 'free-floating', i.e. detached from the frustrating source and discharged upon another person or group. In spite of some methodological problems, this concept of displacement is widely used in social psychology as an explanation for ethnic prejudice, 'scape-goating', racism and other tensions in intergroup relations.[64]

The evidence in Chapter 4 would indicate that the Oriental immigrants in the post-1948 period suffered frustration related to real and relative deprivation. The perceptions of relative deprivation were further enhanced when the initially static and undifferentiated immigrant society broke up because of the accelerated mobility of the Ashkenazi immigrants. The latter were able to utilise personal connections with the Ashkenazi elite and the reparations from Germany in order to move out of the transit camps and development towns, leaving the Orientals behind.

The German reparations received by the Ashkenazi survivors of the Holocaust have apparently had an important, but not sufficiently researched, impact on the differentiation of the society. The individual wealth generated by the reparations enabled their recipients to move out of the working class or to improve their standards of living, leading to an instant 'embourgeoisement' of the Ashkenazi group.[65] Subsequent contacts between the Orientals and the Ashkenazim produced, through the mechanism of the 'demonstration effect', unfulfilled expectations in the lower status group.

In spite of the fact that the standards of living of the Israeli-born Orientals have improved dramatically compared to their parents' generation, their perception of relative deprivation has apparently increased. This stems largely from the phenomenon of *paar adati* (ethnic gap), that is, the fact that ethnic differences have increased in the native-born generation. It should be noted that such a structure of ethnic gap is extremely potent in generating an acute sense of relative deprivation, because most of the gaps are based on *non-malleable* variables. Factors such as poor educational showings, wage differentials, or indirect and subconscious discrimination are not easily corrected through institutionalised intervention, but contribute to the widespread perception by Orientals that they are victims of deliberate discrimination.

Perhaps the most significant implication of the structure of the ethnic gap stems from the fact that the Orientals have profited more from upward group mobility than from individual achievements. The change in group status was caused mainly by the post-1967 influx of Arabs into unskilled positions previously occupied by Orientals. Such mobility patterns have also been characteristic of other immigrant societies. Research shows that this type of mobility, known as 'rationalising unearned status', tends to increase particularistic ethnic identification, to focus diffuse feelings of deprivation, and to turn latent into overt aggression.[66] As Kimmerling pointed out, because the Arab workers came to form the lowest stratum, Oriental Jews had an almost 'vested interest' perpetuating anti-Arab sentiments.[67]

Early empirical studies of intergroup relations among the post-1948 Jewish immigrants reveal a situation of high ethnic tension between the Ashkenazim and the Orientals, with the latter quite often serving as victims of Ashkenazi hostility.[68] Most of the negative encounters were studied in structured situations like mixed housing projects, but Rosenstein suggests that Ashkenazi hostility and prejudice might have been more generalised. For instance, it emerged from the discovery that there were ideologically unacceptable differences in cultural values and skills, 'differences which challenged the initial assumption that all Jews would be somehow alike'.[69] Later studies show more ethnic integration, but the relation indicates a lack of symmetry — the Orientals being normally more keen on integration than the Ashkenazim.[70]

What is especially interesting, though, is that there has been a significant increase in the undercurrent of Oriental hostility towards the Ashkenazim. Whereas the traditional symptoms of lower-stratum Oriental alienation resulted in diffuse aggression, such as violence at soccer games, more recently the Ashkenazim have been specifically targeted. The depth of anti-Ashkenazi feelings is revealed in the use of highly symbolic graffiti demanding a 'final solution to the Ashkenazim' and in swastika-daubing incidents. Such expressions are not limited to the lower classes. *BeMaarcha* and *Afikim*, the two organs of the middle-class 'old Sephardim', have contained occasional classical anti-Semitic language directed against the Ashkenazim.[71]

In such a context of generalised perception of relative deprivation, it would not be uncommon for the Orientals to displace or take out their feelings of frustration and aggression on the Arabs, who are members of a distinctive and hostile outgroup. In many social situations, expressing hostility towards an outgroup is sanctioned as a way of preserving and affirming ingroup solidarity. Undoubtedly, the Arab-Israeli conflict has further legitimised such expressions. In his excellent sociological study of Israeli pluralism, Smooha links the Ashkenazi-Oriental tension to the 'scapegoating' of the Arabs, whereas Lissak argues that a confrontationist stand against the Arabs provides a vent for ethnic frustration and aggressiveness.[72]

Ethnic prejudice and 'scapegoating', generated by feelings of relative deprivation on the part of the lower status groups in a society, are quite often enhanced by an objective clash of interests.

Competition over jobs or mixed housing is a case in point. Higher socio-economic groups do not compete for the same range of jobs and can rely on market mechanisms to protect them from ethnically heterogeneous neighbourhoods. Because of the geographical separation between Jews and Arabs and the long period of economic prosperity, competition has been minimal in the past. However, the current economic crisis may exacerbate the objective clash of interests.

The Marking-Off Perspective. This perspective is based on theories dealing with the formation of the ethnic identity of an individual, as elaborated by Erikson, Lewin and Miller. According to them, identity constitutes both sameness and uniqueness. An individual who possesses a certain ethnic identity is aligned with members of the same group and marked-off from members of other ethnic groups. In the process of developing his ethnic identity an individual becomes conscious of common characteristics shared by the group, while at the same time he erects a barrier between himself and an outgroup which is used to mark off his own identity. Where the marking-off group is negatively assessed, the evaluation of one's own identity is likely to gain by comparison. Distinctive characteristics are likely to be highlighted in order to prevent any mistake about one's own identity.[73]

Both the Oriental and the European immigrants had to assume a new Israeli identity upon arrival. Defined by Jung and others as a commitment therapy, the process is invariably difficult because it involves discarding parts of one's previous ethnic identity. The Oriental immigrants, however, encountered more difficulties than their Ashkenazi counterparts because of two interlocking factors. As pointed out by Sharot in his seminal study on Jewish acculturation in the Diaspora, Middle Eastern Jewish communities were highly assimilated to Arab culture, constituting what is often described as 'Arab Jews'.[74] This in turn aroused fear among the Ashkenazi elite that the influx of Oriental immigrants would 'Levantinise' Israeli society.

In the preceding chapter we have already provided a detailed description of the efforts to 'purge' any 'Arab' characteristics from the emerging Israeli identity of the new immigrants. In shaping this new identity, the Orientals faced an even more insurmountable problem when they tried to conform to the ideal Sabra personality.

Naturally, the native-born offspring of Orientals did not face the same identity problems as their immigrant parents. However, there is evidence to indicate a second-generation identity crisis. Israeli-born Orientals normally define themselves as *yelid ha'aretz* (native-born) rather than as Sabras. Some of them have developed a certain ambivalent tolerance towards their Diaspora heritage. This is reflected in the current revival among Oriental immigrants of festivities and traditions which they practised in Arab countries. Others, mostly lower-class individuals, display symptoms of peripherality — while reaffirming their Israeli identity — and are aware that they are still being perceived as 'Arabs' by the dominant Ashkenazim. Physical resemblance to Arabs enhances the negative valence attributed to Oriental identity.

The findings about the peripheral identity of lower-stratum Orientals takes on an added significance when matched with attitudes towards the Arabs. Peres, a leading proponent of the marking-off perspective, argues that peripheral Orientals use the Arabs as a marking-off group in order to bolster their Israeli identity. Strong anti-Arab prejudice, hostility and hard-line approaches to the conflict are all related. They are used in order to create an appropriate distance from the Arabs and to emphasise the distinctiveness of the holders of Israeli identity.

In surveys which span nearly two decades, Peres found that anti-Arab attitudes are significantly correlated with the 'Arab' physical appearance and Arab-accented Hebrew of his respondents. Likewise, his survey of Oriental literature reveals that peripheral identity can be very traumatic for the Israeli-born generation, thus explaining the strong need to mark-off.[76] Herman's work on Israeli identity bears out Peres's conclusion; he found that the Orientals use the Arabs for a marking-off function far more frequently than the Ashkenazim.[77]

The Political Culture Perspective. Extensive research has established that the Orientals, as a group, have a more rightist political orientation than the Ashkenazim, which has earned them the perceptive name of Israel's 'right wing proletariat'.[78]

A rightist political orientation entails a lack of tolerance towards democratic concepts such as freedom of speech and of the press and the role of a loyal opposition. The Orientals were also found to participate less in politics and to have a lower sense of political efficacy than the Ashkenazim. While there is no evidence to

indicate that the Orientals as a group have an authoritarian personality structure, they often display authoritarian preferences,
and respond more favourably towards authoritarian modes of
political mobilisation, i.e. demagogic and rhetorical leadership
styles.[79] The classic theme of the 'two Israels' is an apparent
reflection of the sharp discontinuities between this type of political
culture and that of the Ashkenazim, which is more in line with the
notion of 'civic culture'.

As a result, the Orientals seem to exhibit a sharper sense of
statism, a political orientation which emphasises the supremacy of
the state over its constituent components. The Orientals express
more pride in state symbols than the Ashkenazim. Because of this
orientation, the Orientals have traditionally responded more posi-
tvely to the Revisionist idea of monism, i.e. the theory that the
national ideal should take preference over all other political and
social ideals in a society.[80]

A strong national commitment means a strong sense of
nationalism in foreign policy. Perceptions of national superiority,
national interests, and national values are universal, and Israelis,
like citizens in other nations, think 'nationalistically'. Yet observers emphasise that the Orientals tend to have a heightened and
more concrete perception of group loyalty, accompanied by a
more acute sense of outgroup competition. They tend to score
higher than the Ashkenazim on the question of the degree of
preference which should be accorded to the competitive interests
of Israel over other nations, and especially over the Arabs and the
Palestinians.[81] In the extreme, heightened perceptions of
nationalism result in chauvinism, disregard for moral standards in
international relations and the companion belief of 'my country,
right or wrong'.

The nationalism of the Orientals is apparently underlaid by two
factors which are inherent in their culture. One is related to the
fact that verbal violence and expressions of hard-line attitudes are
part of a behavioural norm common among the Oriental community, and especially among the most numerous Moroccan
group.[82] The other pertains to the structure of worry among
Israelis. The research of the Israel Institute of Applied Social
Research has repeatedly found that the Orientals tend to worry
more than the Ashkenazim about direct threats such as terrorism,
especially as many of them live in border towns.[83]

The Religious Perspective. The religious perspective is based on the assumption that Oriental attitudes towards the Arabs and the conflict are coloured by religious beliefs. Our methodological discussion of religion emphasised that the degree of orthodoxy among the Orientals may be difficult to ascertain through surveys because these reflect Ashkenazi-oriented Talmudic standards.

Following Deshen's pioneering studies, there has been a growing awareness in the anthropological literature that the orally-based religious value system of the Orientals is more limited and flexible than the Ashkenazi Talmudic perspective. The latter equates with official orthodoxy in Israel, whereas Oriental religiosity is often referred to as traditionalism.

This religious perspective has two important implications. First, in Judaism as in Islam, there is no separation of religion and politics. Religion is the basis of the sociopolitical community. Thus, traditional Orientals, like the orthodox Ashkenazim, have both an extremely strong ingroup orientation and a low tolerance for outgroup members, such as the Arabs. Second, the religious outlook colours the orientation towards the occupied territories, especially the West Bank. On top of any instrumental orientation which they may have, Oriental traditionalists are apparently in the same category as the national-religious camp which has a strongly expressive territorial orientation.

It may even be that the Orientals possess a somewhat stronger expressive orientation than the Ashkenazim. Oriental religiosity is more Biblical-archaic than the Ashkenazi-Talmudic orthodoxy. The former is based on ceremonies which have a distinctive *land* connotation, such as pilgrimages to holy places, burial grounds of holy men, and religious festivals celebrated in designated holy and semi-holy locations.[84] Conversely, some religious critics argue that the Oriental influence was instrumental in evolving an 'animistic' attachment to the West Bank. Although this attachment has not taken a behavioural form — only about eight per cent of the Jewish settlers on the West Bank are Orientals — it provides symbolic and political support to Gush Emunim.

The Delegitimisation of Labour's Foreign Policy: The Breakdown of the National Consensus

The complex network of changes in the public perceptions of the Arab-Israeli conflict has generated considerable pressure on the traditional Socialist Zionist approach to foreign policy. It is customary to assume that, until 1967, Labour's policies were seldom challenged. Although there are no systematic opinion polls in this period, indirect evidence seems to support this assumption. First, the general salience of the conflict as reflected in media coverage was quite low. A content-analysis study based on the leading Israeli newspaper *Haaretz* reveals that in the 1949–66 period the average saliency of the Arab-Israeli conflict, measured on a scale of 0 to 5, was 1.43. Only in 1949 and during the Sinai campaign episode of 1956–7, did the saliency indicator exceed the 2.5 points level. In comparison, since the 1967 war, the saliency indicator has routinely stayed in the 3–4 range.[85] Second, there was little public discussion of foreign policy decisions. The decision-making process concerning the Arab-Israeli conflict was widely perceived as the prerogative of the government and the army. Undoubtedly, this perception was enhanced by the charismatic leadership of Ben-Gurion and the high status enjoyed by the Israel Defence Force.

The breakdown of the national consensus after the Six-Day War accelerated the delegitimisation of the Socialist Zionist belief system. This process was especially severe because it touched upon both the *normative* and the *instrumental* level of Labour's foreign policy ideology.

The normative stress has been expressed in the increasing phenomenon of social anomie in Israel. Using rates of suicide, mental illness, and strikes as an indicator of social anomie, Kimmerling documented that they have been closely correlated with the saliency of the Arab-Israeli conflict. The major conclusion of this study was that the conflict has had a bifurcated impact on the belief system of Israeli society. At the normative level, it has led to disintegration and anomie. At the instrumental level, it has created cohesion which is necessary in order to fight.[86]

Kimmerling's unique study is based on data from the 1949–66 period. It is easy to extrapolate from his research that the post-1967 increase in the saliency of the Arab-Israel conflict has led to more anomie and conflict at the normative level. Since anomie is a leading indicator of delegitimisation, it can be safely assumed that, in spite of the seemingly instrumental cohesion of Israeli society, the dominant belief system started to erode very shortly after the war. Ironically, anomie tends to increase hard-line positions in foreign policy. Aronson and Horowitz, who analysed the patterns of Israel's declared 'strategy of retaliation', concluded that they were influenced by the anomic states of the society. During periods of social instability, the threshold of Israel's sensitivity to outside attack goes down, and the government is forced by public opinion to take military action more frequently.[87]

Another indication of the normative erosion of Socialist Zionism is related to the growing perception that Labour had ceased to be the top-ranking Zionist party. Because Labour was quite hesitant about settling the occupied territories, it was frequently accused by New Zionists of betraying the traditional Zionist values of pioneering and settlement.

These arguments apparently shaped public perceptions during the 1967–73 period. In a 1974 survey of Zionist attitudes of Israeli youth, the present author found that 54 per cent of respondents ranked Likud as the 'most Zionist party', whereas only 36 per cent placed Labour in this category. It is interesting that among those who ranked Likud first, only 31 per cent identified their parents as Likud voters. Conversely, in spite of the poor Zionist ranking of the Labour Party, 56 per cent claimed that their parents supported Labour.[88]

The magnitude of dissonance between Labour's foreign policy and public sentiment, at the instrumental level, has been extensively documented. Various opinion polls of the Israel Institute of Applied Science Research reveal that, in 1962, 42 per cent of respondents supported an aggressive policy towards the Arabs, compared with 61 per cent in 1966 and 70 per cent in 1970.[89] The first academic study of voting behaviour in Israel in 1969 disclosed that 72 per cent of all respondents affirmed their support for an aggressive stand towards the Arabs. Arian, a leading authority on voting behaviour who conducted this research, concluded that the public's hard-line position forced the more liberal parties to adopt a harder anti-Arab stand. On the other hand, left-wing parties such as the Professors List for Peace, which could not adjust their political platform, were apprehensive about their electoral chances.[90]

A secondary analysis of all Arian's polls since 1969 led Etzioni-Halevy to conclude that foreign policy has come to dominate the right-left cleavage in Israel.[91] Virtually all observers accept Arian's conclusion that foreign policy is the most crucial factor in shaping a rightist or leftist political orientation. On top of the other grievances against Labour, the right-wing shift in public attitudes towards foreign policy has delegitimised the last vestiges of Socialist Zionism. There are no empirical studies which weight the relative impact of each of the factors which contributed to Labour's electoral decline, but Arian and others have assumed that the hardening of public opinion towards the Arab-Israeli conflict was the main reason for the ascendancy of Likud.[92]

The developing dissonance between the foreign policy concepts of Socialist Zionism and public perceptions created a painful dilemma for the left-wing parties in general and for Labour in particular. The parties left of Labour faced an agonising choice between policy principles and electoral survival. Some, like *Shelli-Moked*, opted for an ideological stand and lost their parliamentary representation completely. Others, such as *Mapam*, which joined the Labour Party, gave up most of its principles, but secured a modicum of electoral influence within the Labour Alignment.

The Labour Party was presented with an equally painful policy choice. The historical rift between the moderates and the right wing of the party grew wider when the latter used the argument of electoral considerations in order to lobby for a more radical anti-Arab platform. Yet even this shift to the right, which generated internal fragmentation and policy immobilism in the Labour movement, was not large enough to bridge the dissonance gap.

This policy dilemma had a major implication for any Labour coalition government. In the abstract, as Bay observed with insight, 'government policies must be responsive to majority conceptions of what is true and what is just in a world of contending interests and contentious issues'.[93] In the democratic model of executive accountability, it has often happened that governments pursued a hard-line course in face of public opposition. The American war in Vietnam is one widely cited case in point. In Israel, however, the Labour Government seemed to have deviated from executive accountability by conducting a foreign policy which did not live up to the hard-line expectations of the public. Although Bay advocates that in cases 'where individual or collective survival is at stake . . . the government must protect life, rather than follow a majority opinion', in Israel the very core of the foreign policy dispute has focused on the question of what was the best way to protect the survival of the community. In the next chapter we shall discuss the process of transvaluation of the collective belief system, in which the hard-line response to the question of Israel's collective survival emerged.

Notes

1. J. Y. Gonen, *A Psychohistory of Zionism*, (Meridian Books, New York, 1975), p. 198.
2. See footnote 29, chapter 3. After the 1967 war Dayan implemented his idea by settling the Rapha Salient and Gaza Strip.
3. A. W. Bar-On, *The Untold Story: The Diary of the Chief Censor*, (Edanim Publishers, Jerusalem, 1981), p. 151, (Hebrew).
4. B. Kimmerling, *Zionism and Territory: The Socio-Territorial Dimensions of Zionist Politics*, (Institute of International Studies, University of California at Berkeley, 1983), p. 215.
5. Y. Galnoor has argued that the Bible and the Land of Israel are among the dominant themes in the language of the Israeli polity, 'Israel's Polity: the Common Language,' *The Jerusalem Quarterly*, no. 20 (1981), pp. 65–82.
6. Quoted in Kimmerling, *Zionism and Territory*, p. 148.
7. A. Shlaim and a. Yaniv, 'Domestic Politics and Foreign Policy in Israel', *International Affairs*, vol. 56, no. 2 (1980), pp. 242–62.
8. Calculated on the basis of A. Beer, *Settlements* (Eli Printers, Jerusalem, 1981), (Hebrew).
9. C. Kamen, *Attitudes and Behavior of the Public towards Independence Day*, (Israel Institute of Applied Social Research, 1973), p. 7, (Hebrew).
10. M. Peri, 'The Response of the Education Policy Making System in the Ministry of Education Towards Demands in the Field of Education Towards Values', *State, Government and International Relations*, no. 14 (1979), pp. 67–87, (Hebrew).
11. B. Beit-Hallahmi, 'Religion and Nationalism in the Arab-Israeli Conflict', *II Politico*, vol. 38, no. 2 (1973), pp. 232–43.
12. Y. Leibovitz, *Judaism, the Jewish People and the State of Israel* (Shoken Publications, Jerusalem and Tel Aviv, 1979), pp. 233–71, (Hebrew).
13. Z. Verblovsky, 'The Difference between the Secular-Religious Relations in Israel and other Countries' in A. Hareven (ed.), *On the Difficulty of Being an Israeli* (The Van Leer Foundation, Jerusalem, 1983), pp. 201–12, (Hebrew).
14. E. Gellner, 'Concept and Society' in B. R. Wilson (ed.), *Rationality* (Harper and Row, Evanston and New York, 1970), pp. 18–49.
15. C. Ullman, 'Cognitive and Emotional Antecedents of Religious Conversion', *Journal of Personality and Social Psychology*, vol. 43, no. 1 (1982), pp. 183–92.
16. For a good discussion of the theory of symbolic interaction see P. M. Blau, *Exchange and Power in Social Life* (John Wiley & Sons Inc, New York, 1964).
17. N. Kaplowitz, 'Psychological Dimension of the Middle East Conflict: Policy Implications', *Journal of Conflict Resolution*, vol. 20, no. 2 (1976), pp. 279–317.
18. D. Heradstveit, *Arab and Israeli Elite Perceptions* (Universitets Forlaget, Oslo, 1974); D. Caspi, 'How Representative is the Knesset?', *The Jerusalem Quarterly*, no. 14 (1980), pp. 68–81; and A. Yaniv and F. Pascal, 'Doves, Hawks and Other Birds of Feather', *The British Journal of Political Science*, vol. 10, no. 2 (1980), pp. 260–7.
19. N. Kiess, 'The Influence of Public Policy on Public Opinion: Israel 1967–1974', *State, Government and International Relations*, no. 8 (1975), pp. 36–60, (Hebrew).
20. Adopted from A. Stone, *Social Change in Israeli Attitudes and Events 1967–1979* (Praeger Special Studies, New York, 1983), Figure 1.3, p. 38.
21. J. D. Frank, *Sanity and Survival in the Nuclear Age. Psychological Aspects of War and Peace* (Random House, New York, 1982), p. 187.
22. P. S. Lazarus, 'Stress' in D. L. Sills (ed.), *International Encyclopedia of the Social Sciences*, (Free Press, New York, 1972), vol. 15, pp. 337–48.

23. Y. Harkabi, *Arab Attitudes Towards Israel*, (Israel University Press, Jerusalem, 1972).

24. S. Abraham, 'The Jews and the Israelis in Modern Arabic Literature', *The Jerusalem Quarterly*, no. 2 (1977), pp. 119–35.

25. S. Shamir, 'The Palestinians and Israel' in S. Avineri (ed.), *Israel and the Palestinians* (St. Martin's Press, New York, 1971), pp. 133–64; and A. Cohen, 'The Changing Patterns of West Bank Policies', *The Jerusalem Quarterly*, no. 5 (1977), pp. 105–13.

26. R. Patal, *The Arab Mind*, (Charles Scribner and Sons, New York, 1973), pp. 41–72.

27. R. White, *Nobody Wanted War*, (Doubleday, Garden City, NY, 1968), pp. 85–6.

28. R. Jervis, *Perceptions and Misperceptions in International Relations*, (Princeton University Press, Princeton, NJ, 1976), p. 239.

29. Harkabi, *Arab Attitudes*, p. 93.

30. Quoted in M. Brecher, *Decisions in Israeli Foreign Policy*, (Yale University Press, New Haven, CT, 1975), p. 342 and *The Foreign Policy System of Israel*, (Oxford University Press, Oxford, 1972), p. 93.

31. S. Herman, *Israelis and Jews: the Continuity of Identity* (Jewish Publication Society, Philadelphia, 1970), pp. 79, 284.

32. *Haaretz*, 27 July 1984.

33. For a survey of the topic see A. F. Eldridge, *Images of Conflict*, (St. Martin's Press, New York, 1979), pp. 103–32; M. Waltzer, *Just and Unjust Wars* (Basic Books, New York, 1977), p. 203.

34. T. Peled, 'The Impact of Terrorist Activity on the Morale of the Public and Its Attitudes Towards the Arabs: A Longitudinal Analysis,' *State, Government and International Relations*, no. 3 (1972), pp. 129–34 (Hebrew), and S. Levy and E. L. Guttman, *The Feeling of Well Being and Worry Among the Israeli Public* (The Israel Institute of Applied Social Research, Jerusalem, 1973), pp. 20, 40 (Hebrew).

35. A. Merari and N. Friedland, *The Attitudes of the Public Towards Terror* (The Centre for Strategic Studies, Tel Aviv University, 1979), p. 1, (Hebrew).

36. M. Billig, *Social Psychology and Intergroup Relations*, (Academic Press, London, 1976), p. 364.

37. H. Gratch (ed.), *Twenty Five Years of Social Research in Israel*, (Jerusalem Academic Press, Jerusalem, 1973), p. 124.

38. W. E. Lambert and O. Klineberg, *Children's View of Foreign Peoples*, (Appleton Century-Crofts, New York, 1967).

39. K. Benjamini, 'National Stereotypes of Israeli Youth,' *Megamot*, vol. 16, no. 4 (1969), pp. 364–75, (Hebrew).

40. Y. Peres and N. Yuval-Davis, 'Some Observations on the National Identity of the Israeli Arabs', *Human Relations*, vol. 22, no. 3 (1969), p. 219–33.

41. Peled, 'The Impact', pp. 129–34; and Merari and Friedland, *The Attitudes*, p. 1.

42. Israel Institute of Applied Social Research (editorial staff), *Following the Appearance of Yasir Arafat in the General Assembly of the United Nations*, (Israel Institute of Applied Social Research, Jerusalem, n.d.).

43. R. K. White, 'Misperceptions in the Arab-Israeli Conflict', *Journal of Social Issues*, vol. 33, no. 1 (1977), pp. 190–221.

44. M. Billig, *Ideology and Social Psychology, Extremism, Moderation and Contradiction*, (St. Martin's Press, New York, 1982), p. 157; Billig, *Social Psychology*, p. 118; and M. Zuckerman, R. W. Mann, F. J. Bernieri, 'Determinants of Consensus Estimates: Attribution, Salience and Representativeness', *Journal of Personality and Psychology*, vol. 42, no. 5 (1982), pp. 839–52.

45. S. Rakover and A. Yaniv, 'Individual Trauma and National Response to External Threat: the Case of Israel', *Bulletin of the Psychonomic Society*, vol. 16, no. 3 (1980), pp. 217–20.

Foreign Policy and Delegitimisation   185

46. G. M. Wright and L. D. Phillips, 'Personality and Probability Thinking: An Exploratory Study', *British Journal of Psychology*, vol. 70, no. 2 (1979), pp. 295–303.

47. Y. Harkabi, *Arab Strategies and Israel's Responses*, (The Free Press and Collier Macmillan Publishers, New York, 1977).

48. The early hope that the peace process with Egypt would modify the image of the enemy was not warranted. Amir, a leading authority on intergroup relations, and his associates carried out a number of empirical studies on the subject. A major conclusion of this research was that inter-ethnic relations have not improved because of the extremity of the initial attitudes, the poor quality and infrequency of contacts, the lack of institutional support and the status inequalities between the Arab and Jewish groups. Y. Amir, A. Bizman, R. Ben-Ari and M. Rivner, 'Contact Between Israelis and Arabs', *Journal of Cross-Cultural Psychology*, vol. 11, no. 4 (1980), pp. 426–43; A. Bizman and Y. Amir, 'Mutual Perceptions of Arabs and Jews in Israel', *Journal of Cross-Cultural Psychology*, vol. 13, no. 4 (1982), pp. 461–9; Y. Amir and R. Ben-Ari, 'Cognitive Cultural Learning, Intergroup Contact and Change in Ethnic Attitudes and Relations', paper presented at the International Conference on Group Processes and Intergroup Conflict, Shfaim, Israel, October 1983.

49. For a representative article see M. Nissan, 'PLO Moderates', *The Jerusalem Quarterly*, no. 1 (1976), pp. 70–82.

50. D. Bar-Tal, 'Israel-Palestinian Conflict: A Cognitive Analysis', paper presented at the European-Israeli Conference on Group Processes and Intergroup Conflict, Tel Aviv, October 1983.

51. C. Zuckerman-Bareli, 'The Religious Factor and its Impact on Consensus and Polarity Among Israeli Youth', *Megamot*, vol. 22, no. 1 (1975), pp. 62–80, (Hebrew).

52. For instance, see D. Rubinstein, *On the Lord's Side: Gush Emunim*, (Hakibbutz Hameuchad Publishing House, Tel Aviv, 1982), pp. 93–4, (Hebrew).

53. S. Smooha, *Israel: Pluralism and Conflict*, (University of California Press, Berkeley and Los Angeles, 1978), p. 105.

54. Y. Peres, 'Ethnic Relations in Israel', *American Journal of Sociology*, vol. 76, no. 6 (1971), pp. 1021–47 and *Ethnic Relations in Israel* (Sifriat Hapoalim, Tel Aviv, 1977), pp. 93–4, (Hebrew).

55. A. Jacob, 'Trends in Israeli, Public Opinion on Issues Related to the Arab-Israeli Conflict 1967–1972', *The Jewish Journal of Sociology*, vol. 16, no. 2 (1974), pp. 187–208.

56. A. Arian, *The Choosing People*, (Ramat Gan, Massada, 1973), p. 108, (Hebrew).

57. See in particular Jacob, 'Trends', p. 200.

58. S. Smooha, 'Ethnic Stratification and Allegiance in Israel: Where Do Oriental Jews Belong?' *Il Politico*, vol. 41, no. 4 (1974), pp. 635–57.

59. F. Zweig, *Israel: the Sword and the Harp* (Farleigh Dickinson University Press, Rutherford, NJ, 1969), p. 34.

60. O. Mannoni, *Prospero and Caliban*, (Praeger, New York, 1964).

61. N. A. Stillman, 'The Moroccan Jewish Experience: A Revisionist View', *The Jerusalem Quarterly*, no. 9 (1978), pp. 111–23.

62. M. Sharon, 'The Interim Agreement in the Context of Pax Islamica' and S. Ben Shoshan, 'If a Miracle Happens' in A. Ben-Ami (ed.), *The Greater Land of Israel Book* (The Greater Land of Israel Movement and S. Freedman, 1977), pp. 265–8 and pp. 317–20, (Hebrew).

63. G. R. Tamarin, *The Israeli Dilemma; Essays on a Warfare State* (Rotterdam University Press, Rotterdam, 1973), p. 43.

64. For a good summary of the aggression-frustration hypothesis and its variants see H. Tajfel, 'Intergroup Behaviour: A Group Perspective' in H. Tajfel and C.

186   Foreign Policy and Delegitimisation

Fraser (eds), *Introducing Social Psychology*, (Penguin Books, Harmondsworth, 1978), pp. 423–44.

65. For one of the few discussions see D. Bernstein, 'Immigrant Transit Camps — the Formation of Dependent Relations in Israeli Society', *Ethnic and Racial Studies*, vol. 4, no. 1 (1981), pp. 26–43.

66. M. Lissak, *Social Mobility in Israel* (Israel University Press, Jerusalem, 1969), p. 111. A. Rabushka and K. Shepsle make an important theoretical distinction between group and individual mobility. Only the latter, which cuts across ethnic cleavage, promotes true social integration. *Politics in Plural Societies: A Theory of Democratic Instability* (Charles E. Merill Publishing Company, Columbus, OH, 1976).

67. B. Kimmerling, *Zionism and Economy* (Schenkman Publishing Company, Cambridge, MA, 1983), p. 60.

68. J. T. Shuval, 'Emerging Patterns of Ethnic Strain in Israel', *Social Forces*, vol. 40, no. 4 (1962), pp. 323–8; *Immigrants on the Threshold*, (Atherton Press, New York, 1963); and 'Patterns of Intergroup Tension and Affinity,' *International Social Science Bulletin*, vol. 8, no. 1 (1956), pp. 75–103.

69. C. Rosenstein, 'The Liability of Ethnicity in Israel', *Social Forces*, vol. 50, no. 2 (1981), pp. 667–86.

70. For instance, see Peres, *Ethnic Relations*, p. 100 and M. Inbar and C. Adler, *Ethnic Integration in Israel*, (Transaction Books, New Brunswick, NJ, 1977), p. 64.

71. Quoted in Smooha, *Israel*, p. 193.

72. Smooha, *Israel*, p. 104 and Lissak, *Social Mobility*, p. 110.

73. E. H. Erikson, *Childhood and Society*, (Norton, New York, 1950) p. 213; K. Lewin, edited by D. Cartwright, *Field Theory in Social Science*, (Harper and Row, New York, 1951), p. 148; D. R. Miller, 'Study of Social Relationships: Situation, Identity and Social Interaction' in S. Koch, *Psychology: A Study of Science*, vol. 5, (McGraw Hill, New York, 1963), p. 674.

74. S. Sharot, 'Minority Situation and Religious Acculturation: A Comparative Analysis of Jewish Communities', *Comparative Studies in Society and History*, vol. 16, no. 3 (1974), pp. 329–54.

75. The peripheral identity is particularly common among second-generation lower stratum Morrocans, Inbar and Adler, *Ethnic Integration*, p. 64; Peres, *Ethnic Relations*, pp. 83–100.

76. Peres, *Ethnic Relations*, pp. 95–96, (Hebrew).

77. Herman, *Israelis*, p. 64.

78. Y. Yishai, 'Israel's Right-Wing Proletariat', *Jewish Journal of Sociology*, vol. 24, no. 2 (1982), pp. 87–98.

79. For a comprehensive discussion see E. Etzioni-Halevy with R. Shapiro, *Political Culture in Israel: Cleavage and Integration Among Israeli Jews*, (Praeger, New York, 1977), pp. 67–87; D. Nachmias and D. H. Rosenblum, 'Bureaucracy and Ethnicity', *American Journal of Sociology*, vol. 83, no. 4 (1978), pp. 967–74 and Yishai, 'Israel's Right Wing', pp. 87–98.

80. D. Horowitz and M. Lissak, *The Origins of the Israeli Polity*, (Am Oved, Tel Aviv, 1977), pp. 190–2, (Hebrew).

81. Jacob, 'Trends', p. 60; Smooha, *Israel*, p. 112.

82. M. Shokeid, 'Towards Explanation of the Attitudes of Aggression Among Moroccan Immigrants', *Megamot*, vol. 27, no. 4 (1982), pp. 397–412 (Hebrew).

83. Z. Ben-Sira, 'Towards a Facet Theory of a Sequential Order of Societal Needs,' *Quality and Quantity*, no. 13 (1979), pp. 233–53.

84. S. Deshen, 'The Judaism of Middle Eastern Immigrants,' *The Jerusalem Quarterly*, no. 13 (1979), pp. 98–109; A. Stahl, *The Cultural Integration in Israel*, (Am Oved, Tel-Aviv, 1976), p. 35, (Hebrew).

85. B. Kimmerling, 'The Salience of the Arab-Israeli Conflict As a Social Indicator 1949–1970,' *State Government and International Relations*, no. 6 (1974), pp. 100–26, (Hebrew).

86. B. Kimmerling, 'Anomie and Integration in the Israeli Society and the Saliency of the Arab-Israeli Conflict', *Megamot*, vol. 29, no. 4 (1973), pp. 349–74.

87. S. Aronson and D. Horowitz, 'The Strategy of the Controlled Retaliation,' *State, Government and International Relations*, vol. 1, no. 1 (1971), pp. 77–99, (Hebrew).

88. For a full discussion see O. Seliktar, 'Socialization of National Ideology: The Case of Zionist Attitudes Among Young Israelis,' *Political Psychology*, vol. 2, no. 3–4 (1980), pp. 66–94.

89. P. Adi and D. Froelich, *Attitudes Concerning Political Security and Topics of Public Morale in February-March*, (Israel Institute of Applied Social Research, Jerusalem, 1970), (Hebrew).

90. Arian, *The Voting*, pp. 106–7.

91. Etzioni-Halevy with Shapiro, *Political Culture*, p. 61.

92. A. Arian, 'The Electorate: Israel 1977' in H. R. Penniman, *Israel at the Polls: The Knesset Election of 1977*, (American Enterprise Institute, Washington DC, 1979), pp. 59–89.

93. C. Bay, 'Access to Political Knowledge as a Human Right' in I Galnoor (ed.), *Government Secrecy in Democracies* (Harper and Row, New York, 1977), pp. 22–39.

6 THE PROCESS OF TRANSVALUATION: CHANGING PATTERNS OF POLITICAL CULTURE AND FOREIGN POLICY

The delegitimisation of Socialist Zionism was accompanied by a transvaluation of the belief system, into New Zionism. Chapter 1 made it clear that an emerging belief system can be analysed only as a multidimensional phenomenon. In matters of foreign policy, there are three indicative dimensions of transvaluation. The first is the changing style of political mobilisation and political culture. The second is the thrust and themes of the 'crucial discourse' in the foreign policy debate. In Israel, this debate came to be dominated by the military elite. The third pertains to the changing structure of foreign policy advocacy groups. Advocacy or interest groups are an especially useful tool for studying the process of transvaluation, because they generate and propogate new values in society. The flourishing of right-wing interest groups in Israel has been a vital indication of the transition from Socialist Zionism to New Zionism.

The Changing Pattern of Political Mobilisation and Political Culture in Israel

The notion that political culture underlies the belief system of a society is widely accepted. The term has been normally used to describe a set of attitudes and beliefs of individuals towards the political realm. Yet social scientists point out that political culture is shaped by styles of political mobilisation. The most common styles are elitist and pluralistic mobilisation.

Elitist political mobilisation tends to downgrade political cleavages and emphasise a broadly defined consensus. Quite often, the structure of popular commitment is focused on a single dominant party. Pluralistic mobilisation can be either *constitutional* or *populistic*. The former is prevalent in most Western countries; it is based on an orderly interplay between institutions, groups and individuals.[1] The latter is a mixture of patterns, which can range from *populist democracy*, i.e. direct appeals to the people through referenda, to *politicians' populism*, i.e. efforts to overcome social divisions by focusing on an outside enemy.[2]

The style of political mobilisation has a particularly significant implication for societies which are engaged in external conflict. The traditional assumption that external conflict tends to increase internal cohesion has never been decisively proved. Stein, who reviewed the enormous empirical literature on what is known as the 'alliance cohesion' hypothesis, concluded that some intervening conditions can increase internal consensus, but others tend to generate fragmentation.[3] The literature is even less clear with regard to the question of whether different mobilisation styles tend to aggravate external conflict. Yet the theories seem to indicate that in certain types of pluralistic mobilisation an external conflict can be manipulated in order to achieve internal cohesion.

The number of empirical studies which analyse the linkage between the mobilisation style, external conflict and internal cohesion in Israel is limited. However, they can be broadly interpreted to support the hypothesis that, under the elitist political mobilisation of the dominant Labour movement, there was strong pressure to suppress internal divisions and especially the ethnic cleavage. Although the Arab-Israeli conflict has generated a natural consensus, the early Labour elite bolstered internal cohesion through the use of nation-building symbols and non-symbolic politics, such as the manipulation of patronage. The use of these mechanisms generated a degree of internal cohesion large enough to sustain the polity, without resorting to overt manipulations of the external conflict.

The decline in the dominance of the Labour movement has gradually evolved into a pluralistic style of political mobilisation. Scholars have pointed out that the new style has contained elements of both constitutional and populist pluralism. Mendilow, who conducted a longitudinal study of the appeal patterns of Labour and Likud, found that the latter tended to use more populist elements in its election advertising than the Labour Alignment. In a sample taken during the November-December election campaign of 1973, 15.6 per cent of Likud's advertisements emphasised consensus and fear issues, i.e. war, unemployment and danger to democracy. The comparable figures for Labour's appeal were 12.7 per cent and 3.2 per cent respectively.[4]

Other observers noted that the evolution of pluralistic mobilisation hardened the Jewish-Arab divisions. For instance,

Smooha argued that, in spite of the fact that the Arab-Israeli conflict performed a genuine integrative function, the growth of pluralism resulted in inter-Jewish tensions which were released by scapegoating the Arabs.[5] Peres pointed out that the decline in non-symbolic manipulation and patronage politics of the Labour period brought ethnic tensions to bear on the conflict.[6] Etzioni-Halevy, who did an extensive analysis of the relationship between the level of Arab-Israeli conflict, solidarity and protest politics, found a coherent pattern. A higher level of conflict, especially in the major wars of 1967 and 1973, increased the level of cohesion, but in the long run the heightened conflict could not eliminate social protest.[7] The conclusions of Etzioni-Halevy seem to bear out the argument that the relations between pluralism and the Arab-Israeli conflict are circular. The conflict has generated a genuine cohesion, but the rising tension in the ideology of 'social unity' of Israeli society has been increasingly alleviated by the practice of 'unity through conflict'.

The demands of the pluralistic model of mobilisation have often raised speculation that the Israeli Governments might have instigated incidents in order to quell unrest and win public support. These charges were directed particularly at the Likud Cabinet. Some observers noted that selected acts of Israeli belligerency, such as the bombing of PLO strongholds in Lebanon and the destruction of the nuclear facility in Iraq in 1981, have been timed to help Likud's electoral popularity.

There is no conclusive evidence to prove these allegations. It is quite possible that the timing of some incidents involved electoral considerations, but others, such as the raids against the PLO, were prompted by public pressure. The latter was most commonly felt in the heavily Oriental settlements in Upper Galilee which were often shelled by the PLO. Whatever the true motive for Israeli retaliation, there is empirical indication that a heightened level of conflict helped the popularity of the government. In a recent review of public opinion trends since 1973, Louis Guttman, the Academic Director of the Israel Institute of Applied Social Research and a leading authority on public opinion, concluded that the Yom Kippur war had saved the Labour Government of Golda Meir. The air raid on Syria and the destruction of the Iraqi nuclear facility enabled Begin's Cabinet to win the 1981 election. Conversely, the economic concessions of the Likud contributed less to this victory.[8]

The changes in mobilisation style have magnified other features of the political culture which had either a direct or a diffuse impact on the transvaluation of foreign policy beliefs. The most important factor was the decline in the participatory political culture. The only study which replicated Almond and Verba's *Civic Culture* research in Israel found that good citizenship was perceived in terms of obedience to the state rather than in participation. Commitment to the state was emphasised over any other form of political allegiance. For example, 19.6 per cent of respondents reported that the existence of the state commanded their highest pride and 26.3 per cent showed their highest pride in the existence of the Israel Defence Force. By comparison, the political institutions commanded the highest pride of only 8.8 per cent of the representative sample of respondents.[9]

A subsequent survey of Israeli youth revealed a deepening of non-participatory political culture. Loyalty to the state scored highest, whereas the duty of political participation and criticism were ranked as least important by respondents. The democratic principle of tolerance of the political views of others received one of the lowest rankings.[10] Finally, a 1984 survey of democratic attitudes among young Israelis demonstrated that 33 per cent of the sample had democratic attitudes as opposed to 25 per cent who were described as having anti-democratic attitudes. The remaining 42 per cent had mixed attitudes. However, only about half of the sample had democratic attitudes towards Arabs and non-Jews.[11]

Another factor which contributed to the transvaluation of the dominant belief system has been related to the spread of intolerance in Israeli society. Sullivan and his associates, who pioneered work on the psychosocial roots of intolerance, found it related to perceptions of threat. The perception of danger generates anxiety which can be relieved by channelling anger and intolerance against the groups which are deemed to be the source of danger. Sullivan and Shamir, in a series of studies, found that in Israel, which is defined as a 'highly threatened society', there is a high level of 'focused intolerance'. The Jews tend to define Arab groups and pro-Arab left-wing Jewish groups as their least-liked groups. For instance, 29 per cent of respondents choose *Rakach*, the Israeli Communist pro-Arab party, as their least-liked group and 24 per cent choose it as the second least-liked group. The Israeli Arabs tend to dislike most the right-wing Jewish groups, such as Rabbi Kahane's *Kach* and Gush Emunim. Among the

Jews, the proportion of tolerance between right and left groups is 74 to 7 and the proportion of tolerance for Jewish and Arab groups is 64 to 30.[12]

Lack of tolerance affects the norms of democracy. Both Jews and Arabs in Israel have been found to support the notion of democratic rules in the abstract. However, they differ on specific questions of minority rights. The Jews believe more in rights for the majority and the Arabs support more the norms of minority rights. The Jews, however, differentiate more sharply between abstract and applied principles. Some 90 per cent of Jews support abstract democratic rules, but only 63 per cent would like them applied to the Arab minority.[13] Compared to the United States or New Zealand, Israel is the least tolerant country, but the distance between the attitudes of Israelis and Americans is less than expected.[14]

The evolving political culture has had a major impact on a number of issues which are crucial in shaping the foreign policy debate in Israel. First, Israelis have been broadly receptive to the military ethos and the defence needs of the country. In a perceptive remark, Eisenstadt once described Israel as a 'civilian fortress, with a high degree of awareness and sensitivity to defense and yet, with the constant possibility that this element and military considerations would become dominant in the economic and civilian life'.[15]

Empirical evidence bears out the fact that, at least prior to the war in Lebanon, the military domain was highly appreciated by the public. In a survey of public attitudes towards the IDF, Dotan found that between 80 and 90 per cent of the public evaluated the army positively. Most of the respondents felt that the IDF spokesman was more credible than his civilian counterpart. Some 77 per cent of respondents were interested in military information, but 70 per cent declared that they were satisfied with the amount of information which they received.[16] Another study found that in the same period there was a steady decline in the public evaluation of the government's information service.[17]

Israeli society, though not overtly militaristic, has increasingly accepted the continuous conflict. This development is largely due to the effect of the war on the value system of the society, whereby the cumulative number of casualties leads to a perceptual attrition in the sanctity of human life. Some scholars have documented that this attrition has caused a considerable increase in crime rates.[18]

Others, like Friedlander, the Head of the Psychological Services at the Hebrew University, claimed that this phenomenon is demonstrated by the relative equanimity with which Israelis react to the daily count of casualties. Because of the changing value system, most Israelis have accepted the military conflict as inevitable and relatively few speak out for change.[19]

Second, public attitudes touch upon the controversy over the right to know versus governmental secrecy. In the absence of constitutional guidelines, the media and scholars have often complained about the 'credibility gap' and the government's manipulation of information in the name of national security. However, all examination of opinion polls reveals that there is a strong and persistent sentiment against media freedom. An *Yediot Aharanot* poll of 1976, commissioned to gauged the support for a proposed law to stop leaks by broadening censorship, revealed 51.7 per cent supported the measure.[20] A 1983 poll indicated that the number of Israelis who support limitations on the freedom of the press has increased to 65 per cent.[21] Attorney General Yitzhak Zamir and the former chief military censor, Walter Bar-On, claimed that they have received a great number of letters in which the public demanded more censorship.[22]

Third, when military values and norms are accepted as legitimate, there is an increase in the 'monopolisation of patriotism'.[23] Groups which do not share the public consensus are delegitimised and there is a stifling of criticism and dissent. There is no doubt that the political culture in Israel has strongly opposed criticism, which it perceives as a challenge to national unity and harmful to the war effort. Public charges levelled at the Israeli left and the media became particularly prevalent during the war in Lebanon and there were accusations of a 'stab in the back'. Such stifling of criticism is highly regressive in a democracy, yet it is equally true that the Arab states have watched for signs of dissent in order to put pressure on Israel. For instance, prior to the 1984 elections, the *Amal* militia announced that it would increase attacks on the IDF in Lebanon in order to help the Labour Party which was in favour of withdrawal.[24] Whether it is possible to draw a line between legitimate criticism and its harmful effects is a moot point, given the fact that the majority of the Israeli public opposes media criticism.

The existence of a large and intolerant majority in Israel poses a special problem for a country in which there are few legal safeguards for tolerant policies. This difficulty is enhanced by the fact that the intolerant majority is involved rather than apathetic in its attitudes. The tolerant minority is equally outspoken. However, the large intolerant majority can be easily activated by a right-wing political elite. Because of this transvaluation of the political culture, New Zionism became popular among major segments of the society. Likud's traditional emphasis on national consensus and the harmfulness of dissent was so successful because Israelis are particularly sensitive to their historical disasters which were caused by lack of unity.[25]

New Zionist spokesmen have also pointed out that dissent against policies adopted by a democratically elected government which enjoys continuous popular support is anti-democratic. This view has been shared by some of the elites which are not affiliated with the Likud. In one such representative argument Gershon Rivlin, the head of the Ben-Gurion Institute, claimed that those who object to the war and the reserve duty in Lebanon act undemocratically, because the war was decided upon by a democratically elected government.[26]

These claims and counterclaims testify to the difficulty of delineating what constitutes legitimate tolerance for civil rights in a society at war. Such an evaluation has become even more complicated because of the increasing militarisation of the foreign policy debate in Israel.

Militarisation of the Foreign Policy Debate

Research on relations between civilians and the military domain has produced a variety of explanatory models. Scholars have generally agreed that Israel has not become a 'garrison state', but there is not consensus with regard to the question of how permeable the military-civilian sphere is. Using a sociologically oriented analysis, Peri argued that the IDF has increased its influence in important dimensions of the political process, like political thinking, resource allocation and elite penetration.[27]

At the same time, scholars found no evidence to substantiate the hypothesis of the *military mind* phenomenon, which requires the existence of a cohesive group of military which displays hard-line attitudes. On the contrary, Peri's survey of political attitudes among the Israeli military elite reveals that there are no significant tendencies towards conservatism. Among the sample of senior and junior officers, 34 per cent were classified as liberal, 11 per cent as conservative and 55 per cent as having no consistent pattern of attitudes.[28]

An alternative way of ascertaining the impact of the military on society is derived from cognitive psychology. In this model, the military, regardless of its personal views, can influence the foreign policy discourse by casting it in military-strategic terms. Rapoport, a chief proponent of the cognitive approach, argued that, in an extreme case of militarisation of the public discourse, 'foreign policy becomes intellectually indistinguishable from military policy, which by its very nature is essentially strategic'.[29]

The Israeli model of militarisation of the foreign policy debate derives from the fact that the security forces have come to dominate the other crucial elites which normally participate in the legitimisation discourse. There are a number of factors which account for this development. First, the existing laws do not clearly define the relations between the IDF and the government. The armed forces are subordinate to the government through the Minister of Defence. He serves as Commander in Chief of the Armed Forces, although his office does not expressly carry this title. The Minister of Defence need not consult the Cabinet or procure Knesset endorsement before making major decisions, including the mobilisation of reserve brigades. He must refer a mobilisation order immediately to the Knesset Committee on Foreign Affairs and Security, but in practice it is difficult to reverse the decision to mobilise.

Communication between the Chief of Staff, the Minister of Defence, and the Cabinet is not well defined and is mostly informal. This dates back to the days when Ben-Gurion was both Prime Minister and Defence Minister. Ben-Gurion exercised almost exclusive charge over his Chiefs of Staff. Even so, the highly activist Dayan, who served under him, occasionally made independent decisions that jeopardised Ben-Gurion's diplomatic moves. Subsequent Prime Ministers have exercised less control over the military, leading to occasional crises.

The salience of the security effort for Israel's survival has turned the military elite into the most crucial 'social force'. Following Laswell's notion of functional recruitment, whereby elites are chosen from the group whose expertise is most valued in solving the society's problems, senior officers have been regarded as electoral assets. As a result, political recruitment in Israel often involves 'parachuting', that is, a horizontal movement from the apex of the military pyramid to the party pyramid. The transvaluation of the political culture towards a more military value system has created strong popular pressure to include retired officers in the government. The extent of public approval for the military is reflected in a number of opinion polls. For instance, an October 1972 survey indicated that 12.6 per cent of respondents thought the future leaders of the country would be military. Another 26 per cent mentioned politicians and 12.8 per cent opted for scientists.[30]

Third, the reserve system of the Israeli Defence Force has created a particularly permeable boundary between the civilian and the military sectors. In terms of exchange of values, the reserve structure constitutes a two-way process. On the one hand, civilian values penetrate and mitigate the military domain, and, on the other hand, the senior officers have used their military power base to acquire a popular following. Dayan, Rabin and Sharon are the best-known politicians to follow this path, but other high-ranking retired officers have dominated the political scene. Between 1949 and 1981, there were 47 reserve officers in the Knesset and 37 in the cabinet.[31]

The legitimacy of the military elite was greatly enhanced by the Six-Day War. Israel's normative commitment to the occupied territories, and especially the West Bank, has involved the IDF in the most crucial foreign policy debate. Since Israel was forced to accept the status of a 'lawful belligerent occupant', the government could rule the territories only through a Military Administration. As a result, the army acquired extensive administrative, civilian and judicial powers over the local population. The legal guidance for the IDF's activities has been carefully designed to prevent political influence on the part of the military.[32] However, Peri and other scholars of military-civilian relations have documented that the army became a dominant political voice in shaping the debate on the West Bank.[33]

The cognitive model of influence stipulates that, once the military has established itself as a legitimising elite, it will affect foreign policy thinking in a number of ways.

The Paradigm of the Foreign Policy 'Problem'

The militarisation of the paradigm of a foreign policy 'problem' involves four cognitive procedures: (i) the goals are expressed predominantly in terms of power relationships; (ii) an appraisal of means is dominated by military resources; (iii) an appraisal of the adversary's goals and means is also expressed in military terms; (iv) the design for optimisation of the foreign policy process is mostly based on the allocation of military power resources and their implementation.[34]

Empirical identification and measurement of these procedures are extremely difficult. It has been commonplace to argue that post-war foreign policy systems in general have come to be dominated by defence and military thinking. For instance, one prevalent theory holds that, until Vietnam, American foreign policy was dominated by 'battleground conceptions in which communist forces were pitted against those of the United States and the Free World'.[35]

In Israel, the centrality of the security imperative made defence policy virtually synonymous with foreign relations. Epitomised in Dayan's statement that 'small nations do not have a foreign policy . . ., only a defense policy',[36] it was widely accepted by the civilian leadership. However, we have already indicated that, in the early days of the state, the civilian leadership had a fairly strong grip over the military. Even so, Brecher's research and Sharett's diaries provide numerous examples of disagreements between the political leadership and the military.[37]

The balance between military and civilian thinking started to change in the mid-1950s. One reason which accounts for this change is related to the structure of the deterrence process in the Arab-Israeli conflict. In Israel's strategic thinking, deterrence has two major components — general deterrence which seeks to nullify or neutralise the potential threat posed by an enemy *in toto*, and immediate deterrence which can 'nullify a specific type of threat'.[38] From the beginning of terrorist activities in the early 1950s, the problem of general deterrence of the Arab states became compounded by efforts to stop acts of terrorism. The Israeli response to the latter problem has led to a steady increase of retaliatory actions against the Arab countries which harboured Palestinian guerrillas. The policy of retaliation was institutionalised in 1953 when the IDF established the 101 commando unit. In spite of the unit's success at the tactical level, military observers have argued that the policy of *escalating retaliation* failed to deter terrorism. Moreover, there is widespread agreement that this policy led to the upgrading of immediate deterrence to general deterrence. For instance, the failure of the IDF to stop terrorist activities in the early 1950s is recognised as an important component of Ben-Gurion's decision to launch the Sinai campaign of 1956.

Israel's futile efforts to deter Syria from harassing Northern Galilee in the early 1960s is another example of immediate retaliation deteriorating into a general conflict. This process was apparently enhanced when the Chief of Staff Yitzhak Rabin published an article in September 1966 threatening to take action against the Syrian regime. This was followed by the Kineret action in April 1967 where, in response to the shelling of a tractor belonging to the kibbutz Ha'on, Israel shot down four Syrian MIGs. Some Israeli scholars and politicians have speculated that this action, coupled with the fact that the Israeli planes reached Damascus, could have triggered Syrian fears which ultimately led to the Six-Day War.[39]

The difficulties inherent in the structure of deterrence are compounded by the relative absence of civilian channels of communication between Israel and the Arabs. In less acute conflicts, the strategic components of the deterrence are mitigated by civilian and diplomatic communication. Because of the earlier Arab refusal to legitimise any contacts with Israel, the opportunity for structured diplomatic exchange was limited. The use of third-party intermediaries, the United States, the Soviet Union and neutral parties, has often complicated or even distorted the Arab-Israeli dialogue. Such constraints have made the recourse to military options quite commonplace.

This pattern, which can be defined as 'perceptual deadlocking', normally followed a failure in diplomatic activity. In one variant of this pattern, parts of the civilian elite in Israel sided with the military against the more moderate elements in the Cabinet, the success of whose policy was predicated upon a diplomatic breakthrough with the Arabs. One often cited example is the historic rivalry between Ben-Gurion and his moderate Foreign Minister, Moshe Sharett, Shlaim, who reviewed Sharett's diaries and other relevant sources, made a credible argument that Ben-Gurion's decision to attack Egypt in 1956 was partly precipitated by the failure of American mediation efforts in the summer of 1955. The collapse of the Anderson mission undermined the standing of Sharett, and brought Ben-Gurion to support the military, who were apprehensive about the Egyptian arms build-up and exasperated by the failure of their retaliation policy.[40]

In another variant of 'perceptual deadlocking' the civilian elite was forced to accept the military option. A dramatic example of this pattern is provided by the decision-making process before the Six-Day War. In an excellent reconstruction of this process, Gross Stein and Tanter demonstrated how the civilian elite in the Eshkol Cabinet had initially resisted the pressures of the military. But, as the number of diplomatic options decreased, the civilian leadership legitimised the military strategy.[41] A similar development took place during the decision making leading to the Entebbe raid.[42] It is interesting to note that 'perceptual deadlocking' has also been evident in Arab decision making, and especially in the process which led Sadat to the 1973 war.

There is little doubt that, after 1967, there was a serious increase in the militarisation of the paradigm of foreign policy 'problems'. One reason for this increase was functional; the need to occupy a large territory made the military pivotal in any foreign policy debate. A second reason pertained to the newly acquired prestige of the military. Even before 1967, there were occasional instances when the military would publicise its views in order to put pressure on the civilian echelon. For example, in 1957 the then Chief-of-Staff, Dayan, published an Order of the Day criticising the withdrawal of Israeli troops from the Sinai Peninsula.[43] In the early 1970s, however, the public exposure of the military became commonplace. Senior officers were regularly interviewed on political subjects and, according to some reports, generals did not hesitate to lobby ministers.[44] However, the third and most important factor in the militarisation of the paradigm of foreign policy 'problems' relates to the concept of cognitive complexity.

The Military Paradigm of a Foreign Policy 'Problem' and Conceptual Complexity.

Theory postulates that the level of conceptual complexity of any particular discourse is a function of two complaints. The first is the level of cognitive complexity of the individuals involved. The second component is contextual, i.e. it depends on the subject or area of discussion.[45]

Military scholars and psychologists have long pointed out that strategic thinking, which routinely de-emphasises political and social elements, has a relatively low level of conceptual complexity.

One of the most complex issues in defence policy is the proper assessment of an enemy's intentions as opposed to his capabilities. When evaluating threat, strategic thinkers normally emphasise military capabilities. In evaluating capabilities, the ratio between Israel's military hardware capacity and the Arabs' hardware has always been a central part of the strategic thinking in Israel.

The apparent rationale of this stringent emphasis on capabilities derives from the fact that security decisions are structured like choices whose outcomes are not certain. In the Israeli case, the estimates of probabilities are especially crucial because of the widespread perception that the Arabs are bent on destroying the Jewish state. Critics such as Brecher believe that the 'Holocaust fixation', which was justifiable in the earlier days, has become a major psychological obstacle to intelligent and efficient decision making.[46] In other words, the 'Holocaust fixation' has enhanced the propensity of the political system to accept the *worst case scenario* thinking of the military in Israel.

Even if one does not accept this harsh statement, it must be admitted that numerous critics have suggested that the emphasis on military options was detrimental to an analysis of the psychological or political definition of the situation. An interesting case in point was the public debate between Dayan and Yeacov Hasdai, a career officer who, upon his retirement after the 1973 war, became a major critic of the IDF. The evidence in this debate indicates that Dayan, reflecting the prevalent security thinking of his day, limited the definition of the terms 'goals of the war' and 'outcomes of the war' to changes in the military *status quo*.[47]

A more poignant example is the continuing debate over the occupied territories. As the preceding chapter made clear, all initial discussion on the territories was couched in strategic terms. Concepts like 'strategic depths' and 'projectile range' were widely propagated and disseminated through the media. While the normative Land of Israel approach subsequently overshadowed strategic considerations, military thinking is still extensively used in defining the best ways of treating the Palestinian population.

Broadly conceptualised, the military approach used in the administered territories was derived from the model of Military Administration under which the Israeli Arabs lived from 1950 to 1966. Known in the sociological literature as a 'system of control', this model was based on a number of coercive and voluntary mechanisms for keeping the minority quiescent.[48] But conditions in the West Bank and the Gaza Strip, with a large population and relatively free access to the Arab countries, differed sharply from the fate of the tightly controlled Israeli Arabs. Failing to implement any political means of control, the Military Administration increased the use of military options. One consequence of this cognitive style was to avoid a thorough discussion of the psychological sources of civilian unrest and the terrorist acivities of the Palestinians. Normally, these actions were labelled as 'PLO instigation' in the public debate.

The second consequence was an overestimation of the effectiveness of military means to quell the unrest. Whether a more politically oriented approach could have solved the problem of a large population under prolonged military rule is not clear. Those who assume that the West Bank is structurally similar to other superordinate-subordinate situations, such as Algeria or Northern Ireland, argue in the negative. Yet it should be recalled that a review of opinion polls in the preceding chapter indicated that, in the 1970s, the majority of Israelis perceived the treatment of the Palestinian problem in purely military terms.

The Foreign Policy Process and Intelligence

It is generally recognised that intelligence, military and civilian, has become a universal part of the foreign policy making process. Israel's strategic environment poses security problems which are more complex than normal. The strategic parameters were determined by the concept of no-war no-peace with the Arab states and became axiomatic in the doctrine of national security. In addition, strategic space and time resources are perceived as asymmetrical. Before 1967, Israel had the lowest ratio of territory to borders of any state in the Middle East. The ratio improved after 1967, but the return of the Sinai worsened it again. Even more striking has been the asymmetry in the population base of Israel and its neighbours.

Under these circumstances, Israel was forced to create a military establishment with the lowest possible cost in manpower and funds — hence the reserve system. The major weakness of the reserve system was the 48-hour period needed for mobilisation in the event of a surprise attack by the enemy. Thus from the very beginning of independence, intelligence became a focal point in Israeli foreign policy making.

Intelligence collection does constitute a legitimate need of a foreign policy system. Policy decisions, whether diplomatic or military, require detailed information about the external environment. What is more complex, though, is the effort to establish a balance between the intelligence and the civilian components of the foreign policy debate. This problem has two interrelated dimensions: the degree of pluralism of the debate and the degree of its openness.

The Degree of Pluralism. The historical evolution of the national intelligence structure in Israel was largely random and unplanned. In the absence of a National Security Council, intelligence coordination has been conducted by the Cabinet. After the Six-Day War, which enhanced the salience of the military, the Chief of Military intelligence began to act as a *de facto* adviser to the Cabinet. At the same time, there was controversy over the structure of the intelligence community. The three intelligence branches—the *Mossad*, the Military Intelligence (*Aman*), and the General Security Service (*Shin Bet*), have competed for influence and power. The failure of the intelligence community in the 1973 war publicised the debate and revealed the complexity of the problem.

Scholarly research and interviews with past intelligence personnel indicate that Israeli intelligence operates best at the operational and tactical level. Predicting the political-strategic behaviour of the Arab countries has proved more difficult. It is known today that there have been a number of failures: (i) the Rotem Operation of 1960, when Egypt moved troops into Sinai and was forced to withdraw when the IDF countermobilised; the operation was never made public; (ii) the Arab moves which led to the 1967 war were not anticipated before Nasser's highly publicised steps; (iii) the so-called intelligence 'conception' which held that the Arabs states would not attack Israel prior to achieving total combat readiness; this theory was behind the intelligence misperceptions in the 1973 war; (iv) the failure to foresee Sadat's peace initiative; General Shlomo Gazit, a former head of Aman, subsequently admitted that the intelligence community had not developed measures for assessing peaceful intentions.[49]

It is misleading to suggest that all these failures stem from the extremely tight military control of the foreign policy debate in Israel. Extensive research on the psychology of intelligence indicates that most cases of surprise in military history are related to failures in the cognitive processes at either individual or group level. However, the structural dominance of the intelligence community in Israel has amplified these failures. The Agranat Commission which investigated the 1973 war recommended more pluralism and civilian involvement in the foreign policy debate. Presumably, this would have ensured a broader intellectual perspective and prevented the political manipulation of intelligence. As we shall see in the next chapter, the failure to pluralise the debate and the politicisation of the intelligence community played an important role in the decision making which led to the war in Lebanon.

The Degree of Openness. Evaluating the related dimension of the openness of the foreign policy debate is not easy. Galnor argued that the 'culture of secrecy' was inherited from the British Mandate and carried into the independence era.[50] Since security and foreign affairs are matters of survival, there has been widespread agreement that some measure of secrecy is necessary. The former Chief Censor Bar-On acknowledged that most editors have adhered to a policy of voluntary censorship.[51]

On the other hand, there has been an uneasiness among scholars and observers who feel that secrecy and censorship can distort the foreign policy debate. One of the major concerns is the problem of political manipulation of intelligence and censorship. Goren, who studied the media and censorship in Israel, documented the difficulties of differentiating between genuine intelligence concerns and political interest.[52] A catalogue of political uses of intelligence is beyond the scope of the present study, but it should be emphasised that the Mossad took a largely political stand when it supported the decision to invade Lebanon.

Another problem is the occasional incongruence between intelligence and the need to inform the public. For instance, the true story about Eli Cohen, the Israeli spy who was hanged in Damascus was not allowed to be published in Israel. When the case broke open in 1965, the Mossad asked for voluntary censorship. As a result, the public was convinced that the Arabs were hanging an innocent man.[53]

Perhaps the most serious problem involving openness is the degree to which the media are allowed to scrutinise the military. The principal question of whether the media in Israel can criticise the Ministry of Defence was not solved until the spring of 1956. At that time *Haaretz* tried to publish a series of articles about the Ministry of Defence, but they were suppressed by censorship. The subsequent change in this policy brought more media criticism, but the 1973 war created renewed tension between the military and the media. According to accounts published by military correspondents, a number of journalits visited the Southern Command in the Sinai, prior to the Yom Kippur War. Some of the senior officers, including General Albert Mendler, revealed their apprehensions about the possibility of a surprise attack by the Egyptians. Based on these interviews, one of the correspondents, Yaacov Erez of *Maariv*, prepared a detailed report on Egypt's preparation for war. His article was due to be published on 4 October 1973, but the censorship did not approve it.[54] Whether publication of the article could have prevented the surprise attack is doubtful, but the incident illustrates the difficulties in finding an appropriate balance between the need for secrecy and public scrutiny.

This dilemma was highlighted during the preparations for the war in Lebanon. When the original plan for Operation Peace for Galilee was discussed by the Cabinet in 1981–2, a number of journalists like Zeen Schiff from *Haaretz*, Eitan Haber from *Yediot Aharanot* and Hirsh Goodman from *The Jerusalem Post*, wrote about the dangers of a possible involvement. Yet the necessary secrecy surrounding the invasion plan, code-named Big Pine, has prevented a public discussion of its merits.

The Changing Pattern of the Advocacy Groups

The changing pattern of the advocacy groups is a major indicator of the transvaluation of a national belief system. The importance of advocacy groups in foreign policy is best understood in terms of the 'linkage model'. Drawing on the work of Rosenau and Deutsch, Holt and Turner developed a scheme for analysing the impact of advocacy groups on the international behaviour of a country. The crucial factors in this scheme are the number and political orientation of linkage groups and the strength of the ties between the linkage group and the domestic system.[55]

In his extensive study of foreign policy advocacy groups in the 1960s, Brecher found a preponderance of left-of-centre groups. The Greater Land of Israel Movement is the only significant right-wing group listed in Brecher's survey.[56]

The structure of the advocacy groups changed considerably in the 1970s. The most important trend was the polarisation of the interest groups. On the one hand, there has been an increase in the salience of advocacy groups which are broadly representative of Socialist Zionism. The most important of these groups is Peace Now, which was established in an effort to spur the peace process with Egypt. Peace Now has proved itself both durable and capable of mobilising large segments of the Israeli electorate. Peace Now constitutes the most coherent opposition to the occupation of the West Bank and has been active in the opposition to the war in Lebanon.[57]

Other left and liberal groups have been more ephemeral. Soldiers Against Silence, There is a Limit, and Parents Against Silence were established in opposition to the war in Lebanon. They have been either disbanded or absorbed in the Peace Now activities. The new Oriental group, East For Peace, has not made an impact on the Oriental community. The more traditional left-wing groups like *Matzpen, Haolam Hazeh*, and *Ihud* have virtually ceased to exist. The only exception is the *New Outlook* and the recently established International Centre for Peace in the Middle East. Yet in spite of its considerable influence abroad, the *New Outlook* circle has a very limited domestic influence.

On the other hand, there has been a dramatic increase in the number of right-wing and religious groups which have broadly reflected the New Zionist ideology. They can be classified as secular right, religious right and born-again groups.

The Secular Right.   Two loosely co-ordinated coalitions of small groups comprise the active secular right wing. One association is known as the New Israeli Right. This group was founded by a number of Likud MPs headed by Michael Kleiner, and two Russian immigrants, Avigdor Askin and Arieh Vodkah. Another prominent leader of the group is Paul Eidelberg, a former professor from the University of Chicago. Affiliated groups include the Association for the Security of Israel and *Maoz*, an organisation of Soviet Jews.

The New Israeli Right has been financed by Robert Jacobs and has close links to Jerry Falwell's Moral Majority and the conservative Heritage Foundation in the United States. The proclaimed goal of the New Right is to undermine the 'monopoly of the left' in the Israeli media and publishing. To this end, the group plans to establish an institute modelled on the American Heritage Foundation with a projected annual budget of $1 million.[58]

The other group is more diffuse and derives from the estimated 400,000-strong Oriental lower class, many of them dwellers in the big slum areas in Jerusalem and Tel Aviv. In the past, Oriental protest has been left-wing, populist or anti-Ashkenazi. The Black Panthers in the 1970s and the more recent *Ohalim* and *Shahak* movements confined their protest to demands for better housing and education.

In the late 1970s some of this Oriental protest was turned into support for the Likud. On a number of occasions, the Oriental right was engaged in violent participation in political rallies and attacks on Labour and Peace Now activities. Right-wing Oriental violence assumed serious proportions in the 1981 elections, and reached unprecedented levels in the reaction to the largely Ashkenazi anti-war protest in 1982–3. This culminated in the February 1983 protest march in Jerusalem, when a Peace Now activist, Emil Grunzweig, was killed and several people wounded.

There is no conclusive evidence that the Oriental right has a permanent organisation. Police investigations in the past have exposed a number of small underground cells dedicated to vandalism and sabotage. The *Maatz* Gang and the *Shimshon* Soccer Club arms cache are two known cells. An Oriental Jew, Yonah Abrushmi, was convicted of the Grunzweig killing. The trial revealed that Abrushmi was linked to the *Katamon* Gang in Jerusalem, well known for its criminal activities.

The Religious Groups.   This category comprises a wide variety of groups, some loosely co-ordinated and others tightly organised. The most prominent movement is the Gush Emunim, which was established after the 1973 war. The Gush serves as the major lobby for the West Bank; it has generated pressure on the decision-making process, often by establishing illegal settlements. The Gush's settlement organisation, *Amana*, has acted to bolster the existing network of settlements in the West Bank.

Members of Gush Emunim have engaged in vigilante violence in three categories: expropriation of Arab land, retaliation against Arab terror and civilian resistance, and sporadic attacks on IDF soldiers enforcing order. It is unclear whether the attacks are individual or organised acts. Table 6.1, which lists anti-Arab violence in the 1982–3 period, indicates that most of the incidents

Table 6.1: Anti-Arab Violence by Jewish Settlers January
1982 – July 1983

Date	Place	Incident	Casualties Dead	Hurt	Suspects
1982					
Mar.	Sinjil	property vandalised	–	–	unidentified
"	Temple Mount	assault on worshippers	–	3	f. Kiryat Arba
"	Hebron	grenade thrown at house	–	–	unidentified
"	Bireh	20 cars vandalised	–	–	settlers
"	Tulkarem	shots fired at house	–	–	settlers
"	Dahisha	arson at gas station	–	–	settlers
"	Hebron	shots fired at demonstrators	–	7	f. Kiryat Arba
"	Sinjil	arson at generator	–	–	f. Shiloh
"	near Shiloh	shots fired at demonstrators	1	2	f. Shiloh
"	Ramallah	shots fired at demonstrators	–	–	2 settlers
"	Dir Dibwan	2 buses set afire	–	–	*
"	Bitin	2 cars set afire	–	–	*
"	Beni Naim	shots fired at demonstrators	1	–	f. Kiryat Arba
"	?	house windows broken	–	–	f.Kochav Hashahar
"	Halhoul	shots fired at demonstrators	1	–	civillians
"	Taibeh	property vandalised	–	–	settlers
Apr.	?	100 cars vandalised	–	–	settlers
"	Nablus	shots fired at demonstrators	–	2	settlers
"	Nablus	12 children kidnapped	–	–	settlers
May	Ein el Arub	shots fired at domonstrators	1	–	settler
"	3 towns	3 children kidnapped	–	–	settlers
Dec.	Hebron	shots fired at stores	–	–	f. Elon Moreh
"	Hebron	house confiscated	–	–	settlers
1983					
Jan.	Nahlin	trees uprooted, sprayed	–	–	f. Gush Etzion
"	Hebron	elec/tel lines destroyed	–	–	f. Kiryat Arba
"	Hebron	house destroyed	–	–	f. Kiryat Arba
Feb.	Hebron	Purim joy shots fired	–	1	f. Kiryat Arba
"	Hebron	explosion near mosque	–	–	unidentified
Mar.	Hebron	shots fired at tender	–	–	f. Kiryat Arba
"	Yatta	school invaded, 2 girls seized	–	–	settlers "
"	Hebron	shooting in city	–	–	f. El-Kakum
"	Kalandia	invaded camp	–	–	*
Apr.	Hebron	many cars vandalised	–	–	*
May	Bet Jala	40 cars vandalised	–	–	*
"	Hebron	10 cars vandalised	–	–	f. Kiryat Arba
"	Turmus Aiya	crop confiscated	–	–	f. Shiloh
July	Hebron	bus set afire	–	–	unidentified
"	el-Arub	bus set afire	–	–	unidentified
"	Hebron	elec lines destroyed	–	–	f. Kiryat Arba
"	Hebron	marketplace burned	–	–	f. Kiryat Arba

* Incident claimed in name of organised group.

Source: D. Zucher (ed.), *Human Rights in the Occupied Territories*, The
International Centre for Peace in the Middle East, Tel Aviv, 1983.

were carried out by individual settlers. According to Gush spokesmen, the vigilante activities were in retaliation for terrorist and civil resistance on the part of the Palestinians.

Most recently, the existence of a Gush-linked terrorist organisation was revealed. The organisation was charged with the 1980 attack on the West Bank mayors, the 1983 killing of students in the Islamic College in Hebron, and plans to blow up the mosques on Temple Mount. The trial of the 27 suspects, some of them high-ranking in the Gush organisation, established that the terrorist organisation had the tacit support of leading circles in Gush Emunim.

The *Kach* group, founded by Rabbi Meir Kahane, the former head of the US Jewish Defense League, is a much smaller organisation. Kahane, who won a Knesset seat in the 1984 election, has advocated expulsion of the Palestinians from Israel and the West Bank and the formal annexation of the occupied territories.[59] Kach's mostly American members have been involved in dozens of attacks against Arab persons and property in the West Bank. The *El Nakam*, a radical splinter of Kach, was behind the 1984 attack on a bus near Ramallah, in which six Palestinians were wounded. Kach, El Nakam and perhaps Gush Emunim have operated under various names. *Irgun Hamagen* took credit in early 1983 for vandalising cars in Hebron and wounding two Palestinians with a bomb planted in a local mosque.[60]

Another small advocacy group is the Faithful of the Temple Mount. This non-violent movement was organised by former Gush activist Gershon Salamon, by Rabbi Israel Ariel who led the opposition to the evacuation of Sinai, and by Geulah Cohen of the Tehiya Party. The Faithful of the Temple Mount have a youth organisation, *Hashmonaim*, headed by Yoel Lerner, and are supported by the *El Har Hashem*, an organisation established by Israel Medad of Shiloah.

The Faithful and their affiliates want to legalise Jewish access to the area on which the Temple was built. The group differs sharply from the official orthodox view, which imposed a ban on Jews setting foot on the Temple Mount because of its supreme holiness. For Israeli nationalists who participate in the group, the Temple Mount symbolises Israeli sovereignty over the whole of Jerusalem. The ultra-orthodox elements in the movement advocate the rebuilding of the Temple. The 60 or so students of the *Ateret*

Cohanim Yeshiva and others have been preparing plans for re-building the Temple and weaving the ritual garment of the High Priest.[61]

Total membership of the Faithful of the Temple Mount is estimated at 1,500. They have established the Temple Mount Foundation to collect money and have set up activities — trying to tunnel into the site, trying to settle on the Mount, praying outside the walls — to publicise their objective of rebuilding the Temple. The Faithful receive support from fundamentalist groups in the United States. According to newspaper reports, the Faithful are backed by Christian evangelists like Dr Milton Sutton and an Oklahoma millionaire, Terry Risenhoover. Christian evangelists are also linked to the board of the Temple Foundation.[62]

The return to orthodox Judaism, the *teshuva* ('born again') movement, has steadily gained momentum since 1967. According to Aviad, the author of a book on the 'return to Judaism', the movement has attracted a relatively large number of people from secular families who share the feeling that the country has no clear sense of goals.[63] The teshuva movement has been popularised by the conversion of many well-known entertainment, media and military personalities.

The various born-again groups are normally associated with the *yeshivot*, the Talmudic colleges. The *Or Sameah* Yeshiva in Jerusalem is the largest centre for born-again activities. To accommodate the burgeoning movement, Or Sameah opened a number of branches throughout Israel. The *Beltz* Hassidim is another group which, through its *Torah ve Emunah* centres has conducted seminars and other born-again activities. The yeshivot of the *Habad* Hassidic movement have been traditionally engaged in the born-again movement. There is no statistical data about the total number of converts, but one source estimated that there are currently some 4,000 students in these centres, not including the Habad Hassidic movement.[64]

The foreign policy advocacy of the born-again movement is somewhat diffuse. Not all of the sects which attract converts take a clear stand with regard to the Land of Israel issue. Some are anti-Zionist and others do not support the retention of the territories. But the majority of the born-again movement, taking its lead from Agudat Israel, has increasingly come out in favour of the sanctity of the Land of Israel. A major breakthrough in this policy occurred when the ultra-orthodox community built the town

Emanuel in Samaria. The official orthodoxy has also become vocal in sponsoring a variety of Likud's policies, including the war in Lebanon.[65]

Only a tiny minority of the born-again Jews engage in violence or terrorism. One of these groups is *Birchat Avraham* Yeshiva in Jerusalem. The students, followers of Reb Nahman of Bratslav, regularly communicate with God in the open fields and engage in prolonged vociferous prayer. Financed by Rabbi Abraham Dueik, the leader of the Aleppo-Jewish community in the United States, the sect's 100 members have been accused of harassing Arabs. Charges included destruction of Arab property and the brutal beating of a 75-year-old Arab woman.[66]

Another minuscule cell was the *Bnei Yehuda* messianic sect. Its members were born-again Jews with criminal records who lived in an abandoned building in the ruined Arab village of Lifta outside Jerusalem. Led by a Tel Aviv criminal, Shimon Barda, the group was allegedly financed by a Jaffa arms dealer. Five members of the group were involved in the attempt on 27 January 1984 to blow up the Dome of the Rock and the al-Aqsa mosque. It was also reported that the police found a huge arsenal at Lifta.[67]

Still another marginal cell known as the *Ein Keren* Gang was formed by four born-again residents of the Ein Keren neighbourhood. They were accused of numerous attacks on Christian churches and mosques on the Mount of Olives and Mount Zion. The Ein Keren group apparently used the slogan of TNT (a Hebrew acronym for Terror Against Terror) to publicise its activity.[68]

From the model developed by Holt and Turner, it is possible to derive a list of indicators which can measure the strength of the ties between the 'linkage groups' and the domestic system. One indicator is the amount of the political system's support for the advocacy groups. At the legal level, all governments can raise the costs of some collective actions to some groups and lower the costs to others. This can be done by simply tolerating certain activities or by actively encouraging them.[69]

A number of recent studies have found that all Israeli governments have been most lenient in exercising law enforcement with regard to religious groups. Reiser, who used Lehman's data on police response to religious demonstrations, concluded that since 1977, when the National Religious Party took over the police portfolio, the level of tolerance has increased considerably.[70]

Legal tolerance has been carried into the administration of the occupied territories, which created numerous problems of law and order. Efforts to delineate the legal principles in the territories became extremely complicated because of the multiplicity of legal sources. The administered territories are governed according to four legal systems: international law, such as the Fourth Geneva Convention; the legal principles established by the Military Administration; Jordanian law binding on the local population; and Israeli law.

The arrival of the Jewish settlers, following the successful attempt of Rabbi Moshe Levinger in 1968 to break the Israeli government ban on Jewish settlements, has vastly complicated the legal situation. There was a lack of clarity regarding the legal status of the Jewish settlers and the land expropriation undertaken by the government on their behalf. The legal situation was further aggravated when, in response to Arab resistance and terrorist activities, the Jewish settlers embarked on vigilante activities. Jewish attacks on Arabs went largely unpunished, as opposed to the stringent measures taken against comparable Arab activities.

In 1980, the charges that the West Bank had a double legal standard prompted Attorney General Yitzhak Zamir to appoint a special committee headed by his deputy, Yehudit Karp. The Karp Report, which documented numerous cases of Jewish abuse of Arabs, was not acted upon until 1983.

The political system has also encouraged the activity of right-wing and religious groups. In a series of investigative reports on the born-again movement, Ran Kislev revealed that, under former Chief of Staff Raphael Eitan, the Israeli Defence Force opened its gates to teshuva practices. Officers and enlisted men have been invited to participate in seminars conducted by Or Sameah and other yeshivot which sponsor born-again activities. Concurrently, the Ministry of Religious Affairs upgraded the *per capita* allowance for the teshuva students to 150,000 shekel as opposed to 111,000 shekel for regular yeshiva students.[71]

Finally, public opinion has been constantly supportive of the New Zionist advocacy groups and rather hostile to Peace Now and similar groups. According to a *Modiin Ezrachi* poll of July 1983, 53.8 per cent of respondents objected to Peace Now tactics and 13.3 per cent supported the movement. Twenty-seven per cent justified some of Peace Now tactics but objected to others. Demographically, those who opposed Peace Now were predominantly lower-stratum Orientals in the 18–22 age group.[72]

A 1980 survey of the Israel Institute of Applied Social Research revealed that 70 per cent of Israeli Jews question the loyalty of the Arabs, as opposed to 37 per cent who expressed the same negative sentiments in 1970.[73] A PORI poll of 1983 revealed that the public was in line with the advocacy groups which lobby for harsh measures against the Palestinians. Forty-five per cent supported the expulsion of Palestinians to Jordan as a punishment for civilian resistance, 5.3 per cent conditioned the expulsion by the severity of the offence, and 39.7 per cent objected to it.[74]

The more messianically oriented advocacy groups are less popular with the public. A PORI poll of 1983 revealed that only 18.3 per cent of respondents supported the idea of the Third Temple. Forty-eight per cent categorically objected to it and 3.1 per cent argued that the Third Temple should be built only after the coming of the Messiah. The most supportive group was the lower-stratum Orientals, whereas the better-educated Ashkenazim objected to the idea.[75]

In conclusion, the survey of indicators of transvaluation — the changing pattern of political mobilisation and culture, the militarisation of the crucial legitimisation debate, and the realignment of the advocacy group structure — provides empirical evidence about the process through which New Zionism took root in the society. The application of New Zionism to Israel's foreign policy will be examined in the next section.

Notes

1. J. P. Nettle, *Political Mobilization*, (Faber and Faber, London, 1967), pp. 87–8.

2. M. Canover, *Populism* (Harcourt Brace Jovanich, New York and London, 1981), p. 137.

3. A. A. Stein, 'Conflict and Cohesion. A Review of Literature,' *Journal of Conflict Resolution*, vol. 20, no. 1 (1976), pp. 143–72.

4. Adapted from J. Mendilow, 'The Transformation of the Israeli Multi-Party System, 1965–1981' in A. Arian (ed.), *The Elections in Israel, 1981* (Ramot Publishing, Tel Aviv, 1983), Table 3, p. 27.

5. S. Smooha, *Israel: Pluralism and Conflict*, (University of California Press, Berkeley and Los Angeles, 1978), p. 104.

6. Y. Peres, *Ethnic Relations in Israel*, (Sifriat Hapoalim, Tel Aviv, 1977), p. 37 (Hebrew).

7. E. Etzioni-Halevy with R. Shapiro, *Political Culture in Israel*, (Praeger, New York and London, 1977), pp. 112–123.

8. E. L. Guttman, 'Wars and Political Attitudes of the Jewish Public in Israel', paper presented at the annual conference of the Israel Sociological Association, Ber Sheeba, February 1985, (Hebrew).

9. E. Golan, *Political Culture in Israel-Case Study*, (unpublished M.A. thesis, Haifa University, 1977), p. 80, (Hebrew).

10. O. Ichilov and N. Nave, '"The Good Citizen", as Viewed by Israeli Adolescents', *Comparative Politics*, vol. 13, no. 3 (1981), pp. 361–76.

11. Reported in *Haaretz*, 15 October 1984.

12. M. Shamir and J. L. Sullivan, 'The Political Context of Tolerance. Israel and the United States', *American Political Science Review*, vol. 75, no. 2 (1983), pp. 92–106.

13. M. Shamir and J. L. Sullivan, 'Jews and Arabs in Israel: Everybody Hates Somebody, Sometimes', *Journal of Conflict Resolution*, forthcoming.

14. J. L. Sullivan, N. Roberts, M. Shamir and P. Welsh, 'Pluralistic Intolerance, Focused Intolerance and Tolerance: Mass Attitudes in the U.S., Israel and New Zealand', *Comparative Politics*, forthcoming.

15. S. Eisenstadt, 'Change and Continuity in Israeli Society; II Dynamic Conservatism vs. Innovation', *The Jerusalem Quarterly*, no. 2 (1977), p. 8.

16. Y. Dotan, *The Opinions of the Public About the Army and Defense*, (The Israel Institute of Applied Social Research, Jerusalem, 1974), pp. 1–8, (Hebrew).

17. S. Levy and E. L. Guttman, *The Feeling of Satisfaction and Stress Among the Israeli Public*, (The Israel Institute of Applied Social Research, Jerusalem, 1973), p. 25 (Hebrew).

18. G. Fishman, 'On War and Crime' in S. Breznitz (ed.), *Stress in Israel* (Van Nostrand Reinhold Company, New York, 1983), pp. 165–80; and S. F. Landau and B. Beit Hallahmi, 'Israel: Aggression in Psychohistorical Perspective' in A. P. Goldstein and M. H. Segal (eds), *Aggression in Global Perspective*, (Pergamon Press, New York, 1983), pp. 261–86.

19. Reported in *Haaretz*, 23 November 1983.

20. Quoted in A. W. Bar-On, *The Untold Stories, the Diary of the Chief Censor*, (Edanim Publication, Jerusalem, 1981), p. 279.

21. Quoted in *Haaretz*, 3 April 1983.

22. *Maariv*, 8 July 1983; and Bar-On, *The Untold Story*, p. 279.

23. D. Bar-Tal, 'Psychological Analysis of Patriotism' (unpublished manuscript, n.d.).

24. *Haaretz*, 15 July 1984.

25. This theme has been espoused by Israel Eldad, a chief New Zionist spokesman, and other members of the ideological elite of the Greater Land of Israel Movement. The target of most of their criticism has been the Peace Now Movement. For a representative article see I. Eldad, 'How Zionism Failed', *Haaretz*, 5 May 1983.

26. *Maariv*, 3 June 1983.

27. Y. Peri, *Between Battles and Ballots: Israeli Military in Politics* (Cambridge University Press, Cambridge, 1983), pp. 265–85.

28. Y. Peri, 'Ideological Portrait of the Israeli Military Elite', *The Jerusalem Quarterly*, no. 3 (1977), pp. 28–41.

29. A. Rapoport, 'Critique of Strategic Thinking' in R. Fisher (ed.), *International Conflict and Behavioural Science*, (Basic Books, New York, 1964), pp. 211–37.

30. Quoted in Peri, *Between Battles*, p. 119.

31. For a theoretically oriented discussion see M. Lissak, 'The Contact and Conversion Dimensions Between the Civilian Sector and the Military Establishment: The Army of Volunteers and the Conscript Army', *State, Government and International Relations*, no. 12 (1978), pp. 27–45 (Hebrew); D. Zamir, 'Generals in Politics', *The Jerusalem Quarterly*, no. 20 (1981), pp. 18–35. The statistics were calculated on the basis of Tables 4 and 5 in Peri, *Between Battles*, pp. 103–4.

32. For a thorough discussion of the military role in the administered territories, see M. Shamgar (ed.), *Military Government in the Territories Administered by*

Israel 1967–1980, vol. 1, (Hebrew University, Jerusalem — Faculty of Law, Jerusalem 1982).

33. Peri, *Between Battles*, pp. 90–100.

34. Rapoport, 'Critique', p. 225.

35. C. W. Kegley and E. R. Wittkopf, *American Foreign Policy. Patterns and Process* (St. Martin's Press, New York, 1979), p. 66.

36. Quoted in Peri, *Between Battles*, p. 20.

37. Moshe Sharett and Levi Eshkol were two of Israel's Prime Ministers who were particularly undermined by the military.

38. O. Chen, 'Reflection on Israeli Deterrence', *The Jerusalem Quarterly*, no. 24 (1982), pp. 26–39.

39. Peri, *Between Battles*, p. 160; S. Peres, *David's Sling* (Random House, New York, 1970), p. 223; D. Schoueftan, 'Nasser's 1967 Policy Reconsidered', *The Jerusalem Quarterly* no. 3 (1977), pp. 124–44.

40. A. Shlaim, 'Conflicting Approaches to Israel's Relations with the Arabs: Ben-Gurion and Sharett, 1953–1956', *The Middle East Journal*, vol. 37, no. 2 (1983), pp. 180–201.

41. J. Gross Stein and R. Tanter, *Rational Decision Making: Israel's Security Choices, 1967* (Ohio State University Press, Columbus, OH, 1980), pp. 157–213.

42. Z. Maoz, 'The Decision to Raid Entebbe. Decision Analysis Applied to Crisis Behavior', *Journal of Conflict Resolution*, vol. 25, no. 4 (1981), pp. 677–707.

43. Bar-On, *The Untold Story*, p. 89.

44. Y. Elizur and E. Salpater, *Who Rules Israel?* (Harper & Row, New York, 1973), p. 219.

45. P. Suedfeld, P. E. Tetlock and C. Ramirez, 'War, Peace and Integrative Complexity', *Journal of Conflict Resolution*, vol. 21, no. 3 (1977), pp. 427–43.

46. M. Brecher, *The Foreign Policy System of Israel*, (Oxford University Press, London, 1972), p. 514.

47. S. Harlap, 'The Goals of the War and its Outcomes: The Yom Kippur War', *State Government and International Relations*, no. 17 (1981), pp. 68–85; Y. Hasdai, *With Iron Pen* (Kvutzat La'or Publishing, Jerusalem, 1983), (Hebrew).

48. O. Seliktar, 'The Arabs in Israel: Some Observations on the Psychology of the System of Controls', *Journal of Conflict Resolution*, vol. 28, no. 2 (1984), pp. 247–69.

49. Compiled on the basis of M. Hendel, *Israel's Political Military Doctrine*, (Center for International Affairs, Harvard University, Cambridge, MA, 1973), p. 50; Z. Lanir, *Fundamental Surprise: the National Intelligence Crisis*, (Kav Adom, Tel Aviv, 1983), pp. 88–9 (Hebrew); J. Gross Stein, 'The 1973 Intelligence Failure: A Reconsideration', *The Jerusalem Quarterly*, no. 24 (1982), pp. 41–54; A. Haraven, 'Disturbed Hierarchy, Israeli Intelligence in 1954 and 1973', *The Jerusalem Quarterly*, no. 9 (1978), pp. 3–19. The military historian M. Van Creveld pointed out that Israel's performance at the operational and tactical level was much better than at the strategic level, i.e. predicting the overall politico-military-economic situation. 'Military Lessons of the Yom Kippur War', *The Jerusalem Quarterly*, no. 5, (1977), pp. 114–24; S. Green, *Taking Sides: America's Secret Relations with a Militant Israel*, (William Morrow and Company Inc, New York, 1984).

50. I. Galnoor, 'The Right to Know vs. Government Secrecy', *The Jerusalem Quarterly*, no. 5 (1977), pp. 48–65.

51. The media became more critical of censorship in the early 1960s, but the spirit of co-operation prevailed until 1973. Bar-On, *The Untold Story*, pp. 18, 142.

52. D. Goren, *Secrecy, Security and Freedom of Press*, (Magnes Publishers, Jerusalem, 1976), pp. 192–204, (Hebrew).

53. Bar-On, *The Untold Story*, p. 180.

54. Y. Erez, 'To be a Military Correspondent', *Maariv*, 24 June 1983.

55. R. T. Holt and J. K. Turner, 'Insular Politics' in J. N. Rosenau (ed.), *Linkage Politics*, (The Free Press, New York, 1969), pp. 199–238.

56. Brecher, *The Foreign Policy System*, pp. 134–82.

57. For a good discussion of the Peace Now movement see R. J. Isaac, *Israel Divided: Ideological Politics in the Jewish State*, (Johns Hopkins University Press, Baltimore, MD, 1976).

58. Based on a series of articles by J. Winkler in *Haaretz*, 25 and 29 Novermber, 2 December 1983, also *Haaretz* 18 July 1983.

59. For a programmatic statement see Rabbi M. Kahane, *They Must Go*, (Grosset and Dunlop, New York, 1981).

60. *The Jerusalem Post*, 8–14 May 1983.

61. A. Elon, 'The Builders of The Third Temple', *Haaretz*, 3 March 1983.

62. *Jerusalem Post*, 17–24 June 1984.

63. J. Aviad, 'From Protest to Return: Contemporary Teshuva', *The Jerusalem Quarterly*, no. 16 (1980), pp. 71–82.

64. R. Kislev, 'How Much Does it Cost Us', *Haaretz*, 5 April 1984.

65. For instance, the two Chief Rabbis Mordechai Eliahu and Abraham Shapira have claimed that the war in Lebanon is part of the redemption of the Land of Israel. An interview in *Haaretz*, 25 November 1983.

66. *Haaretz*, 6 December 1983.

67. *Maariv*, 9 March 1984.

68. *The New York Times*, 10 April 1984.

69. C. Tilly, *From Mobilization to Revolution*, (Addison Wesley, Reading, MA, 1978), p. 106.

70. S. Reiser, 'Cultural and Political Influences on Police Discretion: The Case of Religion in Israel', *Police Studies*, vol. 6, no. 1 (1983), pp. 13–23.

71. *Haaretz*, 4–5 April 1984.

72. *Jerusalem Post*, 28 August 1983; 9 September 1983.

73. *Haaretz*, 3 March 1983.

74. *Haaretz*, 3 July 1983.

75. *Haaretz*, 12 May 1983.

PART THREE

7 NEW ZIONISM AND MODELS OF FOREIGN POLICY CONDUCT: THE APPLICATION OF THE IDEALISTIC-INITIATING MODEL TO THE FOREIGN POLICY OF LIKUD

Traditional approaches to foreign policy have seldom explained the linkage between the dominant belief system of a society and the conduct of its foreign policy. The 'cognitive map' perspective introduced in Chapter 1 requires a more systematic analysis of the relationship between the dominant belief system and the decision-making process in Israel.

At the most general level such an inquiry is concerned with the *modus operandi* of the foreign policy establishment. It comprises two interrelated dimensions. The first is the particular mix of pragmatism and idealism in foreign policy thinking and the second is the balance between the initiative and the responsive elements of the system.

The first section of this chapter analyses the *modus operandi* of the foreign policy system under Likud and will demonstrate that New Zionism has emphasised idealism and initiative as opposed to the pragmatic and largely responsive foreign policy of the Labour era. The second section analyses the application of the new *modus operandi* to a redefinition of some key areas in Israel's foreign policy. The third section analyses the culmination of these policies in the war in Lebanon.

Pragmatism and Idealism in the Foreign Policy System in Israel

Foreign policy theorists have argued that most nations adapt to the limitations imposed on them by the international system. Yet occasionally actors find their international environment unsatisfactory and may want to modify it.[1] Analysed as a continuum, the behaviour of states may range from adopting a foreign policy which would give maximum consideration to the international environment to fashioning a course designed to change the international environment completely. *Realpolitik* is the term often used to describe the art of striking the delicate balance between the external exigencies and the internal needs of a nation.

Yet any attempt to define what constitutes *Realpolitik* involves a large element of arbitrariness. Methodologically, *Realpolitik* is based on the notion that there is a realistic or rational strategy for balancing external and internal needs. Chapter 1 made it clear that the most popular concept of rationality involves a process of means-ends analysis. Presumably, an actor can perform this calculation by determining whether his means are adequate to achieve his foreign policy goals. Yet the 'cognitive map' approach recognises that each collective belief system contains two sets of propositions: empirical propositions which define the 'real life' conditions and normative propositions which are value judgments about what 'reality' should be.

The latter concept raises serious problems when applied to means-ends rationality, because actors use normative beliefs often as historical analogies for assessing current situations. Moreover, decision makers seldom search through a number of historical experiences in order to select an analogy which best fits the current decision-making problem. More often they select those historical analogies which Jung described as 'archetypal situations', i.e. powerful historical events which had an immense or even mythical cross-generational influence on their society.

The question of what constitutes a 'realistic' assessment of Israel's needs as opposed to the limitations of the international system has been the object of a particularly sharp debate in Israel. In a historical survey of this debate, Vital pointed out that, in the formative stage of Zionism, the idea of a Jewish state was perceived by most Jews and Gentiles as an utterly impossible dream.[2] In other words, the needs of the Jews so vastly exceeded their foreign policy means that the creation of a state was evaluated as an event of extremely low probability.[3]

The *modus operandi* of the Socialist Zionist heirs of Herzl's Zionism has always been plagued by tension between those who cautioned against policy designs which would exceed the limited means of the Yishuv and those who advocated a more audacious course of action. Traditional Israeli historiography normally associates Ben-Gurion with the stand of 'courage' as opposed to Sharett, who advocated 'caution,' i.e. greater acceptance of international limitations. Ben-Gurion's thinking can be discerned from some of his well-publicised statements. In an Independence Day speech on 27 April 1965, he emphasised that what the Jews do is more important than what the Gentiles say. In another of his images about the international system, he referred to the United Nations in a derogatory way as 'oum shmoun'.[4]

Some observers have even claimed that Israel under Labour had a messianic streak in its foreign policy. It had its philotheological origin in the designation of the Jews as a Chosen people, and both Ben-Gurion and Chaim Weitzmann have written extensively about the role of Israel as the Light unto the Nations.[5] However, most of the messianic elements were confined to the internal matter of building a model society rather than to defying or challenging the international system. Abba Eban, one of the major spokesmen for pragmatism, described foreign policy decision-making in Isral as a very delicately balanced act. The most important goal was to achieve a Jewish state; subsequently 'we aimed to get as big a home as *reality* would allow us to have'.[6] Whatever the periodical deviations from this perception of reality, we may accept Avineri's argument that the Socialist Zionist *modus operandi* in foreign policy was pragmatic, that is, based on the perception that there were limits to what Israel could implement and achieve.[7]

From its very inception, Revisionism and its ideological heir, New Zionism, have adopted an idealistic approach to foreign policy thinking. Yuval Neeman, the leader of the Tehiya Party, provided the best description of this mode. 'In order to agree on national goals we need vision.' Vision is not a blind faith in the future but a creative evaluation of feasibilities. The assessment of the probabilities for fulfilling the relevant goals is based on three elements; the present indicators, the internal and international processes, and the ability to create processes which will increase the chances of success.[8]

Translated into terms of decision making, the idealistic *modus operandi* is based on two elements: high risk-taking and the calculation of the probabilities of success based on standard means as well as such 'intangibles' as motivation, destiny or even the help of God.[9] As Eldad, one of the chief ideologues of New Zionism put it:[10]

Zionism is the process of turning a dream into reality which should not be suffocated because of the limitations of reality. Our existence and redemption rejects everything that is 'real' and 'rational'.

The onset of the idealistic approach to foreign policy under Likud provoked a lively public debate about the merits of pragmatism versus idealism and the use of historical analogies in evaluating current situations. The exchange between Harkabi and Eldad over the merits of the Bar-Kochba revolt provided the most interesting insight into this debate. Bar-Kochba was the legendary leader of the rebellion against the Romans which contributed to the destruction of the Second Temple in 70 AD.[11]

According to Harkabi, the Bar-Kochba revolt represented a misguided idealistic approach to foreign policy. In this image, Bar-Kochba was lacking in realism, i.e. he misjudged his ability to achieve his ends with the means at his disposal, causing the destruction of the Second Temple and the Dispersion of the Jewish people.[12] Harkabi, giving the Bar-Kochba revolt as an example of the dangers involved in high-risk decision making, warns that contemporary Israel should not adopt historical analogies where the Jews won against extreme odds. Instead, the author suggests the model of the prophet Jeremiah, who represents 'political realism'.[13]

On the other hand, the New Zionist spokesman Eldad views all of Jewish history as an example of survival against extreme odds. In his view, the question of whether a certain political act has a fair chance of success should be evaluated only at the end of the process. The faith and motivation generated during a revolutionary or political struggle may or may not increase the chances of success.[14]

Although the historical debate was conducted in generalities, what was at stake were the contemporary issues in Israel's foreign policy. Harkabi accused the Likud of being unrealistic enough to retain the occupied territories. Other critics complained about the aggressive foreign policy style of Likud. In order to understand these issues better it is necessary to look at the initiative versus reactive elements in New Zionist foreign policy thinking.

It is widely acknowledged that the foreign policy behaviour of an actor constitutes a sequentially ordered chain of initiative and reactive behaviour. The balance between reaction and initiation is normally dictated by the status of the actor in the global system. Big powers possess more initiating capabilities than smaller actors, who are normally more reactive to the global constraints. Yet subjective perceptions derived from an idealistic *modus operandi* can prompt even a small actor to adopt a largely initiating foreign policy posture.

Applying the Idealistic-Initiating Model to Likud's Foreign Policy

The three areas in which New Zionism took a highly idealistic-initiating stand were: (i) a re-evaluation of Israel's method of integration in the Middle East region; (ii) a new definition of relations with the United States; (iii) a new policy towards the occupied territories.

New Zionism and the Image of Israel's Integration in the Middle East

From the very beginning, the Revisionist school of Zionism differed from Socialist Zionism in its vision of Jewish integration in the region.

One of the differences pertained to the image of geopolitical space in the Middle East. Whereas the Socialist Zionists viewed the Middle East as a relatively homogeneous Arab entity, the Revisionists emphasised the fragmented ethno-religious character of the region. This view was fully elaborated by Jabotinsky's son Ari, who became a Knesset member for Herut. He argued that the Arab world is an artificial imperialist creation, achieved through the subjugation of sizeable non-Arab and non-Muslim minorities. The prevalent Pan-Arab image has glossed over the considerable tension between Christians, Muslims, Shiites and Sunnis. Both Ari Jabotinsky and the ideologues of the Greater Land of Israel Movement, Zvi Shiloah and Eliezer Livneh, argued that religious tension in general and the Shiite-Sunni cleavage in particular would ultimately lead to an explosion in the Middle East.[15]

A logical corollary of this perception was the belief that these centre-periphery fissures in the Middle East would be used to facilitate Israel's integration into the Middle East subsystem. Since the 1950s, the New Zionists have argued that Israel should establish an active alliance with the Shiite and Maronite periphery. Moreover, Shiloah, Ezrah Zohar and other New Zionists have frequently predicted a Shiite upheaval in the region.[16] The Iranian Shiite revolution has been perceived by the Likud elite as a vindication of this belief. Iranian anti-Israel rhetoric notwithstanding, Israel enhanced its regional standing by virtue of becoming a balancing influence in the Iran-Iraq war as well as America's only reliable ally.

This belief was part of a more fundamental image of Israel's integration strategy in the Middle East. It was based on the assumption that an appropriate 'mix' of conditions would eventually persuade the Arabs to reconcile themselves to the existence of a Jewish state. The most important of these conditions was the readiness to use military power to achieve political aims.

In a perceptive analysis of the relationship between political aims and military objectives, Lanir argued that there have been two types of security orientations in Israel. One is related to Clausewitz's concept that war is the alternative means of diplomacy. Under certain circumstances, a country finds it necessary to use military power in order to achieve political objectives. The other orientation is denial of the war option which derives from the philosophy that defence is the only morally permissible use of military force. The denial approach, which was closely associated with Labour, was based on the acceptance of the *status quo* between Israel and the Arab countries. With the brief exception of the 1956 Suez campaign, only after the Yom Kippur War, which dealt a shattering blow to the denial strategy, was there a reversal to the Clausewitzian concept of using war and diplomacy interchangeably.[17]

Likud's policy since 1977 has been increasingly Clausewitzian. Begin's government broke with Labour's philosophy of the *status quo* by negotiating a peace treaty with Egypt. At the same time, there was growing emphasis on the use of force to effect geopolitical changes in the Middle East. The establishment of a Druze state as part of Syria and Lebanon, a dominant Maronite state in Lebanon or a multi-ethnic federation in Iraq were among the options historically discussed in New Zionist circles. However, the intervention in Lebanon was the only option which became crystallised in Likud's thinking and subsequently carried out.

Israel and the United States: A Re-evaluation of Traditional Client-Patron Relations

A historical analysis of Revisionist perceptions on Jewish-Great Power relations reveals a certain lack of consistency. On the one hand, Jabotinsky was the most forceful spokesman for the doctrine of Jewish self-reliance, self-sufficiency and self-development in foreign policy. This was part of his broader theory about the psychological transformation of the Jews from a passive and inferior Diaspora people to an active and sovereign nation, master of its own affairs. On the other hand, the Revisionist leaders emphasised the crucial role of the Great Powers in the establishment of a Jewish state.

New Zionism has reflected this inherent contradiction. Since the early 1950s, Begin's Herut party has advocated Israel's need for complete military self-reliance and for economic self-sufficiency. Herut was also opposed to any type of contractual security. Both the civilian and the military elites associated with New Zionism have customarily denounced all American plans based on contractual security for Israel; a characteristic example was Begin's rebuttal of Reagan's proposals, to the effect that 'there is no guarantee that can guarantee a guarantee'.[18]

Concomitantly, however, Herut criticised Labour's efforts to fashion a non-aligned foreign policy and advocated a close alliance with the United States. After Likud came to power in 1977, it vigorously pursued a strategic alliance with the United States, which resulted in the 1981 'mutual understanding' agreement signed by Sharon and the US Secretary of Defense, Weinberger. Above all, Likud's economic policies, which brought in a chronic three-digit inflation and a mounting foreign debt in excess of $22 billion in 1984, undermined the goal of self-reliance.

There are two theoretical explanations for these inconsistencies. One is provided by the psychological perspective of dependence in subordinate-superordinate relations. Long-term dependence creates psychological sensitivity, frustration and hostility in the subordinate client. This mind set can manifest itself in an 'irrational' pattern of response, alternating between compliance and a show of independence. This perspective can be gleaned in the *dependencia* writing of Latin American scholars and observed in case studies of long-term beneficiaries of US aid, including former Marshall Plan clients.[19]

A more sophisticated explanation is derived from the structural-functional analysis of the asymmetrical dyads literature. According to this, a subordinate client may choose among a number of strategies ranging from reinforcement, i.e. a desire to increase relations with the superordinate power, to intermittent accommodation, i.e. a wish to reconcile the competing aims of increasing and restricting relations with the superpower. The accommodation is not 'irrational', but its corollary behaviour over short periods of time may create the appearance of inconsistency.[20]

Given the New Zionist belief system, it can be assumed that Likud broke with Labour's tradition of compliance with the United States. The strategy of intermittent accommodation which Likud adopted in 1977 called for placing US-Israeli relations on a more equitable footing. In the cognitive image of the Likud elite, there were a number of positive as well as negative inducements which could justify this new relationship.

On the positive side, the Likud elite listed a number of interrelated propositions. Israel is a major American asset in the Middle East. As the only stable and democratic system, it acts as a bulwark against communism and fundamentalist destabilisation in the region. Israel's wars serve as a testing ground for American military hardware; it makes American military technology more marketable and provides cyclical financing for the American military industry. It acts as a proxy for American interests, which for either domestic or global reasons the United States cannot pursue directly.[21]

The negative inducements are based on the 'coercive stance' which could be utilised by Israel. The foreign policy thinking behind this concept includes two contingencies. American failure to provide conventional military assistance would force Israel to use nuclear weapons. Although Israel has used the 'bomb in the basement' approach to nuclear deterrence, and has never acknowledged the existence of such an arsenal, the country's considerable nuclear capabilities are widely recognised.[22] Alternatively, Israel might have to take sweeping pre-emptive measures to eliminate the threat of an Arab build-up, an alternative which is possible only as long as the IDF enjoys superiority over the adversary. According to intelligence estimates, this superiority will taper off in the late 1980s. It is known that this message was conveyed to a visiting American delegation a few years ago,[23] and was reaffirmed more recently through Tom Dine, the Director of AIPAC — the official pro-Israeli lobby in Washington.[24]

The 'equal partnership' perspective was used by the New Zionist elite to redefine a key aspect in the client-patron relationship which predicates the level of assistance by the patron on the degree of compliance of the client. Unlike its Labour predecessor, Likud has never assumed that US military and economic aid should be conditioned upon Israel's willingness to follow the American lead. It is also of interest that a reported simulation exercise in the Israeli Ministry of Foreign Affairs estimated that no American administration would be able to sustain long-term pressure on the Likud Government. Israel would revert to its old 'underdog' image, which would trigger public opinion and the Jewish vote.[25] Although one may question the correctness of this perception, Likud was the first political party in Israel to elaborate the premise that US aid should not be used to pressure Israel.

The Occupied Territories: De Jure and De Facto Annexation

New Zionist orientation towards the West Bank has undoubtedly constituted the most striking break with traditional Labour foreign policy. Labour's policy in the territories was largely reactive. It has already been mentioned that its only initiating moves were the decision to settle the Jordan Rift Valley along the lines of the Allon Plan and Dayan's advocacy of a 'security space' in Sinai. The latter resulted in the settlement of the Rapha Salient and the building of the towns of Yamit and Otira on the Straits of Tiran. Unable to reach a decision about the final disposition of the territories, it temporised and succumbed to the increasing Jewish pressure to settle the West Bank, often producing confusing and contradictory policies.

Likud's approach to the West Bank has been initiating almost from the very beginning. The Jerusalem Law was passed in 1980, and the Golan Heights were annexed in 1982. The plan to settle the West Bank evolved over a number of years and included three dimensions.

The first dimension involved the institutionalisation of the process of land expropriation. According to Pleah Albek, a Ministry of Justice official in charge of West Bank land policy, the Ministry followed the 1977 decision of the Begin Cabinet to start a massive settlement drive with a comprehensive survey to identify public land. According to the Ministry's definition, 2.7 million dunams (one acre equals four dunams), or 37 per cent of the total 7 million dunams of the West Bank, have been designated as public land available for expropriation. In addition, Likud abolished Labour's Military Administration Order no. 25 which barred private Israelis from buying land in the occupied territories.[26] It was estimated that, up to 1982, some 30,000 dunams of private Arab land had been sold to Jews.[27]

The second dimension involved decisions about the various strategies for settling the West Bank. The initial settlement drive was pioneering and spearheaded by the Gush Emunim, but its human reserve was judged to be limited to about 20,000 settlers. To bolster this number, the government decided on a largely urban type of settlement. This was made attractive to non-ideological settlers through a combination of mortgage and tax subsidies, larger than average housing units, and high quality living conditions. Michael Dekel, the former Deputy Minister of Agriculture in charge of settlements, estimated in 1982 that this new plan would bring 100,000 Jewish settlers by the end of the 1980s.[28]

The third dimension involved a discussion of the appropriate strategies for dealing with the Palestinian population. In place of Dayan's traditional policy of 'benevolent neglect', the Likud Government decided to intervene in the political process in the West Bank. To this effect it established the Civilian Administration, headed by Sharon's appointee, Menachem Milson. The Civilian Administration, which nominally replaced the Military Administration, was charged with purging PLO supporters and independent nationalists from among the West Bank leadership. In order to fill the void and develop a new cadre of leadership which would collaborate with the Israeli authorities, the Civilian Administration tried to bolster the standing of the Village Leagues. This group of small rural organisations carried little weight with the traditional urban centres of power in the West Bank.

To quell political unrest and terrorist activities, Sharon and his Chief of Staff, Eitan, developed a 'stick-and-carrot' policy, loosely modelled on the early Israeli experience of administering the Arabs within the Green Line. Palestinians who collaborated with the Israeli authorities were rewarded by direct patronage or through the perquisites distributed by the Village Leagues. On the other hand, security measures aimed at civilian demonstrators and terrorists were tightened. Among these measures were collective and individual punishments, preventive arrests, curfews, harassment of suspected troublemakers, and economic sanctions against villages where unrest occurred. A complementary, non-institutionalised measure involved tolerating the Gush Emunim and Kach vigilante activities against Palestinians.[29]

Tackling the PLO Issue: A Military Solution to a Political Problem

The initiating posture in Likud's policy in the West Bank could not be accomplished without a radical solution to the PLO problem. From its inception in 1964, the Palestinian Liberation Organisation has aspired to become the political and military representative of the Palestinian people. The PLO is a loosely knit organisation consisting of four major factions — Al Fatah, Al Saiqa, the Popular Democratic Front for the Liberation of Palestine and the Popular Front for the Liberation of Palestine — General Command. They are represented on the Palestinian National Council, the Executive Council of which is headed by Yasir Arafat. The military arm of the PLO is the Palestinian Liberation Army, which has branches in several countries.

The PLO had three major goals. The first was to establish itself as the legitimate representative of the Palestinian people and take a major part in the political process in the West Bank. The organisation became increasingly successful, when it managed to replace the popular allegiance towards the traditional *hamulah* leaders. Diskin and Mishal, who analysed the voting patterns in local elections in the West Bank, found that by the mid-1970s the pro-PLO vote was considerable.

The second goal was to establish international credibility by receiving *de facto* recognition from a large number of states. The hallmark of this international effort was Arafat's appearance at the United Nations in 1974. The PLO subsequently received the status of observer at the UN.

The third goal in the PLO's strategy was to launch acts of internal and international terrorism. To this end the organisation had to develop a military force. Since it failed to establish an underground organisation in the occupied territories, it strove to acquire a territorial base in Jordan. The efforts of the PLO to establish itself in Jordan led to a growing tension between the organisation and the Hashemite monarchy, culminating in the 1970 civil war, in which about 30 per cent of the combat members of the organisation were killed. The PLO bases were closed and some 150,000 PLO fighters, sympathisers and their families were expelled.[31]

Lebanon became the next territorial base of the PLO. Under the terms of the 1969 Cairo Agreement which Nasser imposed on Lebanon, the PLO was granted operational immunity by the Lebanese Government. The Cairo Agreement paved the way for creating a PLO 'state-within-a-state' in Lebanon, which upset the delicate balance between the various sects in the country. In the resulting exacerbation of the civil war in 1975, the PLO became allied with the predominantly Muslim left and threatened the

Christian dominance. Syrian intervention checked the PLO threat to the Maronite-dominated government, but left intact the considerable territorial stronghold of the organisation in the South of Lebanon.

The military deployment of the PLO in Lebanon spread from Beirut to the Israeli border, with a heavy concentration in the refugee camps around the coastal towns of Beirut, Damour, Sidon and Tyre. The estimated strength of the PLO was 15,000 — some in guerrilla units which were integrated within the civilian population and some in semi-regular army formations. The three infantry brigades — Karameh, Yarmuk and Kastel — had several artillery units and a number of antiquated Soviet T-34 tanks.

There is little doubt that the military strength of the PLO was no match for the far superior IDF. However, politically and strategically the PLO 'mini-state' in Lebanon posed major problems for the Israeli foreign policy system. First, the PLO exerted a major influence on the political process in the West Bank. Both Sharon and Eitan have made it clear that the existence of a strong PLO would hamper the planned political reforms in the West Bank and jeopardise the moves for a *de facto* annexation of the territories. PLO activists and supporters in the West Bank have often intimidated and killed Palestinians who were willing to collaborate with the Israeli administration. The Israeli authorities also claimed that the PLO was behind the civilian unrest which increased under the Sharon-Eitan regime.

Second, denying a territorial base to the PLO has been a longstanding tenet in Israel's strategic thinking. The South of Lebanon was ideally situated for harassing the Jewish settlements in Upper and Western Galilee. In one particularly dramatic exchange, the 'Two-Week War' of July 1981, the PLO shelled a string of settlements in the area, causing a major exodus of the population. But even the more routine PLO shelling and terrorist raids created heavy political pressure on all the Israeli governments to eradicate the territorial base of the Palestinians. The sporadic Israeli retaliation raids and the 'mopping-up' Litani Operation of 1978 had proved ineffective in curbing the military and political power of the PLO.

Third, Israeli intelligence and defence sources apparently accepted the Maronite argument that the continued presence of the PLO in Lebanon would lead to the total collapse of Christian dominance in the country. According to the authoritative account of the war in Lebanon by Schiff and Ya'ari, until the spring of 1976 the Maronite leaders, Gemayal and Chamoun, were confident that Syria would be able to restrain the PLO. However, after a few weeks in which reassurances were given but not fulfilled, the Maronites became convinced that even the Syrians would not be able to scuttle the budding alliance between the PLO, the leftist Shiite Moslems, and the Druze. Israel accepted the Maronite estimate that the success of such an alliance would turn Lebanon into a confrontationist country and further bolster the power and legitimacy of the PLO.[32]

The War in Lebanon: Carrying Out the 'Grand Design' Policy

The collective 'cognitive map' of New Zionism has been analysed in a preceding section. Yet, as our introductory chapter made clear, foreign-policy decisions at the operational level are not an automatic translation of the cognitive map. Such a decision may be defined as an effort to implement select elements of the 'cognitive image' of the belief system. The selection of any particular option out of the set of choices at a given time depends on a number of factors — the foreign policy making elite, the perceived strategic and political importance of the plans, and the perceived international environment.

We shall begin with the attitudes and relationships of the foreign policy elite at the time of the decision to launch Operation Peace for Galilee. The three most important actors involved in the decision were Prime Minister Begin, Defence Minister Sharon and Foreign Minister Shamir. Chief of Staff Eitan, the Head of the Mossad and the Chief of Intelligence, Yehoshua Saqui, played important secondary roles, whereas the Cabinet was relegated to a relatively minor position.

A probe into the 'cognitive map' of Begin, Sharon, Shamir, and Eitan reveals that they shared a basic consensus on the question of using force in order to bring about political changes in the region. The public proclamation of Begin, Sharon and Eitan and the secret reports from Cabinet meetings, revealed in the Schiff and Ya'ari book, indicate that they were all committed to the New Zionist notion of *optional use* of military force in order to achieve political objectives. The exact stand of the Cabinet is difficult to determine, but it would seem that no major objections were raised against this *modus operandi*.[33]

The perceived strategic goal of the decision to invade Lebanon has proved more confusing. There were three different plans circulated among the civilian and military leadership. The first plan was minimalistic — it called for an invasion of southern Lebanon in order to eliminate the PLO's threat to Northern Galilee. The plan did not envisage an engagement with Syrian troops and was basically an expanded version of the 1978 Operation Litani which limited the IDF movement to 40 km, i.e. to the Litani River.

The second plan was more ambitious. It aimed at destroying the infrastructure of the PLO up to Beirut, but wanted to avoid combat with Syrian forces. This modified plan relied on the Phalangist forces to eradicate the PLO from Beirut. The political aim of the second plan was to fragment or destroy the PLO, in order to facilitate the *de facto* annexation of the West Bank.

The third and most ambitious plan, code-named by the IDF the 'Big Pine' operation, envisaged a combined action against the PLO and the Syrians. The IDF was expected to fight in Beirut in co-operation with the Phalangist forces. The political goal of the plan was far-fetched. It called for the establishment of a strong Christian Government; Israeli support would help to preserve its hegemony over the increasingly assertive Muslim population. In due time the Maronite Government was expected to become the second Arab government to sign a peace treaty with Israel. The prospect of averting the radicalisation of Lebanon was apparently well received by the US Secretary of State, Alexander Haig. According to Schiff and Ya'ari, Haig gave tacit approval to Sharon to carry out the third plan which would have also dealt a serious blow to the PLO.[34]

There is a considerable amount of confusion surrounding the actual process of decision making on the three plans. Newspaper accounts, the Kahn Commission Report and a number of books published after the war indicate that no final decision on the plans was reached before the attempted assassination of the Israeli ambassador to London, Shlomo Argov, on 3 June 1982.

The debates prior to the decision imply that the Cabinet, under the influence of military intelligence which objected to the maximalist plan, rejected the Sharon-Eitan-sponsored proposal. Begin and the civilian leadership apparently favoured the minimalist plan, with some small modifications which would have brought the IDF somewhat closer to Beirut.

It is not entirely clear how the limited plan expanded into a full-fledged war. There are two possible explanations. If we assume that Begin was initially committed to a 40-km operation, then his public announcements to this effect were quite sincere. However, when, on 9 June, the confrontation expanded to include the Syrians, the limited plan was undermined by the strategic realities of the war theatre and Begin and the Cabinet were forced to go along with them.

The other possibility, which is strongly supported by Schiff and Ya'ari, holds that Sharon and Eitan misled the Cabinet about the real aims of the 'limited incursion'. The Israeli claim of 'forty kilometers' thus became a camouflage for a comprehensive campaign, which would bring the IDF to the Bekaa Valley and the outskirts of Beirut.

The evidence from the decision-making process which led to the war in Lebanon provides some interesting insights on the linkage between a collective belief system, the *modus operandi* of the foreign policy system, and the executive elite. First, it conforms to our notion that the formulation of high policy decisions is derived from the set of options included in the 'collective cognitive map'. This feature is particularly noticeable when compared to the Socialist Zionist image, which depicted the Middle East as a relatively homogeneous Muslim entity. Ben-Gurion and other Labour leaders had always believed that Israel's best chance of integrating itself into the region would be through a peace treaty with the Muslim countries. Although the Labour Government extended small-scale help to the Kurds in Iraq and the Christians in Lebanon, Ben-Gurion had turned down a number of proposals for massive intervention in Lebanon.[35]

Second, the idealistic-initiating *modus operandi* in Likud's foreign policy made the use of military force for political purposes normatively acceptable. Even before Likud came to power in 1977, there were indicators that offensive strategic thinking was on the increase. The failures of intelligence to provide an advance warning about the enemy forced the IDF to rely more heavily on offensive tactics. Coupled with the more general difficulty of modern intelligence in distinguishing between offensive and defensive military moves, it led Likud policy-makers to decide on a preemptive strike strategy well in advance to forestall any developing threat to Israeli security.

The 'surgical strike' concept associated with the former Chief of

Staff, Raphael Eitan, and Sharon had a *temporal* as well as a *spatial* tactical dimension. For instance, the bombing of the nuclear facility in Iraq in 1981 was a temporal application of the concept. The Sharon-Eitan agreement to bomb Iraqi military convoys destined for an Eastern Front deployment in either Jordan or Syria were examples of a *spatial* application of the 'surgical strike'. Although the 'surgical strike' was limited in scope, the broader implication of such thinking was that offensive uses of power are also morally justified for more ambitious targets.

Third, analysis of the interaction of the executive elite reveals that the developments which generated a full-fledged war in Lebanon were contingent upon two elements. The first element was structural and pertained to relations among Begin, Sharon, and Eitan. Begin was known to rely completely on the military expertise of Sharon and Eitan. The Chief of Military Intelligence, Saqui, and the Communications Minister, Mordechai Tzipori, who objected to the maximalist venture, were in a subordinate relationship to Begin and Sharon, and their opposition did not carry enough weight to sway the Cabinet into making a *positive decision* in favour of the 'minimal incursion' plan.

The second element derives from the psychological process of 'groupthink', Janis's notion that, in group situations, there may be a shift towards a risky solution. This is especially helpful in understanding the group dynamics of the Israeli Cabinet.[36] In the absence of a strong opposition to the Sharon-Eitan team and because the Cabinet was cognitively conditioned by the collective belief system, a 'risky shift' occurred by default. In other words, the Cabinet did not take the necessary legal steps which could have prevented Sharon from carrying out his maximalist design.

The cognitive dynamics involved in the process of decision making makes the evaluation of Sharon's role in instigating the war difficult. Analysed at the structural-legal level, it can be argued that the Sharon-Eitan team was largely responsible for the ambitious scheme in Lebanon. Yet, the 'risky shift' concept would indicate that the whole Cabinet was susceptible to a relatively quick cognitive transformation from the 40-km plan to a large-scale offensive operation.

Whatever the personal role of Sharon, the Cabinet's behaviour constituted a drastic break with the traditional policy of Labour. Instead of striving to impose peace *through deterrence*, Likud tried to impose peace by waging an actual war. According to Abba

Eban, the opposition Labour leaders Shimon Peres, Yitzhak Rabin and Chaim Bar-Lev objected to a full-scale invasion but their objections were not taken into account.[37] As a consequence, Operation Peace for Galilee was also the first Israeli war which was fought without a national consensus.

The War in Lebanon: A Cost-benefit Evaluation of the Military and Political Goals

The tactical plan for Operation Peace for Galilee divided the war theatre into three zones. The western sector followed the coastal road from the Israeli border to Beirut. The central sector ran from Marj Ayoun north up to the Shouf Mountains and cut through the Beirut-Damascus highway. The eastern sector embraced the environs of Lake Qaraoun and reached towards the centre of the Bekaa Valley.

The major goal in the western and central sectors was to trap the PLO forces and destroy their infrastructure. The IDF contingent in the eastern sector was charged with blocking the Syrian forces at the southern end of the valley and mounting a subsequent two-pronged flanking movement to the north in order to cut off their retreat route to Damascus. To this end, Israel assembled some seven divisions. The bulk of the force — four divisions comprising 800 tanks and some 38,000 men — was designated to fight in the eastern sector.

By and large, the IDF accomplished the military goals of the war. It destroyed most of the infrastructure of the PLO in Lebanon and captured a massive arsenal of its weaponry. The Israelis acquired intelligence material which helped them to identify and round up PLO fighters and sympathisers. According to some sources, out of the estimated 15,000 PLO guerrillas in southern Lebanon, some 1,000 were killed or captured in the campaign and an additional 1,700 were identified among the some 5,000 Palestinians detained in the Ansar Camp. The most successful Israeli ploy was the forced evacuation of some 11,000 PLO fighters after the August siege of Beirut.[38]

The rating of IDF performance with regard to the Syrian forces was mixed. The IDF destroyed the SAM missile batteries in the Bekaa Valley and some 85 Syrian airplanes. However, in spite of the fact that the Syrians were forced to retreat in the Beirut-Damascus highway battle, their losses were only moderate. For instance, the Syrians lost some 10 per cent of their manpower, i.e.

1,200 dead and some 3,000 wounded out of a 30,000-strong battle force. Both Israeli intelligence and foreign observers agreed that Syrian performance in terms of discipline and morale was good.[39]

In terms of human costs the military operation was rated as excessively high. The most questionable aspect was the number of civilian casualties. Since most of the PLO camps were located in densely populated areas, the IDF could not avoid engaging in urban combat. Although there is an impression that the IDF tried to minimise the damage to the civilian population, the combat conditions often turned into a zero-sum choice between Israeli and Palestinian casualties. The actual estimates of civilian Palestinian casualties are hotly contested.

The PLO-supplied figures stated the number of deaths at 10,000 and the number of homeless at 600,000. The Speaker of the Israeli Knesset estimated that there were 800 dead in the south and 40,000 left homeless. *Time's* Jerusalem bureau arrived at the conclusion that between 3,000 and 5,000 were killed and 70,000–80,000 lost their homes. The siege of Beirut added 10,000–12,000 to the civilian death toll and some 20,000 were wounded.[40]

One of the most serious calamities of the war was the Sabra and Shatila massacre, in which a detachment of Phalangists killed some 700 civilian Palestinians on 16–18 September 1982. The massacre had a profound impact on Israeli public opinion and seriously undermined the moral stature and the rationale of the war. The subsequent Kahn Commission of Inquiry implicated the Israeli civilian and military elite in the massacre and recommended that Sharon should be relieved of his post as Defence Minister.

The implementation of the political goals of the so-called 'grand design' in Lebanon proved to be more difficult. After the expulsion of the PLO, Israel tried to promote a new realignment in Lebanon's intricate sectarian political system. The first step in this design was to elect Bashir Gemayel as a President who could form a strong Maronite Government. Bashir Gemayel was elected President on 23 August 1982, but his narrow political base made open support for Israel difficult. In fact, some of the statistical data available would suggest that the 'grand design' was not particularly realistic. For instance, after the invasion an Israeli-conducted census revealed that only some 30–40 per cent of the Lebanese population were Christian. A survey analysis conducted during the civil war disclosed that only 20 per cent of the upper-income groups (i.e. Maronites and Sunni) expressed support for the Maronite-dominated national pact. On the other hand, most of the lower-class Sunnis and Shiites demanded Maronite subservience.[41]

During the meeting between Gemayel and Begin on 30 August 1982, the Lebanese President-elect undertook to work for an official peace treaty with Israel. In a meeting with Sharon on 12 September Gamayel repeated his pledge to start negotiations. However, on 14 September Gemayel was assassinated, according to Schiff and Ya'ari by members of the Syrian Socialist Nationalist Party, a small radical splinter of the Phalange which advocated a confederation between Lebanon and Syria.

The death of Bashir Gemayel upset Israeli plans for a negotiated peace with Lebanon. The new President, Amin Gemayel, who has never been a strong supporter of Israel, had links with the Syrian Government. Although his political support was broader than that accorded to his brother Bashir, the Syrian and domestic constraints weighed heavily on Israeli-Lebanese negotiations. Syria increased its military presence in Lebanon and provided aid to the Lebanese Druze, who posed the most serious threat to the Maronite hold on the government.

The final agreement, which was signed on 17 May 1983, fell short of most Israeli expectations. First, the agreement was composed of a series of secret documents and third-party (American) guarantees. The only open clauses were those which were palatable to Lebanese public opinion and Syria. Second, Israel gave up on most of its earlier conditions for safeguarding the South of Lebanon, such as a direct presence or surveillance stations. The new formula called for joint Israeli-Lebanese patrols. Third, instead of full peaceful relations between the two countries, the agreement did not commit Lebanon to an open border policy and envisaged a supervisory committee instead of a diplomatic mission. Finally, the end of belligerency between Israel and Lebanon was contingent on the withdrawal of Syrian forces, although Syria was not a party to the agreement.

The agreement proved to be a short-lived victory for Israel. The factional strife between the Druze and the Maronites in the Shouf Mountains forced the IDF in August 1983 to withdraw unilaterally to the Awali River. The last vestige of Gemayel's influence was dissipated, when he was forced to appoint a pro-Syrian Cabinet led by Rashid Karame. The appointment of Karame reflected both the growing influence of Syria and the political-demographic changes in the country, whereby the Christians lost control relative to the Shiite Muslims and the Druze. Israel, which still had a nominal alliance with the Maronites, was forced to close its liaison bureau in the Christian sector near Beirut. The only official remaining linkage has been the Lebanese Christian Agency in Jerusalem, headed by Pierre Yazbeck, a known supporter of Israel.

The situation in the South of Lebanon has proved even more difficult. Approximately 24,000 Israeli troops faced 60,000 Syrian soldiers in the Bekaa Valley. The IDF has also attempted to stop the re-infiltration of the PLO. According to Israeli intelligence reports, since their expulsion in 1982, some 6,000 guerrillas have returned via the Bekaa Valley.[42] The IDF was also forced to make a number of incursions north of the Awali in order to defend the Christians.

The most serious threat to the IDF came from the radicalisation of the Shiites, who constitute a majority of the estimated 700,000 people who live in the South. The Amal Party, led by Nabih Berri, and the local Shiite clergy have taken a lead in promoting anti-Israeli sentiments. The Shiite Mufti in Lebanon, Sheikh Muhammad Madhi Shamseddin, issued a *fatwa* — a religious ruling — ordering a comprehensive civil resistance against Israel. There have been a number of terrorist groups operating against the IDF — *Hezzballah* (the Party of God), *Ghanad Allah* (the Soldiers of God) and Islamic *Amal* which seceded from the Amal party. All are affiliated with Iran. The main Amal party has also participated in these activities. In addition, there are three tiny leftist groups which have carried out attacks in the south: the Organisation for Communist Action in Lebanon, the Lebanese Communist Party and the Socialist Nasserites.

To sum up, in spite of considerable military means, all the political goals involved in the grand Israeli design for Lebanon failed. Although the ascendancy of the Druze and the Shiites was inevitable in the long run, the Israeli intervention accelerated this process. In addition, the war turned the Shiites into an extremely hostile element in South Lebanon. It was estimated that about 90 per cent of the attacks on the IDF are carried out by the Shiites.[43] It is not clear whether the Shiites are likely to carry their anti-Israeli activities into Upper Galilee after the IDF withdrawal from the area. Finally, Israeli intervention has enhanced the status of Syria in both Lebanon and the whole Middle East region.

The political goal of undermining the PLO has been more successful. In spite of the return of some guerrillas, the war caused a major disintegration of the PLO. The only two bodies which support Arafat are Al Fatah and the Arab Liberation Front, which is backed by Iraq. The National Alliance, which opposes Arafat and any peace process, is composed of the pro-Syrian Al-Fatah rebels, led by Saed Musa, the Popular Front for the Liberation of Palestine — General Command, headed by Ahmed Jabril, and the Popular Struggle Front, which is a small pro-Syrian group led by Samir Gosheh.

The Democratic Alliance has also criticised Arafat and his plans for peace talks, but objects to a formal split in the PLO. The Alliance is composed of the Popular Front for the Liberation of Palestine of George Habash, the Democratic Front for the Liberation of Palestine, led by Nayef Hawatmeh, and the Palestine Liberation Front of Talat Yacoub. The headquarters of the Democratic Alliance is in Damascus, but most of its supporters come from guerrillas exiled to South Yemen and Algeria.

From an Israeli point of view, the exile of the PLO and the split in its ranks present a number of advantages. The destruction of the PLO infrastructure in the South of Lebanon has curtailed the danger to the Galilee. The factionalisation of the PLO has impaired its decision-making ability. The Aden Agreement of July 1984 between the Democratic Alliance and the PLO provided for sweeping changes in the structure of the organisation, which curbed Arafat's freedom of action. The radicalisation of the organisation was evident at the November 1984 meeting of the Palestine National Council. In spite of the fact that Arafat retained his leadership, he was able to obtain only a limited mandate to join King Hussein in negotiating over the future of the West Bank. Moreover, because of the outcome of the war, Syria acquired a major say in any possible negotiations between Israel and the Hussein-Arafat team.

Notes

1. For a good survey of the literature on realism and idealism (utopian approach) see J.G. Dougherty and R.L. Pfaltzgraff, *Contending Theories of International Relations* (Harper and Row, New York, 1981), pp. 84–6; J. D. Singer, 'The Global System and its Subsystems: A Developmental View' in J. N. Rosenau, *Linkage Politics*, (The Free Press, New York), pp. 21–43.

2. D. Vital, 'The Definition of Goals in Foreign Policy', *State, Government and International Relations*, no. 13 (1979), pp. 5–16 (Hebrew).

3. For an interesting discussion of the Zionist prophecy see A. Ilan, 'The Prophecy of a Jewish State and its "Fulfillment", 1941–1949', *The Jerusalem Quarterly*, no. 33 (1984), pp. 125–44.

4. M. Brecher, *The Foreign Policy System of Israel*, (Oxford University Press, London, 1972), p. 235.

5. S. Decalo, *Messianic Influences in Israeli Foreign Policy*, (University of Rhode Island, Kingston, RI 1967).

6. *Maariv*, 6 June 1969.

7. S. Avineri, *Essays on Zionism and Politics*, (Sifrei Mabat, Tel Aviv, 1977), p. 86.

8. Y. Neeman, 'National Goals' in A. Hareven (ed.), *On the Difficulty of Being an Israeli*, (The Van Leer Foundation, Jerusalem, 1983), pp. 257–74.

9. Idealistic or messianic concepts in foreign policy thinking are quite prevalent. Interviews with Poles during the heyday of the Solidarity movement revealed that many used the historical analogy of 'God or a miracle which saved Poland in the past' to bolster their expectation that Poland would be freed from Russian domination. *The New York Times Magazine*, 7 August 1983.

10. I. Eldad, *A Controversy: Our Perceptions of the Destruction of the Second Temple and of Bar Kochba's Revolt*, (The Van Leer Foundation, Jerusalem, 1982), pp. 84–85, (Hebrew).

11. Throughout Jewish history Bar-Kochba and his spiritual mentor Rabbi Akiba have hardly even been mentioned. The interest in Bar-Kochba was awakened after the Six-Day War when Israel occupied Betar, the last stronghold of the rebellion. The latest round of excavations revealed that Bar-Kochba put up a formidable defence before surrendering to the Roman legions of Hadrian. Bar-Kochba has always been a legendary hero in the Revisionist ideology and the Revisionist youth movement *Betar* adopted the name of his last stronghold. *The Jerusalem Post*, 24 November 1984.

12. Y. Harkabi, *Vision, No Fantasy; Realism in International Relations* (The Domino Press, Jerusalem, 1982), (Hebrew).

13. Y. Harkabi, *Facing Reality, Lessons from Jeremiah, the Destruction of the Second Temple and Bar-Kochba's Rebellion*, (The Van Leer Foundation, Jerusalem, 1981), (Hebrew).

14. Eldad, *A Controversy*, pp. 1–83.

15. A. Jabotinsky, 'The Territories Held by Arab Imperialism', *Zot Haaretz*, 2 May 1969; Z. Shiloah, 'The Goals of Greater Israel in the Land of the Fathers' in A. Ben-Ami (ed.), *The Greater Land of Israel Movement Book*, (Greater Land of Israel Movement and S. Freedman, Tel Aviv, 1977), pp. 213–26, (Hebrew); and E. Livneh and S. Katz, *The Land of Israel and its Borders*, (The Greater Land of Israel Movement, Tel Aviv, 1968).

16. E. Zohar, 'Israel and the Periphery Against Arab Pan-Arabism', in Ben-Ami, *The Greater Land*, pp. 227–41.

17. Z. Lanir, 'Political Aims and Military Objectives — Some Observations on the Israeli Experience' in Z. Lanir (ed.), *Israeli Security Planning in the 1980s*, (Praeger, New York, 1984), pp. 14–47.

18. Quoted in *The Jerusalem Post*, 27 February–5 March 1983.

19. For a survey of *dependencia* writing see J. Caporoso, 'Dependence, Dependency and Power in the Global System: A Structural and Behavioural Analysis: Notes Toward Precision of Concept and Argument', *International Organization*, vol. 33, no. 1 (1978), pp. 13–43.

20. B. W. Tomlin, M. Doland, H. von Rickhoff and M. Appel Molot, 'Foreign Policies of Subordinate States in Asymmetrical Dyads', *The Jerusalem Journal of International Relations*, vol. 5, no. 4 (1981), pp. 14–40.

21. Compiled from S. Erlich, 'The Price of Aid', *Haaretz*, 13 March 1983 and S. Katz, 'The Defense of American Folly,' *The Jerusalem Post*, 6–12 February 1983.

22. For instance see I. Dueti, 'The Nuclear Policy of Israel', *State, Government and International Relations*, no. 7, (1975), pp. 5–27, (Hebrew); S.J. Rosen, 'A Stable System of Mutual Nuclear Deterrence in the Arab-Israeli Conflict', *American Political Science Review*, vol. 71, no. 4 (1977), pp. 1367–83;; P. Pry, *Israel's Nuclear Arsenal* (Westview Press, Boulder, CO, and Croom Helm, London, 1984).

23. Erlich, 'The Price of Aid'.

24. W. Blitzer, 'Collision Course', *The Jerusalem Post*, 6–12 March 1983.

25. Quoted in *Haaretz*, 6 February 1983.

26. An interview in *Haaretz*, 11 February 1983.

27. *Jerusalem Post*, 9–15 January 1983.

28. An interview in *Maariv*, 1 October 1982.

29. For a discussion of Israel's policy in the West Bank see I. S. Lustick, 'The West Bank and the Gaza Strip in Israeli Politics' in S. Heydemann (ed.) *The Begin Era: Issues in Contemporary Israel* (Westview Press, Boulder, CO, and London, 1984), pp. 79–98.

30. S. Mishal and A. Diskin, 'Palestinian Voting in the West Bank: Electoral Behavior in a Traditional Community Without Sovereignty', *Journal of Politics*, vol 44, no. 2 (1982), pp. 538–58.

31. R. A. Gabriel, *Operation Peace for Galilee: The Israeli-PLO War in Lebanon*, (Hill and Wang, New York, 1984), p. 34.

32. For a good survey of the Lebanese crisis see I. Rabinowitch, *The War for Lebanon 1970–1983*, (Cornell University Press, Ithaca NY, 1984).

33. L. Schiff and E. Ya'ari, *Israel's Lebanon War*, (Simon and Schuster, New York, 1984), pp. 97–131; see also Gabriel, *Operation Peace*, pp. 60–74.

34. Schiff and Ya'ari, *Israel's War*, pp. 63–77.

35. A recently declassified document from the Foreign Ministry disclosed that the links between Israel and the Phalange go back to 1948. However, a memo of 28 December 1950 submitted to Walter Eytan, Director General of the Foreign Ministry, suggested that, even if the Christians were to dominate politics in Lebanon, it was unlikely that they would sign a peace treaty with Israel because of Muslim pressure. *The Jerusalem Post*, 3–9 July 1983. According to Avi Valentin, in 1955 Ben-Gurion rejected Dayan's plan to set up a Christian puppet government in Lebanon, *Haaretz*, 5 November 1982.

36. I. L. Janis, *Victims of Groupthink: A Psychological Study of Foreign Policy Decisions and Fiascos*, (Houghton Mifflin, Boston, MA, 1972).

37. A. Eban, 'Twenty Months of Dread', *Maariv*, 2 February 1983.

38. Gabriel, *Operation Peace*, p. 116.

39. *Ibid.*, p. 121.

40. *Ibid.*, pp. 121, 165.

41. H. Khashan and M. Palmer, 'The Economic Basis of Civil Conflict in Lebanon: A Survey Analysis of Sunni Muslims', in T. E. Farah (ed.), *Political Behavior in the Arab States*, (Westview Press, Boulder, CO, 1983), pp. 67–81.

42. *Haaretz*, 2 July 1984.

43. *The New York Times Magazine*, 20 January 1985.

8 CHANGES IN THE NEW ZIONIST BELIEF SYSTEM IN THE AFTERMATH OF THE LEBANON WAR

The constant process of legitimisation and transvaluation of the dominant belief system in a society is normally accelerated by wars or other major social traumas. The war in Lebanon has provided the Likud with an opportunity to test and validate its basic assumptions in foreign policy.

There is a certain difficulty in analysing the impact of the war in Lebanon on New Zionism. The war and its consequences are still evolving. The long-term influence will ultimately depend on a number of dynamically related factors, such as the degree of success in settling the Lebanese problem and perceptions of the human and economic costs of the war. In the meantime, a few preliminary observations can be offered with regard to the three major dimensions of New Zionist foreign policy which were tested by Lebanon. The first is the idealistic-initiating *modus operandi* in Israeli foreign policy, the second involves the Israeli-American alliance, and the third pertains to the debate about the future of the territories.

Idealistic-Initiating Model of Foreign Policy Revisited

The failure of the 'grand design' has undermined the New Zionist assumption that military force can be used to create favourable political conditions in Lebanon. The outcome of the war was especially damaging to Likud's claim that it could improve on Labour's performance in turning military success into political gains. Instead, the idealistic-initiating model was delegitimised in two major ways.

The Costs of the War

There were a number of issues involved in the debate over the costs of the war. Understandably, the human cost has come to dominate the public debate. Although the war was originally en-visaged as a low-cost operation, the initial round of hostilities alone claimed 368 dead and wounded. The redeployment south of the Awali did not diminish the numbers of casualties, because the IDF has been increasingly exposed to attacks by remnants of the PLO and the Shiites. By the end of March 1985, the war had resulted in more than 630 Israeli dead and some 300 wounded. These numbers constitute 3.4 per cent of the 18,000 soldiers killed and 10.3 per cent of the 24,000 wounded since 1948. The casualty rate in the current war is almost comparable to that of the Six-Day War in 1967.

The war has also been financially devastating. Cost estimates for the invasion include $650 million in domestic outlays and $850 million for imported weapons and ammunition. Indirect costs, through loss of production and reduction of tourism, have been calculated at $425 million.[1] The initial daily cost of keeping the 36,000 troops in Lebanon was put at $1 million per day. More recently, the Defence Ministry estimated the annual cost at $130 million. Coupled with the reduction of the military budget, these costs forced the IDF to eliminate some programmes and lay off 1,000 civilians and military personnel.[2]

The deployment in Lebanon introduced severe constraints on the training and reserve system of the IDF. Since the war, IDF units have had increasingly to be trained in urban guerrilla tactics, at the expense of the more traditional skills needed in conventional warfare. In addition, reserve duty, which is normally devoted to training, has been 'eaten up' by police duties in Lebanon. Following the war, the reserve tour of duty was increased, but it still left the IDF with little time margin for training, which is a serious impediment in a citizens' army.

The military performance of the IDF and its ability to launch a sustained campaign in difficult conditions has become a major topic of controversy. According to Schiff and Ya'ari, who interviewed dozens of military personnel, there were numerous complaints about strategic co-ordination and the poor performance of individual units. Some of the problems stemmed from the political design of the war, which did not allow for an optimal operational deployment, but others were attributed to tactical failures and poor training.[3] Van Crevland, a military historian, noted that the traditional superiority of individual Israeli troops and crews over their Arab opponents had declined sharply since the 1973 war.[4] An analysis of the casualty lists released by the IDF, matched against the various theatres, indicates that Israel sustained most of its casualties — 69.2 per cent of its total dead and 64.4 per cent of its wounded — in battles with Syrian soldiers. This is a higher casualty rate than that sustained against Syria during the Yom Kippur War.[5]

Other, unsubstantiated reports evaluated Israeli performance even more harshly. *The Washington Times*, a small newspaper owned by the Unification Church, alleged that a secret Pentagon report had revealed that 20 per cent of the Israeli casualties were caused by IDF fire.[6] In September–October 1984 Shlomo Aronson, a professor of political science at the Hebrew University, published four articles in *Haaretz*, in which he criticised the performance of the IDF and the General Staff. Aronson quoted unspecified reports by a private American research organisation on the West Coast. These findings were denied by the Chief of Staff and produced a journalistic furore, when Aronson was accused of using non-existent data.[7]

Perhaps the most important cost of the war was the damage to the moral and ethnical consensus that had prevailed in earlier wars. In legitimising a war, a society uses two criteria. The first refers to the reasons for fighting, or *jus ad bellum*, and the second to the means applied in the fighting, that is *jus in belli*.[8] In terms of *jus ad bellum* the Israelis' self-perception in all their previous wars was highly moral, because they fought in self-defence.

But there has also been an emphasis on morality of means known as *tohar haneshek* (purity of arms). Its application became increasingly difficult after the Six-Day War. A number of books published after the 1967 war revealed the dissonance between the demand for moral conduct during the war and the actual combat conditions. The war in Lebanon was the first military operation in which the morality of the act has been increasingly questioned. This was compounded by the fact that the principle of purity of arms had to be compromised because of the urban and guerrilla character of the operation.

The moral implications of the war have badly politicised the IDF. Peace Now, Soldiers Against Silence, Parents Against Silence, There is a Limit and a number of other anti-war groups have actively denounced the war. Some of them spearheaded a drive of conscientious objection to service in Lebanon. About 140 reservists have been tried for refusing their tour of duty there. Numerous officers and soldiers have written to Begin and his successor, Shamir, to protest against the war. On one occasion a whole reserve unit turned up to protest outside the Prime Minister's home. These actions came on top of the highly publicised year-long vigil of anti-war activists outside Begin's residence.

The delegitimisation of the war in Lebanon was dramatised by internal dissent among high-ranking officers. One of them, Colonel Eli Geva, resigned, creating the most publicised event of the 'moral crusade' against the war. In a less publicised event, Chief of Staff Eitan was forced to delay the call-up of a reserve battalion in order to avert public embarrassment.

Perhaps the most delegitimising type of protest against the war came from parents whose sons were killed in action. One of them was Gurni Harnik, a Peace Now activist and a major in an elite paratrooper unit who was killed during an assault on the Beaufort Castle, a major PLO stronghold. In a letter to the press, his mother described the death of her son as a futile act in a 'cynical political war'. The parents of Yaron Zamir, an officer in an elite unit who died with Harnik on the *Beaufort*, criticised Begin in an open letter for causing 'bereavement and agony' to both Israelis and Lebanese.[10]

The moral question exposed the limits of the use of military power in the Likud model of foreign policy. At the immediate level, the lack of legitimisation has affected the morale of the troops. Research in the United States and Europe indicates that if a war is viewed as 'colonial', rather than defensive, combat motivation and performance suffer drastically. The difficulties of the British in the Boer War, the Russian embroilment with the Japanese and the American problems in Vietnam are but a few historical instances where low motivation forced the termination of the conflict by the initiating country.

The extent to which the moral delegitimisation affected the IDF's performance in Lebanon is difficult to assess. Some of the previously cited examples would indicate that low morale created by confusion and dissent affected combat ability and troop cohesion. The rate of 'combat refusal', although low by American standards in Vietnam, was unprecedented in Israeli military history. The rate of psychiatric casualties, another indication of low morale, was 26 per cent, compared to some 3.5–5 per cent in the Yom Kippur War, which was fought in exceedingly difficult conditions. On the other hand, the suicide and attempted suicide rates in the 1982–3 period were lower than the average IDF rate in the preceding ten years. These rates compare favourably with both the American figures in Vietnam and Russian statistics in Afghanistan.[11]

Furthermore, a survey of IDF combat troops conducted in January 1983 by the Department of Behavioral Science has revealed a reasonably high level of morale and cohesion. For instance, 60 per cent of the soldiers claimed high or very high morale and 80 per cent expressed confidence in their superiors. However, 40 per cent were not satisfied with their level of physical fitness during the war.[12]

The long-term implications of the morality issue are even more complex. Since the draft in Israel is compulsory, objection to the war was expressed through a drop in the number of youths who volunteered for elite combat units and officer training. Known in Israel as the 'small head' syndrome, this drop (from 40 per cent in 1975 to 18 percent in 1985) was particularly widespread among kibbutz members and middle-class Ashkenazim who have traditionally formed the backbone of elite units in the IDF.[13] Although the 'small head' syndrome is at least partially related to general changes in the Israeli value system, it has been recognised as a form of political protest against the war in Lebanon, particularly because many members of the elite units have been active in Peace Now and other anti-war groups.

The IDF and the kibbutz movement launched a campaign to combat this phenomenon, mostly through meetings between senior officers and pre-draft kibbutz members. However, in one of these symposiums entitled 'Military Service: Necessity or Vocation', young kibbutz members complained that they had to fight in spite of the fact that they were often abused by Likud supporters and called 'PLO sympathisers', a derogatory term commonly used against Peace Now activists.[14]

It is too early to estimate whether the 'small head' syndrome is a temporary protest phenomenon, or is indicative of a long-term trend in passive resistance to 'colonial' uses of military power. According to Yossi Elder, the Chief Educational Officer of the IDF, the phenomenon is already tapering off. The latest figures released by the IDF indicate that volunteering for elite combat unit is up; in the paratroopers there were five times as many volunteers as were needed and the Givati and Golani units were 81 per cent volunteer.[15]

A longitudinal survey released by the IDF shows that the motivational level of young Israelis has not changed over time. In

1984, 80 per cent of the recruits expressed pride in the service, the same proportion as in 1974. Seventy-one per cent intended to volunteer for an elite unit; 70 per cent did so in the earlier period. Thirty-two per cent in 1984 and 31 per cent in 1974 revealed that they would try to avoid serving in a combat unit.[16] There are no equivalent surveys for reservists, but journalists' reports indicate that the motivation there has been lower. Another phenomenon which is apparently related to the problem of ethics and morale can be observed in the re-enlistment rate of career officers. Although there are no numbers available, some military observers report that officers in combat units and even pilots choose to terminate their commission after the minimal time period.[17]

Whatever the actual level of motivation may be, there is a broad consensus that Israel would find it difficult to fight another 'colonial' war. In other democratic countries the military is normally professional and the combat units are made up of volunteers who espouse the 'military spirit'. The structure of the IDF, whose officer corps and combat units include a high percentage of kibbutz members and peace activists, makes far-flung military ventures difficult to carry out. The high rate of casualties among the officers, i.e. 25.1 per cent in the Peace for Galilee operation, poses a painful question in distributive justice. Although distributive justice is normally associated with allocation of resources for existence, in the case of war it hinges upon the probability rates for mortality in certain groups in the society. In the case of Israel, this probability is skewed towards the Ashkenazi group which has not been supportive of Likud's foreign policy.

Failure of Israeli Policy Objectives in Lebanon: Undermining the 'Grand Design' Theory

The limits of the idealistic-initiating posture of Likud's foreign policy have become dramatically manifest in the circumstances which led Israel to decide to leave Lebanon. After months of frustrating negotiations with the weak and fragmented Lebanese Government and with Syria, the Israeli Cabinet decided on 15 January 1985 to withdraw unilaterally from Lebanon. The pullback was envisaged as a three-stage process. The first stage involves a withdrawal to the Litani-Nabutije region. In stage two, the IDF pulls back from the Bekaa Valley and the Mount Baruka range. In stage three the Israeli forces will return to the international border, while maintaining a security zone manned by the

South Lebanese Army led by General Antoine Lahad. The withdrawal was expected to be accomplished in six to nine months. However, because of the increase in terrorist activities against the IDF, the final pullout was rescheduled for August 1985. Nevertheless, the acts of terrorism continued, forcing the IDF to a final pullout in June 1985. Currently, Israel has a small mobile force which together with the South Lebanese Army supervises a security zone in southern Lebanon.

Analysis of the background of the decision reveals that the Unity Government came to acknowledge that all the premises which guided the 'grand design' were untenable. The most important change in Israeli thinking was the Cabinet's recognition that, due to demographic changes, Lebanon was becoming transformed from a Christian country into a Shiite one. The war, which speeded up the growing dominance of the Shiites, has resulted in shifting Israeli attention from the Palestinian danger to what is described as 'Little Teheran' on the Israeli border. The Likud elite still adheres to the theory that the biggest threat from Lebanon will be posed by Palestinian guerrillas, but there is a growing realisation that a hostile Shiite population may supersede this danger. According to Israeli intelligence estimates, the Shiite guerrilla threat against the Galilee cannot be ruled out even after a complete IDF withdrawal.

The second change in Israeli thinking stems from a better understanding of the psychological consequences of military actions. In Chapter 6 we pointed out that the militarisation of the foreign policy paradigm had left little room for considering the psychology of the occupied population. The rapid radicalisation of the Shiites in southern Lebanon has demonstrated to the Israeli decision makers that occupation can produce a dynamic resistance movement. The relatively moderate mainstream Shiite Amal organisation of Nabih Berri has been undermined by radical clergy such as Sheikh Mohammed Mahdi Shamseddin and the fundamentalist movement *Hezzballah*, the Party of God.

The third and related change in Israeli thinking pertains to the future function of the IDF. It has already been noted that the war in Lebanon has turned the Israeli army into a police force. Such a function could hardly be sustained over a long time period because of the reserve structure of the force. The Cabinet decision signifies a return to the more traditional methods of dealing with guerrillas, such as preventive surgical strikes and retaliatory raids.

The fourth and perhaps most interesting change in Israeli perceptions is the renewed emphasis on contractual security. Since the Secretary-General of United Nations, U Thant, withdrew the UN forces at Nasser's request in 1967, the Israeli foreign policy establishment has had little faith in peace-keeping forces. Israel criticised most strongly the performance of the UNIFIL forces stationed in Lebanon prior to the 1982 war. The decision to withdraw, after the failure to reach an agreement with both Lebanon and Syria, indicates that Israel has been forced to accept the concept of UN protection. This message was communicated to UN Under-Secretary-General, Brian Urquhart, although Israel received no assurances that Syria and Lebanon would permit the deployment of the peace-keeping force.

US-Israeli Relations: An Emerging Strategic Alliance

The US commitment to Israel dates back to the decision of President Truman to support the 1947 UN partition resolution on Palestine and his subsequent move to recognise the State of Israel in May 1948. In spite of this fact, the two countries have never signed a security pact. The major objection came from the US Department of State, the Defense Department and other segments in the foreign policy establishment which viewed Israel as a liability for American political and strategic interests in the Middle East. Establishing a contractual recognition of Israeli-US ties was perceived as detrimental to American credibility with the moderate Arab countries.

This view was accepted, by and large, by the traditional Labour leadership in Israel. Since the old Socialist Zionist elite were also apprehensive about a potential Soviet reaction, they refrained from any formal strategic co-operation with the United States.

The cognitive outlook of the Likud was influenced by Jabotinsky's dictum that Israel, which is the only European state in the Middle East, should be turned into a major Western asset in the region. The Likud's new design was ambitious in its psychological objectives rather than aimed at an incremental change in Arab perceptions of power relations in the Middle East; its objective was to establish the Americans as the only actor with credibility and influence in the area. A corollary of this policy was to forge a strategic alliance with the United States.

The new national security orientation was rapidly put into effect. Even before Likud came to power, Sharon, who acted as a security adviser to the Rubin Cabinet, devised the framework for a strategic dialogue with the Americans which started in 1975. After 1977, pursuit of a strategic alliance with the United States received high priority. In March 1979 Ezer Weitzmann signed an agreement with his American counterpart, Harold Brown, on a Defence Trade Initiative. In November 1981, Sharon and the new American Defense Secretary, Alexander Haig, signed a low-key strategic agreement, known as the Memorandum of Understanding on Strategic Co-operation.

Likud's policy soon suffered major setbacks. Following Israel's annexation of the Golan Heights in December 1981, the strategic agreement was almost immediately suspended. With the outbreak of the war in Lebanon, relations between the two countries reached their nadir. The decision to start the war had at least the tacit approval of the former Secretary of State, Alexander Haig, but after his removal the American Government reacted sharply to the Israeli drive towards Beirut. The bombing of civilian targets in Beirut and the massacres in the Sabra and Shatila camps were seen as particularly harmful to American interests.

Israeli-American relations continued to be strained even after the war. The major critic of Israeli foreign policy in the Reagan administration is Defense Secretary Caspar Weinberger, who adheres to the theory that the Soviet threat in the Middle East can be best contained by cultivating moderate Arab regimes. According to some administration officials, Weinberger held up the delivery of 75 new F-16 fighters and was behind the proposal to freeze military assistance to Israel at the $2.5 billion level of 1982. Moreover, in February 1983 Weinberger rejected the intelligence agreement with Israel, negotiated by Andrew W. Marshall, a noted US intelligence expert, in November 1982.[18]

Changes in Israel's top leadership have had some effect in improving the climate of the relationship. The appointment of Moshe Arens to replace Sharon as the Defence Minister and the choice of Yitzhak Shamir as the new Prime Minister in September 1983 led to a new dialogue. An agreement to reactivate the strategic memorandum was reached in November 1983, when Shamir and Arens visited Washington. Subsequent discussions by political and military commissions have generated policies which indicate that there may be a significant change in the American perception of Israel's strategic utility in the Middle East.

In fact, some Israeli and American observers believe that the US is on its way to integrating Israel into its global defence system. The Brookings Institute places Israel immediately after Central America, Japan, Canada and Europe, in terms of strategic importance.

If this assessment is correct, then Likud has managed to validate its claim that Israel and the United States can enjoy a more equitable relationship in spite of the Arab-Israeli conflict. Most of the information on evolving strategic co-operation is secret, but a careful analysis of the published sources reveals that there are two major reasons which have changed American perceptions.

The American foreign policy establishment has become disillusioned with the ability or willingness of the Jordanian and Palestinian actors to follow up any new peace initiative, which would have halted Israeli settlements in the West Bank and brought a solution to the Palestinian problem. The success of the Reagan peace initative of September 1982 was contingent on an initial agreement by King Hussein and Arafat to join the talks. The Americans apparently hoped that Arab consent to that initiative would generate enough domestic and international pressure on Israel to overcome Begin's expected refusal. There is indirect evidence to suggest that this policy was encouraged by the Labour Party, whose Jordanian option has been traditionally discredited by Likud on the ground that it is not acceptable to Hussein and the Palestinians. Shultz revealed some of his exasperation with the Palestinians when he publicly complained that 'we are constantly following the will-o'-the wisp of what Arafat thinks lately. It is always very, very difficult to pin down.'[19]

An even more crucial consideration in the changing US perspective stemmed from the progressive destabilisation of the situation in the Middle East. Initiated by the Iranian revolution, this process has dramatically underlined the vulnerability of American interests in the region. The fundamentalist revolution has demonstrated the somewhat tenuous quality of the moderate regimes in the area. It has undermined the traditional theory that the Arab-Israeli conflict is the only threat to the moderate regimes, and has overshadowed the concerns generated by the historical clash between Jews and Arabs.

American decision makers perceive the Iranian revolution as

potentially destabilising to the moderate regimes in the area. The official estimate is that fundamentalism may spread through the region, by means of direct Iranian 'export' or by spontaneous emulation. The 'amplification effect' has been so far limited because of the Iranian war effort, but it cannot be ruled out in the future, especially if the fundamentalist regime survives the war with Iraq.

A demographic analysis of the Gulf countries bears out this prediction. Most of the principalities have Shiite minorities, although the Sunnis monopolise political power. Shiite unrest was behind the bomb attacks against the US Embassy in Kuwait and other targets.[20] The Gulf countries, including Saudi Arabia, have large 'guest worker' populations, a mixture of Palestinians, Egyptians, Pakistanis, and non-Muslims. These people have no political rights, in spite of the fact that many occupy high-ranking positions in the economy. A drive for political equality of the second 'guest' generation might prove highly destabilising. This trend will undoubtedly be enhanced by the differential fertility rates of the Shiites and the immigrant population, which may alter the demographic balance in these countries sooner than expected.

Given the destabilisation of the Middle East, Israel's strategic status has increased in the eyes of US policy makers. Israel is particularly appreciated for undermining the credibility of Russian weapons systems. Ever since Israel fought the Russian-equipped Egyptian forces in the Suez campaign of 1956, consecutive generations of Russian weapons have been proved inferior, first to French and subsequently to American systems at the disposal of the IDF. This trend intensified in the war in Lebanon, where the Air Force put out of commission the Syrian-operated SAM surface-to-air-missile system and shot down 85 Soviet built MIG-23s without suffering any losses.

The continuous out-performance of the Soviet weapon systems by Israeli arms has a more global strategic implication for the United States and NATO. Admiral Elmo Zumwalt, the former Chief of Naval Operations and a past member of the Joint Chiefs of Staff, has pointed out that the Israeli performance may force the Soviet Union to rethink the entire concept of its conventional air-defence system in Eastern Europe. The Warsaw Pact relies heavily on the same interceptors and ground-based missiles as are used by Syria.[21] More recently the combat data provided by the Israelis on the performance of American vs. Soviet weapon systems have been useful in improving American arms. There are grounds for believing that the US Air Force System Command has used the considerable Israeli expertise in the Stealth Project, which is aimed at developing designs for radar-evading aircraft.[22] Meir Rosenne, the Israeli Ambassador to Washington, revealed that the data on Soviet weapons provided to the US have been worth $50 billion.[23]

Israel is apparently being considered in American contingency planning for the defence of the Persian Gulf and the Mediterranean. The details of the co-operation are kept secret, but it is known that a number of initiatives have been undertaken. Assistant Under-Secretary of Defense for Policy and Research, Dov Zakheim, revealed that General Donald Keith, Commander of the US Army Military Readiness and Development Command, has visited Israel to discuss joint military exercises, strategic stockpiling and medical co-operation.[24] The US Defense Department also confirmed that American and Israeli naval vessels conducted an anti-submarine exercise in the Mediterranean.[25]

The evolving strategic co-operation has already led to a major revision in the terms of economic aid to Israel. A report prepared by the General Accounting Office in 1983 reveals that US assistance to Israel totalled $24 billion in the 1948–82 period. This assistance was administered under the Foreign Military Sales (FMS) and Economic Support Fund (ESF). Israel has been the largest single recipient of US aid, followed by Egypt. The special relationship between the two countries is demonstrated by the liberal terms and purchasing flexibility of the FMS loans. The ESF aid is not linked to any specific projects, as customarily required by the US Agency for International Development which administers the programme.[26]

Although the special economic relationship began under Labour, Likud can point to the fact that the United States did not use economic aid to put pressure on Israel. Table 8.1 indicates that since Likud came to power in 1977, the amount of US aid has increased steadily. Moreover, the Likud Government, facing major economic difficulties, has been able to secure loan forgiveness, which in effect converts part of the loan into grants. Since 1976, about half of the FMS loan was turned into a grant, whereas the ESF aid has been mostly disbursed in grant form.

Likud's success was particularly remarkable in face of the past efforts of the Labour opposition to persuade the American Gov-

Table 8.1: US Aid to Israel 1950–84

FMS (US$bn**)

Type	1950–71	1972	1973	1974	1975	1976	1977	1978	1979	1980	1981	1982	1983	1984
Guaranteed Loan	0.14	0.15	0.15	0.30	0.20	0.85	0.50	0.50	2.70	0.50	0.90	0.85	0.95	0.85
Direct Loan	0.68	0.15	0.15	0.68	0.10	*	*	*	*	*	*	*	*	*
Payment Waived	*	*	*	1.60	*	0.85	0.50	0.50	0.60	0.50	0.50	0.55	0.75	0.85
TOTAL	0.82	0.30	0.30	2.58	0.30	1.70	1.00	1.00	3.30	1.00	1.40	1.40	1.70	1.70

ESF (US$m)

Type	1950–71	1972	1973	1974	1975	1976	1977	1978	1979	1980	1981	1982	1983	1984
Grant		50.0	50.0	50.0	375.0	94.5	490.0	525.0	525.0	525.0	525.0	764.0	806.0	910.0
Grant Portion of Loan		*	*	*	14.5	130.5	132.3	150.8	161.2	182.0	764.0	806.0	785.0	*
Non-Grant Portion of Loans		*	*	*	10.5	94.5	112.7	109.2	98.8	78.0	*	*	*	*
TOTAL		50.0	50.0	50.0	400.0	319.5	735.0	785.0	785.0	785.0	1289.0	1570.0	1591.0	910.0

GRAND TOTAL (US$bn)

	1950–71	1972	1973	1974	1975	1976	1977	1978	1979	1980	1981	1982	1983	1984
GRAND TOTAL (US$bn)	0.82	0.35	0.35	2.63	0.7	2.02	1.74	1.79	4.09	1.79	2.69	2.97	3.29	2.61

** thousand million
* no data provided; also no data for FMS and ESF for the 1948–50 period.

Source: Adapted from a Report of the General Accounting Office.

ernment to cut back on aid to Israel in order to stop the settlements on the West Bank.[27] In November 1983, some fifty Israeli politicians and financial leaders, many representing the Labour Party, met the US Ambassador in Israel, Samuel Lewis, in order to protest at what they described as indiscriminate American aid, which facilitates the consumption-oriented policy of the Likud.[28]

More recently, the American Government has tried to use economic aid to put pressure on Israel to institute a radical reform of its economic system. The economic team appointed by Secretary of State Shultz urged Israel to end the system of indexation which ties wages and benefits to the rate of inflation, which reached 48.6 per cent in 1984. It also requested that Israel trim its 1985 budget to $2.3 billion. In spite of this, the Congress may approve part of the request for emergency assistance of $800 million, which is in addition to the $2.6 billion already approved by the Congress for the fiscal year 1985. The Israeli request of $4.05 billion for 1986 is the largest ever made. Moreover, Israel is the first country to negotiate a free-trade agreement with the United States. Under the terms of the agreement all tariffs will be phased out over a 10-year period.

The Debate Over the West Bank

The Peace For Galilee operation was the first attempt by any Israeli government to formulate a clear policy for the occupied territories. Indeed, both Sharon and Chief of Staff Eitan made it clear that the war in Lebanon should be perceived as a major struggle for Judea and Samaria. The preceding chapter, which traced the 'cognitive map' of the decision to invade Lebanon, demonstrated the linkage between the PLO and the annexation of the territories. In the Likud vision, the destruction of the PLO would have led to a change in the leadership structure in the West Bank, a realignment in the political loyalties of the Palestinians, and a reduction in terrorist activities and civilian unrest.

The war in Lebanon inflicted heavy damage on the PLO, but did not validate any of the political assumptions of New Zionism. First, in spite of Palestinian disappointment with the PLO, Arafat and local leaders associated with the movement have retained high popularity in the West Bank. A PORI poll of March 1982 revealed that 86 per cent of the Palestinians wanted a PLO leadership for their future state. Bassem Schakaa, one of the leaders of the National Palestinian Committee and the former mayor of Nablus, was chosen by 68 per cent of respondents as the most popular local politician. On the other hand, Mustafa Dudin, the head of the Israeli-sponsored Village League, with 0.2 per cent support, was viewed as the least popular leader.[29]

The most recent opinion poll commissioned by *Al-Bayader Assiyasi*, a news magazine which appears in the occupied territories, shows that 92.1 per cent of the Palestinians, regard Arafat as their leader, 71.9 per cent of respondents supported the continuation of the Jordanian-Palestinian dialogue, but only 27.6 per cent believed that the United States would exercise any pressure on Israel to relinquish the territories.[30]

Second, there are no indications that the disintegration of the PLO has diminished terrorist activity and civilian unrest. Although the Civilian Administration does not release full statistics, a *Jerusalem Post* report would seem to suggest that there have not been significant changes in these trends since 1978.[31] In any case, establishing a direct correlation between the existence of the PLO and resistance activity is extremely difficult, because there are additional factors which can interfere with the statistics. Some of them can be random, such as political assassinations, whereas others are related to the more structured patterns of demography and employment. For instance, a 1984 report of the Bank of Israel found that the economic slump in the Gulf countries and Israel had affected the level of employment in the territories. It is quite conceivable that high unemployment rates in the West Bank would create civilian unrest.

Ironically, the failure to translate the military victory of the PLO into a political success in the West Bank spurred the ongoing debate on the future of the occupied territories. Although the debate is often confusing and overlapping, two major issues may be identified.

The Demography of the Occupied Territories

Likud's declared policy of *de facto* annexation of the West Bank has raised the question of the demographic balance between the Jews and the Arabs. However, as the political scientist Ezrachi pointed out, under Likud there has been a steady depreciation of the scientific elements in this debate, coupled with an idealistic emphasis on Jewish faith and destiny.[32]

The various New Zionist spokesmen who did address themselves to the 'demographic danger' claimed that it was overestimated by the politically-motivated Labour arguments. Government sources pointed out that the pace of voluntary emigration increased in the 1970s and that 94,000 Palestinians departed between 1974 and 1980. It was also hoped that attractive land prices would tempt many Palestinians to sell out and leave.

For instance, Yedidya Atlas from Elon More, a spokesman for the settlers, has argued that the Arabs have always followed more attractive economic conditions and thus have become a society of emigrants. Atlas also produced statistics which showed that the population of the West Bank grew from 1,131,100 to 1,145,100 in the 1979–82 period.[33] These statistics were based on the findings of the research division of the Bank of Israel, which also noted that, because of emigration and lower fertility rates, the overall level of population growth in the occupied territories was exceptionally low.[34]

However, the 1984 report of the Bank of Israel indicates that the trends which generated a low level of population increase in the 1970s are being reversed. The rate of annual increase in the 1981–2 period was 2.1 per cent, compared to 1.9 per cent in the late 1970s. The higher growth rate was caused by two interdependent factors. One is the increase in the birth rate. The total live birth rate for Israel was 23.6 per cent in 1981; the combined live birth rate for the West Bank, Golan and Gaza for the same period was 45.7 per cent, almost twice the Israeli rate. The second factor is a decline in the rate of emigration from the West Bank, which is attributed to the decline in the economy of the Gulf states. Thus, the approximately 800,000 Palestinians in the West Bank in 1983 constitute an increase of 138,000 over the 1976 figures. There are 476,000 Palestinians in the Gaza Strip. The decline in emigration, coupled with the fact that 69 per cent of the population in the occupied territories is less than 24 years old, may increase future fertility rates.[35]

The most comprehensive data on future population trends are included in a report by the Center of International Research, US Bureau of the Census. Using medium fertility rates, the report estimated that by the year 2010 there would be 1,569,510 Palestinians in the West Bank and 1,119,518 residents in the Gaza Strip. The total number of Israelis would reach 5,985,000 — 4,485,000 Jews, 1,400,000 Israeli Arabs and 100,000 Arab residents of East Jerusalem.[36] These projections indicate that, if the administered territories are retained, there will be 4.48 million Jews and 4.18 million Arabs by the year 2010.

The Future of the Territories

The prospect of Israeli rule over a large Palestinian population, which may become a majority, has intensified the debate about its various costs to the Jewish state. The most immediate issue is the problem of law and order. The preceding chapters have made it clear that the prolonged occupation has created numerous problems of law and order which were aggravated by the arrival of the Jewish settlers. These difficulties have quickly spread to the Green Line and resulted in the phenomenon of Jewish terrorism.

According to an investigative report in *Haaretz*, the first efforts to establish what was called a Jewish 'counterterror organisation' started in 1972. Amichai Faglin, a high-ranking officer in the Irgun, was accused of smuggling arms for the Kach group of Rabbi Kahane. In 1974 the Israeli police arrested four suspects who had tried to hit Arab targets in retaliation for Arab terrorist activities in Kiriyat Shmona, Maalot and kibbutz Shamir. The Jewish terror became more organised in 1975, and in 1983 the existence of a Jewish terrorist underground was discovered. The *Haaretz* article implied that the head of the General Security Service, the *Shin Beit*, resigned in protest over the Likud Government's policy of delaying an investigation of the Jewish terrorist organisation.[37]

However, the widespread deterioration in law and order on both sides of the Green Line and the spectre of Jewish racism, as embodied by the Kach party, have prompted the authorities to take a number of steps. The Military Government, acting together with the Ministry of Justice, the Interior Ministry and the police, moved to implement the findings of the Karp Committee. The belated but speedy crackdown on the Jewish terrorist group is but one indication of this new trend. Perhaps the most significant development is the official recognition that right-wing radicalism threatens the very foundations of Israeli democracy. In an unprecedented act, Attorney General Yitzhak Zamir came out against what he described as Kahanism, or the spread of anti-democratic and racial ideas in Israel.[38]

A related issue is the financial cost of keeping the occupied territories. Few would disagree with the proposition that opportunity costs associated with military expenditures may hinder the development of social and welfare programmes. Since public demand for social and welfare programmes normally exceeds the budgetary resources of a country, popular tolerance for defence spending is frequently short-lived. Israel has always been regarded as an exception to this pattern, because of the perceived threat of physical annihilation. The country's current economic situation, which involves chronic three-digit inflation, a huge external debt and spreading unemployment may have changed this trend.

There is evidence to indicate that some areas of defence costs, and especially the war in Lebanon, have been subjected to public criticism. There is also a growing perception of a linkage between the cost of settling the administered territories and the public and private welfare of Israeli citizens. Peace Now was among the first organisations to raise the issue of this clash of interests, but it was only after the deterioration of the economy that the problem became publicised. According to Shimon Peres, Likud has spent a total of $3.4 billion on the settlements, but a British geographer estimated that in the 1978–83 period, the expenditure reached $8 billion.[39]

There are two views on the reaction of the public to what seems to be an obvious trade-off between investment in the West Bank and budgetary limitations within Israel proper. One view holds that in overall terms the West Bank and Gaza are an economic asset to Israel. Van Arkadie, who did an early study on the benefits and burdens of the administered territories, and the Israeli economist Bregmen concluded that the occupation did not place any overall burden on the Israeli economy.[40]

On the other hand, Goldberg and Ben Zadok report that there is ongoing tension between the populations of the largely Oriental development towns and the settlers over the budget.[41] Only 8 per cent of Oriental Jews live on the West Bank, and in the climate of Ashkenazi-Oriental tension, budgetary allocations could become an additional source of friction. The only survey data available come from a 1979 opinion poll which shows that the Orientals are more willing than the Ashkenazim to give priority to settlements in the national budget. Sixty-six per cent born in Asia-Africa and 77 per cent of Israelis of Oriental background stated that the national preference should be for settlement, but only 50 per cent of Ashkenazim were of the same opinion.[42] However, the recent economic problems, which hurt the lower-class Oriental stratum most, may have changed these attitudes.

Whatever the public attitudes, financial difficulties have forced the Israeli Government to cut down on West Bank investments. The 1983 and 1984 budgets revealed that there was a cumulative decrease of 38 per cent in investments in the West Bank, a 27 per cent decrease for the Jordan Valley, and a 30 per cent decline for the Katif Gush.[43]

Undoubtedly, the most crucial part of the debate has focused on the question of controlling the large Palestinian population. In an age of decolonisation and growing ethnic strife, Israel is almost unique in converting from a relatively homogeneous state into a bi-national society. The manifold implications of this move have made the debate between the annexationists and the anti-annexationists extremely bitter.

An analysis of the cognitive map of the annexationists reveals some interesting features. Some annexationist circles exhibit 'millenarian rationality' in the sense that they emphasise the metaphysical link to Eretz Israel. For instance, the philosopher and writer Pinches Sade, who is associated with Gush Emunim circles, has argued that Eretz Israel is the Land of the Bible, regardless of who occupies it. Even though it belongs to the Jews, the Arabs are also sons of Abraham and they have to accept the Biblical nature of the Land of Israel.[44] The metaphysical annexationists are not policy-oriented and do not propose any specific solutions for the Palestinian problem.

Other annexationists are highly policy-oriented. The small Kahane movement advocates expulsion or voluntary emigration of the Arabs. Gush Emunim, which conducted a conference on the issue in Guni Tol in 1981, seems to be split. Some Gush circles close to Rabbi Levinger incline towards induced emigration, but a majority have adopted the Biblical concept of *ger toshav*, i.e. alien residents. This concept of citizenship would give the Palestinians limited personal liberties but would preclude political rights.[45] Yuval Neemen, the head of the Tehiya party, has expressed the opinion that there should be a large voluntary emigration. The remaining Palestinians should be offered a permanent alien resident status. Alternatively, the occupied territories could be turned into an autonomous area resembling the commonwealth of Puerto Rico.[46]

The anti-annexationists, who hail from parts of the Labour movement and the Israeli left, are equally divided. The official position of the Labour Party is based on the Allon Plan, which would leave some 30 per cent of the Palestinians under Israeli rule. The rest of the occupied territories would be returned as part of a Jordanian-Palestinian federation. Only the tiny Israeli left supports the option of an independent Palestinian state.

Yet all the anti-annexationists are united in the perception that the retention of a huge Arab population would undermine Israeli democracy. Ben-Gurion and Sapir were among the first to point out that the annexation of the territories, due to the influx of Arab manual labour, would undermine the Jewish character of the state and reverse the process of social redemption.[47] *Haaretz*, a vocal opponent of annexation, argued in one of its editorials that the Likud proposals for autonomy were equivalent to the creation of homelands in South Africa.[48] The 1983 screening in Israel of Gulio Pontecorvo's film, *The Battle of Algiers*, was used by *Haaretz* as an analogue for Israeli colonisation.[49]

Underlying the discussion about the disposition of the territories has been the so-called 'point of no return' debate. In a 1984 report, Miron Benvenisti, a specialist on the West Bank, argued that, in terms of the Jewish infrastructure, the annexation was not reversible. According to the report, the number and the location of the settlements would make it very difficult for any Israeli Government to negotiate over the West Bank.[50]

The geographer Elishe Efret recently demonstrated that, in numerical terms, the Jewish settlement drive has been a failure. Since the Six-Day War, exclusive of the Jordan Valley, 112 settlements have been built with a population of 23,000. Jews represent only 3.5 per cent as compared with the Arab population of 800,000 settled in more than 450 villages and towns. Most of the Jewish settlements are in the vicinity of the Green Line and Gush Etzion. Averaged over the 1967–84 period, this amounts to only 1,750 settlers a year. On average, the Arab population has grown in this period seven times faster than the Jewish one.[51]

Whatever the technical details of the 'point of no return' debate may be, they are less crucial than their psychological implications for the Israeli foreign policy system. In an analysis full of insight, Lustick argued that, technically, territories can be changed, carved up and rearranged in numerous ways. Psychologically, though, annexation involves two cognitive thresholds. The first one is reached when the dominant belief system makes it difficult to disengage, without undermining the democratic rules of the game. The second one is reached when the issue of the annexation ceases to dominate the political agenda, that is, when the 'ideological hegemony' of annexation has been achieved.[52] In the concluding section of this chapter we shall trace the changes in the dominant belief system in order to determine whether the first threshold has already been reached.

Public Opinion and the Modification of New Zionism

In the introductory section of this book, we have already mentioned that a transvaluation in a belief system will sooner or later manifest itself in changing patterns of public opinion. In spite of the short time span, it is quite clear that certain modifications have taken place in public support for New Zionism.

The most striking change took place in the public approval of the idealistic-initiating model of New Zionist foreign policy. A PORI opinion poll conducted in the first round of the war, in July 1983, showed that Begin's approval rate had risen from 47.7 per cent at the war's outset to 57.6 per cent. The support for Sharon in the equivalent period went up from 48.9 per cent to 56.6 per cent.[53] In January 1983, 40.7 per cent of respondents justified the 'grand design' war, as opposed to 38.4 per cent who supported a limited 40-kilometer operation.[54] However, only 23 per cent of the respondents of another PORI poll wanted the IDF to stay in Lebanon, whereas 53.5 per cent supported an immediate with-drawal.[55] The Cabinet decision of 15 January 1985 to leave Lebanon has been supported by an overwhelming majority of Israelis.

The pressure to withdraw stemmed more from the human cost of the war to Israel than from issues of morality. A PORI poll taken after the Sabra and Shatila massacres found that Likud lost 4.5 per cent of support, whereas Labour gained 2.8 per cent.[56] The publication of the Kahn Report which implicated some Israeli leaders in the massacres did not change these public perceptions. A *Modiin Ezrachi* poll found that 51.7 per cent of respondents thought that the report was too harsh, 31.4 per cent thought that it was fair and only 2.7 per cent claimed that it was too lenient.[57] The role of the press in uncovering the Beirut massacre and the cover-age of the Kahn Report has created an apparent backlash against the media. In April 1984 a *Monitin* poll reported that 56 per cent of respondents argued that the media hurt the national interests.[58]

The intensive debate over the costs of keeping the occupied territories has produced some interesting changes in public attitudes. Whereas before the war in Lebanon a majority of Israelis (58.3 per cent in October 1981) supported annexation, recent developments have decreased this number to 48.5 per cent in 1982 and 1983.[59] A *Modiin Ezrachi* poll of October 1983 revealed that 42.3 per cent of respondents objected to any territorial concessions, 41.1 per cent would give up parts of Judea, Samaria and Gaza, and 9.3 per cent would agree to withdraw without giving up Jerusalem. Only 3.2 per cent of respondents supported a retreat to the 1967 borders.[60]

The high cost of the war in Lebanon and the economic difficulties have further dampened support for the settlements. A January 1985 PORI poll revealed that 51.7 per cent objected to new settlements in Judea and Samaria and 35.9 per cent supported them. In October 1981 only 29.2 per cent objected to the settlements as opposed to 58.2 per cent who supported them.[61]

These numbers indicate that, for the first time in a number of years, there is a majority against the policy of creeping annexation. In a straightforward application of the rules of democracy, such a majority should be enough to cause a disengagement from the West Bank. However, National Religious circles, and Gush Emunim in particular, have often implied that they would resist a withdrawal, even if it were agreed by a democratic majority. Gush spokesmen have intimated that their fierce resistance to the evacuation of the Jewish settlements in the Sinai Desert should be construed as a warning against a similar effort in the West Bank. The spectre of *Kulturkampf*, which this threat evokes, makes it doubtful whether a Jewish withdrawal from Judea and Samaria can be achieved without undermining some of the democratic rules of the polity.

An alternative way of discerning changes in the New Zionist belief system is by an analysis of electoral behaviour. The July 1984 elections were generally considered as one of the most crucial electoral contests in Israeli history. First, the elections tested the durability of the new partisan alignment which brought Likud to power in 1977. It was commonly argued before the election that Oriental support was contingent on Likud's manipulation of the economy, or due to the personal appeal of Begin. Alternatively, the blame was put on the Labour Party, which was badly split, or failed to promote Sephardi politicians.

All these circumstances were absent in the 1984 elections. The election campaign, from which Begin was absent, was conducted in a highly orderly manner. The Labour Alignment was unified and its list of candidates included many repsectable Sephardi politicians, including the former President Yitzhak Navon. The election campaign was especially designed to attract Oriental voters. Yet in spite of all these efforts, which came on top of the slumping economy, there is no indication that Labour increased its support among the crucial electoral groups.

Preliminary surveys and aggregate electoral results indicate that, in spite of its fragmentation, the right-wing vote has actually increased among the up and coming groups in the electorate. Moreover, there was a switch to ultra-right parties among the Oriental and younger voters. A breakdown of the electoral results with respect to the army, which is young and 60 per cent Oriental, is indicative of this trend; 40 per cent of its vote went to Labour, *Shinui* and the Citizens Right Movement. Likud and Tehiya received 48 per cent and Rabbi Kahane's Kach got 2.5 per cent of the vote, twice its national average.[62] Nationwide, Likud, Tehiya and Kach drew disproportionately high support from development towns and urban slums which have a high concentration of Oriental voters. The largest support for Kach came from development towns in the heavily Arab-populated Galilee.[63]

The July election was also seen as a crucial referendum on the occupied territories. It was the first election campaign in Israel's electoral history in which the two major options were clearly spelled out. Labour reaffirmed its support for the Allon Plan, whereas Likud stressed its commitment to the retention of the territories and the speeding-up of the settlement process.

The outcome of the election confirmed the observation that the Jewish electorate is almost equally divided on the issue. Out of the 114 Knesset mandates which were held by the Jewish parties, 58 seats were captured by parties which oppose territorial concessions (Likud, Tehiya, Kach, *Morasha*, National Religious Party, *Ometz* and Shas). The parties which support territorial compromise obtained 53 mandates (Labour, Mapam, Shinui, *Ratz* and *Yahad*). The position of Agudat Israel and *Tami* which won 3 mandates is hard to determine.

The polarised outcome of the election, which led to the creation of the National Unity Government, tends to confirm the impression that the overall modification in the New Zionist belief system was relatively moderate. In spite of the tremendous political and economic difficulties under Likud, there was no backlash against right-wing politics. On the contrary, in so far as opinion polls are indicative of a belief system, the trend towards the ultra-right has increased. For instance, a September PORI poll showed that in the event of new elections, the Kach party would almost double its vote from 1.2 per cent to 2.2 per cent.[63] A December PORI poll indicated that Tehiya's support increased from 4.0 per cent at the election to 4.3 per cent and Kach went up to 2.9 per cent.[64]

The extent and pace of the future delegitimisation of New Zionism will depend on a number of factors. Continuing economic difficulties may persuade the adherents of New Zionism that the expenditures required to deepen the annexation infrastructure in the West Bank are too high to bear. The political and moral cost of keeping the growing Palestinian population quiet can undermine some of the normative commitment to Judea and Samaria.

The future popularity of New Zionism is also related to the stand of the Labour movement. The capacity of Socialist Zionism to win over Oriental and young voters and restore co-operation with the moderate religious bloc will be an important factor in efforts to transvaluate the popular belief system.

Above all, though, Labour will have to offer a viable alternative to the annexationist view of New Zionism. The validity of the Labour vision — the surrender of part of the West Bank and the foundation of a Jordanian-Palestinian Federation in exchange for peace — hinges upon Arab consent. Thus, ultimately, the future success of Socialist Zionism will depend on the same factor which caused its failure in the past — the Arab ability or willingness to accept the co-operative solution to the conflict as defined by the more moderate camp of the Israeli polity.

Notes

1. The data were gathered by SIPRI, quoted in *Haaretz*, 26 June 1984.
2. The figures were released by Deputy Chief of Staff, David Ivri, *Maariv*, 20 April 1984.
3. T. Schiff and E. Ya'ari, *Israel's Lebanon War*, (Simon and Schuster, New York, 1984).
4. *The Jerusalem Post*, 19–23 December 1983.
5. R. A. Gabriel, *Operation Peace for Galilee, The Israeli-PLO War in Lebanon* (Hill and Wang, New York, 1984), p. 182.
6. Reported in *Haaretz*, 28 August 1984.

7. U. Benziman, 'The Secret Research of Aronson', *Haaretz*, 16 December 1984.

8. M. Waltzer, *Just and Unjust Wars*, (Basic Books, New York, 1977), p. 16.

9. For a good discussion of Israeli responses to the dilemma of the war see A. Elon, *The Israelis*, (Sphere Books Limited, London, 1971), pp. 154–192.

10. Quoted in Gabriel, *Operation Peace*, pp. 88, 91.

11. Based on information provided by the military journalist Hirsh Goodman to Gabriel, *Operation Peace*, p. 189.

12. Adapted from *Ibid.*, Table 9, p. 236.

13. The IDF does not release figures on the ethnic composition of officer corps and elite combat units, but our figures in Chapter 4 indicate that the spread of this syndrome could hurt its combat readiness. *Haaretz*, 2 Aug 1985; see also D. Horowitz, 'Is Israel a Garrison State?', *The Jerusalem Quarterly*, no. 4 (1977), pp. 58–75.

14. *Haaretz*, 26 June 1984.

15. *Haaretz*, 16 May and 28 August 1984.

16. *Haaretz*, 17 June 1984.

17. M. Garti, 'The Young Leave the IDF', *Haaretz*, 27 July 1984.

18. *The New York Times*, 10 February 1983.

19. *The New York Times*, 6 March 1983.

20. *The New York Times*, 12 July 1984.

21. *The New York Times*, 19 November 1982.

22. *The New York Times*, 3 May 1984.

23. *Haaretz*, 10 February 1985.

24. *The Jerusalem Post*, 13–20 May 1984.

25. *The Jerusalem Post*, supplement 22 December 1984.

26. The US General Accounting Office, *U.S. Assistance To the State of Israel*, first released on 24 June 1983.

27. This message was apparently conveyed to Max Frankel who interviewed senior Labour members in 1982. 'Help Us By Cutting Aid', *The New York Times*, 16 November 1982.

28. R. Man, 'Do Not Shower Us Mindlessly with Dollars', *Maariv*, 18 November 1983.

29. Quoted in N. Chomsky, *The Fateful Triangle. The United States, Israel and the Palestinians*, (South End Press, Boston, MA, 1983), p. 55.

30. *Al Bayder Assiyasi*, 2 July 1983.

31. *The Jerusalem Post*, 27 May-3 June 1984.

32. Y. Ezrachi, 'The Gap Between the National Vision and Science in the Israeli Democracy' in A. Hareven (ed.), *On the Difficulty of Being an Israeli*, (The Van Leer Jerusalem Foundation, Jerusalem, 1983), pp. 213–23.

33. Y. Atlas, 'The West Bank: A Threat That Wasn't', *The Jerusalem Post*, 19–25 February 1984.

34. *Haaretz*, 26 December 1982.

35. *Haaretz*, 16 and 22 August 1984. For a comprehensive analysis see F. A. Gharaibeh, *The Economies of the West Bank and Gaza Strip* (Westview, Boulder, CO, and London, 1985).

36. M. Roof, *Detailed Statistics on the Population of Israel By Ethnic and Religious Group and Urban and Rural Residence 1950 to 2010*, Center for International Research, US Bureau of the Census, 1984. The statistics on the Palestinian population were provided by the author from unpublished sources.

37. *Haaretz*, 4 May 1984.

38. Y. Zamir, 'The Danger of Kahanism', *The Jerusalem Post*, 22 December 1984.

39. *Haaretz*, 12 July and 23 October 1984.

40. B. Van Arkadie, *Benefits and Burdens: A Report on the West Bank and Gaza Strip Economies since 1967*, (Carnegie Endowment for International Peace, New

York, Washington, DC, 1977); Bregman's argument is quoted by B. Kimmerling, *Zionism and Economy*, (Schenkman Publishing Company Inc., New York, 1983), p. 62.

41. G. Goldberg and E. Ben Zadok, 'Regionalism and the Evolving Territorial Cleavage: Jewish Settlement in the Occupied Territories', *State Government and International Relations*, no. 21 (1983), pp. 94–6, (Hebrew).

42. Y. Yishai, 'Israel's Right-Wing Proletariat', *The Jewish Journal of Sociology*, vol. 24, no. 2 (1982), pp. 87–98.

43. *Haaretz*, 23 February 1983.

44. An interview in *Haaretz*, 1 July 1983.

45. D. Rubinstein, *On the Lord's Side: Gush Emunim*, (Hakibutz Hameuhad Publishers, 1982), p. 90, (Hebrew).

46. Y. Neeman, 'National Goals' in Hareven, *On the Difficulty*, pp. 174–5, 266–7, (Hebrew).

47. M. Brecher, *The Foreign Policy System of Israel* (Oxford University Press, Oxford, 1972), p. 315.

48. *Haaretz*, 22 January 1984.

49. *Haaretz*, 20 December 1983.

50. M. Benvenisti, *The West Bank Data Project: A Survey of Israel's Policies*, (American Enterprise Institute, Washington DC and London, 1984).

51. E. Efrat, 'Where and How Many Are Settling in the West Bank', *Haaretz*, 24 May 1984.

52. I. S. Lustick, 'The West Bank and Gaza in Israeli Politics' in S. Heydemann (ed.), *The Begin Era, Issues in Contemporary Israel* (Westview Press, Boulder, CO, and London, 1984), pp. 79–98.

53. *The New York Times*, 23 August 1983.

54. *Haaretz*, 28 March 1983.

55. *Haaretz*, 27 December 1982.

56. *Haaretz*, 7 November 1982.

57. *The Jerusalem Post*, 3–9 April 1983.

58. *Maariv*, 13 April 1984.

59. *Haaretz*, 28 December 1983.

60. *Haaretz*, 18 November 1983.

61. *Haaretz*, 3 February 1985.

62. *Maariv*, 27 July 1984.

63. G. Berger, 'Where Did They Vote Kach?', *Maariv*, 3 August 1984.

64. *Haaretz*, 18 September 1984.

65. *Haaretz*, 19 December 1984.

9 CONCLUSIONS

This book was conceived as a comprehensive inquiry into the relations between the collective belief system of a society and its conduct of foreign policy. The time span of this inquiry has been extremely broad — from the evolution of the traditional Jewish belief system in the Diaspora into modern Zionism and its contemporary variants. A major attempt has been made to discern the psychological underpinning of the Zionist ideology and the policy choices which it generated. Yet reconstruction of the psychology of a broad and often diffuse belief system poses formidable problems in integrating ideas, facts and decisions with their psychological antecedents. To solve these problems a special research design was developed. A short recapulation of its main points is in order.

A collective belief system was defined on the basis of the interactionist view. This view holds that each society has a complex set of symbols which are used to interpret reality. Such a set is both a product and a determinant of individual beliefs generated through continuous social interaction. A dominant belief system serves as a 'collective cognitive map' of the foreign policy system.

A decision-oriented approach to a collective belief system is best suited to the analysis of a society's foreign policy system. Such a conceptualisation of a belief system has several advantages. The beliefs (options) are treated as a set of probabilistic rather than deterministic events, and the notion of a range or set of alternatives can instruct us as to the choices which the foreign policy elite would pursue in response to certain given contingencies in the external and internal environments. This approach is most appropriate for complex political systems in which personalities, social and political structures, role definitions and external circumstances mediate the relationship between the range of beliefs and the policy decisions of the elite.

One of the most difficult research problems in this undertaking is the identification of the political beliefs of a society. This difficulty stems from the fact that a collective belief system has to be analysed through a duality of focus between the psychological states of an individual on the one hand and the macrosociological realities on the other. This process is circular: psychological states, in constant interaction with the sociopolitical environment, consolidate beliefs into ideology which generates, sustains and changes the social order.

To facilitate the identification of the evolving belief system we have used the methodological constructs of legitimisation, delegitimisation and transvaluation. Legitimisation is the process through which a society conceptualises its group identity/ membership and the criteria which govern its rules of distributive justice. Delegitimisation is based on the aggregate results of personal psychological states. Individuals' beliefs and values are likely to be discarded when they come into conflict with new realities. If enough individuals in a society go through the same dissonant process, they eventually delegitimise the old belief system. Transvaluation is a companion process of delegitimisation, whereby the society sanctions new and more consonant values to replace the old beliefs.

Following this design the analysis proceeded in three parts. In Part I we described the evolution of the Jewish collective system in the Diaspora, which culminated in Zionism. This part focused on the analysis of Socialist Zionism and its ideological successor, New Zionism. In Part II we analysed the long and extremely complex process through which Socialist Zionism was delegitimised. The growth of new beliefs and values which formed the core of the transvaluation process paved the way for the ascendancy of New Zionism. In Part III we applied our analytical framework to the operational environment of Israel's foreign policy system. New Zionism, which has traditionally included the option of creating a new political order based on the non-Muslim periphery of the Middle East, served as the collective 'cognitive map' for the decision to invade Lebanon. In line with our theoretical assumptions that wars serve as occasions to validate extant belief systems, Part III of the book also examined the modification of New Zionism in the aftermath of the war in Lebanon.

Based on this extensive empirical analysis a number of findings can be offered.

1. The two thousand years of existence as an oppressed minority in the Diaspora have created a major sociopolitical predicament for the Jews. As long as the Jews lived in the medieval Gentile societies, they were able to deal with the harshness of their existence through the combination of deep religious beliefs and

the corporate and religiously sequestered social structure of feudalism. Even then, their reaction to this predicament erupted in periodical millenarian ferment which culminated in the seventeenth-century Sabbataian movement. The collapse of the false Messiah and the onset of the modern age exposed the Jews to the full implications of the marginal person syndrome., The long search for a new Jewish identity which would enable the Jews to exist as equal members in their societies led them to embrace the ideas of such movements as the Enlightenment and Socialism.

2. Modern political Zionism has arisen out of the failure of the Jewish collective to achieve a fully equal civic status in Europe. The double spectre of anti-Semitism and assimilation, which threatened the Jewish identity, gave birth to the idea that Jews can become 'normal' and equal to Gentiles only in a state of their own.

3. From its very beginning, the Zionist movement was deeply split over the fundamental ideology and operational-level policies which should be pursued in order to turn the Jews into a 'nation like all other nations'. The Socialist Zionists, who dominated the Zionist movement in Palestine, advocated social redemption and a compromise solution to the evolving Arab-Israeli conflict. The Revisionists emphasised the achievement of national sovereignty as the best way of 'normalising' the Jewish people. Based on a pessimistic zero-sum evaluation of the Arab-Israeli conflict, the Revisionists advocated a hard-line position towards the Arabs. They strove to establish a Jewish state on both banks of the Jordan River and called for large-scale immigration to Palestine in order to save the East European Jews.

4. The Revisionists lost in the power struggle with the Socialist Zionists during the Yishuv period. However, the Holocaust, the Arab refusal to accept the compromise UN Partition Proposal of 1947, and the subsequent 1948 war undermined the validity of some key claims of the Socialist Zionist belief system. Although the Labour movement retained its political dominance, the Revisionist belief system, augmented by Neo-Revisionism and a growing National Religious movement, slowly gained legitimacy as the New Zionist belief system.

5. An analysis of the delegitimisation of the dominant Socialist Zionist belief system reveals the extraordinary complexity of this process. The dissonance between the Socialist Zionist ideology and the Labour Government praxis undermined the legitimacy of key elements in the belief system. The growth of new demographic

groups in the society — the orthodox and the Oriental Jews — further undermined the definition of the group identity of Socialist Zionism and brought into question the norms of distributive justice of this ideology.

6. This disappointment with Socialist Zionism was accompanied by a growing legitimisation of some of the basic tenets of New Zionism. The turning-point in this process came after the Six-Day War, which exposed the Israelis in a concrete way to their historical-religious heritage. The Land of Israel, which under Labour was relegated to the status of a national symbol, has been turned by New Zionism into an active quest to establish the State of Israel within what was seen as its proper Biblical borders. The activities of Gush Emunim and nationalist circles in the right-wing parties have transformed the public perception of the occupied territories from a largely instrumental to a normative one. Whether interpreted as part of the process of Redemption, or viewed as the historical-normative centre of Jewish existence, the quest for the Land of Israel has taken a deep psychological root in the society. In fact, during the peak of Likud's popularity the millenarian claim to Eretz Israel superseded the more utilitarian notions of the instrumental-strategic and bargaining value of the administered territories.

7. The widespread popularity of New Zionism was facilitated by the transvaluation of the popular value system. Hardened by the harsh experience of the continuous Arab-Israeli conflict and enhanced by the threatening image of the enemy, the political culture in Israel became less tolerant and more receptive to the language of New Zionism. The militarisation of the foreign policy debate legitimised some of the oldest Iron Wall tenets of Revisionism and their zero-sum game view of the conflict. This process of transvaluation was not entirely spontaneous. The legitimising debate was structured by numerous right-wing groups which in words and deeds spread the new values among the general population. The rapid growth of the right-wing movement has altered the traditional structure of the advocacy groups and has come to dominate the foreign policy system in Israel.

8. New Zionism, which generated a highly idealistic-initiative *modus operandi* in foreign policy, broke sharply with the more cautious management tradition of Labour's international relations. Contrary to some popular beliefs that the war in Lebanon was almost entirely engineered and carried out by Sharon and his

Chief of Staff Raphael Eitan, our analysis shows that the 'grand design' theory for Lebanon has enjoyed a long tradition in Revisionist thinking. While Sharon and Eitan may be held procedurally or legally responsible for the war, their plans were facilitated by the fact that the 'grand design' was a part of the collective 'cognitive map' of the Likud leadership. The cognitive approach to the analysis of foreign policy decisions makes it clear that collective shifts toward high-risk policies are more likely to occur when the option is included in the range of options of a given belief system.

The cognitive analysis also illuminates the psychological intricacies of decision making. The detailed examination of the behaviour of the Israeli Cabinet during the planning and invasion stages indicates that the very existence of the 'grand design' option in New Zionist thinking might have facilitated a decision by default. This ideological imperative apparently created a degree of ambivalence in the attitudes of the Likud Cabinet toward the evolving invasion. In turn, this ambivalence has led to immobilism in decision making and *de facto* delegation of power to the defence and military establishment, which proceeded to carry out the 'grand design' in Lebanon.

9. It is too early to assess the full impact of the war in Lebanon on New Zionism. As in the case of Socialist Zionism, the delegitimisation of New Zionism may take many years and include factors which go beyond the implications of the war. At the moment only a few tentative observations can be offered. The war in Lebanon failed to validate any of the 'grand design' tenets of New Zionism. The high human and economic cost of the war, the moral implications of a 'colonial' war, and the political structure of the IDF will undermine the idealistic-initiating style in Israel's foreign policy. The most obvious outcome of these developments will be the delegitimisation of the use of an offensive war in the pursuance of political goals.

At the same time, Israel will remain a highly visible and strong actor in the area. Likud's belief in Israel's vital strategic role in the Middle East has been vindicated by the political destabilisation of the region. Most notably, the spread of the Shiite fundamentalist movement, which was predicted by New Zionism, has posed a threat to the moderate Arab regimes and enhanced the need for Israel's strategic services. Conversely, the growth of the Shiite movement in general, and in the South of Lebanon in particular, may even strengthen the already existing Israeli image of the enemy as implacably hostile and immensely threatening. A genuine Shiite threat to Israel would redefine any future conflict from a 'colonial' to a defensive one, and legitimise once again the hard line of New Zionism. In a conflict as complex and dynamic as the Arab-Israeli struggle, the lines between what is offensive and defensive often become blurred in public perceptions.

Finally, the outcome of the war has failed to produce a serious change in attitudes towards the occupied territories. The public is deeply split on what undoubtedly constitutes the most crucial issue in the legitimisation debate in Israel. On the one hand, there is the moderate camp, which argues that the retention of more than one and a half million Palestinians would doom both the Jewish and the democratic character of the Israel polity. On the other hand, there is the New Zionist camp, which views annexation as an inevitable move in the process of turning the State of Israel into the Land of Israel. In the concluding section of the preceding Chapter we pointed out that the debate between these two belief systems is at its peak. The large number of factors which can influence this debate makes prediction of the outcome difficult. Whatever final view prevails, it will affect the Jewish State for generations to come.

APPENDIX
THE DECISION TO INVADE LEBANON:
CHRONOLOGICAL SURVEY

Table A1: Events Preceding the Decision to Invade Lebanon: A Chronological Survey

Date	Domestic Environment	Regional Environment	International Environment
March 1976		Abu Halil, a representative of the Phalange Party, approached Israel for help against the Palestinian – Druze leftist Muslim Alliance.	
June 1976		The beginning of Syrian intervention in the Civil War in Lebanon.	
August 1976	The Labour Cabinet decided against the request to help the Phalangists.		
August 1976		Prime Minister Yitzhuk Rabin met with Camille Chamoun, but refused to commit Israel.	
September 1976		Syrian offensive against the PLO halted the Civil War in Lebanon.	
September 1976		The Riyadh Agreement recognised Syria as a peace-making force in Lebanon.	
May 1977	Likud formed a coalition government.		
February 1978	Likud Cabinet decided to retaliate against the increased harassment of Galilee by the PLO.		

March 1978	Operation Litani – Israel invaded the South of Lebanon in order to eliminate the PLO bases.
Summer 1978	Following the murder of Tony Frangieh, a Christian ally of Syria, by the Phalangists, Syria stepped up its attacks on Maronites.
Autumn 1978	Bashir Gemayel, the head of the Phalange movement, secured the Israeli pledge for arms support.
December 1980	The Israeli Cabinet agreed to provide air cover in the event of a Syrian attack against the Phalange.
April 1981	Following a Maronite-Syrian incident near Zahle, the Syrians besieged the city which was a Maronite stronghold.
April 1981	On the apparent initiative of Israel's Defence Minister, Ariel Sharon, and the Chief of Staff, Raphael Eitan, the IDF shot down two Syrian helicopters on Mount Senin, near Zahle.
April 1981	Following the shooting down of the helicopters, Syria installed SAM-6 missiles near Zahle.

May 1981	Mount Senin, the Phalangist stronghold, was captured by Syrians.	
December 1981		Sharon met with Philip Habib and the American Chargé d'Affaires, William Brown, to discuss a possible action against the PLO build-up in Lebanon.
February 1982	The talks between Bashir Gemayel and the PLO collapsed. The Phalange became convinced that Arafat would not negotiate with Israel.	The Israeli Chief of Intelligence, Yehoshua Saguy, met secretly with the American Secretary of State Alexander Haig to discuss possible action against the PLO.
April 1982		NBC evening news disclosed the details of the planned Israeli operation in Lebanon.
May 1982		Sharon met Alexander Haig and obtained an understanding that Israel could reserve its right to attack the PLO in the event of a clear provocation.
May 1982		Haig sent a mildly worded letter to Begin on the subject of a possible invasion.

May 1982	Begin and his supporters in the Cabinet interpreted Haig's letter as a tacit approval of a possible venture in Lebanon.		
May 1982	Following another round of PLO activities in southern Lebanon, Israel bombed PLO targets in the region.	PLO, under pressure from its extreme wing, retaliated by bombing targets in Upper Galilee.	
May 1982	The Big Pine operation (code name for the invasion of Lebanon) was discussed at a Cabinet meeting. The Chief of Intelligence and a number of ministers disagreed and no decision was reached.		

Table A2: The Implementation of the Decision

Date	Domestic Environment	Regional Environment	International Environment
3 June 1982	An assassination attempt on the Israeli ambassador to London, Shlomo Argov.	The Palestinian National Liberation Movement, an extremist group lead by Abu Nidal, was behind the attack. This action was apparently supported by Syria which hoped that Israel would retaliate against the PLO.	

4 June 1982	An 8:30 a.m. emergency Cabinet meeting to discuss the incident. Begin stated that Argov was chosen as a target because he was a Jew and a symbol of the State of Israel. The various plans for the invasion were discussed, but no decision was made. The Cabinet ordered heavy air attacks on PLO strongholds in Lebanon.	
5 June 1982		PLO retaliated with a heavy artillery barrage across Western and Northern Galilee.
5 June 1982	At a night session the Cabinet decided to move into Lebanon. There are conflicting reports about the scope of the plans of the invasion. Most diplomatic and journalistic sources claim that Begin and the Cabinet approved a modified version of the 40km plan, i.e., a quick drive into southern Lebanon, possibly beyond the Awali River. The Cabinet did not authorise an attack against the Syrians or the entry into Beirut.	

5 June 1982	Throughout the night the Chief of Staff conducted briefings of the IDF forces scheduled to participate in the invasion.
6 June 1982	The crossing of the border into Lebanon began at 11:00 a.m. Philip Habib telephoned Begin to find out about the scope of the invasion. Begin assured him that the 40 km invasion would take 72 hours. It is not clear whether Begin was sincere or tried to deflect possible American pressure against a larger scale operation.
7 June 1982	IDF was engaged in heavy fighting against the PLO. During an Israeli air raid on Beirut, Syria decided to counteract and lost some MIGs.
8 June 1982	Syrian forces began a move to block an apparent Israeli move to cut the Beirut-Damascus highway.

9 June 1982	Begin gave final authorisation to destroy the Syrian SAM missiles, in the Bekaa Valley. This decision was an apparent victory for Sharon. In 1981 the Defence Ministry had ordered a study of long-term Syrian security threats, which predicted that Syria might attack Israel in 1984 or 1985. The conclusions of the intelligence report were accepted by Sharon, who pressed for a pre-emptive strike.
9 June 1982	In an afternoon raid, the IDF destroyed 17 out of the 19 Syrian missiles and shot down a large number of MIGs. The raid initiated the war with Syria.
11 June 1982	Syria and Israel agreed on a cease-fire which did not include the PLO.
13 June 1982	The Israeli-Syrian cease-fire broke down.

22,24 June 1982

The battle for the Beirut -
Damascus highway ended in
Syrian withdrawal.

25 June 1982

The official Israeli campaign in
Lebanon was accomplished. The
IDF controlled a large part of
Lebanese territory; the line
extended from Beirut across the
Bekaa Valley up to Kfar Anoq in
the West. The PLO infrastructure
in these territories was destroyed.

1 July 1982

The siege of Beirut began. There
were approximately 14,000 PLO
guerrillas and 500,000 Palestinians
mostly in the West Beirut camps
of Sabra, Shatila and Bourje el
Barajneh.

4 July 1982

In order to exert pressure on the
PLO, Israel cut off supplies to
West Beirut.

7 July 1982

Following an urgent message
from President Reagan, Israel
restored supplies to West
Beirut.

22–28 July 1982	Israel staged concentrated attacks on the Syrian and PLO forces in Beirut.
29 July 1982	The Arab League formally endorsed a proposal under which the PLO would withdraw from Beirut.
4 August 1982	Following the slowdown of negotiations on the withdrawal, the Israeli Cabinet decided on renewed pressure on the PLO.	The decision was implemented by a concentrated aerial, naval and infantry attack on West Beirut and the port area.
5 August 1982		President Reagan expressed extreme anger at Israeli incursion into West Beirut.
8 August 1982		Habib reached an agreement with the Lebanese Government and the PLO on the terms of withdrawal.
9 August 1982	The Cabinet was formally presented with the Habib agreement, but demanded that a complete list of the PLO evacuees should be attached.

12 August 1982	IDF conducted a day-long bombing of West Beirut. According to some sources the bombing was enhanced by sonic booms to apply psychological pressure on the PLO.	The bombing drew a sharp reaction from the United States and the international community.
14 August 1982	The Syrians publicly announced their agreement to withdraw from Beirut.	
19 August 1982	The Cabinet formally approved the agreement for the evacuation of the PLO.	
21 August 1982		The contingent of the multinational force arrived in Beirut to oversee the withdrawal.
21 August 1982	The withdrawal of the PLO and Syrian forces implemented.	

BIBLIOGRAPHY

Abelson, R. P. 'Script Processing in Attitude Formation and Decision Making' in J. S. Carrol and J. W. Payne (eds), *Cognitive and Social Behavior*, (John Wiley and Sons, New York, 1976), pp. 33–45.

Abercombie, N. and S. B. Turner, 'The Dominant Ideology Thesis', *The British Journal of Sociology*, vol. 29, no. 2 (1978), pp. 149–67.

Abraham, S., 'The Jews and the Israelis in Modern Arabic Literature', *The Jerusalem Quarterly*, no. 2 (1977), pp. 119–35.

Adams, H., 'Survival Politics: Afrikanerdom in Search of a New Ideology', *The Journal of Modern African Studies*, vol. 16, no. 4 (1978), pp. 657–69.

Adar, Z., *Jewish Education in Israel and the United States*, (The School of Education and the Institute of Contemporary Jewry of the Hebrew University, Jerusalem, 1977).

Adorno, T. W., E. Frankel-Brunswick, D. J. Levinson and N. Sanford, *The Authoritarian Personality*, (Harper and Row, New York, 1965).

Adi, P. and D. Froelich, *Attitudes Concerning Political Security and Topics of Public Morale in February — March* (Israel Institute of Applied Social Research, Jerusalem, 1970), (Hebrew).

Allport, G. W. *The Nature of Prejudice*, (Addison Wesley, New York, 1979).

Almond, G. *The Appeals of Communism*, (Princeton University Press, Princeton, NJ, 1965).

—— and S. Verba, *Civic Culture*, (Little, Brown and Company, Boston, MA, 1965).

Almog, S. (ed.), *Zionism and the Arabs*, (The Historical Society of Israel and the Zalman Shazar Center, Jerusalem, 1983).

Amir, Y., A. Bizman, R. Ben-Ari and M. Rivner, 'Contact Between Israelis and Arabs', *Journal of Cross-Cultural Psychology*, vol. 11, no. 4 (1980), pp. 426–43.

—— and R. Ben-Ari, 'Cognitive Cultural Learning, Intergroup Contact and Change in Ethnic Attitudes and Relations', paper presented at the International Conference on Group Processes and Intergroup Conflict, Shfaim, Israel, October 1983.

Antonovsky, A. 'Israeli Political-Social Attitudes', *Amot*, vol. 1, no. 16 (1963), pp. 11–22, (Hebrew).

Apter, D. E., *The Politics of Modernization*, (University of Chicago Press, Chicago and London, 1965).

Arendt, H. *Eichmann in Jerusalem. A Report on the Banality of Evil*, (Viking Press, New York, 1963).

—— 'The Jewish State: Fifty Years After — Where Have Herzl's Politics Led?' in G. V. Smith (ed.), *Zionism: The Dream and Reality*, (David and Charles, Newton Abbot, London and New York, 1974), pp. 67–80.

Arian, A., *Ideological Change in Israel*, (Case Western Reserve University Press, Cleveland, OH, 1968).

—— *The Choosing People*, (Ramat Gan, Massada, 1973), (Hebrew).

—— 'The Electorate: Israel 1977' in H. R. Penniman, (ed.), *Israel at the Polls: The Knesset Election of 1977*, (American Enterprise Institute, Washington, DC, 1979), pp. 59–89.

—— and M. Shamir, 'The Primary Political Function of the Left-Right Continuum' in A. Arian (ed.), *The Elections in Israel — 1981*, (Ramot Publishing, Tel Aviv, 1983), pp. 258–79.

287

288   *Bibliography*

Arlow, J. A., 'Ego Psychology and the Study of Mythology', *Journal of the American Psychoanalytical Association*, vol. 9, no. 3 (1967), pp. 371–93.

Arnoni, M. S., *Rights and Wrongs in the Arab-Israeli Conflict*, (The Minority of One Press, Passaic, NJ, 1968).

Aronson, S., *Conflict and Bargaining in the Middle East, An Israeli Perspective*, (Johns Hopkins University Press, Baltimore and London, 1978).

—— and D. Horowitz, 'The Strategy of the Controlled Retaliation', *State, Government and International Relations*, vol. 1, no. 1 (1971), pp. 77–99, (Hebrew).

Asad, T. 'Anthropology and the Analysis of Ideology', *Man*, vol. 14, no. 4 (1979), pp. 607–27.

Ashcroft, R., 'Political Theory and the Problem of Ideology', *The Journal of Politics*, vol. 42, no. 3 (1980), pp. 687–721.

Aviad, J., 'From Protest to Return: Contemporary Teshuva', *The Jerusalem Quarterly*, no. 16 (1980), pp. 71–86.

Avigal, S., 'Morrocan Dybbuk?', *The Jerusalem Quarterly*, no. 2 (1981), pp. 48–54.

Avineri, S., *Essays on Zionism and Politics*, (Sifrei Mabat, Tel Aviv, 1977), (Hebrew).

—— 'The Political Thought of Vladimir Jabotinsky', *The Jerusalem Quarterly*, no. 16 (1980), pp. 3–26.

Axelrod, R., 'Structure of Public Opinion on Policy Issues', *Public Opinion Quarterly*, vol. 31, no. 2 (1967), pp. 51–60.

Bar-On, A. W., *The Untold Story. The Diary of the Chief Censor*, (Edanim Publications, Jerusalem, 1981), (Hebrew).

Bar-Tal, D., 'Israel-Palestinian Conflict: A Cognitive Analysis', paper presented at the European-Israeli Conference on Group Processes and Intergroup Conflict, Tel Aviv, October 1983.

—— 'Psychological Analysis of Patriotism', unpublished manuscript, n.d.

Bay, C., 'Access to Political Knowledge as a Human Right', in I. Galnoor (ed.), *Government Secrecy in Democracies*, (Harper and Row, New York, 1977), pp. 22–39.

Beer, A., *Settlements*, (Eli Printers, Jerusalem, 1981), (Hebrew).

Beit-Hallahmi, B., 'Religion and Nationalism in the Arab Israeli Conflict', *Il Politico*, vol. 38, no. 2 (1973), pp. 232–43.

Bell, D., 'The Depressed' in D. Bell (ed.), *The Radical Right*, (Anchor Books, New York, 1964), pp. 1–45.

Benedict, R. F., *Patterns of Culture*, (Penguin Books, New York, 1946).

Ben-Ezer, E. 'War and Siege in Hebrew Literature After 1967', *The Jerusalem Quarterly*, no. 9 (1978), pp. 20–37.

Ben-Meir, Y. and P. Kedem, 'A Measure of Religiosity for the Jewish Population in Israel', *Megamot*, vol. 24, no. 3 (1978), pp. 352–62, (Hebrew).

Benjamini, K., 'National Stereotypes of Israeli Youth', *Megamot*, vol. 16, no. 4 (1969), pp. 364–75, (Hebrew).

Ben Shoshan, S., 'If a Miracle Happens' in A. Ben-Ami (ed.), *The Greater Land of Israel Book*, (The Greater Land of Israel Movement and S. Freedman, Tel Aviv, 1977), pp. 317–20.

Ben-Sira, Z., *Interethnic Cleavage, Stress, Coping and Compensatory Mechanism: The Case of Israel*, (The Israel Institute of Applied Social Research, Jerusalem, 1983).

—— *The Jewish Society in Israel: Ethnic Relations*, (The Israel Institute of Applied Social Research, Jerusalem 1983), (Hebrew).

—— 'Towards a Facet Theory of a Sequential Order of Societal Needs', *Quality and Quantity*, no. 13 (1979), pp. 233–53.

Benvenisti, M., *The West Bank Data Project. A Survey of Israel's Policies*, (American Enterprise Institute, Washington DC, and London, 1984).

Bernstein, D., 'Immigrant Transit Camps — The Formation of Dependent Relations in Israeli Society', *Ethnic and Racial Studies*, vol. 4, no. 1 (1981), pp. 26–43.

—— 'Immigrants and Society. A Critical View of the Dominant School of Israeli Sociology', *British Journal of Sociology*, vol. 31, no. 1 (1980), pp. 246–64.

Billig, M., *Ideology and Social Psychology. Extremism, Moderation and Contradiction*, (St. Martins, New York, 1982).

—— *Social Psychology and Intergroup Relations*, (Academic Press, London, 1976).

Bizman, A. and Y. Amir, 'Mutual Perceptions of Arabs and Jews in Israel', *Journal of Cross-Cultural Psychology*, vol. 13, no. 4 (1982), pp. 461–9.

Blau, P. M., *Exchange and Power in Social Life*, (John Wiley & Sons, New York, 1964).

Booth, K., *Strategy and Ethnocentrism*, (Holmes and Meir Publishers, New York, 1979).

Borthwick, B. M., 'Religion and Politics in Israel and Egypt', *The Middle East Journal*, vol. 33, no. 2 (1979), pp. 144–63.

Boulding, K. N., 'National Images and International Systems', *Journal of Conflict Resolution*, vol. 3, no. 2 (1959), pp. 120–37.

—— *The Image: Knowledge in Life and Society*, (University of Michigan Press, Ann Arbor, MI, 1963).

Brecher, M., *Decisions in Israeli Foreign Policy*, (Yale University Press, New Haven, CT, 1975).

—— *The Foreign Policy System of Israel*, (Oxford University Press, London, 1972).

—— 'Towards a Theory of International Crisis Behavior', *International Studies Quarterly*, vol. 21, no. 1 (1977), pp. 39–74.

Brenner, L., *Zionism in the Age of the Dictators*, (Croom Helm, London, 1983).

Buber, M., 'Nationalism' in G. V. Smith (ed.), *Zionism: The Dream and Reality*, (David and Charles, Newton Abbot, London and New York, 1974).

Burnstein, P., 'Political Patronage and Party Choice Among Israeli Voters', *The Journal of Politics*, vol. 38, no. 4 (1976), pp. 1024–32.

—— 'Social Network and Voting: Some Israeli Data', *Social Forces*, vol. 54, no. 4 (1976), pp. 833–47.

Campbell, D. J. and D. Fiske, 'Convergent and Discriminant Validation by Multitrait Multimethod Matrix', *Psychological Bulletin*, vol. 56, no. 1 (1959), pp. 81–104.

Canover, M., *Populism*, (Harcourt Brace Jovanovitch, New York and London, 1981).

Caplan, N., 'Negotiations and the Arab Israeli Conflict', *The Jerusalem Quarterly*, no. 6 (1978), pp. 3–19.

Caporoso, J., 'Dependence, Dependency and Power in the Global System: A Structural and Behavioral Analysis: Notes Towards Precision of Concept and Argument', *International Organization*, vol. 33, no. 1 (1978), pp. 13–43.

Caspi, D., 'How Representative is the Knesset?', *The Jerusalem Quarterly*, no. 14 (1980), pp. 68–81.

Chen, O., 'Reflection on Israeli Deterrence', *The Jerusalem Quarterly*, no. 24 (1982), pp. 26–37.

Chomsky, N., *The Fateful Triangle: the United States, Israel and the Palestinians*, (South End Press, Boston, MA, 1983).

Cohen, A., 'The Changing Pattern of West Bank Policies', *The Jerusalem Quarterly*, no. 5 (1977), pp. 105–13.

Cohen, A. A., *The Natural and Supernatural Jew. A Historical and Theological Introduction*, (Pantheon Books, New York, 1962).

Converse, P., 'The Nature of Belief Systems in Mass Publics' in D. E. Apter (ed.), *Ideology and Discontent*, (The Free Press, New York, 1964), pp. 206–61.

Coser, L. A., *The Function of Social Conflict*, (The Free Press of Glencoe, New York, 1964).

290   *Bibliography*

Czudnowski, M., 'Legislative Recruitment Under Proportional Representation in Israel: A Model and a Case Study' in M. Lissak and E. Guttman (eds), *Political Institutions and Processes in Israel*, (Akademon, Jerusalem, 1975), pp. 348–82.

Daaldar, H. 'The Netherlands: Opposition in a Segmented Society' in R. Dahl (ed.), *Political Opposition in Western Democracies*, (Yale University Press, New Haven, CT, 1966), pp. 232–53.

Dallak, R., *The American Style of Foreign Policy*, (Alfred A. Knopf, New York, 1983).

Decalo, S., *Messianic Influence in Israeli Foreign Policy*, (University of Rhode Island, Kingston, RI, 1967).

Dela Pergola, S., 'Immigration, Emigration and Other Demographic Problems' in A. Hareven, *On the Difficulty of Being an Israeli*, (The Van Leer Foundation, Jerusalem, 1983), pp. 225–56, (Hebrew).

Derber, M., 'Israel's Wage Differential: A Persisting Problem' in S. N. Eisenstadt, R. Bar-Yosef and C. Adler (eds), *Integration and Development in Israel*, (Praeger and Pall Mall, New York and London, 1970), pp. 185–201.

Deshen, S. A., *Immigrant Voters in Israel*, (Manchester University Press, Manchester, 1970).

—— 'Israeli Judaism: Introduction to the Major Patterns', *International Journal of Middle East Studies*, vol. 9, no. 2 (1978), pp. 141–169.

—— 'The Judaism of Middle Eastern Immigrants', *The Jerusalem Quarterly*, no. 13 (1979), pp. 48–109.

Deutsch, M., *The Resolution of Conflict: Constructive and Destructive Processes*, (Yale University Press, New Haven, CT, 1973).

Diamond, S., 'Kibbutz and Shtetl: The History of an Idea', *Social Problems*, vol. 5, no. 2 (1957), pp. 71–99.

Dimont, M. I., *Jews, God and History*, (Simon and Schuster, New York, 1962).

Dotan, Y., *The Opinion of the Public About the Army and Defense*, (The Israel Institute of Applied Social Research, Jerusalem, 1974), (Hebrew).

Dougherty, E. J. and R. L. Pfaltzgraff, Jr., *Contending Theories of International Relations*, (Harper and Row Publishers, New York, 1981).

Douglas M., 'Social Preconditions of Enthusiasm and Heterodoxy' in R. F. Spencer (ed.) *Forms of Symbolic Action*, (University of Washington Press, Seattle, WA, 1969), pp. 69–80.

Dueti, I., 'The Nuclear Policy of Israel', *State Government and International Relations*, no. 7 (1975), pp. 5–27, (Hebrew).

Eisenstadt, S. N., 'Change and Continuity in Israeli Society. II Dynamic Conservatism vs. Innovation', *The Jerusalem Quarterly*, no. 2 (1977), pp. 3–11.

—— 'Communication Process Among Immigrants in Israel', *Public Opinion Quarterly*, vol. 16, no. 1 (1952), pp. 42–58.

—— *Israeli Society*, (Weidenfeld and Nicolson, London, 1967).

—— 'The Place of Elites and Primary Groups in the Absorption of New Immigrants in Israel', *American Journal of Sociology*, vol. 57, no. 3 (1951), pp. 222–31.

—— 'The Process of Absorption of New Immigrants in Israel', *Human Relations*, vol. 5, no. 2 (1952), pp. 223–46.

Eldad, I., *A Controversy: Our Perceptions of the Destruction of the Second Temple and of Bar-Kochba's Revolt*, (The Van Leer Foundation, Jerusalem, 1982).

—— 'Jabotinsky Distorted', *The Jerusalem Quarterly*, no. 16 (1980), pp. 27–39.

Eldridge, A. F., *Images of Conflict*, (St. Martin's Press, New York, 1979).

Elizur, Y. and E. Salpater, *Who Rules Israel?* (Harper and Row, New York, 1973).

Elkins, D. J. and R. E. B. Simeon, 'A Cause in Search of its Effects or What Does Political Culture Explain', *Comparative Politics*, vol. 11, no. 2 (1979), pp. 127–46.

Elliot, P. E. and P. Schlesinger, 'On the Stratification of Political Knowledge', *Sociological Review*, vol. 27, no. 1 (1979), pp. 55–81.

Elon, A., *The Israelis*, (Sphere Books Limited, London, 1971).

Erikson, E. H., *Childhood and Society*, (Norton, New York, 1950).

Ettinger, S., 'Anti-Semitism in Our Time', *The Jerusalem Quarterly*, no. 23 (1983), pp. 95–113.

Etzioni-Halevy, E. with R. Shapiro, *Political Culture in Israel: Cleavage and Integration Among Israeli Jews*, (Praeger, New York and London, 1977).

Ezrachi, Y., 'The Gap Between the National Vision and Science in the Israeli Democracy' in A. Hareven (ed.), *On the Difficulty of Being an Israeli*, (The Van Leer Jerusalem Foundation, Jerusalem, 1983), pp. 213–23.

Farago, U., 'The Perception of the Holocaust Among Israeli Students — 1983', *Dapim Le Mehkar Hasho'a*, November 1983, pp. 117–128, (Hebrew).

Festinger, L., *A Theory of Cognitive Dissonance*, (Stanford University Press, Stanford, CA, 1957).

Fishelson, G., Y. Weiss and N. Mark, 'Ethnic Origin and Income Differentials Among Israeli Males, 1969–1976' in A. Arian (ed.), *Israel — A Developing Society*, (Van Gorcum, Assen, 1980), pp. 253–77.

Fishman, G., 'On War and Crime' in S. Breznitz (ed.), *Stress in Israel*, (Van Nostrand Reinhold Company, New York, 1983), pp. 165–80.

Frank, J. D. 'Nature and Function of Belief Systems: Humanism and Transcendental Religion', *American Psychologist*, vol. 32, no. 7 (1977), pp. 555–9.

—— *Sanity and Survival in the Nuclear Age: Psychological Aspects of War and Peace*, (Random House, New York, 1982).

Fraser, J., 'Validating a Measure of National Political Legitimacy', *American Journal of Political Science*, vol. 18, no. 2 (1974), pp. 117–34.

Frassie, P., *The Psychology of Time*, (Harper and Row, New York, 1963).

Friedlander, S., 'Some Aspects of the Historical Significance of the Holocaust', *The Jerusalem Quarterly*, no. 1 (1976), pp. 36–59.

Gabriel, R. A., *Operation Peace for Galilee: The Israeli-PLO War in Lebanon*, (Hill and Wang, New York, 1984).

Galnoor, I, 'Israel's Polity: The Common Language', *The Jerusalem Quarterly*, no. 20 (1981), pp. 65–82.

—— 'The Right to Know vs. Government Secrecy', *The Jerusalem Quarterly*, no. 5 (1977), pp. 48–65.

Galtson, W. A., *Justice and the Human Good*, (University of Chicago Press, Chicago, 1980).

Gellner, E., 'Concept and Society' in B. R. Wilson (ed.), *Rationality*, (Harper and Row, Evanston and New York, 1970), pp. 18–49.

Gerber-Talmon, Y. and Z. Stup, *Secular Ascetism: Patterns of Ideological Change* in S. N. Eisenstadt, S. Bar-Yosef and C. Adler (eds), *Integration and Development in Israel*, (Pall Mall, New York, 1970), pp. 469–504.

Gertz, N., 'Israeli Novelists', *The Jerusalem Quarterly*, no. 17 (1980), pp. 66–77.

Gharaibeh, F. A., *The Economies of the West Bank and Gaza Strip*, (Westview, Boulder, CO, and London, 1985).

Goffman, E., *The Presentation of Self in Everyday Life*, (Doubleday Anchor, Garden City, 1959).

Golan, E., *Political Culture in Israel — Case Study*, unpublished M. A. thesis, Haifa University, 1977, (Hebrew).

Goldberg, G. and E. Ben Zadok, 'Regionalism and the Evolving Territorial Cleavage: Jewish Settlement in the Occupied Territories', *State, Government and International Relations*, no. 21 (1983), pp. 94–6, (Hebrew).

Goldberg, G. and S. A. Hoffman, 'Nominations in Israel: The Politics of Institutionalization' in A. Arian (ed.), *The Elections in Israel — 1981*, (Ramot Publishing Co, Tel Aviv, 1983).

Goldberg, H., 'Ethnic Groups in Israeli Society', *Ethnic Groups*, vol. 1, no. 3 (1977), pp. 163–86.

Gonen, J. Y., *A Psychohistory of Zionism*, (Meridian Books, New York, 1975).
Gordon, L., 'Reflections on Inter- and Intra-Group Relations in Israeli Society', *Jewish Social Studies*, vol. 36, no. 3–4 (1974), pp. 262–272.
Goren, D., *Secrecy, Security and Freedom of Press*, (Magnes Publishers, Jerusalem, 1976), (Hebrew).
Gratch, H. (ed.), *Twenty-Five Years of Social Research in Jerusalem*, (Jerusalem Academic Press, Jerusalem, 1973).
Green, S., *Taking Sides: America's Secret Relations With a Militant Israel*, (William Morrow and Company, New York, 1984).
Greenstein, F., 'The Impact of Personality and Politics: An Attempt to Clear Away the Underbrush', *American Political Science Review*, vol. 61, no. 4 (1967), pp. 629–41.
Gross Stein, J., 'The 1973 Intelligence Failure: A Reconsideration', *The Jerusalem Quarterly*, no. 24 (1982), pp. 41–54.
—— and R. Tanter, *Rational Decision Making. Israel's Security Choices 1967*, (Ohio State University Press, Columbus, OH, 1976).
Gurr, T. R., *Why Men Rebel*, (Princeton University Press, Princeton, NJ, 1970).
Guttman, E. L., 'Wars and Political Attitudes of the Jewish Public in Israel', paper presented at the annual conference of the Israeli Sociological Association, Ber Sheeba, February 1985, (Hebrew).
Guttman, J., *Philosophies of Judaism*, (Schocken Books, New York, 1973).
Ha'am, Ahad, *All Writings of Ahad Ha'am*, (Hebrew Publishing, Jerusalem, 1956), (Hebrew).
Habermas, J., *Legitimation Crisis*, (Beacon Press, Boston, MA, 1975).
Handel, W., 'Normative Expectations and the Emergence of Meanings as Solution to Problems: Convergence of Structural and Interactionist Views', *American Journal of Sociology*, vol. 34, no. 4 (1979), pp. 855–81.
Hareven, A., 'Disturbed Hierarchy. Israeli Intelligence in 1954 and 1973', *The Jerusalem Quarterly*, no. 9 (1978).
Harkabi, Y., *Arab Attitudes Towards Israel*, (Israel University Press, Jerusalem, 1972).
—— *Arab Strategies and Israel's Responses*, (The Free Press and Collier MacMillan Publishers, New York, 1977).
—— *Vision, No Fantasy. Realism in International Relations*, (The Domino Press, Jerusalem, 1982), (Hebrew).
—— *Facing Reality. Lessons from Jeremiah, the Destruction of the Second Temple and Bar-Kochba's Rebellion*, (The Van Leer Foundation, Jerusalem, 1981), (Hebrew).
Harlap, S., 'The Goals of the War and its Outcomes: The Yom Kippur War', *State Government and International Relations*, no. 17 (1981), pp. 68–85.
Hasdai, Y., *With Iron Pen*, (Kvutzat La'or Publishing, Jerusalem, 1983), (Hebrew).
Heider, F., 'Social Perception and Phenomenal Causality', *Psychological Review*, vol. 51, no. 3 (1951), pp. 358–76.
Hendel, M., *Israel's Political Military Doctrine*, (Center for International Affairs, Harvard University, Cambridge, MA, 1973).
Heradstveit, D., *Arab and Israeli Elite Perceptions*, (Universitets Forlaget, Oslo, 1974).
Herman, S. N., *Israelis and Jews. The Continuity of an Identity*, (The Jewish Publication Society of America, Philadelphia, 1970).
—— 'In the Shadow of the Holocaust', *The Jerusalem Quarterly*, no. 3 (1977), pp. 85–97.
—— *Zionism and Pro-Israelism. A Social Psychological Analysis*, (The Institute of Contemporary Jewry, Hebrew University, Jerusalem, 1976).
—— U. Farago and Y. Harel, *Continuity and Change in the Jewish Identity of High*

School Youth in Israel 1965–1974, (Eshkol Institute, Hebrew University, Jerusalem, 1976), (Hebrew).

—— Y. Peres and E. Yuchtman, 'Reaction to the Eichmann Trial in Israel: A Study in High Involvement', *Scripta Hierosolymitana*, vol. 14 (1965), pp. 98–119.

Hertz, J. H., 'Legitimacy: Can We Retrieve It?', *Comparative Politics*, vol. 10, no. 3 (1978), pp. 317–44.

Herzog, Y., *A People That Dwells Alone*, (Maariv Publishing, Tel Aviv, 1976), (Hebrew).

Hilberg, R., *The Destruction of the European Jews*, (Quadrangle Press, Chicago, 1967).

Holt, R. T., and J. K. Turner, 'Insular Politics' in J. N. Rosenau (ed.), *Linkage Politics*, (The Free Press, New York, 1969), pp. 199–238.

Horney, K., *Neuroses and Human Growth: The Struggle Towards Self-Realization*, (Norton, New York, 1950).

Horowitz, D. L., 'Ethnic Identity' in D. Glazer and D. P. Moynihan (eds), *Ethnicity, Theory and Experience*, (Harvard University Press, Cambridge, MA, 1975), pp. 111–40.

Horowitz, D., 'Is Israel a Garrison State?', *The Jerusalem Quarterly*, no. 4 (1977), pp. 58–75.

—— and M. Lissak, *The Origins of the Israeli Polity. The Political System of the Jewish Community in Palestine Under the Mandate*, (Am Oved, Tel Aviv, 1977), (Hebrew).

Ichilov, O. and N. Nave, '"The Good Citizen" as Viewed by Israeli Adolescents', *Comparative Politics*, vol. 13, no. 3 (1981), pp. 361–76.

Ilan, A., 'The Prophecy of a Jewish State; Its "Fulfillment", 1941–1949', *The Jerusalem Quarterly*, no. 33 (1984), pp. 125–44.

Inbar, M., and C. Adler, *Ethnic Integration in Israel*, (Transaction Books, New Brunswick, NJ, 1977).

Isaac, R. J., *Israel Divided: Ideological Politics in the Jewish State*, (Johns Hopkins University Press, Baltimore, MD, 1976).

—— *Party Politics in Israel*, (Longman, New York, 1981).

Israel Institute of Applied Social Research, (editorial staff), *Following the Appearance of Yassir Arafat in the General Assembly of the United Nations*, (Israel Institute of Applied Social Research, Jerusalem, n.d.).

Israel Pocket Library, *Immigration and Settlement*, (Keter Books, Jerusalem, 1973).

Jacob, A., 'Trends in Israel, Public Opinion on Issues Related to the Arab-Israeli Conflict 1967–1972', *The Jewish Journal of Sociology*, vol. 16, no. 2 (1974), pp. 187–208.

Janis, L. I., *Victims of Groupthink: A Psychological Study of Foreign Policy Decision and Fiascos*, (Houghton, Mifflin, Boston, MA, 1972).

Jarvie, I. C., 'Explaining Cargo Cults' in B. R. Wilson (ed.), *Rationality*, (Harper and Row, Evanston and New York, 1970), pp. 50–61.

Jervis, R., *Perceptions and Misperceptions in International Politics*, (Princeton University Press, Princeton, NJ, 1976).

Johnson, C., *Revolutionary Change*, (Little Brown, Boston, MA and Toronto, 1966).

Kahane, M., *They Must Go*, (Grosset and Dunlop, New York, 1981).

Kamen, C., *Attitudes and Behavior of the Public Towards Independence Day*, (The Israel Institute of Applied Social Research, 1973), (Hebrew).

Kammen, M. P., (ed.), *The Past Before Us: Contemporary Writings in America*, (Cornell University Press, Ithaca, NY, 1980).

Kaplowitz, N., 'Psychological Dimensions of the Middle East Conflict: Policy Implications', *Journal of Conflict Resolution*, vol. 20, no. 2 (1976), pp. 279–317.

Katz, J., *No Daring and No Glory*, (Dvir, Tel Aviv, 1981), (Hebrew).
—— *Exclusiveness and Tolerance*, (Schocken, New York, 1962).
Kav-Venaki, S. and A. Nadler, 'Trans-Generational Effects of Massive Psychic Traumatization: Psychological Characteristics of Children of Holocaust Survivors', paper presented at the annual conference of the International Society of Political Psychology, Mannheim, West Germany, June 1983.
Kayyali, A. W., 'The Historical Roots of the Imperialist-Zionist Alliance' in A. W. Kayyali (ed.), *Zionism, Imperialism and Racism*, (Croom Helm, London, 1979).
Kedem, P., 'A Measure of Religiosity for the Jewish Population in Israel', *Megamot*, vol. 24 (1978), pp. 353–62, (Hebrew).
Kegley, C. W. and E. R. Wittkopf, *American Foreign Policy. Patterns and Process*, (St. Martin's Press, New York, 1979).
Khashan, H. and A. Palmer, 'The Economic Basis of Conflict in Lebanon: A Survey Analysis of Sunni Muslims' in T. E. Farah (ed.), *Political Behavior in the Arab States*, (Westview Press, Boulder, CO, 1983), pp. 67–81.
Kiess, N., 'The Influence of Public Policy on Public Opinion: Israel 1967–1974', *State, Government and International Relations*, no. 8 (1975), pp. 36–60, (Hebrew).
Killion, M. L., 'The Respect Revolution: Freedom and Equality' in H. D. Laswell, D. Lerner and H. Speier (eds), *A Pluralizing World in Formation* vol. 3, *Propaganda and Communication in World History*, (University Press of Hawaii, Honolulu, HI, 1980), pp. 43–147.
Kimmerling, B., 'Anomie and Integration in the Israeli Society and the Saliency of the Arab-Israeli Conflict', *Megamot*, vol. 29, no. 4 (1973), pp. 349–74.
—— 'The Salience of the Arab-Israeli Conflict As a Social Indicator 1949–1970', *State Government and International Relations*, no. 6 (1974), pp. 100–26.
—— *Zionism and Economy* (Schenkman Publishing Company, Cambridge, MA, 1983).
—— *Zionism and Territory. The Socio-Territorial Dimension of Zionist Politics*, (University of California, Institute of International Relations Studies, Berkeley, CA, 1983).
Kolatt, I., 'The Zionist Movement and the Arabs' in S. Almog (ed.), *Zionism and the Arabs*, (The Historical Society of Israel and the Zalman Shazar Center, Jerusalem, 1983), pp. 35–72.
Kuhn, T. S., *The Structure of Scientific Revolution*, (University of Chicago Press, Chicago and London, 1962).
Lambert, W. E. and O. Klineberg, *Children's View of Foreign Peoples*, (Appleton Century-Crofts, New York, 1967).
Landau, S. F., and B. Beit-Hallahmi, 'Israel: Aggression in Psycho-historical Perspective' in A. P. Goldstein and M. H. Segal (eds), *Aggression in Global Perspective*, (Pergamon Press, New York, 1983), pp. 261–88.
Lane, R. E., *Political Thinking and Consciousness*, (Markham Publishing Company, Chicago, 1969).
Langer, S. K., *An Introduction to Symbolic Logic*, 3rd Revised Edition, (Dover Publications, New York, 1967).
Lanir, Z., *Fundamental Surprise. The National Intelligence Crisis*, (Kav Adom, Tel Aviv, 1983), (Hebrew).
—— 'Political Aims and Military Objectives — Some Observations on the Israeli Experience' in Z. Lanir (ed.), *Israeli Security Planning in the 1980s*, (Praeger, New York, 1984), pp. 14–47.
Laqueur, W. *A History of Zionism*, (Weidenfeld and Nicolson, London, 1972).
Lazarus, P. S., 'Stress' in D. L. Sills (ed.), *International Encyclopedia of the Social Sciences*, (Free Press, New York, 1972), pp. 337–48.
Lee, E. S., 'A Theory of Migration', *Demography*, vol. 3, no. 1 (1966), pp. 47–57.

Leibovitz, Y., *Judaism, the Jewish People and the State of Israel*, (Shoken Publications, Jerusalem and Tel Aviv, 1979), (Hebrew).

Leviatan, U., 'The Attitudes of the Jewish Public Towards the Kibbutz Movement and the Possibility of Living in a Kibbutz', *Megamot*, vol. 26, no. 2 (1980), pp. 232–37, (Hebrew).

Levy, S. and E. L. Guttman, *The Feeling of Well Being and Worry Among the Israeli Public*, (The Israel Institute of Applied Social Research, Jerusalem, 1973).

—— *The Values and Attitudes of Israeli Students*, vol. 2, (The Institute of Applied Social Research, Jerusalem, 1976), (Hebrew).

—— *Towards A Prediction of Election to the Next Knesset*, (The Israel Institute of Applied Social Research, Jerusalem, 1979), (Hebrew).

Lewin, K., *A Dynamic Theory of Personality*, (McGraw Hill, New York, 1935),

—— *Field Theory in Social Science*, edited by D. Cartwright, (Harper and Row, New York, 1951).

—— *Resolving Social Conflict*, (Harper and Row, New York, 1948).

Levite, A. and S. Tarrow, 'The Legitimation of Excluded Parties in Dominant Party Systems. A Comparison of Israel and Italy', *Comparative Politics*, vol. 15, no. 3 (1983), pp. 295–327.

Liebman, C., 'The Development of Neo-Traditionalism Among the Orthodox Jews in Israel', *Megamot*, vol. 27, no. 3 (1982), pp. 231–251.

—— and E. Don-Yehiya, *Religion and Politics in Israel*, (Indiana University Press, Bloomington, IN, 1984).

—— *The Civil Religion in Israel: Traditional Judaism and Political Culture in the Jewish State*, (University of California Press, Berkeley, CA, 1983).

Lijphart, A., *The Politics of Accommodation: The Dutch and West New Guinea*, (Yale University Press, New Haven, CT, 1966).

Linton, R., *The Cultural Background of Personality*, (Prentice Hall, London, 1945).

Lissak, M., *Social Mobility in Israeli Society*, (Israel University Press, Jerusalem, 1969).

—— 'The Contact and Conversion Dimension Between the Civilian Sector and the Military Establishment: The Army of Volunteers and the Conscript Army', *State, Government and International Relations*, no. 12 (1978), pp. 27–45, (Hebrew).

Livneh, E., *Israel and the Crisis of Western Civilization*, (Shoken Publishing, Tel Aviv, 1972), (Hebrew).

—— 'The Spiritual Meaning of the Six-Day War' in A. Ben Ami (ed.), *The Greater Land of Israel Book*, (The Greater Land of Israel Movement and Freedman Publishers, Tel Aviv, 1977), pp. 22–6, (Hebrew).

—— and S. Katz, *Land of Israel and its Borders*, (The Greater Land of Israel Movement, Tel Aviv, 1968), (Hebrew).

Lukes, S., 'Some Problems About Rationality' in B. R. Wilson (ed.), *Rationality*, (Harper and Row, Evanston and New York, 1970), pp. 295–327.

Lustick, I. S., 'The West Bank and Gaza Strip in Israeli Politics' in S. Heydemann (ed.), *The Begin Era, Issues in Contemporary Israel*, (Westview Press, Boulder, CO, and London, 1984), pp. 79–98.

Luttwak, E. N. and D. Horowitz, *The Israeli Army 1948–1973*, (Abt Books, Cambridge, MA, 1983).

McClosky, H., 'Personality and Attitude Correlates of Foreign Policy Orientation' in J. Rosenau, *Domestic Sources of Foreign Policy*, (The Free Press, New York, 1967), pp. 51–107.

Magnes, J. L., 'A Solution Through Force?' in G. V. Smith, *Zionism: the Dream and the Reality. A Jewish Critique*, (David and Charles, Newton Abbot, London and New York, 1974).

Maier, C. S., 'The Politics of Inflation in the Twentieth Century' in F. Hirsch and J.

H. Goldthorpe (eds), *The Political Economy of Inflation*, (Martin Robertson, London, 1978), pp. 37–72.

Mannheim, K., *Ideology and Utopia*, (Harvest HBJ Books, New York, 1955).

Mannoni, O., *Prospero and Caliban*, (Praeger, New York, 1964).

Manor, R., 'Perceptions, Decision Making and Feedback in Israeli Foreign Policy: The Forming of the Israeli Border Map During the War of Independence', *State, Government and International Relations*, no. 13 (1979), pp. 17–51, (Hebrew).

Maoz, Z., 'The Decision to Raid Entebbe, Decision Analysis Applied to Crisis Behavior', *Journal of Conflict Resolution*, vol. 25, no. 4 (1981), pp. 677–707.

Marmorstein, E., *Heaven at Bay: Kulturkampf in the Holy Land*, (Oxford University Press, London, 1969).

Matras, J., *Social Change in Israel*, (Aldine, Chicago, 1965).

Melikian, L. H., Authoritarianism and Its Correlates in the Egyptian Culture and in the United States', *Journal of Social Issues*, vol. 15, no. 1 (1959), pp. 58–69.

Menachem, N., *Ethnic Tension and Discrimination in Israel. Socio-historical Perspective*, (Rubin Publishing, Ramat Gan, 1983), (Hebrew).

Mendilow, J., 'The Transformation of the Israeli Multi-Party System 1965–1981' in A. Arian (ed.), *The Election in Israel 1981*, (Ramot Publishing Co., Tel Aviv, 1983), pp. 15–37.

Merari, A. and N. Friedland, *The Attitudes of the Public Towards Terror*, (The Centre for Strategic Studies, Tel Aviv University, Tel Aviv, 1979), (Hebrew).

Merhav, P., *The Israeli Left. History, Problems, Documents*, (A. S. Barnes and Company, San Diego and New York, 1980).

Merton, R. K., *Social Theory and Social Structure. Towards the Codification of Theory and Research*, (The Free Press, Glencoe, IL, 1949).

Middle East Research Institute, *MERI Report: Israel*, (Croom Helm, London, 1985).

Miller, D. R., 'The Study of Social Relationships: Situation Identity and Social Interaction' in S. Koch (ed.), *Psychology. A Study of a Science*, vol. 5, (McGraw Hill, New York, 1963).

Mishal, S. and A. Diskin, 'Palestinian Voting in the West Bank: Electoral Behavior in a Traditional Community Without Sovereignty', *Journal of Politics*, vol. 44, no. 2 (1982), pp. 538–58.

Nachmias, C., 'The Status Attainment Process: A Test of a Model in Two Stratification System', *The Sociological Quarterly*, vol. 18, no. 4 (1977), pp. 589–607.

Nachmias, D, and D. H. Rosenblum, 'Bureaucracy and Ethnicity', *American Journal of Sociology*, vol. 83, no. 4 (1978), pp. 967–74.

Neeman, Y., 'National Goals' in A. Hareven (ed.), *On the Difficulty of Being an Israeli*, (The Van Leer Jerusalem Foundation, Jerusalem, 1983), pp. 257–74, (Hebrew).

—— 'Sovereignty and Territories' in A. Ben Ami (ed.), *The Greater Land of Israel Book*, (The Greater Land of Israel Movement and Freedman Publishers, Tel Aviv, 1977), (Hebrew).

Nettle, P. J., *Political Mobilization*, (Faber and Faber, London, 1967).

Nini, Y., 'Immigration and Assimilation: The Yemenite Jews', *The Jerusalem Quarterly*, no. 2 (1981), pp. 85–98.

Nisbett, R. and L. Ross, *Human Inference: Strategies and Shortcomings of Social Judgment*, (Prentice Hall, Englewood Cliffs, NJ, 1980).

Nissan, M., 'PLO Moderates', *The Jerusalem Quarterly*, no. 1 (1976), pp. 70–82.

Olsen, M. E., 'Alienation and Political Opinion', *Public Opinion Quarterly*, vol. 29, no. 2 (1965), pp. 200–12.

Oz, A., *A Journey in Israel Autumn 1982*, (Am Oved Publishers, Tel Aviv, 1983), (Hebrew).

Parsons, T., *The Social System*, (The Free Press, New York, 1964).

Patai, R., *Israel Between East and West*, (Greenwood Publishing Corporation, Westport, CT, 1970).

—— *The Arab Mind*, (Charles Scribner and Sons, New York, 1973), pp. 41–72.

—— *The Jewish Mind*, (Charles Scribner and Sons, New York, 1977).

Peled T., 'The Impact of Terrorist Activity on the Morale of the Public and Its Attitudes Towards the Arabs. A Longitudinal Analysis', *State, Government and International Relations*, no. 3 (1972), pp. 129–34, (Hebrew).

Peres, S., *David's Sling*, (Random House, New York, 1970).

Peres, Y., *Ethnic Relations in Israel*, (Sifriat Hapoalim, Tel Aviv, 1977), (Hebrew).

—— 'Ethnic Relations in Israel', *American Journal of Sociology*, vol. 76, no. 6 (1971), pp. 1021–47.

—— and S. Shemer, 'The Ethnic Factor in Elections to the Tenth Knesset' in D. Caspi, A. Diskin and E. L. Gutmann (eds), *The Source of Begin's Success*, (Croom Helm, London, 1984), pp. 89–112.

—— and N. Yuval-Davis, 'Some Observations on the National Identity of the Israeli Arabs', *Human Relations*, vol. 22, no. 3 (1969), pp. 219–33.

Peri, M., 'The Response of the Education Policy Making System in the Ministry of Education Towards Demands in the Field of Education Towards Values', *State, Government and International Relations*, no. 14 (1974), pp. 67–87, (Hebrew).

Peri, Y., *Between Battles and Ballots. Israeli Military in Politics*, (Cambridge University Press, Cambridge, 1983).

—— 'Ideological Portrait of the Israeli Military Elite', *The Jerusalem Quarterly*, no. 3 (1977), pp. 28–41.

Pettigrew, T. F., 'Personality and Sociocultural Factors in Intergroup Attitudes: A Cross-National Comparison' in R. S. Sigel (ed.), *Learning About Politics: A Reader in Political Socialization*, (Random House, New York, 1970), pp. 491–8.

—— G. W. Allport and E. O. Barnett, 'Binocular Resolution and Perception of Race in South Africa', *British Journal of Psychology*, vol. 49, no. 2 (1958), pp. 265–79.

Pinsker, Y. L., *The Road to Freedom*, edited by B. Netanyahu, (Scopus Publishing Company, New York, 1944).

Pry, P., *Israel's Nuclear Arsenal*, (Westview Press, Boulder, CO, and Croom Helm, London, 1984).

Przeworsky, A. and M. Teune, *The Logic of Comparative Social Inquiry*, (Wiley, New York, 1970).

Rabinowitch, I., *The War for Lebanon 1970–1983*, (Cornell University Press, Ithaca, NY, 1984).

Rabushka, A. and K. Shepsle, *Politics in Plural Societies: A Theory of Democratic Instability*, (Charles E. Merrill Publishing Company, Columbus, OH, 1976).

Rakover, S. and A. Yaniv, 'Individual Trauma and National Response to External Threat: The Case of Israel', *Bulletin of the Psychonomic Society*, vol. 16, no. 3 (1980), pp. 217–20.

Rapoport, A., 'Critique of Strategic Thinking' in R. Fisher (ed.), International Conflict and Behavioral Science, (Basic Books, New York, 1964), pp. 211–37.

—— *Strategy and Consciences*, (Shaven Books, New York, 1969).

Reiser, S., 'Cultural and Political Influence on Police Discretion: The Case of Religion of Israel', *Police Studies*, vol. 6, no. 1 (1983), pp. 13–23.

Richardson, B. M., 'Party Loyalties and Party Saliency in Japan', *Comparative Political Studies*, vol. 8, no. 1 (1975), pp. 32–57.

Rim, Y., 'National Stereotypes in Children', *Megamot*, vol. 10, no. 1 (1968), pp. 45–51, (Hebrew).

—— and R. Aloni, 'Stereotypes According to Ethnic Origin, Social Class and Sex', *Acta Psychologica*, vol. 31, no. 4 (1969), pp. 312–25.

Rokeach, M., *The Open and Closed Mind*, (Basic Books, New York, 1960).

Rolle, A., 'The Historic Past of the Unconscious' in H. D. Laswell, D. Lerner and H. Speier (eds), *A Pluralizing World in Formation*, vol. 3, *Propaganda and Communication in World History*, (University of Hawaii Press, Honolulu, HI, 1980), pp. 403–60.

Roof, M., *Detailed Statistics on the Population of Israel by Ethnic and Religious and Urban Residence and Rural Residence: 1950–2010*, (Center for International Research, US Bureau of the Census, 1984).

Rose, N. A., *The Gentile Zionists*, (Frank Cass, London, 1973).

Rosen, S. J., 'A Stable System of Mutual Nuclear Deterrence in the Arab-Israeli Conflict', *American Political Science Review*, vol. 71, no. 4 (1977), pp. 1367–83.

Rosenau, J. N., 'Foreign Policy as an Issue Area' in J. N. Rosenau (ed.), *Domestic Sources of Foreign Policy*, (The Free Press, New York, 1967), pp. 11–50.

—— (ed.), *Linkage Politics*, (The Free Press, New York, 1969).

—— and O. R. Holsti, 'US Leadership in a Shrinking World: The Breakdown of Consensus and the Emergence of Conflicting Belief Systems', *World Politics*, vol. 35, no. 3 (1983), pp. 368–92.

Rosenblatt, P., 'Origins and Effects of Group Ethnocentrism and Nationalism', *World Politics*, vol. 16, no. 1 (1964), pp. 146–81.

Rosenblum, G., *Immigrant Workers: Their Impact on American Radicalism*, (Basic Books, New York, 1970).

Rosenstein, C., 'The Liability of Ethnicity in Israel', *Social Forces*, vol. 50, no. 2 (1981), pp. 667–86.

Rotenstreich, N., *Examining Zionism Today*, (The Zionist Library, Jerusalem, 1977), (Hebrew).

Roumani, M., 'An Effort to Advance and Integrate the Underpriviliged Population in IDF and Israeli Society', unpublished report, n.d.

—— *The Contribution of the Army to National Integration in Israel*, (Foundation for the Study of Plural Societies, The Hague, 1979).

Rubinstein, A., *From Herzl to Gush Emunim and Back*, (Shoken Publishing House, Tel Aviv, 1980), (Hebrew).

—— *To Be a Free Nation*, (Shoken Publishing House, Jerusalem and Tel Aviv, 1977), (Hebrew).

Rubinstein, D., *On the Lord's Side: Gush Emunim*, (Hakibbutz Hameuchad Publishing House, Tel Aviv, 1982), (Hebrew).

Rubinstein, E., 'Zionist Attitudes on the Jewish Arab Conflict Until 1936' in S. Almog (ed.), *Zionism and the Arabs*, (The Historical Society of Israel and the Zalman Shazar Center, 1983).

Sandler, S. and H. Frisch, *Israel, the Palestinians and the West Bank; A Study in Intercommunal Conflict*, (Lexington Heath, New York, 1984).

Schiff, Z. and E. Ya'ari, *Israel's Lebanon War*, (Simon and Schuster, New York, 1984).

Schmid, H., 'On the Origin of Ideology', *Acta Sociologica*, vol. 24, no. 1 (1981), pp. 57–73.

Schoueftan, D., 'Nasser's 1967 Policy Reconsidered', *The Jerusalem Quarterly*, no. 3 (1977), pp. 124–44.

Schweid, E., *Homeland and a Land Promise*, (Am Oved Publishers, Tel Aviv, 1979), (Hebrew).

Segre, D. V., *A Crisis of Identity: Israel and Zionism*, (Oxford University Press, Oxford, 1980).

Seliger, M., 'The Two Principal Dimensions of Political Argumentation', *Policy Sciences*, vol. 1, no. 4 (1970), pp. 325–38.

Seliktar, O., 'Acquiring Partisan Preferences in a Plural Society: The Case of Israel', *Plural Societies*, vol. 11, no. 4 (1980), pp. 3–19.

—— 'Israel: Electoral Cleavages in a Nation in Making' in R. Rose (ed.), *Electoral Participation. A Comparative Analysis*, (Sage Publications, Beverly Hills, CA and London, 1980).

—— 'Israel: Fragile Coalitions in a New Nation', in E. C. Browne and J. Dreijmanis (eds), *Government Coalitions in Western Democracies*, (Longman, New York and London, 1981), pp. 283–315.

—— 'New Zionism', *Foreign Policy*, no. 51 (1983), pp. 118–38.

—— 'Socialization of National Ideology: The Case of Zionist Attitudes Among Young Israelis', *Political Psychology*, vol. 2, no. 3–4 (1980), pp. 66–94.

—— 'The Arabs in Israel. Some Observations on the Psychology of the System of Controls', *Journal of Conflict Resolution*, vol. 28, no. 2 (1984), pp. 247–69.

—— and L. E. Dutter, 'Israel as a Latent Plural Society' in W. C. McCready (ed.), *Culture, Ethnicity and Identity*, (Academic Press, New York and London, 1983), pp. 301–26.

Selzer, M., 'Politics and Human Perfectability: A Jewish Perspective' in G. V. Smith (ed.), *Zionism: The Dream and Reality*, (David and Charles, Newton Abbot, London and New York, 1974), pp. 285–303.

Shama, A. and M. Iris, *Immigration Without Integration*, (Schenkman Publishing Company, Cambridge, MA, 1977).

Shamgar, M. (ed.), *Military Government in the Territories Administered by Israel 1967–1980*, vol. 1, (Hebrew University of Jerusalem, Faculty of Law, Jerusalem, 1982).

Shamir, M. and A. Arian, 'The Ethnic Vote in Israel's 1981 Elections' in A. Arian (ed.), *The Elections in Israel–1981*, (Ramot Publishing, Tel Aviv, 1983), pp. 91–111.

—— and J. L. Sullivan, 'Jews and Arabs in Israel: Everybody Hates Somebody, Sometimes', *Journal of Conflict Resolution*, forthcoming.

—— 'The Political Context of Tolerance. Israel and the United States', *American Political Science Review*, vol. 75, no. 2 (1983), pp. 92–106.

Shamir, S., 'The Palestinians and Israel' in S. Avineri (ed.), *Israel and the Palestinians*, (St. Martin Press, New York, 1971), pp. 133–64.

Shapiro, A., *Berl Katzenelson. A Biography*, vol. 1, (Am Oved, Tel Aviv, 1981), (Hebrew).

Shapiro, Y., 'Generational Units and Intergenerational Relations in Israeli Politics' in A. Asher (ed.), *Israel — A Developing Society*, (Van Gorcum, Assen, 1980), pp. 161–180.

Sharon, M., 'The Interim Agreement in the Context of Pax Islamica' in A. Ben-Ami (ed.), *The Greater Land of Israel Book*, (The Greater Land of Israel Movement and S. Freedman, 1977), pp. 265–8, (Hebrew).

Sharot, S., *Messianism: Mysticism and Magic. A Sociological Analysis of Jewish Religious Movements*, (University of North Carolina Press, Chapel Hill, NC, 1982).

—— 'Minority Situation and Religious Acculturation: A Comparative Analysis of Jewish Communities', *Comparative Studies in Society and History*, vol. 16, no. 3 (1974), pp. 329–54.

Shavit, Y., *From Hebrew to Canaanite*, (The Domino Press, Tel Aviv, 1984), (Hebrew).

—— *Revisionism in Zionism. The Revisionist Movement: The Plan for Colonizatory Regime and Social Ideas 1915–1935*, 2nd Edition, (Hadar Publishers, Tel Aviv, 1983), (Hebrew).

—— 'Revisionism's View of the Arab National Movement' in S. Almog (ed.), *Zionism and the Arabs*, (The Historical Society of Israel and the Zalman Shazar Center, 1983), pp. 73–94.

Sheffer, G., 'The Confrontation Between Moshe Sharett and D. Ben-Gurion' in S. Almog (ed.), *Zionism and the Arabs*, (The Historical Society of Israel and the Zalman Shazar Center, 1983), pp. 95–147.

Shem-Ur, O., *The Challenges of Israel*, (Shengold Publishers Inc, New York, 1980).

300 *Bibliography*

Shils, E., 'Charisma, Order and Status', *American Sociological Review*, vol. 30, no. 2 (1965), pp. 199–213.
Shiloah, Z., 'The Goals of Greater Israel in the Land of the Fathers' in A. Ben-Ami (ed.), *The Greater Land of Israel Movement Book*, (The Greater Land of Israel Movement and S. Freedman, Tel Aviv, 1977), pp. 213–26, (Hebrew).
Shlaim, A., 'Conflicting Approaches to Israel's Relations With the Arabs: Ben-Gurion and Sharett, 1953–1956', *Middle East Journal*, vol. 37, no. 2 (1963), pp. 180–201.
— and A. Yaniv, 'Domestic Politics and Foreign Policy in Israel', *International Affairs*, vol. 56, no. 2 (1980), pp. 242–62.
Shmueli, E., *Seven Jewish Cultures. A Reinterpretation of Jewish History and Thought*, (Yahdav, Tel Aviv, 1980), (Hebrew).
Shokeid, M., 'Towards Explanation of the Attitudes of Aggression Among Moroccan Immigrants', *Megamot*, vol. 27, no. 4 (1982), pp. 397–412.
Sholem, G., *Sabbatai Sevi: The Mystical Messiah 1626–1679*, (Princeton University Press, Princeton, NJ, 1973).
Shuval, J. T., 'Emerging Patterns of Ethnic Strain in Israel', *Social Forces*, vol. 40, no. 4 (1982), pp. 323–8.
— *Immigrants on the Threshold*, (Atherton Press, New York, 1963).
— 'Patterns of Inter-Group Tension and Affinity', *International Social Science Bulletin*, vol. 8, no. 1 (1956), pp. 75–103.
— 'Value Orientations of Immigrants to Israel', *Sociometry*, vol. 20, no. 1 (1983), pp. 247–59.
Shwartzwald, Y. and Y. Yanon, 'Symmetry and Asymmetry in Ethnic Pereptions', *Megamot*, vol. 24, no. 1 (1978), pp. 45–52, (Hebrew).
Simon, L., *Ahad ha-Am (Asher Ginsburg). A Biography*, (Jewish Publication Society, Philadelphia, 1960).
Singer, J. D., 'The Global System and Its Subsystems: A Developmental View' in J. N. Rosenau, *Linkage Politics*, (The Free Press, New York, 1969), pp. 21–43.
Sivin, N., 'Chinese Conception of Time', *The Ertham Review*, vol. 1, no. 1 (1960), pp. 82–92.
Smith, D. E., *Religion and Political Development*, (Little Brown, Boston, MA, 1970).
Smooha, S., 'Ashkenazi Hegemony', *New Outlook*, July-August, 1981, pp. 17–21.
— 'Ethnic Stratification and Allegiance in Israel: Where Do Oriental Jews Belong?', *II Politico*, vol. 14, no. 4 (1974), pp. 635–57.
— *Israel: Pluralism and Conflict*, (University of California Press, Berkeley and Los Angeles, CA, 1978).
Spengler, J. J., 'Rising Expectations: Frustration' in H.D. Laswell, D. Lerner and H. Speier (eds), *A Pluralizing World in Formation*, vol. 3, *Propaganda and Communication in World History*, (University of Hawaii Press, Honolulu, HI, 1980), pp. 37–93.
Spicer, E. H., 'Persistent Cultural Systems', *Science*, vol. 174, no. 4011 (1971), pp. 795–830.
Spiro, M. E., 'The Sabras and Zionism: A Study in Personality and Ideology', *Social Problems*, vol. 5, no. 2 (1957), pp. 100–10.
Sprout, H. and M. Sprout, 'Environmental Factors in the Study of International Politics' in J. N. Rosenau (ed.), *International Politics and Foreign Policy*, (The Free Press of Glencoe, IL, 1961), pp. 106–19.
Stagner, R., *Psychological Aspects of International Conflict*, (Brooks Cole, Belmont, CA, 1967).
Stahl, A., *The Cultural Integration in Israel*, (Am Oved, Tel Aviv, 1976), (Hebrew).
Stein, A. A., 'Conflict and Cohesion. A Review of Literature', *Journal of Conflict Resolution*, vol. 20, no. 1 (1976), pp. 143–72.

Stillman, N. A., 'The Moroccan Jewish Experience: A Revisionist View', *The Jerusalem Quarterly*, no. 9 (1978), pp. 111–23.

Stinchcombe, A. L., 'Some Empirical Consequences of the Davis-Moore Theory of Stratification', *American Sociological Review*, vol. 28, no. 5 (1963), pp. 805–90.

Stone, A., *Social Change in Israeli Attitudes and Events 1967–1979*, (Praeger Special Studies, New York, 1983).

Stonquist, E. V., *The Marginal Man: A Study of Personality and Cultural Conflict*, (Charles Scribner and Sons, New York, 1937).

Strachey, A., *The Unconscious Motives of War*, (International Universities Press, New York, 1957).

Suedfeld, P., P. E. Tetlock and C. Ramirez, 'War, Peace and Integrative Complexity', *Journal of Conflict Resolution*, vol. 21, no. 3 (1977), pp. 427–43.

Sullivan, J. L., N. Roberts, M. Shamir and P. Welsh, 'Pluralistic Intolerance, Focused Intolerance and Tolerance: Mass Attitudes in the U.S., Israel and New Zealand', *Comparative Politics*, forthcoming.

Swirski, S., *Orientals and Ashkenazim in Israel. The Ethnic Division of Labor*, (Machbarot Le'mechkar u'Lebikoret, Haifa, 1981), (Hebrew).

Szalay, L. B. and R. M. Kelley, 'Political Ideology and Subjective Culture: Conceptualization and Empirical Assessment', *The American Political Science Review*, vol. 76, no. 4 (1982), pp. 585–602.

—— and T. W. Moon, 'Ideology: Its Meaning and Measurement', *Comparative Political Studies*, vol 35, no. 2 (1972), pp. 151–73.

Tajfel, H., 'Intergroup Behaviour: A Group Perspective' in H. Tajfel and C. Fraser (eds), *Introducing Social Psychology*, (Penguin Books, Harmondsworth, Middx, 1978), pp. 423–44.

—— 'The Structure of Our Views About Society' in H. Tajfel and C. Fraser (eds), *Introducing Social Psychology*, (Penguin Books, Harmondsworth, Middx, 1978), pp. 302–19.

Talmon, J. L., *Political Messianism: The Romantic Phase*, (Praeger, New York, 1960).

Tamarin, G. P., *The Israeli Dilemma. Essays on a Warfare State*, (Rotterdam University Press, Rotterdam, 1973).

Tilly, C., *From Mobilization to Revolution*, (Addison Wesley Publishing, Reading, MA, 1978).

Tockatli, R., 'Party Distances in Israel, 1969', *Megamot*, vol. 20, no. 2 (1974), pp. 136–54, (Hebrew).

Toennis, F., *Community and Association*, (Routledge and Kegan Paul, London, 1955).

Tomlin, B. W., M. Doland, H. von Rikhoff and V. Appel Molot, 'Foreign Policies of Superordinate States in Asymmetrical Dyads', *The Jerusalem Journal of International Relations*, vol. 5, no. 4 (1981), pp. 14–40.

Tucker, R. C., *Stalin as a Revolutionary*, (Norton, New York, 1973).

Turkel, G., 'Privatism and Orientation Towards Political Action', *Urban Life*, vol. 9, no. 2 (1980), pp. 217–35.

Ullman, C., 'Cognitive and Emotional Antecedents of Religious Conversion', *Journal of Personality and Social Psychology*, vol. 43, no. 1 (1982), pp. 183–92.

Van Arkadie, B., *Benefits and Burdens: A Report on the West Bank and Gaza Strip Economies Since 1967*, (Carnegie Endowment for International Peace, New York and Washington, 1977).

Van Creveld, M., 'Military Lessons of the Yom Kippur War', *The Jerusalem Quarterly*, no. 5 (1977), pp. 114–24.

Verblovsky, Z., 'The Difference Between the Secular-Religious Relations in Israel and Other Countries' in A. Hareven (ed.), *On the Difficulty of Being an Israeli*, (The Van Leer Foundation, Jerusalem, 1983), pp. 201–12, (Hebrew).

Vinokur, A. and E. Burstein, 'Effects of Partially Shared Persuasive Arguments on Group Induced Shifts: A Group Problem-Solving Approach', *Journal of Personality*, vol. 29, no. 3 (1974), pp. 305–15.

Vital, D., 'The Definition of Goals in Foreign Policy', *State, Government and International Relations*, no. 13 (1979), pp. 5–16, (Hebrew).

—— *The Origins of Zionism*, (At the Clarendon Press, Oxford, 1975).

Von Neumann, J. and V. Morgenstern, *The Theory of Games and Economic Behavior*, 2nd Edition, (Princeton University Press, Princeton, NJ, 1947).

Wagner, Y. and E. Kaphafi, *The Sources of the Dispute: The Historical Quarrel Between the Labor Movement and the Revisionists*, (Am Oved, Tel Aviv, 1982), (Hebrew).

Waltzer, M., *Just and Unjust Wars*, (Basic Books, New York, 1977).

Weber, M., *Economy and Society*, edited by G. Roth and C. Wittich, (Bedminister Press, New York, 1968).

—— *The Theory of Social and Economic Organization*, (The Free Press of Glencoe, IL, 1957).

Weingrod, A., 'The Two Israels', *Commentary*, vol. 33, no. 4 (1962), pp. 313–19.

Wiesel, E., 'The Death of My Father' in J. Riener (ed.), *Jewish Reflection in Death*, (Schocken Books, New York, 1976), pp. 35–9.

White, R. K. 'Misperceptions in the Arab-Israeli Conflict', *Journal of Social Issues*, vol. 33, no. 1 (1977), pp. 190–221.

—— *Nobody Wanted War*, (Doubleday, Garden City, NY, 1968).

Wilner, D., *Nation Building and Community in Israel*, (Princeton University Press, Princeton, NJ, 1969).

Wilson, B. R., 'A Sociologist's Introduction' in B. R. Wilson (ed.), *Rationality*, (Harper and Row, Evanston and New York, 1970), pp. vviii-ix.

Wright, G. M. and L. D. Phillips 'Personality and Probability Thinking: An Exploratory Study', *British Journal of Psychology*, vol. 70, no. 2 (1979), pp. 295–303.

Wuthnow, R., 'Comparative Ideology', *International Journal of Comparative Sociology*, vol. 22, no. 3–4 (1981), pp. 121–40.

Yaniv, A. and F. Pascal, 'Doves, Hawks and Other Birds of Feather', *The British Journal of Political Science*, vol. 10, no. 2 (1980), pp. 260–67.

Yanon, Y., A. Avnad and A. Heirar, 'Indirect Measurements of Ethnic Prejudice Among Young Western Israelis Towards Oriental Jews', *Megamot*, vol. 21, no. 3 (1975), pp. 314–23, (Hebrew).

Yishai, Y., 'Israel's Right Wing Proletariat', *Jewish Journal of Sociology*, vol. 24, no. 2 (1982), pp. 87–98.

Yogev, A. and H. Ayalon, 'The Impact of Sex and Ethnic Origin on Expectations for Higher Education in Israel', *Megamot*, vol. 27, no. 4 (1982), pp. 349–69, (Hebrew).

Young, T. R., 'The Division of Labor in the Construction of Social Reality', *Urban Life*, vol. 9, no. 2 (1980), pp. 135–62.

Yuchtman-Yaar, E., 'Differences in Ethnic Patterns of Socio-economic Achievement in Israel: A Neglected Aspect of Structured Inequality', *International Review of Modern Sociology*, forthcoming.

—— and M. Semyonov, 'Ethnic Inequality in Israeli Schools and Sports: An Expectation State Approach', *American Journal of Sociology*, vol. 85, no. 3 (1979), pp. 576–90.

Zamir, D., 'Generals in Politics', *The Jerusalem Quarterly*, no. 20 (1981), pp. 18–35.

Zelniker, S. and M. Kahan, 'Religion and Nascent Cleavages: The Case of Israel's National Religious Party', *Comparative Politics*, vol. 9, no. 1 (1976), pp. 21–48.

Zenner, W. P., 'Ambivalence and Self Image Among Oriental Jews in Israel', *Jewish Journal of Sociology*, vol. 5, no. 2 (1963), pp. 214–23.

Zohar, E., 'Israel and the Periphery Against Arab Pan-Arabism' in A. Ben-Ami (ed.), *The Greater Land of Israel Movement Book*, (The Greater Land of Israel Movement and S. Freedman, Tel Aviv, 1977), pp. 227–41, (Hebrew).

Zucher, D. (ed.), *Human Rights in the Occupied Territories*, (The International Center for Peace in the Middle East, Tel Aviv, 1983).

Zucker, N. L., *The Coming Crisis in Israel: Private Faith and Public Policy*, (MIT Press, Cambridge, MA, 1973).

Zuckerman, M., R. W. Mann, F. J. Bernieri, 'Determinants of Consensus Estimates: Attribution, Salience and Representativeness', *Journal of Personality and Psychology*, vol. 42, no. 5 (1982), pp. 839–52.

Zuckerman, A. S., 'The Limits of Political Behavior: Individual Calculations and Survival During the Holocaust', *Political Psychology*, vol. 5, no. 1 (1984), pp. 37–52.

Zuckerman-Bareli, C., 'The Religious Factor and Its Impact on Consensus and Polarity Among Israeli Youth', *Megamot*, vol. 22, no. 1 (1975), pp. 62–80, (Hebrew).

Zweig, F., *Israel: The Sword and the Harp*, (Farleigh Dickinson University Press, Rutherford NJ, 1969).

INDEX

advocacy groups 12, 188, 204,
    208–12, 271
agrarianism 55, 56, 77
Agudat Israel Party 97,124, 126–8,
    209, 264
aliyah 62, 155
Allon Plan, The 157, 227, 260, 267
Amal 193, 238, 248
annex, annexation 156, 157, 161, 206,
    227, 228, 230, 232, 250, 255, 256,
    260–3, 265, 273
anomie 24, 180
anti-Arab sentiment 84, 169, 171,
    174, 177, 181, 207
anti-Semitism 3, 5, 32, 44, 48–51, 53,
    64, 74, 75, 93, 101–4, 107, 209, 270
Arab, Arabs x, 57–70, 78, 81–6,
    88–91, 94, 96, 99, 101–3, 107, 109,
    130, 135, 154–7, 160, 163–6,
    168–79, 181, 189, 190–3, 197–203,
    206, 208, 210–12, 223, 224, 226,
    232, 239, 243, 249–51, 256–8, 260,
    261, 264, 265, 270, 272
Arab-Israeli conflict, Arab-Jewish
    relations x, 58–65, 68–70, 89, 90,
    95, 101, 163, 164, 167, 170, 173,
    175, 179, 180, 182, 189, 190, 197,
    198, 251, 270, 271, 273
Arafat, Yasser 164, 167, 229, 239,
    251, 255, 256
Arens, Moshe 164, 250, 252
ashkenazim, ashkenazi 27, 42, 63,
    100, 128, 129, 131–3, 135–8, 140,
    141, 145, 147, 148, 169–72, 174–9,
    206, 212, 246, 247, 259
assimilation 47, 48, 50, 53, 54, 93,
    129, 130, 176, 270
authority system 18–22, 25, 84

Balfour Declaration 52, 65, 81
Begin, Menachem 85, 91, 92, 104,
    146, 190, 224, 225, 227, 231–4, 237,
    244, 245, 251, 263, 264
belief system x, 1–18, 22–4, 26, 27,
    29–32, 41, 44, 49–51, 55, 56, 58, 59,
    70, 74, 75, 82, 86, 88, 91, 92, 99,
    101, 107, 108, 115, 116, 118, 120–2,
    124–8, 131, 132, 135, 139, 147, 156,
    161, 169, 180, 182, 188, 191, 192,
    200, 204, 219, 220, 225, 231, 233,
    234, 242, 261–5, 268–70, 272, 273

Ben-Gurion, David 55–7, 59, 60, 62,
    65, 66, 68, 70, 91, 105, 124, 129, 135,
    144, 156, 180, 190, 194, 198, 220, 233
'born-again' Jews 126, 209–11
boundary 2, 5, 19, 99, 155, 156, 196
Brit Habyrionim 84, 85, 88
Brit Shalom 67, 88
Buber, Martin; Buberism 67, 70, 88

censorship 193, 203, 204
Christians, Christianity 42, 45, 46, 48,
    52–4, 102, 209, 210, 223, 230, 232,
    233, 236, 238, 248
cognitive 1, 9, 46, 59, 62, 64, 87, 90,
    104, 105, 144, 161, 168, 169, 196, 199,
    203, 226, 231, 234, 249, 261, 272
    dissonance 10, 15, 25–7, 32, 144
    maps 1, 2, 5, 16, 219, 220, 231, 233,
    255, 260, 268, 269, 272
    psychology 2, 14, 16, 25, 26, 50, 157,
    195
    style 7, 10, 201

Dayan, Moshe 86, 130, 156, 157,
    195–7, 199, 200, 228
Deir Yassin 69
delegitimisation x, 23–9, 32, 64, 91,
    108, 115–18, 120, 121, 125, 133, 135,
    139, 144, 148, 154, 156, 168, 179, 180,
    182, 188, 242, 245, 265, 269, 270, 272
Democratic Movement of Change 146
Diaspora 32, 41–5, 50, 51, 53–6, 61, 74,
    75, 102, 106, 124, 154, 176, 224, 268,
    269

Eban, Abba 130, 164, 221, 234
Egypt 91, 94, 102, 157, 162, 169, 198,
    202, 204, 205, 224, 252, 253
Eitan, Raphael 211, 228, 230–4, 245,
    255, 272
elite(s) 1, 4, 14, 22, 25, 27, 29–31, 41,
    62, 63, 65–8, 78, 81–3, 86, 87, 93,
    102–4, 115, 116, 121, 124, 129, 154,
    161, 174, 176, 188, 189, 194–6, 198,
    199, 223, 225, 226, 231, 233, 234, 236,
    245, 246, 248, 249, 268
Enlightenment, enlightened 44, 46, 48,
    49, 52, 54, 55, 270
Eretz Israel 80, 86, 92, 97, 99, 155, 271
    see also Greater Land of Israel
ethnic 17, 47, 52, 77, 79, 81, 127, 129,

305